BLOCKCHAIN WARS:

The Future of Big Tech Monopolies and the

Blockchain Internet

Evan McFarland

To the administration of my alma mater: It was a firsthand look at your organization that inspired my search for solutions.

CONTENTS

CHAPTER 1:

THE INTERNET LANDSCAPE

Blockchain is not a literal *chain of blocks*. Granted, Satoshi Nakamodo's Bitcoin introduced the actual coining of the term *blockchain* because it relied on a chain of information "blocks," but that concept is very limiting.[1] Nowadays, blockchain's utility is in the origins of its philosophy more than Bitcoin's consensus mechanism.

I'm not downplaying the significance of revolutionary technology, but this book is for someone who wants to understand big-picture blockchain concepts. Many blockchain-related books, academic journals, course lectures, cryptocurrency white papers, and similar documents begin by explaining how the Bitcoin Blockchain works and then develop some grand idea that uses blockchain technology potentially to solve a world problem, but these projects often raise the same question: What part of that was blockchain?

The usual answer is that it is *all on the blockchain*, *powered by blockchain*, or something similar, but those statements would be equally accurate if the word *blockchain* was swapped with *the Internet* or *the personal computer*. The grandiose concepts that emerge from blockchain startups are analogous to hardware companies introducing their initiatives with an explanation of the Turing Machine, or website homepages presenting a brief history of the Internet before moving to company-specific content. There must be a better way to demystify the blockchain concept.

Blockchain is a Fancy Database—with All the Problems that Entails

Blockchain is just a fancy database, even though it is now often used to refer to much more than that. To understand why these fancy databases initiated a global movement, we will consider an analogy that, while not perfect in that it squeezes together many types of databases, will help clarify the nature of a blockchain.

A spreadsheet is an example of a rudimentary database. You've probably manually entered data into them and retrieved it later using the Ctrl + F command. Things become more complicated if you want to use data from other spreadsheets made by other people—that's where a database comes in. A typical database would look like your spreadsheet if it had 100 columns, 1,000 rows, and 100 similar spreadsheets stacked on top of it. (A technical note: Instead of using Ctrl + F to retrieve data from individual cells, you would probably use some version of Structured Query Language to remove 3-dimensional cross sections of cell groupings.)

In the past two decades, digital data has grown exponentially in both quantity and value for reasons that will become apparent throughout this book. But databases have not changed much in that time, and we still use programming logic from the 1990s for the use of that data.

Database problems begin with a general inability to validate data-entry endpoints. A clerk can enter typos into a spreadsheet. Anyone with spreadsheet access could manipulate data at will. The overall structure of databases also tends to be sloppy because they must encompass missing data and incompatible datapoints. These errors get factored into every process that uses the data.

Since our paychecks, property ownership details, medical records, criminal records, and entire online lives are recorded in databases, the consequences of mistakes can be devastating. Even with less crucial data, database limitations have severe consequences. Either machine-learning algorithms will be unusable because they can't register typos, or, worse yet, inaccurate data will yield faulty analytics.

We tend to deal with these problems by throwing more people and resources (usually redundant information) at them. The idea is if a data source could be compromised, then about five disparate data sources should be used to verify the information. That's why (1) you must jump through different hoops to verify your identity for various entities, (2) it takes banks and credit card companies multiple days to validate your transactions, and (3) why supply chains must transfer a stack of mutable documents 100 times to ship a single container.

Blockchain removes the need for data redundancy by being an entirely different kind of database. A blockchain is just like that stack-of-spreadsheets database, except that blocks, which are like single spreadsheets in the larger stack, are all attached with a "chain." Chains can be thought of as cryptographic locks that keep those blocks of data locked in place forever.

Running with the stack-of-spreadsheets as a database example, we'll imagine you're contributing to a blockchain instead of a conventional database. In the blockchain case, when you enter a new piece of data into your spreadsheet, you request to add it to a *master spreadsheet* that everyone shares. Because of this, your data entry is checked by every single person who is involved in making spreadsheets. Once everyone agrees on the spreadsheet's accuracy, it is added to the stack, and the process repeats.

In real blockchains, spreadsheets are blocks: Data is appended automatically by networks and machines, not manually by humans, and accuracy is verified by a consensus mechanism rather than popular opinion.

Two remarkable things happen here. First, the information in those spreadsheets/blocks becomes perfect: no typos, no errors, no subjectivity—just raw truth. Second, none of that spreadsheet/block data can be deleted, duplicated, or disputed in any way on its respective blockchain. These two unique features are a result of blockchain's general transparency and decentralization.

That is the gist of what blockchain is. Of course, there are many technical details that we are ignoring at this point, but the central concept is spot-on. But even though the two mentioned features are significant, they don't explain the forthcoming blockchain revolution that technologists promise.

A Brief History of Bitcoin

In 2008, a decentralized payment network called Bitcoin was released, and it is now considered the first blockchain ever, but blockchain's story doesn't start here. The governing technology behind Bitcoin is *cryptography*, the mathematical framework that allows blockchain's network consensus to be achieved in a decentralized and pseudonymous manner, and it is nothing new. Cryptography long predates the Internet, and its application to currency is nothing extraordinary: About 100 notable cryptographic payment systems were attempted in the 20 years before Bitcoin came out.[2] Bitcoin's decentralized network concept is nothing new either: Platforms such as Napster, BitTorrent, and Grokster enabled anonymous P2P data transfer with far more usability than blockchain-based equivalents. Using encryption techniques for online anonymity is also not unique to blockchain and has already been made surprisingly easy with standards such as Tor.

You might notice that the projects mentioned in the preceding paragraph except Bitcoin are slowly fading or have completely died out. Online services now primarily involve centralized systems hosted by private companies. This evolutionary path for the Internet makes perfect economic sense. The software as a service model can produce revenue from subscription packages or advertisements. A decentralized protocol that runs on itself leaves no monetary incentive for its creators.

Take Spotify, for example, which built a multi-billion dollar revenue model for the music industry that funnels money to its creators in direct proportion to the success of the service. Napster and similar copycats enabled completely free music sharing but never provided a way to pay platform contributors. Napster is not only missing the resources required to compete with Spotify, but it has absolutely no reason to do so.

Thus, the centralized models have won. The Internet now has a centralized and capitalistic business model based on advertisements and subscriptions. Bitcoin is an interesting case because it was the decentralized standard that thrived while most others were failing. One school of thought attributes this success to a perfectly-struck balance in Bitcoin's level of anonymity and decentralization.[3] Bitcoin is decentralized enough to never be broken or sued but does not have the perfect decentralization that would degrade system design qualities. Bitcoin is also pseudonymous, which sacrifices perfect user anonymity for unparalleled network transparency. No network before Bitcoin meets both criteria.

Bitcoin's uniqueness does not make it practical by any standards. Being the first blockchain, Bitcoin is a terrible poster child for the technology. Bitcoin is not user friendly. It's slow, inefficient, and expensive, which only gets worse as the network grows. Bitcoin's fancy database features are almost unrecognizable because system intricacies make broader applications seem impossible. The Bitcoin Blockchain is only compatible with itself, which means all projects with Bitcoin interoperability are forever tied to an outdated codebase. And all of these detrimental problems with Bitcoin can never be fixed without compromising system integrity.

Even though these facts will make some crypto folks cringe, the shortcomings should be obvious. The world didn't ignore Bitcoin for nearly a decade by mistake. Only recently has its primary use case switched from being a payment medium for criminals to a store of value for investors. No innovation occurred in Bitcoin since its creation, and seemingly out of nowhere, a late 2017 media frenzy had industry leaders preaching about the revolutionary potential of blockchain technology. So what happened to blockchain from 2008 to 2017?

From Bitcoin to Blockchain

While crooks were enjoying the fruits of an anonymous payment system, small bands of technologists continued to work on the bigger picture: a fancy database that could be used to build unbreakable networks without 3rd parties. These developer communities show a shocking resemblance to the innovators behind Napster, BitTorrent, and Grokster, sharing a mentality and ambition that often gets intertwined with decentralized technologies. The difference this time around was that they found an economic model and monetary incentive for developing distributed technologies. By attaching a cryptocurrency to a network as the native token, online services no longer needed a revenue model based on subscriptions and ads, or even the parent company. This newfound approach cracked the economics piece of the puzzle that gave Internet freedom fighters the resources needed to improve blockchain technologies.

Developer activity in the blockchain space increased in proportion to the number of people who realized the opportunity. Bitcoin's impractical speed and efficiency was a good starting point for improvement. Tweaking the mathematical rules and design tradeoffs of blockchain consensus mechanisms fixed that problem for later blockchains. Cryptography improved as a result, along with the methods for using it in peer-to-peer applications.

Another step was the construction of a blockchain with an associated Turing complete programming language. Ethereum, the second-largest cryptocurrency by market capitalization, was the pioneer of this innovation. The project proved that it is possible to build and host any imaginable web application with just a peer-to-peer network of computers and a blockchain as the underlying data structure.

The ability of Ethereum and similar projects to build what's essentially a decentralized equivalent of the Internet brought up a new set of technical demands and practical concerns. These blockchains began as very inefficient, bad at interacting with non-blockchain technologies, and were inconvenient to use. Since the potential applications for these blockchains are nearly unlimited, and every mathematical tweak comes with a design tradeoff, there can be no uniform fix for blockchains. Making different blockchains for unique purposes is now the predominant workaround for their technical limitations.

Notable innovations have come out of experimenting with the possible types of blockchains. Interoperability-focused blockchain startups created blockchains where the associated programing language is generic enough for functions to work with disparate blockchains and even conventional Internet infrastructure. Many companies created blockchains that did away with the chain of blocks concept but used an alternative structure that preserved the qualities of our fancy database. Some went so far as to make private blockchains, which kept the chain-of-blocks structure but removed user anonymity, network transparency, and decentralized consensus.

It's now commonplace for platforms to offer developer tools so simple that anyone can write software and build platforms that utilize blockchain. To keep these platforms aligned with blockchain's core principles, startups took blockchain-like techniques to make a decentralized version of the "cloud" that hosts these platforms. In combating blockchain's rigidity, those same platforms have created entire network democracies dedicated to adding a human element to their design. These examples barely scratch the surface of what comprise leading advancements in the so-called blockchain industry, and yet let's not forget that blockchains still have far more problems to solve than completed solutions.

Does Anyone Understand What Blockchain *Really* Is?

If you still don't understand what blockchain is, you are exactly where you should be. If you already have a deep understanding of blockchain technology or are an astute reader, you may see what's going on here: Like so much other writing about the concept, the more we investigate blockchain, the more we seem to diverge into a host of related topics and technologies.

We humans really can't agree on what blockchain is or what it is for. The most competent industry leaders recycle misinformation about blockchain's relationship to their business models even though the two are generally irreconcilable. No enthusiasts want to admit what blockchain is either.

So let's return to the following description: Bockchain is still just a fancy database, and that's it. Though the word *blockchain* has become increasingly vague and ambiguous, the term still does generalize a complex industry and reminds us of the common ancestor that newly-revived decentralized technologies share. For the rest of this book, *blockchain* is defined in a way that aligns with how it is generally employed: any technology or set of technologies used in conjunction with anything that shares the principles of a fancy database.

With those preliminaries out of the way, it is now possible to summarize what blockchain *really* is. Blockchain technology is pretty much where Napster, BitTorrent, and Grokster-like technologies intersect with cryptography. They are peer-to-peer protocols with a unique underlying data structure. It sounds simple at this point, but this is still a broad categorization—so broad, in fact, that when you run with it, you quickly realize that it is the bedrock for a whole other Internet.

The term to describe the vision of this decentralized Internet is *Web3*. Web3 can theoretically recreate any existing Internet service with open-source software: that is, the services provided by Big Tech are all replaceable. Distributed networks of collaborating peers can replace centralized hardware infrastructure. On-chain governance mechanisms can replace corporate and bureaucratic hierarchies. Parent companies and governments lose jurisdiction in these environments, and their departure coincides with lower barriers to entry for platform creators.

As you continue exploring this Web3 territory, it appears that two incompatible Internets exist: the centralized one and the decentralized one. We are most familiar with the centralized one because it has two decades of privately-funded development behind it. But increased fear surrounding the power Big Tech has over the Internet is now helping decentralized alternatives gain favor. We are starting to see inklings of Web3's success as fresh money has led to advancements exceedingly more interesting than the Napster-like protocols of the early Internet. We will always have Bitcoin to thank for the resurgence of societal interest in distributed technologies.

The narrative for blockchain's history stops here in the eyes of your typical enthusiasts. They tend to assume a gradual transition toward Web3 will ensue until we end up with a fully decentralized Internet. The full story indicates a far more precarious future for blockchain technology.

A brief history of Bitcoin and blockchains doesn't give due consideration to the centralized Internet's developmental history, which is full of benevolent innovations that don't always translate well to Web3. The story also doesn't answer to the fleet of resource-rich incumbents that dominate the technology sector and who have nothing to gain and everything to lose from a true Web3.

Another big problem is that we have no idea how to distinguish decentralized technologies from centralized ones. The words *centralized* and *decentralized* often are wrongly conflated when Internet technologies are discussed because the topics are complicated. The largest tech companies often succeed by adopting decentralized elements, and the vast majority of blockchains are heavily centralized. How can we make accurate claims about Web3 when only ambiguous or vague words can describe it? People have no idea how to answer this question, suggesting that blockchain's decentralized vision for the Internet is far from inevitable. The current landscape looks more like an ideological battle over Internet control than an evolutionary step for technology.

Some objective context needs to be added before exploring Web3 beyond the confines of socially-driven narratives. The next section will describe the technical construction of Web3 in the context of our fancy database. After that, you will probably know more about blockchain than 99.9% of the population.

Structuring Web3

To understand the relevance of Web3, we must first understand how the Internet is constructed. It starts with clients (computers). Your PC, smartphone, and tablet are all examples of clients. When you go on the Internet, your client is constantly requesting access to information that is inside various servers.

Servers are pieces of hardware or software that host networks—that is, they store all the data of a network. You might know of them as *server farms* or the tech company computer rooms with black cubes stacked by the thousands. Those black cubes are servers.

Clients make requests while servers grant them, which is how information is exchanged between hardware. There can be thousands of clients to a single server, all sharing a universal protocol that writes the rules for how they can interact. The combination of clients and servers with a protocol is called *the client-server model*, and it keeps our smartphones and laptops from having to store the data and run the computations that uphold the Internet.

Once a system for hardware communication has been established, there exists a network, which gives programming languages and their associated software packages a place to run. They are used to build platforms, which is the part that you see (websites and applications).

When you combine thousands of networks, you get the Internet that we all know and love (or sometimes hate). These aspects of the Internet are consistent across both the Web3 and the legacy system versions. Figure 1 depicts a typical network structure and the characteristic differences of both versions.

Figure 1

Internet Infrastructure

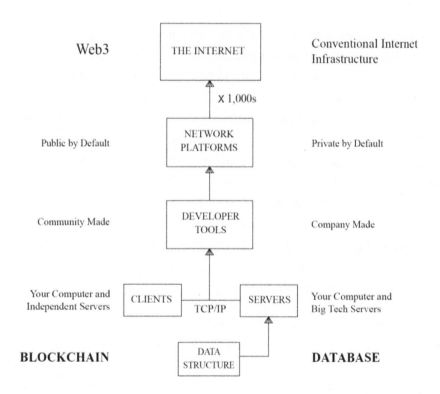

Blockchain only makes a difference for one small part of the Internet. Since servers exist to fill the requests of clients, one of their responsibilities is storing data, which is generally done with a database. Web3 merely swaps out the database with a blockchain. Other differences in Web3 come from subsequent technologies that are made newly available to the Internet. To understand why this is, let's look at why today's Internet evolved in the way that it did.

In the legacy system, most of the Internet's constituent parts are privatized, which came about through a natural evolutionary process. To demonstrate why, we'll use a hypothetical scenario from the 1990s where modern Internet infrastructure doesn't exist yet, but where involved parties fully understand the client-server model.

Alice is a software developer and wants to launch a web application. For Alice to make her app publicly accessible, she needs to find a server or servers to host her app's code. It's expensive and impractical to build the hardware infrastructure herself, so she looks for 3rd-party help. Alice is referred to Bob, who recently opened a small business that runs servers specially designed for people like Alice. Unfortunately, Bob's setup poses many risks for Alice that all stem from a lack of trust. The obvious issue is that Alice doesn't trust Bob enough to give him free rein over her app's database. Even if Bob is an honest guy, he doesn't have the resources or know-how to implement the security measures necessary for preventing cyberattacks. If Bob loses power or goes out of business, then Alice's app will become inoperable. If Alice's app grows beyond Bob's server capacity, Alice's app will again shut down. Alice can't trust the human or the technology necessary for creating her app.

Luckily, Alice finds Dave, an IBM consultant, who is able to alleviate all her concerns. Dave explains how his team provides unlimited server space protected by top-notch firewalls and backup systems, which brings her platform risk to near zero. Alice moves from having to trust Bob's word to trusting industrial-scale servers backed by the full faith and credit of IBM. Alice finishes coding her web app and is ready to launch thanks to the help of IBM.

Everyone who builds on the Internet makes the same choice of sticking with the most prominent service providers. Centralized actors are now the Internet's bedrock because they provide the Internet's trust.

As we now know, IBM was not the company to monopolize the Internet because it failed to realize that mainframes wouldn't build the Internet. It was primarily Google, Microsoft, and Amazon that came to dominate the Internet because they created the "Cloud," which is another way of saying Big Tech's servers.

Before diving into the Cloud, we have to take a step back. The client-server model is the winning standard for connecting networks, but it doesn't create anything useful until you add developer tools. I'm using term *developer tools* to cover some of the many other components that go into making the Internet. Operating systems, programming languages, compilers, Application Programming Interfaces (APIs), software development kits, load balancers, browsers, search engines, and content delivery networks are some examples of developer tools. Thirty years ago, it was not in any way obvious that those tools would be around, but today's Internet treats those tools as general standards.

Google, Microsoft, and Amazon didn't initially succeed as cloud companies. Instead, they built Internet services in vastly different domains: search, software as a service, and e-commerce, respectively. There was also no straight path to building an Internet company at the time; there was no easy way to host a network and no useful developer tools for making platforms on those networks. Big Tech companies of today either became the best at using available developer tools or making the best ones from scratch.

Now let's look at how Alice would create her web application in 2020. She starts with a programming language, which is her specialty—it is where the logic of her entire app is coded. This part is just like how it was done in the 1990s; it doesn't require 3rd-party help because many programming languages are open source. For Alice to build a network that runs her software logic—that is, get her app on the Internet—she needs to find servers to host her app's code. This process is similar to what Alice could do with Bob and Dave, except that this time she doesn't have any good options outside of the Big Tech cloud.

Alice's earlier analogy left out all the extra baggage that comes along with today's developer tools. 1990's Alice would be nearly finished with her app at this point because developer tools were sparse, but this convenience would do no favors for Alice's web application. The app would probably be complicated to use, even harder to find, and wouldn't easily integrate with similar networks. In short, Alice from the early Internet probably wouldn't attract any users beyond friends and family.

Big Tech is so big because of what they do for Alice and developers like her. To prove this point, let's look at the additional steps Alice would take in the 2020 Internet after setting up her app with the Cloud. First, she would need a database for the servers. She could make one herself, but the all-around better choice is to share an existing Big Tech database because it will take care of logistics and security for her. The one security measure Alice must take is setting up username and password access controls that are compatible with single sign-ons like Google accounts. Alice also needs to set up a payment method, and she will probably use something like Amazon API Gateway, which takes care of everything e-commerce in one fell swoop. To make sure people find her app, Alice must construct the whole thing in a manner that caters to the Google Search algorithm. Attracting users probably requires a Facebook presence at the very least, but the superior choice for Alice is building on a bigger platform with something like Microsoft's LinkedIn API. Alice then needs to make a separate mobile app that meets the guidelines for Apple App Store and Google Play. Similar subsequent processes follow for mobile versions using Apple Pay and Google Pay for paid services and catering to app store search algorithms. Alice must also ensure the compatibility of her app and any downloadable software with the various competing operating systems.

As Alice takes these extra steps on top of coding her app, she is just adding pre-packaged pieces of software that are owned and controlled by someone else. In this sense, Internet apps relate to the Ship of Theseus thought experiment: As you keep restoring parts of this ancient ship, at what point is it no longer Theseus's ship? As Internet apps become increasingly composed of 3rd-party parts, at what point are they no longer owned by creators like Alice? If you want to look at this paradox practically, I think the answer depends on how much you trust Big Tech.

The Internet is the result of combining tens of thousands of networks like Alice's. They are all private by default, restricting interactions to those granted by a complex set of permissions. Of course, this is not a comprehensive explanation of the Internet. Instead, it is focused on the parts that change in a Web3 transition. Now that we have a handle on what is meant by "the Internet," viewing the centralized and decentralized versions can be done more literally.

The Internet that Alice has been working with is heavily centralized relative to the Web3 vision. Its lowest layer is a data structure, which is almost always a centralized database. Alice's app data is in one place and controlled by a single entity for the same reasons Alice chose Dave's IBM database over Bob's homemade database. The next Internet layer is servers that compose the hardware for the data structure. They transmit data to clients and are owned by the same companies that host the databases. The servers hold all the programming logic that makes Alice's network and platform, including Alice's app code and all the software packages that connect to it.

If Alice used Google Cloud to make her app and you were using it, this means your computer would be requesting data from a database that Google owns through a server that Google owns and with the developer tools that Google owns, hence the centralization. We will talk about the Internet power triangles relating to this later. For now, we will look at how the entire structure changes when adding blockchain.

In Web3, the data structure is composed of a blockchain instead of a mere database, roughly speaking. The old data structure had to be owned by a company to be kept secure, but this new data structure is protected because a company cannot own it. The reason for this, if you'll remember, is located in the two unique features of our fancy database (a blockchain): Its data is perfect because it is mathematically required to reject all errors, and all its data is immutable, making it a kind of eternal truth. For Alice, the blockchain data structure option is more reliable and potentially cheaper.

The next Web3 component is a hardware infrastructure for connecting the app data structure to users. The client-server model is the typical way to do this, except servers must be distributed in the Web3 environment so that networks will favor Bob's handmade setup over Dave's industrial design. Since the servers are hosting secure by default blockchains, Bob doesn't need any extra security measures, and if he loses power, other people like him all over the world will pick up the network's slack. IBM's server rooms now look outdated, with unnecessary cybersecurity protection and single points of failure dictated by geographical limitations. What's more, Web3 can explore client-to-client models since, if networks are efficient enough to dispense with server compute resources, clients can freely interact without trusting each other because they trust the underlying data structure.

Developer tools can make networks into unique and useful platforms. Comparing Web3 developer tools to those of the familiar Internet is almost impossible at this stage because no clear standards exist, and there is no certainty that they will. They will also be built on an infantile stage infrastructure that is, in many ways, incomparable to the old infrastructure. The following explanation of Web3 developer tools is mostly theoretical and based on the goals of many leading startups.

Web3 networks like Alice's application are public by default. This means usernames and passwords don't make sense, nor do APIs that connect platforms with permissioned controls. These things are built-in and occur automatically. An Internet without usernames or passwords begins to make sense when blockchain identities dictate access controls, which is a can of worms that won't be opened until Chapter 6. APIs also make less sense when you are working with public networks. For example, apps that would previously take additional steps imposed by Big Tech would now have them as built-in and unconditionally-free modules. For Alice, this means that many of those app add-ons are pre-packaged code that she doesn't need to remake, and if she makes an original add-on (which today would look like a unique API for her app), then it would be pre-packaged for everyone else just the same.

No one has to reinvent the wheel. And no, this will not sabotage Alice's or anyone else's revenue model or intellectual property. Just as Facebook only benefits when Zynga used their API to make apps like Farmville, Alice will benefit when others use her pre-packaged code—only this time around, Alice and Zynga don't need to trust a profit reaping puppet master like Facebook to run their apps.

Collectively, tens of thousands of these public-by-default networks create Web3.

Can We Forecast Blockchain's Future?

This chapter provides a technical overview of blockchain and its significance for the future Internet. It also idealizes` Web3 as a sort of online utopia because, well, it doesn't exist yet, and idealized concepts brush aside all complexity-related problems with the assumption that they will be simplified over time. This assumption is very wrong.

An even more pervasive and imprudent idea is that Web3 will grow without external influence from prior generations of the Internet. A true Web3 makes the big five Internet companies look outmoded, but some simple math tells us that those companies are more formidable than this idea gives them credit for. The combined value of all cryptocurrencies, which has only a small fraction of its value dedicated to Web3, at the time of this writing is one-twentieth the size of the big five Internet companies by market capitalization. Are we expected to believe that Big Tech will roll over and die by the hands of un-owned networks? How about governments and the capitalist system, which by their very nature must privatize and control things?

Questions like these drill down to the core of something that is technically legitimate and socially nonsensical. When members of the technology sector are confronted with this, they are forced to lean toward one of two polarized camps: the technocratic libertarian looking for a blockchain-based future, and the conformist incumbent who considers the hype around blockchain to be laughable. These are the extremes of a vital spectrum. Interestingly, these ideologies are both held by hypercompetent people, but each camp denies the existence of the other, or at the very least, doesn't understand the other's position. What's funny is that most people in the middle of this spectrum who just don't care about blockchain will correctly tell you that both sides are wrong.

Both sides are increasingly forced to merge as innovation continues. Anonymous cryptographers and small startups drove most innovation occurring in the first decade since Bitcoin's release. Only recently have large companies and venture capital projects started taking over the show.

Mainstream depictions of the blockchain industry highlight the technocratic libertarians, probably because the conformist incumbents won't elicit any reaction. Granted, blockchain can be argued to have started with anarchistic developers, but those radical groups are now an exceedingly small and harmless minority. At this stage in blockchain's developmental history, the conformist incumbents are becoming an overrepresented majority. They should be classified as radicals too because they claim to utilize blockchain technology but dispense with all axioms on which its original design is predicated.

Private blockchains, which are the predominant choice for companies using blockchain, are a prime example of this. They solve the scalability and governance problem by giving ownership and consensus controls to a single entity, usually the parent company. Incumbent industry experts love to tout the superiority of private blockchains over public blockchains (the type we've been talking about) as if they achieve the best of both worlds. But a private blockchain is really just another database with an especially funky structure. Private blockchains do not share either of the two unique features of our fancy database, and they do not contribute to Web3. To a casual observer, this movement turns blockchain technology into an easy-to-use developer tool. To a seasoned technologist, this is an attempt at privatizing blockchain technology and represents the antithesis of a blockchain revolution.

You might be wondering why the beginning of this section postulates that Web3 will be loaded with complexity. Isn't Web3 supposed to remove complexity so people like Alice don't have to take a dozen ancillary steps to deploy a web app? Aren't these all-in-one solutions?

The all-in-one solution idea is full of contradictions. There's no all-in-one package for Internet services. Software packages provide the tools necessary for one solution, but an Internet user is solving dozens of problems that each require an independent solution. Just think about how many platforms you have a username and password for.

Web3 is trying to be a truly independent all-in-one solution, and this may unfortunately be its downfall. Ironically, open systems, including blockchain technologies, are inherently bad at cooperating. This is a lesson about open systems that humanity keeps forgetting, and evidence for this long predates the failed Napster-like protocols. It took the whole latter half of the 20th century for technologists to learn the detrimental flaw of decentralized systems.

Protocols were briefly mentioned as what write the rules for how clients and servers interact. Today, the Internet's universal protocol is Transmission Control Protocol/Internet Protocol (TCP/IP), but it wasn't always this way. Exploration of standards to connect hardware devices started before 1950. After decades of trial and error, Open Systems Interconnect (OSI) was the apparent global protocol standard supported by major governments and corporations. As the name suggests, OSI was dedicated to openness, modularity, and permissionlessness (just like blockchain). All this equates to an all-in-one solution: that is, companies with many disparate computing devices could connect them into a network using only OSI. It was the would-be Internet's bedrock, but come the early 1990s, the tides began to shift toward the simpler and less comprehensive alternative that is TCP/IP.

The unanticipated transition from OSI was ironically a result of its inability to interconnect. General Motors (GM), one of OSI's early proponents, demonstrates this perfectly with its experience. Across the company's many plants using thousands of pieces of incompatible hardware and software, GM set out to create a digital connection for all of its operations.[4] Given its tremendous resources, the company used OSI to create a network from the bottom up that was perfectly customized to its needs. Many companies followed this process. The finished product was always a unique network that wasn't designed to cooperate with other networks.

TCP/IP is a simple load-it-and-go type of protocol and is the mechanism behind today's client-server model (the Internet's lowest level from Figure 1). This availability made TCP/IP the popular choice for network initiatives, especially small-scale ones. Once this was realized, anyone who used OSI would alienate themselves from the rest of the Internet.

The TCP/IP victory should be celebrated, but the tradeoff was a lack of built-in developer tools. This leads right back to the problem with the 1990s Alice: Her web app is useless without developer tools, which were hard to come by for the early Internet. The developer tool gap left by TCP/IP provided room for private companies to monopolize the Internet. Instead of using OSI's open-source building blocks to make systems, TCP/IP users could just link up to existing company software services. Instead of GM building their own custom network, they were better off connecting with the same software services that everyone used, such as Microsoft Office. This trend has since accelerated, and its remnants can be seen in all the additional steps 2020 Alice takes when creating a web app.

If we fast forward to the blockchain world of 2020, there is a striking resemblance to the mid-1980s when OSI adoption appeared inevitable. Both

OSI and Web3 are incessantly dedicated to openness and completeness, so everything you need to build a custom network is available in one place. Comprehensive protocols are incredible in theory until you realize dozens of uniquely constructed Web3 startups are bad at connecting, and users could only work with one at a time. Since these networks are independent, they will never agree on standardizing one. OSI failed because competitors would not concede to another's network standards. Ford would never adopt the GM network, and IBM wasn't about to share its software service stack with Microsoft. Imagine how poorly this would work across industry verticals. Instead of paying attention to this problem, Web3 and blockchain startups make a new blockchain for every possible use case.

The Internet's solution to the problem of disparate networks is platform proprietors. The idea is that you create a single company that provides all the developer tools so that they don't clash with each other. The more people use them, the more standardized the developer tools become, and the closer you get to an all-in-one solution. By being simple and available for everyone, Big Tech's proprietary tools have conquered the Internet's real estate. Today's Internet connects so well because it is all made of the same Big Tech stuff. Of course, there are disadvantages to this Internet oligopoly that will become apparent in the subsequent chapters, but we are forced to accept the Internet as it is.

Blockchain technology is perhaps the best attempt in history at providing freedom for the Internet, but there may not be enough resources within the space for this to matter. Web3 poses an existential threat to Big Tech; meanwhile, the whole industry's valuation is a drop in the bucket for technology companies.

If history is any indication, the blockchain industry's future will look something like the following. Leading startups will continue to accomplish technological feats that preserve blockchain's fundamental principles, and their completeness will continually place roadblocks in the way of widespread adoption. Big Tech will be there to repurpose any notable successes into centralized developer tools, all under the flag of blockchain technology. No one will understand the difference, and everyone will opt for the simple, available, and interoperable Big Tech version.

Since the terms *decentralized*, *open*, *comprehensive*, *permissionless*, and *blockchain* are full of contradictions, it is hard to stop those trying to privatize them. Real blockchain applications are embedded in the Internet's bedrock, not developer tool add-ons. Restructuring Internet infrastructure isn't sustainable with the data-centric blockchains, which was this chapter's focus and the general focus of Web3 leaders. It instead requires mostly non-blockchain computer science innovations that maintain the core features of data-centric blockchains.

There are technological workarounds to make such a future possible (and on which this book will focus), but they don't give enough credit to the social element. If we are to reallocate the Internet's resources to supporting Web3 instead of suppressing it, industry leaders need to understand misconceptions surrounding blockchain technologies. User decisions also determine the bulk of technology's progression. It is paramount that the public understands the tremendous impact of their online activity.

Hopefully, we don't look back at early blockchains in the same way we view Napster-like protocols: a failed attempt at a peer-to-peer Internet. This book serves to outline possible paths for blockchain technologies in the many places where they apply.

A Guide for Reading this Book

The idealized Alice and Bob–style analogies used in this chapter aren't meant to prove particular claims but rather to help us grasp complex and conflicted narratives without stripping too much nuance from the relevant science and engineering. There's a tricky tradeoff when summarizing abstract concepts like this; for example, you just got a concise and high-level overview of Web3 and upon finishing this book you should have a perspective that makes this chapter seem flaw-ridden and oversimplified. This book will now attempt to prove very particular and perhaps radical claims, which means it is about to become much less ambiguous in its overall style.

Your time is valuable, and I want to disclose this entire book's structure, everything you should expect to take from it, and the shortcuts available based on your objective.

The book is designed to be read consecutively. Each chapter opens with a concept or question that wraps around full circle to a conclusion or answer through a very carefully woven chain of logic—order matters. Every chapter is meant to be read in the context of itself and all the preceding chapters. That said, some chapters work as standalone chapters for those willing to accept conclusions at face value. For example, you can skip to, read, and fully understand chapters 9 and 10 which walk through the vision and process for restructuring Big Tech with a blockchain Internet, but you won't know why it is true or important without the rest of the book. Below is a breakdown of all the chapters to be used as a guide.

Chapters 2, 3, and 4 outline problems with the legacy Internet, the best available solutions offered by blockchain technologies, and new difficulties posed by implementing those blockchain solutions. Keep in mind these chapters attempt to hit *all* the best solutions to *all* the biggest problems. These solutions are usually found deeply entrenched in academia and will often carry with them deeply controversial implications. For you, the reader, this means that some examples will be technical and complex because Alice and Bob style analogies no longer have legitimacy when referring to controversial and technologically specific topics. Although each chapter builds on the previous one, it is not a requirement to understand every example to profit from reading this book. In other words, feel free to skip over or skim the heavily-cited technical jargon of these chapters in order to follow the main argument.

Chapter 5 is about governance mechanisms, which is a very meta way of looking at the societal importance of blockchain technologies and why it is an irreplaceable tool for the collaboration of the masses. It describes what is, in many ways, the final frontier for blockchain technologies and what should be the highest priority goal for technologists.

Chapters 6, 7, and 8 cover the preliminary steps that must be taken in key industries to make earlier solutions a reality. These chapters don't try to evaluate every available blockchain solution but instead take a linear path through related solutions that create the most optimistic outcomes for each industry. They also flow with the implication that these solutions will happen sequentially: For example, Chapter 7 would not be complete without using the technology depicted in Chapter 6.

Chapter 8 is about how blockchain technology applies to the physical world, such as IoT devices and machines. Those solutions aren't practical on any large scale without blockchain solutions for identity and finance from Chapters 6 and 7. Here you will begin to grasp how widely used blockchain can become by reading summaries of all the most effective pilot programs and startup initiatives. These chapters serve as a literature review and are quite dense. Although blockchain solutions for identity, finance, manufacturing, and supply chain demonstrate the usefulness of later Internet solutions, the final chapters are written to be comprehensible without prerequisites. If you don't care about a chapter's particular industry, feel free to read only the first and last sections.

Chapters 9 is all about what Big Tech would look like if it implemented blockchain solutions. It runs through an idealized version of each of the Big Five Internet companies, what it would take to get there, and what they could do to stop decentralization and privatize the blockchain space. This chapter's grandiose and fanciful visions are grounded with technological legitimacy by the context from previous chapters.

Chapter 10 is about how the entire blockchain and Web3 narrative of today does not provide any realistic way to decentralize the Internet or take on Big Tech. Yet the technological features promised by the blockchain narrative and provided throughout this book are still possible with a better Web3 infrastructure proposal. This chapter explains the Internet Computer, which is one such proposal, and the only one I have found that is capable of restructuring today's Internet. Finally, global implications for a scenario that sticks with Big Tech and one that moves toward a blockchain Internet are both evaluated.

CHAPTER 2:

THE DEATH OF PRIVACY

Chapter 1 provided an overview of Web3—and it is clear that there is a long road to actually creating Web3. At present, we cannot even guarantee what parts of Web3 will be better than the current Internet because the technology it uses is still so young. If decentralized technologies are challenging to implement and not necessarily better than centralized technology, why should we bother putting so much effort into improving them?

The answer is entirely out of view for a typical Internet user because the dangerous aspects of a centralized Internet are happening behind the scenes: namely, a loss of privacy. Alan Watts perfectly captured the dangers of privacy loss in his 1966 *The Book: On the Taboo Against Knowing Who You Are:*

> By means of scientific prediction and its technical applications, we are trying to gain maximum control over our surroundings and ourselves. In medicine, communications, industrial production, transportation, finance, commerce, housing, education, psychiatry, criminology, and law we are trying to make foolproof systems, to get rid of the possibility of mistakes. The more powerful technology becomes, the more urgent the need for such controls…. The trend of all this is towards the end of individual privacy, to an extent where it may even be impossible to conceal one's thoughts. At the end of the line, no one is left with a mind of his own: there is just a vast and complex community-mind, endowed, perhaps, with such fantastic powers of control and prediction that it will already know its own future for years and years to come.[5]

The trend toward increasing certainty Watts proposed has only since accelerated. Loss of individual privacy and the rise of a community mind are the two outlined possibilities, with the latter being a result of the former. We can see both playing out almost exactly on the Internet, but not in the way most might suspect.

Pornography research alludes to the core reasons for a distorted public perspective on privacy protection and its perpetrators. Beyond personally identifiable information (PII), one's porn history is ordinarily the most sensitive personal data. When someone searches for online privacy solutions, porn was likely the chief motivation (this is, of course, not a target audience thing but rather a blunt conclusion that anyone would draw from a glance at porn statistics). Public concern regarding privacy protection is unfortunately driven by individual porn usage and other less than productive activities, diverting attention away from more pressing communal privacy issues.

When we think of surveillance, we incur debates surrounding what should be considered appropriate levels of surveillance by the state. Surveillance in the private sector lacks that type of public accountability.[6] Publicity regarding the Snowden accusations and several related occurrences in government mass surveillance should raise severe concerns at the federal level.[7] More general usage of online government tactics has been well documented and studied.

A comparative analysis of declassified documents utilizing Internet metadata in the context of International Data Privacy Law produces the following conclusion: In most countries, there is a general lack of transparency and behavior that is inconsistent with published law, which in turn violates standards of international human rights.[8]Findings in this area are unfortunate but offer few solutions beyond calls for "robust global debate."[9] Given that the original issue is perpetrator recidivism, it's hard to consider increased awareness and more laws as viable solutions. Although these are concerning issues, there continues to be tremendous resources dedicated to providing checks for the state's technology usage. Since the Internet is also borderless, tyrannical utilization of the Internet by one government does not protect it from the rest of the world.

Fortunately or unfortunately, depending on your perspective, the threat of privacy loss through government action pales in comparison to that posed by tech companies. This claim would only be wrong if some massive classified program(s) surpassed the powers of Big Tech while keeping the public oblivious, which, if true, would make talking about it a useless pursuit. It's typical to think of a world where Big Brother surveillance has no boundaries, but the present circumstances leave governments with no jurisdiction or reason for intrusions without severe criminal activity. Rare situations where governments violate privacy have harmed individuals but are not that dire on a global scale (with a few exceptions such as China's mass surveillance). United States legislation effectively prevents government intrusion but still does little to shield the average Internet user from private actors.[10]

Our brave new world looks more subtle. The personal data we create is not individually targeted, but instead is collected in terabytes and used for something closely resembling a complex community-mind.

To establish why private corporations have the means and motive to violate privacy well beyond governments, let's run with the porn example. A study scanning 22,484 porn sites found a 93% data leak, 79% of which came from 3rd-party cookies and trackers, often from our beloved data behemoths (e.g., Facebook and Google), even though these platforms supposedly don't support adult websites.[11] Boundless statistics from Internet companies (not governments) have yielded hundreds of porn statistics in a single study.[12] Shortly, it will become clear how analytics companies could determine and monetize individual porn histories with this data alone.

Examples like this are unsurprising given their frequency in Big Tech, but if word got out that a National Security Agency (NSA) employee hacked and viewed a single computer's history without permission, the public backlash would be fierce. An unauthorized hack by the NSA faces more repercussions because it can get wrapped up in a relatable story about a victim who is not all that different from you. Governments are held to high privacy standards, and tech titans fly under the radar while conducting this behavior on the scale of millions.

Keep in mind that government data from the international privacy study was primarily obtained from the private sector.[13] Governments have no incentive for discovering data like porn preferences for average citizens, but Internet companies have everything to gain.

A complex community-mind is the probable outcome of Internet privacy loss, and governments are not the culprits. Internet infrastructure was built on the backs of private companies, the same companies that now control it. For the remainder of this book, Facebook, Apple, Amazon, Microsoft, and Google will be referred to as FAAMG.

Cambridge Analytica

Cambridge Analytica is the American brand of the English-based Strategic Communication Laboratories (SCL) group and also the most widely-publicized analytics firm for their utilization of Big Data. Although just a small and typical Big Data operation, they are the most infamous firm of their kind as a consequence of their role in the U.S. 2016 presidential election. Politics is irrelevant to the analysis of this event: Instead, it is significant as proof that human behavior is reducible to bits. Evaluating the Cambridge Analytica (CA) operation is dependent on the hearsay of conflicting testimony, but this explanation will not go into detail beyond what is accepted as corroborated by the relevant literature.[14]

CA is an analytics company that worked to maximize the effectiveness of online advertisements. Its data collection consisted of demographic data (race, gender, age, income, geographic features, etc.) and psychographic data (advertising resonance, lifestyle data, consumer confidence, etc.), amounting to as many as 5,000 data points on 220 million Americans. With a sample size somewhere in the millions, data was collected with online quizzes measuring levels of what behavioral psychologists call the big five personality traits: Openness, Conscientiousness, Extroversion, Agreeableness, and Neuroticism (OCEAN).[15] Cross-referencing the resulting behavioral data with that of social networking sites (SNS) provided the algorithmic precondition for personality blueprints from SNS data alone. In other words, someone who took the personality test that was high in agreeableness will have measurably different clicking patterns than someone who was scored as disagreeable. This was done with individual traits, but with the unique combinations formed from all five. After analyzing thousands of test-takers and their online activity, every clicking behavior could be accurately linked to personality traits. You no longer need to take a personality test for companies to understand you: Just browsing the web is sufficient. Personality profiling results were then used to connect offline data with the cookies of different sites to deliver individualized ads.

Former CEO of CA, Alexander Nix, gave an example of how digital profiling was used in the Ted Cruz campaign during the Iowa Caucus. CA started by isolating a persuasion group: 45,000 swing voters with a high chance of election turnout.[16] Analysis of this group generated likely personality traits: above-average conscientiousness, low neuroticism, low openness, etc. The primary issue of concern with the group was gun rights. These combined factors laid the foundation for successful ads. Within this target audience, breaking down groups further to the individual level is possible with CA's estimated 4,000-5,000 data points on individual Americans.[17]

No doubt, CA had a brilliant strategy methodology, and it was no secret. The above explanation was well documented, and no one cared. Nix described this exact strategy on stage and was commended for it until President Trump was elected, at which point a long series of allegations were made.[18] Investigations generally concluded that the manner in which data was obtained was legal, but the way it was exploited was not transparent, making the data transactions illegal. Lack of proper vetting on the part of data brokers led to a series of fines for involved parties.[19] CA was permanently shut down. Data retrieved by CA from Facebook catalyzed the Facebook (FB) Federal Trade Commission (FTC) investigation.[20]

News outlets conveniently leave out the more banal components of this story.[21] CA was a relatively small analytics company acting in the same way similar companies do. Elections are just one area of advertising CA operated in, and the company has been involved in over a hundred elections before the U.S. 2016 election.[22] U.S. military defense agency DARPA funded AggregateIQ (an organization under the CA umbrella) in contributing to the Ripon Project for the purposes of combating terrorism.[23] DARPA also validated counter-terrorism work developed by the Behavioral Dynamics Institute, which relied on the same technology underpinning CA's tactics.[24] Behavior was reasonably consistent across each circumstance and not surreptitious or unique to CA.

Accusations against the company were primarily baseless but stuck around long enough to destroy its reputation. For example, Nix's voluntary testimony to the Digital Culture Media and Sport Committee was over three hours of collusion accusations (most of which were false) with no mention of behavioral microtargeting or its implications.[25] Much of the hoopla encompassing CA's services probably surfaced as a result of media outlets looking for reasons to discredit President Trump.[26] While CA's behavior was not ethically justifiable, it also wasn't intentionally nefarious, as its practices followed the standard procedures of Big Data analytics.

After enduring prolonged investigations, company algorithms remain top secret, and the extent to which Big Data can control elections remains virtually incalculable. Perhaps conceptualizing the scale of CA in the grand scheme of things is possible by evaluating their economics. The first U.S. candidate to use CA was Senator Ted Cruz, whose campaign contributed $5.8 million for the company's services.[27] His campaign saw tremendous progress through the course of its collaboration with CA. Donald Trump's payments to CA amounted to $6 million over the last five months of his campaign.[28] Assuming the deal was profitable, CA purchased all related data for less than the payment received.

To Facebook (FB), these figures are a crumb of a crumb. The Cambridge Analytica Scandal is one of many SNS data leaks where the tactics of 3rd-party beneficiaries were just small-scale reflections of FB's own targeting.[29]

CA initiated a snowball effect that culminated in FB policies and procedures for Big Data investigations. To recapitulate FTC documents succinctly, FB clearly monetizes user behavior through mass surveillance. Privacy policies are intentionally vague: for example, protecting interactions with user interface components are outlined, but the mechanisms that collect data circumvent application platforms in obtaining device data.[30] This system's sole purpose is to maximize engagement by using past behavior to influence future behavior.[31]

As for the government's role in protecting human rights online, legislation can only do so much. The FTC Facebook settlement cost them penalties but did not change core practices.[32] Enforcement agencies call for more specificity in policies available to their users. Still, increasing user awareness will probably change nothing given that the manner in which Mark Zuckerberg drank water during his testimony got more attention than the testimony itself. Let us not forget that no one cared about CA practices until it became politically convenient. As evident in their attempts, legislators are unlikely to keep up with the speed and obscurity of Big Data tactics.

Even after incidents and guilty rulings, we never see the algorithms. The public has still never seen behind the curtain of the platforms they use. Companies themselves would have to surrender their competitive edge (and reputations) by revealing their techniques. However, tracking a single device has given us a rough idea of what data outputs are available to these service providers. The 2019 study "Google and Facebook Data Retention and Location Tracking through Forensic Cloud Analysis" proved exactly what does stay private for a typical Samsung Galaxy Note 5 user. Researchers did this by rooting the phone to gain access to the memory, files, and partition encryption of Samsung,

Google, and Facebook. Two weeks of phone use with Facebook and Google applications combined with forensics software revealed the following: Every interaction that occurred on Facebook, nearly all intimate details from Google apps, and a location timeline regardless of locations services being turned off was all retrievable data.[33] To simplify, next to no application data was protected. Google and Facebook are not transparent about how they can obtain such data, a situation best summarized by the words of Congressman Bob Goodlatte during the testimony of Google's CEO: "Google is able to collect an amount of information about its users that would even make the NSA blush."[34]

All this is scary to an individual, but fearful reasoning blocks progress toward a benevolent version of that complex community-mind. In terms of ethics, behavioral microtargeting is exceptionally complex. Threats posed are a reduction in privacy and human autonomy. These adverse outcomes at first glance are seen through different eyes when the harsh realities begin to sink in. Not even blockchain can put the mass data collection genie back in the bottle, and the extent to which we produce data will only increase. Facebook, for example, will always monetize data, but if the company disappeared, data collection wouldn't just stop. Data is becoming a new world currency, and curators will always be there to fill the gap.

Correspondingly, every major industry has its fair share of sleazy elements coupled with entirely genuine intentions. For instance, researchers in Big Data don't pursue a career in research for wealth or fame, yet their success is dependent on an ability to secure external funding. For these professors and researchers, large-scale grants and opportunity for influence pigeonholes their research conclusions.[35] Whether individual professors or entire corporations, both work toward a cause under the gun by adversaries eager to pick up wherever they leave off. FAAMG will continue to prevail in some form, and as they navigate further into uncharted technological territories, clear-cut legislative boundaries become increasingly blurred.

Data behemoths can't even get their stories straight—they have mutually exclusive philosophies. Apple wants nothing to do with user data: It's a liability.[36] Facebook believes "the future is private," and the company's job is to ensure this vision.[37] Google intends to embrace data usage for altruistic motives and maximizing user benefit.[38] [39] Who's right?

Assuming the reduction in people's privacy and autonomy caused by CA was immoral, complications entangled in that assumption are endless. DARPA and CA targeted Islamic extremists, intending to manipulate them into adopting a more conventional belief system by the same micro-level tactics.[40] Are we saying Islamic extremists are too unintelligent to come up with the *right* belief systems? If not, behavioral microtargeting should be seen as immoral. If so, what distinguishes it from elections? Not much beyond the differing ideologies.

Socrates reminds us that democracy's limitation lies in the foolishness of its voters.[41] How about the hundreds of minuscule decisions we make every day? At what point does autonomy reduction in cereal choices become too much? Should we restrict discussion to these high-stake examples and exempt low-stake equivalents? Lawmakers and technologists are the ones that will have to answer these questions, but as current models indicate, legislative mandates have low penetration without organizational transparency.

This preliminary summary of how companies use data is not an attempt to demonize them. Global-scale improvements in efficiency and value production are positive consequences that should not be marginalized. The economic value created by Big Data spans every sector with figures approaching the hundreds of billions in each. This book does not harp on industry benefits of Big Data because blockchain solutions do not jeopardize them.

Internet of Things Sensors

Data collection in web interactions and wearable devices is still just scratching the surface. Roughly 90% of this data is currently wasted, but analytics companies are still in the nascent stage and will only drop this percentage.[42] Data creation is also no longer restricted to these sources. Internet of Things (IoT) devices are rapidly intruding on every intimate aspect of human life. Device growth went from 500 million in 2003 to 8 billion in 2017 and is projected at 50 billion in 2020.[43] Now omnipresent technologies such as RFID, NFC, actuator nodes, and sensors, in general, have their data collected and monetized. Internet technologies will involve device-to-device value transactions with anything enclosing a circuit.[44]

The last chapter described Web3 as the vision for a decentralized Internet, but since it does not exist yet, it can mean completely different things depending on what future Internet is imagined. In this chapter, I will refer to different stages of the Web as they are used in the conventional Internet literature. Web3 is not used here to describe the decentralized Internet, but instead a different sort of stage. Keep in mind that Web generations are just loosely-defined metaphors.

One school of thought conceptualizes the transition to IoT as three successive stages: Web1 (static webpages), Web2 (social networking), and Web3 (ubiquitous computing web). Web3 consists of wireless sensor networks (WSN): spatially dispersed devices seamlessly integrating with the physical environment.[45] Web3 also demands a system for data analytics, which brings us to the Cognitive IoT era and potentially Web4. Cognitive computing infuses intelligence from the physical world to move systems toward data-driven decision making. IBM predicts these systems will "learn at scale, reason with purpose, and interact with humans naturally."[46] This potential for tremendous progress makes long-term consequences easy to overlook. Cognitive IoT is just one of many names providing a similar interpretation of future directions. Whatever does come next will essentially be the Web3 version of what CA and Facebook became relying on Web2 level data.

Entering the cognitive era of the Internet assumes the last stage we can reasonably estimate. The Internet of Autonomous Things, the Internet of Robotic Things, and the Autonomous System of Things are a few of many eventual prospects. All of these necessitate network device hyperconnectivity with data controlled and utilized by artificial intelligence.[47] This is not a direction that can be stopped, but it should warrant proceeding with caution. We still have minimal control over even data analytics that come directly from humans. When smart toilets start checking you for hemorrhoids and your Alexa integrated toaster serves as your psychologist, you will want to control what happens to that data.

Web3 digitization of the physical world is becoming evident in smart cities. As we move from the Big Tech behemoths of Web2 into the dispersed brick and mortar IoT infrastructure of Web3, there are significant security threats that non-specialized companies are not equipped to handle. Data from devices controlling homes and facilities are now at stake. Smart cities are susceptible to threats on availability, integrity, confidentiality, authenticity, and accountability.[48] Traditional security mechanisms remain insufficient in addressing these same concerns where blockchain is specifically tailored.[49]

The current smart-city ecosystem is suffering from a higher frequency of indiscernible attacks. The response has been increasing security system complexity, making hacks more sophisticated and harder to detect.[50] Innovators attempting to revamp this model are converging on the same solution techniques used in Big Data. Rebounding on support from Big Data is the predominant option for making smart-city initiatives feasible.[51] [52] Security Information Management Systems have already benefited from adopting Big Data principles in large-scale testing environments.[53] It makes perfect sense that Internet companies would want to gobble up all this data. Control is the motive of Internet companies, and the operations of entire cities offer a powerful spectacle. The dark side of smart cities is their failure to recognize solutions outside of Big Data analytics.

The Future of Privacy

The CA scandal is an infamous example of Big Data usage that incurred global debate, and the whole thing was a $6 million service. The Big Data industry is worth around $50 billion now and sees rapid growth due to IoT sensors and AI.[54] Who's keeping tabs on the societal impact of the other $49,994,000,000 worth of Big Data analytics? The fact is that no one is moderating this industry, and its global influence remains incalculable.

Until now, there has existed a boundary between online life and the physical world. The extent to which data is collected about you used to stop when you disconnected from devices. A near future with ubiquitous machine computing will break down the physical barriers that allowed people to disconnect from the Internet. China is a pioneer of this new age, having developed a state surveillance infrastructure with ubiquitous facial recognition cameras being the most popular of many data collection techniques.[55]

The extent to which acquired data gets used by the public and private sectors is unknown. Still, its intent is undeniably a politically-motivated means of growing power for the communist party. Furthermore, China now has created and mastered the best developer tools for this very sophisticated surveillance system, which has become their export because it can add a government surveillance layer to the Internet for any willing country.[56] It should come as no surprise that Big Tech is the force helping build this digital totalitarian state.

Even though it was just a few years ago, the CA scandal now looks like a child's play version of Big Data analytics. CA made people mad at the time, but it seems we are becoming desensitized to nefarious Big Data tactics in proportion to the rate at which they advance. Especially now, since data scientists—who led the development of Big Data analytics—have the most sought-after job in America.[57]

A future with conventional Internet infrastructure does not look private. No, governments and corporations won't seek out your porn history, but they will collect everyone's porn history and every other piece of information you create that converts to power or money. Maybe we shouldn't worry too much about this, because the trend toward utilizing communal data and growing a collective community-mind will just leave everyone docile and happy with the eventual state of affairs.

Potential Blockchain Solutions

Ironically, governments appear as the only possible opponents of Big Data. Investigations have concluded that these tech companies are potentially dangerous, but governing bodies have trouble implementing explicitly actionable restrictions. At present, democratic governments can do little more than encourage FAAMG to play nice under the threat of litigation war. Another approach, like that of China, is if you can't beat em, join em. The next chapter will discuss the regulatory response to Big Tech's alarming growth and centralization at length.

There is one other possible and underrecognized opponent of Big Data that is far more relevant to these problems and this book than are governments. Technologists themselves and their solutions offer the best ways to counteract other nefarious technologies.

Fully Homomorphic Encryption, Multi-Party Computation, and Zero-Knowledge Proofs are some advancements enabling useful outputs from completely confidential data. Provenance tracking and data authenticity from network endpoints can be ensured by unclonable identifiers linked with blockchain transactions. Decentralized storage and computing cultivate immutability, auditability, and simultaneous private-transparency. A decentralized network of peers accompanied by a public ledger does not offer an exhaustive solution, but there is a compilation of under-recognized tech plugging away at infringement in the data economy.

Isolated data sets provide the most prominent functioning examples—adding one or more of these technologies as a feature—to date. Electronic Medical Records (EMRs) are instrumental and sensitive datasets that crave innovation. These consist of information from individual specialists—for example, dentists, orthopedics, and surgeons. Legislation such as the Health Insurance Portability and Accountability Act (HIPAA) protects patient privacy somewhat but disallows system interoperability, so specialists can't exchange research. Data collection then becomes limited to silos because EMRs are not shareable. Notice that this is a microcosm for the problem with conventional networks: They can't interact because their data is private by default. The legacy system protects patient data, and rightfully so. It's important to keep EMRs confidential to the standards of the corresponding patient. An ideal system utilizes all the data transparently without violating privacy.

Solving this starts with creating and storing unique pathways to EMRs on a blockchain while leaving the actual EMRs in the same traditional database. Since those digital pathways, or pointers, are cryptographically attached to EMRs with a hash function, any change to the EMR will change the pointer. Once you put pointers in the hands of their patients, they can then access their own records, control how it is shared and used, and alter their set of permissions at any time. This solution is a serious contender for tackling the Office of the National Coordinator for Health Information Technology's (ONC's) interoperability challenges and would offer vast amounts of genetic, lifestyle, and environmental data for medical research.[58]

This blockchain solution for patient-centric EMR management has already been seen in practice. MedRec is a medical data management system born out of MIT Media Lab. Patients are given the ability to grant data access through smart contracts that issue traceable addresses for EMRs. The MedRec Blockchain does not store EMRs; instead, it keeps metadata and pointers for locating them.[59] Metadata makes the original copies tamper-proof because any changes are detectable in the blockchain. Network miners could secure the chain in an entirely distributed and anonymous fashion, or the current and more economically feasible method is delegating trust to already established service providers.[60] Patients involved benefit from a full picture of accurate health data and control who can receive what.[61] As similar alternatives become universal, patients could leverage the management of their own valuable data to demand compensation.

This is by no means a comprehensive blockchain solution in the medical industry. There are currently over a thousand health-related blockchain startups. MedRec offers slightly more transparency, privacy, and data utilization to a single set of records. More broadly, MedRec is a proof of concept that made distributed data unified across disparate service providers. Any group of related accounts can apply this technology to connect and protect users. Records from financial accounts, insurance companies, Internet services, etc., would all benefit by using blockchain as a trusted mechanism for interoperability.

Despite the MedRec blockchain serving as a trustless (capable of functioning without needing trust) delegator, there are lapses in trust in the conventional IT infrastructure that it rests on. MedRec only tweaks the legacy system and still stores raw data with 3rd parties, relying on arbitrary record keepers. EMRs still lack authenticity, secure storage, provenance tracking, auditability, data entry verification, and private analytics. In the case of EMRs, these are expendable features because we tend to trust the healthcare industry. The everyday data that we generate lands inevitably on centralized servers, which warrants some upgrades.

Blockchain cloud storage is prevalent in Ethereum's Swarm, InterPlanetary File System, Filecoin, Storj, Sia, and MaidSafe. Each work according to similar principles: Files uploaded to the network are hashed and given a "digital fingerprint"; the data is fragmented across many nodes with all locations filed, and the nodes recombine all pieces upon retrieval, yielding that same digital fingerprint.[62] This process does not need to occur in centralized databases, which is why the blockchain cloud is reserved for when trust and robustness are of utmost importance,[63] at least until its efficiency surpasses that of the Big Tech cloud.

In many respects, the security of blockchain storage is already superior to the silos of the conventional cloud.[64] All these startups are making strides toward the blockchain cloud, bringing it into the realm of unparalleled robustness. Walled gardens such as Google Cloud require consumer trust to function, while blockchain provides it as an inexorable prerequisite. The Internet's cavalier approach to data protection raises the demand for trust and robustness, thus increasing the importance of decentralized storage solutions.

Both centralized and decentralized storage options offer privacy but can't provide a route for data audits and can't ensure authenticity. If Facebook is suspected of selling a sample of user data it is not authorized to share, the company has two choices: Maintain integrity by withholding exonerating data, or prove a negative by exposing the very data it is committed to protecting. In Facebook's current state, the latter is not a viable option because its databases are mutable, meaning an audit of exonerating data would not provide definitive proof because it could have been altered after the fact.

The Provchain data provenance architecture is one solution example that would offer the best of both worlds. Built on blockchain, Provchain offers private and immutable cloud storage with added auditability. The auditability feature is only possible thanks to blockchain identities, which is discussed in Chapter 6; for now, we assume they are sets of online personally identifiable information (PII) that interact with blockchain. Provenance auditors can analyze the data in question using the associated hash of a block-identity, thus preserving privacy while verifying source authenticity.[65]

A hash is similar to the MedRec pointers in that even the slightest change to the underlying data will completely change the hash/pointer; this way, no alteration goes unnoticed. Every provenance data entry has a receipt confirmation that verifies its permanent state and access control parameters.[66] Applied to

Facebook, this would cryptographically link posts to the real person who posted it and restrict access to that data based on controls set by the content creator. Provchain has yet to take root outside the testing environment. Mass market adoption is likely too big an undertaking for Provchain and similar startups. The concept works but will not be commercially available until it starts interacting with incumbent systems.

Applying Provchain and similar systems to the different stages of the Web will carry various intricacies for each case. These systems fit Web1 like a glove: Content creators and developers can have their independence without many technical obstacles. This already exists in the form of dapps (decentralized applications) and decentralized storage. Web2 (social networking) has its fair share of challenges. The vast majority of this data doesn't call for robustness and trust. Auditability and analytics for this metadata are only useful at scale— that is, Facebook data is useful when combining thousands of accounts, not when singling out individual ones (later, I will discuss options for solving the leftover flaws in Web2 data protection/usage). Web3 (IoT device) data is utilized in the same universal way once it reaches a database. Standardizing the way it is produced and processed is the new frontier.

Proof of authenticity comes from provenance tracking, which is only possible through legitimate blockchain identities. IoT devices can comply with decentralized database infrastructure by generating non-fungible identifiers. Physically Unclonable Functions (PUFs) have been successfully used to register digital fingerprints for manufactured devices on a global blockchain (identity API connecting all PUF enabled public blockchains).[67] Trust is at first delegated to original manufacturers because they ensure the quality of a given product. After initial registration, device IDs act as a tamper-proof certificate of product authenticity. Illegitimate devices are prevented because the real manufacturers have a special mathematical relationship to generated keys, making them the sole entity that can create device IDs.[68] A Web3 using devices having blockchain IDs will ensure data integrity long after they leave the factory. The result would be safer supply chains and smart cities.

Every incremental stage in the Internet's development corresponds with exponential growth in data creation. Robustness and trust from decentralized storage come at the expense of higher resource intensity. Web3 devices have excess resources that can be cultivated to keep up with their colossal data generation volume. Object-based computing power and memory space could allow sensors to accomplish their functions without releasing heaps of useless outputs. *Sapphire* is a blockchain-based storage system that uses typical IoT devices to perform smart contract execution. Instead of a sensor sending all outputs to a server for analysis and having a decision routed back to the device circuit, this is all handled internally.[69] For example, if sensors in your home tracked activity to control lighting, they would have enough reserve storage to run an independent program that determines when each light is on or off. They could sync with each other to optimally function but would not need to send data inputs to another computing device (your phone) to determine the state of each light. The only data sent off the sensors is a finalized result (the state of each light switch). *Sapphire* system architecture tailors smart contracts with an on-screen display, so devices remain physically controllable.[70]

In practice, this means that when strolling home from work, your fingerprint enabled doorknob could auto-sync with your smart appliances independent of your browsing history from that day. It will set up your home based on preset conditions controllable by you with no control given to Big Tech. Freely configurable IoT devices are efficient and transparent in their operation because they operate in a closed system. Embracing this concept is one way to keep Big Data tactics from infiltrating smart home devices and smart cities in general.

Web3 is coming, and many more solutions have yet to be explored. Web2 is of more imminent concern because it's already dominated by organizations too big to fail. Controllers of Web2 are building Web3 on the same principles.

Secure information storage and access have been addressed, but once the data is accessed from its silo, blockchain can no longer preserve it. Secondary markets can prey on the reproducibility of data. It's most apparent in the music and movie industries where online pirating is a casual occurrence. Bitcoin's solution to the double-spend problem solved this for currency, but more generic content does not share a universal ledger. In other words, copying bitcoins onto your database is useless because people only believe data on the Bitcoin blockchain, but for movies, this is harder because copied movie data is usable in many different forms. To fix the double-spend problem for movies, movie data would need to be in blockchain form and readable by something like a blockchain-based Netflix.

Solving the double-spend problem for generic data starts with making public who owns what data. Let's step into the shoes of CA while assuming incumbent systems perfectly integrated MedRec/Provchain-like solutions. Facebook would still have collected massive data samples in whatever ways smart contracts deemed permissible. CA access to data bundles would be transparent from the start if it participated in the network. Otherwise, a secondary source providing CA with data would leave no blockchain footprints. Regardless of how it was obtained, CA's use of data would remain private. Demand for indefinite privacy while keeping data usable is blockchain's next big challenge.

Enigma, the MIT Media Lab–based startup, is surfacing implementations of this idea. Using Distributed Hash Tables, they scalably store all relevant data on-chain. Keys generated by compressing data with a hash function are propagated through the network, making data retrievable. Generating readable analytics is accomplished through Multi-Party Computation where distributed nodes draw algorithmic conclusions with unreadable data bundle pieces. Results improve already existing algorithms and never reveal raw data. User permissions allow full reversibility of available data and unauthorized reproduction becomes impossible.[71] The primary project initiative is to advance medical trials at scale by extracting statistics from newly usable data.[72] Beyond health records,

Enigma use cases extend to genomics data computations, credit assessments/lending, identity verification, and machine data marketplace management.[73] Bureaucratic hindrances like HIPAA and GDPR are bypassed without jeopardizing any involved parties. This could yield a credit score or contribute to genetic research without ever showing companies your information.

Enigma and other projects cryptographically securing usable data are still in the development/piloting phase. Creating that privacy layer comes at the expense of prolonged time to market. The Medical Internet of Things is veering toward Big Data analytics for its miraculous capabilities such as "analytical capability for patterns of care, unstructured data analytical capability, decision support capability, predictive capability, and traceability."[74] Comparable to smart cities, the medical industry Internet layer will opt for the most readily available developer tools. Big Tech couldn't be more enthusiastic about adding this additional stepping stone en route to the cognitive era.

Although these solutions don't directly address Big Tech, they are what is on the horizon. The medical industry makes a great example because it is an excellent place for new technology to mesh with public and private actors. So much work with blockchain is being done in health care because of its commitment to patient rights. Medical institutions are similar in structure to Internet service providers in that they have disparate systems with useful data that need ways to interact that don't compromise ethics. If Internet companies were to take user rights as seriously as patient rights, they should view the above solutions as parts of an exemplary data protection system.

Big Data Solutions

Proof of concepts directly challenging Google and Facebook must take root in standalone platforms because Big Tech is not ready to start adding decentralized elements. Blockchain startups have done just that and provide the decentralized equivalent of popular online services. These projects introduce eminent technology options to a world that needs them but are probably not themselves serious competitors of incumbents.

FAAMG consumes approximately 70% of all online ad spending.[75] Data analytics yielding beguiling advertisements makes for a troubling business model. Built-in Chrome and Safari ad blockers have been a means to accentuate their own ads and trackers while crimping the efficacy of 3rd-party equivalents. The Brave Browser combined with Basic Attention Token has created an alternative.

Brave is an ad-blocking browser with no ulterior motives. Unlike Chrome extensions, Brave has a native implementation in C++ (not JavaScript), which precludes automatic jumps to insecure communication lines (HTTPS upgrades) and blocks trackers through unconventional means. Simply put, it is far superior to a traditional ad blocker and is already built into the browser. This blocking precludes much of the unwarranted data collection that websites conduct. Brave also adds an advertising model that exclusively comprises advertisers, content creators, and users with no Big Tech involvement. These ads efficiently target audiences in an entirely unintrusive fashion. Instead of collecting and analyzing data on centralized servers, Brave ads use machine-learning algorithms executing on device browsers with locally-stored data.[76] Browsers see everything in real-time: active tabs, intent signals, browsing history, keyword searches, click logs, etc.[77] Algorithms can also optimize ad timing and placement based on active/inactive features, tabs in focus, length of the session, etc.[78] Algorithms that utilize this data are computed locally on your device. Privacy is ensured because user data never leaves the device. It is a closed system. Since Brave doesn't have to pay Big Tech, its decentralized model shares the excess ad revenue with users in the form of Basic Attention Token, their native cryptocurrency.[79]

Although Brave is outsmarting 3rd-party advertisers, FAAMG's 70% dominance over online advertising is not addressable. The Brave browser still offers Google and Facebook services, and it's where its jurisdiction seemingly comes to a halt. It is unclear how much user data is protected by Brave, but it does not supersede traditional browser extensions in every way. Even if the number of Brave users exploded, Google Search would still use Adwords/Adsense, and Facebook would still profile users.

The brilliantly-constructed Brave advertising model is essentially being built on top of the already existing model. Because problems are rooted in the application layer, adoption at that same layer is vital for progress, so a decentralized alternative to Facebook is the only way to remove Facebook ads. Facing FAAMG head-on is not a prudent route for this startup. Instead, assimilating the public with the concept and technology is the success that will incorporate it in grander-scale Internet applications.

Social Networking Sites thrive on interlacing user data with clever advertising. Centralized platforms have no other economically feasible option, though decentralized systems are challenging this model. Steemit is a blockchain-based social medium with functionality like Reddit and Facebook. All blog posts have their text content logged on the Steem blockchain (pictures and videos are projected to be added on IPFS at a later date).[80] What Facebook stores on centralized servers, Steemit stores across 21 witnesses (delegated node operators) that are supported with only 10% of network proceeds. The remaining resources are broken down as follows: 10% delegated to the Steem Proposal System (developers improving the network), 15% to holders staking Steem tokens, and 65% to content creators and curators.[81] No presumptuous data collection or advertisements of any kind. This economic model is not at all intuitive, just like online advertising was at first a bizarre approach but is now driving trillion dollar companies. So where does the money come from, and why isn't Steemit beating Facebook?

Advertising is about attention, and through its evolution, discrete attention diversion with the help of Big Data integration has been FAAMG's recipe for success. Blogs are voluntarily viewed ads that have an agenda in the least annoying way possible. The Steemit cryptocurrency Steem, which is earned or bought, can be converted to Steem Power for increased content visibility and platform influence.[82] Used correctly, Steem Power could turn modern advertising on its head. Instead of Nike buying Instagram ads, they can create a Steemit blog with its visibility correlating to investments. An elaborate rewards system would redistribute rewards to viewers. If the Nike blog provides value to users, it will drive revenue from increased engagement. Being otherwise stingy with valuable content would lower the blog's reputation.

Steemit is a fully functioning, transparent, and immutable content database with over 1 million registered accounts.[83] Users own the data they create and get rewarded for it but still can't compete against existing social media giants. One reason for its stagnant user base is the inferior peer-to-peer value compared to existing frameworks. The walled gardens of leviathans create this barrier to entry for every newcomer. Even without this barrier, Steemit can't compete with the addictive properties of its personality-profiling counterparts. Algorithms have gone so far as to exploit profile pictures to classify personalities, extract interaction style traits, and use them to construct the ideal user experience.[84] Steemit algorithms are open-source, completely transparent, and unequivocally direct; they provide what you search for. Facebook's opaque algorithms perpetuate emotional states by snowballing insular results. Facebook is addictive because it gives you what it already knows you want, making Steemit respond like a comparatively dull research site.

Projects displayed thus far are narrowly creating isolated blockchain substitutes. All are limited by adherence to concepts with a single application and the inability to reach legacy systems. Restructuring a secure and honest Internet will require independent architecture thriving from its own decentralization. Oasis Labs is one platform for decentralized storage and computing. Decentralized applications (dapps) can be made with the same functionality as centralized applications/websites without reliance on Amazon Web Services/Google Cloud/Microsoft Azure. Computations and storage on the Oasis platform are secure from the hardware level up to the application layer. They even offer analytics with a similar style as Enigma, which opens a wider variety of uses for sensitive data. Dapp development, in general, can be similarly purposed for making decentralized equivalents of any centralized platform. Ethereum, Cardano, Hedera Hashgraph, Neo, Blockstack, EOS, and Dfinity are all notable competitors also building dapps.

Dapps are now rapidly being built but remain dormant and devoid of users. To the average user, there is no reason to fix a system that isn't broken. Solutions in this chapter cover technologies that are often framed as Big Data competitors instead of upgrades. With this outlook, they are likely to fail because you can't convince a market to renounce its conventions based on unevaluated dangers. Establishing an explicit set of universal concerns in the data economy is a start. Watt's collective community-mind metaphor gets pretty close to the core of these concerns: As advertising and human decision making become increasingly data-driven, centralized platforms will gain prodigious amounts of unchecked power.

This leads us to a paradoxical issue because getting social support for technological solutions requires convincing communities to take responsibility for personal data through participation in sub-par (non-FAAMG) services. The next chapter will paint a picture of why this is a doomed pursuit. Only after understanding the nature of heavily centralized tech companies can we start hybridizing data-based organizations with decentralized upgrades.

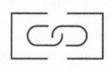

CHAPTER 3:

THE CENTRALIZED LENS

Many of the solutions from Chapter 2 are still science fiction, not because of technical problems, but because of the competitive Internet structure. There is an insurmountable concentration of power in legacy Internet infrastructure that opposes decentralization both systematically and culturally. If blockchain technologies indeed have the technological means to decentralize the Internet, then deciding blockchain's societal relevance has everything to do with hierarchy.

Global structures have become overly centralized, making us view everything through a centralized lens. We tend to either turn a blind eye to organizational centralization or detest it—both conceptions result from ignorance. Centralization is a beast of a topic and has delicate implications when discussing what can replace it. For this reason, explanations in this chapter are not exhaustive but are thorough enough to justify the need for decentralized solutions in the way that they are proposed.

Time and time again, the staple holding together acclaim for blockchain buzz has been the topic of decentralization. Top-down leadership in the corporate world is demonized as if blockchain networks are a candidate for replacing them. Although a popular Web3 notion, it will become abundantly clear in the next chapter why a blockchain-based approach to removing hierarchy will not only fail, but will never see a legitimate attempt. Centralization, of course, has its fair share of malevolent offshoots but removing them is rarely practical.

Centralization results from hierarchy. Truly decentralized systems must strip away all forms of hierarchy. But hierarchy is inevitable. It's ubiquitous in nature. Evolutionary speaking, humans couldn't survive in tribes over 100 without the introduction of a formal hierarchy.[85] The agricultural revolution occurred thanks to humanity's ability to adopt hierarchical structures and cooperate within them.[86] Development of cities and governments arose as 100+ person hierarchies became 1,000+ person hierarchies.[87]

The world's past several centuries were arguably the most decentralized centuries since tribal periods because there never existed a more significant number of interconnected hierarchies. Perhaps we can call this a *decentralized set of hierarchies*. People in the developed world have more opportunities to transcend their current socioeconomic class than ever before. People now compete in different hierarchies and have the option to switch between them as they please. Changing occupation can be done across various industries, corporations, and governmental organizations, which are all independent hierarchies.

Humanity now faces a different problem with regard to hierarchy. The Internet and other technological innovations make the world increasingly borderless, which breaks down barriers between hierarchies. Since hierarchies grow until they find boundaries, the Internet poses a new challenge. Boundaries for hierarchies have previously been geographical. This restriction was especially pronounced in previous centuries when the size of a hierarchy depended on physical infrastructure. The modern arrangement encourages the merging of organizational structures into a set of fewer and larger hierarchies (acquisitions, for example, demonstrate how corporate hierarchies always steepen to favor large companies). This is especially prevalent in the technology industry, where there are no physical borders to put a cap on growth. Dangerously fast growth rates of Internet companies have now increased the appeal of decentralized equivalents, but even those don't know what strategy can compete with incumbents.

So what's to stop the largest companies from growing? Well, aside from governments, there doesn't seem to be much. Instead of playing these guessing games, we will refocus on some fundamental truths about hierarchy to determine what aspects of centralized organizations are mutable. Luckily, centralized structures all follow statistically explainable laws that cannot be detached from the fabric of civilization.

The bell curve or normal distribution is the most popular way to explain universal behaviors. Its symmetry or "fairness" makes it broadly appealing, but hierarchies operate in an almost opposite manner that is explainable with the Pareto distribution. The Pareto principle or 80/20 rule is more popular, stating that 20% of people account for 80% of the useful work in an organization and vice versa.

Figure 2

The Pareto Distribution

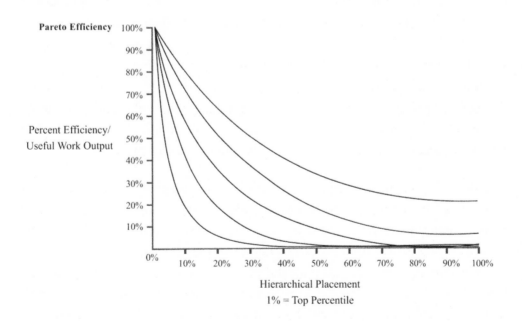

What most people ignore is that the trend continues up to the extreme percentiles. Its formation is self-evident in a simple experiment where 1,000 people each with $10 continually place dollar bets on a coin toss. Immediately a normal distribution is generated.[88] Some people win, some lose, most stay the same or close to it. This result is to be expected, but over time this game generates a Pareto distribution.[89] The vast majority are left with little to nothing, and a lucky few end up with all the money. Thus 85% of the world's wealth is held by the top 10% of people not because of a rigged game,[90] but because it's natural. Successful in modeling both useful output and achievement, the Pareto distribution is not only natural, but it's also necessary.

Figure 2 displays five different Pareto distributions, the center curve representing the conventional nature of hierarchical structures. Higher, more shallow curves resemble smaller, more disparate frameworks, and larger hierarchies ride closer to the X and Y axis as they grow. Of course, there is a deep-rooted problem when the curve gets too steep. Before the 14th century, hierarchies of modern humans were disparate across continents. Small pools of competing Pareto distributions worked just fine. Borders were relevant, and hierarchies balanced each other's size. Technological paradigm shifts gave these hierarchies space to grow by closing various gaps between people. The printing press closed the knowledge gap, giving birth to new industries, augmenting world trade, popularizing scientific breakthroughs, and distributing literature. This renaissance sprung us out of the Middle Ages by combining feudal hierarchies into cities. The world became a smaller place.

The steam engine initiated a paradigm shift, closing the distance gap with trains and ships. Industrialization followed, which yielded new industries and monopolistic hierarchies led by Ford, Vanderbilt, and Rockefeller. The immense progress of these times resulted from the efficient (left) side of each curve becoming concentrated with the most resources. Luckily, governments have always kept a hold on brick-and-mortar monopolies. Insurance, medical, real estate, and banking industries are all kept in check with heavy regulation. The Internet paradigm shift was powerful enough to make borders irrelevant and has few physical components to rectify. The Internet started as a humble decentralized architecture closing the communication gap. With the rise of information and communication technologies went the loss of barriers for Internet company growth.

From 1988 to 2016, the American top 1% of people went from controlling just under 30% of the wealth to 39% while the bottom 90% went from holding 33% to less than 23% of the wealth.[91] It's no coincidence that the five largest companies in the S&P 500 by market capitalization are Facebook, Apple, Amazon, Microsoft, and Google (FAAMG).[92] They remain immune to crisis: As the COVID-19 pandemic destroys entire industries, Big Tech continues to see rapid growth in wealth and power. FAAMG is the top 1% of the global wealth Pareto distribution, the steepest corporate Pareto distribution in history. This idea of paradigm shifts closing gaps is credited to author Richie Ethwaru, who asserts that blockchain will be the paradigm shift to close the trust gap between organizations and their consumers.[93]

Here's a refresher from Chapter 1. Before the year 2000, people could create and run software but had no easy way to succeed on the Internet. The Cloud solved this problem by providing computational power, storage, and a place to host software. This opened a new doorway for data sharing and is the bedrock of the Internet today. It also stripped users and developers of any power they might have had. This kick-started a positive feedback loop, funneling all the Internet's leverage into today's cloud giants.

Monopolistic Subsidies

It's not so obvious that hierarchy on the Internet bears relevance to other heavily-regulated industries. After all, their competitive elements are immaterial. A parallel example of hierarchies having abnormal growth because of the Internet paradigm shift is evident in the food industry. Individual/local food distributors (mom-and-pop shops) were ubiquitous until the late 19th century.[94] Commercializing wholesale was made possible by disseminating the tin can and cardboard box, which arguably closed the quality gap by giving rise to brand names. Large-scale distribution channels made chain stores the economical option by mitigating risk. Then chains killed off most mom-and-pop shops by the late 20th century.[95]

Now, most food and drink brands are under the umbrella of ten companies, and chains are now retail's only competitive option.[96] Consumers benefit from this arrangement because chains would rather endure low profit margins to grow market share. On average, grocery store chain profits ranged between 0% and 2% of annual revenues for the past three decades.[97] It's an infamously harsh industry, but massive revenues make it desirable. All major sectors have seen similar centralization of market players. This bigness has its fair share of short-term benefits but discourages newcomers.

Internet behemoths mastered the ability to delay gratification. FAAMG continues to slim down margins and lower prices purely for control. Giant incumbent industry players, like grocery chains, create a convenient opportunity for those on the Pareto distribution's most powerful fringes. Take, for example, the resource requirements for building a new supermarket brand. Not many entrepreneurs are eager to enter an industry where profits cap at 2% and no venture capitalist would support them anyway. That 2% margin becomes worthwhile when risk is distributed across hundreds of locations or when a financial means to wait out initial losses has been established. Thus, the opportunity is available only to the big guys. With more resources and innovative ability than anyone, FAAMG fits this category like a glove.

Cynicism is not the goal of FAAMG or my representation of them. If adequately controlled, this transition will be globally favorable. We have already seen constructive outcomes in Amazon's absorption of Whole Foods. Consumers are thrilled to have efficient delivery for the lowest-priced foods. AmazonFresh is their grocery distribution program, and although specific figures have not been released, this is likely an unlucrative venture.[98] A similar story exists in the FAAMG community for dozens of subsidiaries. Take Amazon's tablet initiative, for example. Amazon sells the Fire Kindle Tablet for less than the cost of its raw materials.[99] This is a substantial and dramatic loss that only increased with sales. Google also goes to extreme lengths for its free services: YouTube doesn't turn a profit because Google pays for uploading, storage, and streaming for even the lowest value customers.[100] Most Google apps operate on the same principle. Even Microsoft has proven abstemious when carrying on with Xbox after enduring the project's hundreds of millions in net loss.[101] Apple Pay, Android Pay, Google Pay, Samsung Pay, and Microsoft Wallet are analogous attempts at control in the financial sector: Their respective parent companies won't miss an opportunity to seize control over user spending endpoints too, even if it means losing money.[102] All this means to users is that FAAMG services are usually fantastic and entirely free.

Transitioning from individual food distributors to grocery chains is a microcosm for what's happening in technology. In one sense, this is pro-competitive conduct where giants force each other to scrape by while pricing products as low as possible. In another sense, this is exceedingly anti-competitive because the game only has five players. As amalgamating hierarchies reach new levels, so do barriers to entry. Any company that wants to compete with FAAMG needs insurmountable resources just for a seat at the table. These giants succeed so spectacularly because they know when to lose money. Control has been the motive of all these companies, and the short-term gains of high premiums leave unwanted room for competition. Tech titans are the only ones that can do this because they already control the technology sector's most lucrative avenues.

In the meantime, investors pick up slack as seen in many stock metrics—for example, dangerous price-to-sales ratios are apparent in all FAAMG stocks (earnings do not correlate with stock valuations). Most freemium models are on the dime of venture capitalists at first, and publicly traded companies have inflated investor stockpiles to buffer losses. Even still, they each need to save face with some profitability. Microsoft and Apple have fairly straightforward income sources; they charge high premiums for hardware and software with freemium products as a side benefit. Facebook and Google earn by monetizing data. Amazon is a special case, having dominant control over e-commerce but choosing to make so little money from it. They are ready to jack up prices at will, but profits are ultimately dependent on the Cloud. Amazon Web Services is the rapidly growing cloud storage, computing, and content delivery platform that made the bulk of Amazon's 2018 income.[103] The runner-ups are Microsoft Azure and Google Cloud, giving the big trio a majority share in the global Cloud.[104]

Beyond size and control, FAAMG wins by optimizing technology and minimizing overhead better than anyone. Their software can be copied virtually for free, and it scales to infinity. Customers do the work to improve existing systems by providing their data. Digital labor theory validates the idea that users can inadvertently act as workers, especially in social media.[105] FAAMG users are the product, not the customer. The economic proof is apparent when comparing annual economic value per worker in traditional companies to tech titans, such as GM and Facebook: Economic value is $231,000 per GM employee and is $20.5 million per Facebook employee.[106]

All the unbounded success from this section is just a representation of size. Monopolistic subsidies are just one hurdle faced by FAAMG's competition. If size was the only issue, any odious shifts in FAAMG's far-reaching branches could be balanced by venture capitalist funded startups. Tech titans exercise little concern for financial control, and it's no mistake. Once they establish irrevocable control over the Internet, then reasons for lowering prices will diminish. The biggest problem with this is FAAMG's inherent ability to always win by leveraging what they already control.

The Monopolistic Power of Data

Let's jump back to retailers and their data-based logistics or efficient consumer response (ECR) standards, specifically grocery chains, because their strategies are detailed enough to administer urgency for perishable items. Supermarket chains have a problematic relationship with suppliers. Entire commodities markets are dedicated to predicting price fluctuations in various food groups. Retailers need to couple this data with in-house data to optimize pricing and purchasing decisions. In a store, they determine what foods sell at what times on a seasonal and weekly basis.[107] What customers will pay, where to place in-store, and what brands to use are all questions that retailers must answer. Results prevent overbuying and overselling. With an expected 1–2% profit margin, any tweaks are highly valued.

Since stores aren't capable of mass Internet surveillance, they rely on loyalty/rewards participation for ECR programs.[108] Retailers can build purchasing profiles in participants from electronic point of sale and shipping data.[109] No further explanation is needed for these efforts to be laughable in the eyes of data behemoths. While in-store data collection is based on purchases, Amazon collects data on every step of the journey, and it doesn't even need to reward customers for it. Searches, clicks, purchases, streams, account details, etc., are all subject to collection for bettering the user experience.[110] This tactic is just one aspect of Amazon's unparalleled efficiency that no challenger can match.

Brands are mostly unaffected by this at first, so long as they register with Amazon Brand Registry. They can concurrently embrace online retail and traditional retail without batting an eye. Of course, sellers can still participate without joining Amazon Prime, but will suffer from decreased platform visibility.[111] So if Nike wants to sell on Amazon, it can either register the brand or lose sales from reduced search engine optimization on the platform.

Online retail, being controlled by Amazon, opens new doors for the company as an independent brand. Take headphones, for example. Many brands sell headphones on Amazon with different prices and features. When cross-referencing data points, Amazon can determine what features are most desirable and for what price. The result creates an impeccable blueprint for the perfect headphones with solely internal market research. AmazonBasics is starting this trend as an independent everything brand able to outsell everyone.

Facebook and Google have a forthright justification for data usage. Users feed data to have compelling advertisements fed back, all in a single platform. In controlling most of online advertising, they can essentially choose winners and losers. This isn't limited to paid advertising either. Everything on these platforms has visibility controlled by algorithms. Competitors are at the mercy of giants in helping them get exposure. One more novel component of the Facebook and Google data advantage is its aging process, which only improves services with time.[112] How can others compete with a project's continual data-driven refinements 20 years in the making?

FAAMG's data advantage is something any competition, even blockchain ones, will have to grapple with. The one disadvantage of FAAMG is that people are beginning to dislike how they hoard data that isn't theirs and selectively distribute content in an unfair way. It's such a bizarre concept because FAAMG opened up near-infinite data access to the public for free, which we definitely want to keep. The problem is that global risks are imposed when the information issuing party increases public influence without increasing organizational transparency.[113] Since no content provider ever had a similar role as FAAMG, it's hard to find a reference point for an appropriate level of transparency or even a way to measure it. Governments are the only entities that can boast comparable size and social responsibility to FAAMG.

Enormous government power and influence—especially with consideration to new data collection methods—require openness as a means to avert tyranny.[114] Luckily, efforts have yielded successful measurements of government transparency with 3rd-party checks. Results prove that organizations can protect trade secrets while using different levels of transparency for the public good. The Global Open Data Index (GODI) and Open Data Barometer (ODB) have established objective parameters of organizational transparency by evaluating dozens of components in 94 governments.[115] From factors such as government spending, draft legislation, land ownership, and national statistics,

objective results were compiled to give a comprehensive overview of governmental transparency.[116]

Data transparency is an open conversation for governments that haven't yet reached the private sector. Every organization that utilizes the public's data should be held to standards of openness similar to those outlined by GODI and ODB. Any practical approach applying similar standards to the Internet must (1) be driven by decentralized architecture and (2) align with corporate interests.[117]

Platform Advantage

Marauding for the home-field advantage is what spurs FAAMG's generosity. At the dawn of the Internet age (Web1), the exploration of static webpages began. Since then, Internet components have branched out to make webpages easier to find and run similarly offline. In centralizing these access control methods, a ranking system that we call the Internet hierarchy developed as depicted in Figure 3. Insurmountable levels of competition can be understood by observing how FAAMG maneuvers around this pyramid.

Figure 3

The Internet Hierarchy

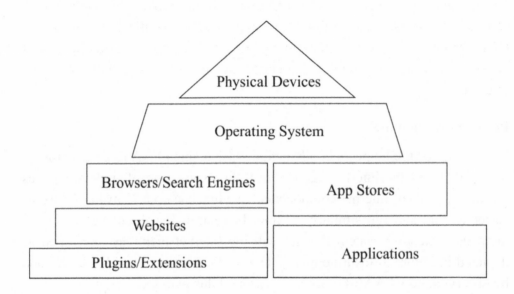

Starting on the left side, plugins and extensions are software add-ons that add functionality to existing programs. They are at the mercy of their host platform for functionality. Luckily, they usually fly under FAAMG's radar, but when on the cusp of any considerable success, their business models get crushed as they are added by software giants as defaults.

In the case of browsers, most design characteristics emulate a previously existing extension/plugin. Additional extensions are accessible through the browser itself—for example, the Chrome Web Store. It's hard to argue with this convenience, but it is also hard to endorse when knowing how much power it lends to FAAMG. Facebook offered a VPN called Onavo to "increase privacy," and it turned out to be collecting data from apps that were diverting attention from Facebook's own app.[118] It has since been discontinued because of privacy policy violations.

Websites can usually disable plugins, which is why they outrank them on the Internet hierarchy, but Google gets around this. Google is committed to maintaining the safety and security of users, which gives them the authority to block malicious extensions.[119] Although not deliberately preventing 3rd-party ad blockers, Google benefits from planting its own version in the place of whatever it blocks. Google Ad Blocker, for example, blocks localized website ads while prioritizing its own. The Google AMP (accelerated mobile page) Extension excludes junk when loading web pages in Chrome. This junk can be any website resources that Google doesn't like and has been criticized for basically dictating how websites *should* be built and forcing publishers into committing to the Google search engine. Websites can either participate in AMP or suffer decreased search engine optimization by opting out. In a much broader sense, website traffic and visibility are entirely dictated by search engines.

Let's be clear: Excluding Onavo, none of this is malevolent behavior. All the above scenarios have the best interest of end-users at heart because keeping customers happy aligns with FAAMG's goal of maximizing control. Small-scale developers end up as the only casualties here. As long as this model is centralized, the hierarchy will not change. It may instead cause developers to shift toward decentralized variants.

Google may be the puppet master for the lower left side of our Internet hierarchy, but it still gets beaten down by those above. Dozens of off-brand browsers and search engines are the bargaining chips giving operating systems power over Google. Apple's iPhone (the pyramid's apex predator) uses an independent operating system (iOS) and browser (Safari). Safari can choose to preset any search engine and threatens the use of Microsoft's Bing. Google Search stays as Safari's default because Google pays Apple a fat annual check: $12 billion in 2019.[120] Microsoft's Windows OS and Edge browser have this same leverage. Physical devices and operating systems preloading don't just pick the winning search engine. Software in general no longer gains market share through merit, but instead by being preinstalled when you buy the device. This preloading is taken to its next extreme when shifting to the right side of the Internet hierarchy.

Google doesn't thrive on hardware lines or own an operating system, but the company has its hands in a different cookie jar that helps it retaliate. Google's Mobile Application Distribution Agreement (MADA) allows it to shove device manufacturers in their back pocket. Samsung builds phones using the open-source Android OS. For Samsung to deliver the full functionality of a compelling phone, they need preloaded applications. Google offers a full suite of apps or Google Mobile Services (GMS), which includes Google Play Store, Chrome, Drive, Gmail, Maps, YouTube, Music, Photos, and a few others. Samsung gets free permission to preinstall the suite when following MADA requirements. The agreement mandates Google as the network location provider, requires features like voice search and assist to use Google, and includes specifics on-app positioning.[121]

Lastly, all MADA participants must sign anti-fragmentation agreements that prohibit the distribution of hardware running Android forks (altered versions of Android OS unaffiliated with Google).[122] This arrangement favors manufacturers and users with free premium (freemium) apps that have seamless interoperability. Google wins too because users commit time and data across interconnected apps, making them cumbersome to leave, not to mention that a presence at the top of the Internet hierarchy (with physical devices) maintains power in its lower portions. Apple uses this same tactic, just with a smaller market share. Their hardware lines, App Store, and iOS trio allow them to exclusively expand their application services to millions with relative ease. Once personalizing these platform bundles, you have to start from scratch by moving elsewhere. Third-party alternatives are available to consumers through the arbitration of application gatekeepers or app stores.

Google Play and the Apple App Store are rightfully the leading market players, not only because of dominance concerning operating systems but because they offer the most apps by far.[123] Each app store has authority over app listings for reasons of censorship. Banned apps are predominantly malicious or salacious, but this power is not constrained to misbehavior.[124] It's hard to decipher cases removing bias, but dozens have been reported: for example, a tech education app did not meet Apple App Store guidelines until removing its Android learning component.[125]

Application visibility is under the heel of yet another one of FAAMG's dials with app store search engines. The concern is otherwise not with the current app store conduct as much as with the capacity for misbehavior. The intention of these app stores is quite simple at present: Prioritize the best apps to grow user bases and their 30% cut on purchases.[126] [127]

Individual apps receive ample opportunity here—until they appear on FAAMG's radar. Exceedingly popular app designs all get added to the OS. Music, streaming, email, photo, GPS, and messaging apps are just some examples. FAAMG has another trick up their sleeves in case anything gets too big to crush. They just buy it. Here are the most prominent examples of FAAMG app acquisitions: Google's YouTube and Waze; Apple's Shazam; Amazon's Twitch; Microsoft's LinkedIn, Skype, and GitHub; and Facebook's WhatsApp, Instagram, and Oculus. These mega-platforms are not too accepting of rejected acquisitions either. Take Snapchat's choice to remain an independent company after receiving multiple offers from Facebook. Facebook retaliated by gathering Snapchat data via Onavo and mimicking their most popular features on its own platforms.[128] It simultaneously decreased the visibility of Snapchat posts and disabled links to the app on Instagram.[129]

Most platform acquisitions are not out of fear of a dark horse takeover; actually, most of these procurements are not with direct competitors. The anti-competitive nature of platform acquisitions relates to their data stockpiles. LinkedIn was by far Microsoft's largest acquisition, and they were not even in competition, yet this is inherently anti-competitive conduct.[130] LinkedIn consists of a user base concentrated with likely Microsoft users (business professionals) and has all the intimate details of their professional lives, giving its data exorbitant exclusionary potential.[131] This puts every Microsoft competitor at a substantial disadvantage in both production and marketing SaaS packages.

The Internet hierarchy has become so rigid that seasoned tech titans can't even breach it. Amazon's attempt to enter the smartphone space posed two major complications: hardware and software challenges, which are both not Amazon's strong suit. Outsourcing hardware development to a prominent manufacturer was not an option because they are all tethered to Google's MADA. Operating system choices were scarce because popular ones are exclusive. Amazon independently overcame this with the Amazon Fire Phone, built on an Android fork operating system. Preloading was restricted to "off-brand" app bundles, and the Amazon App Store offered only one-third the options of Google Play.[132] If consumers independently downloaded the typical freemium apps, they would suffer from software bloat as similar apps competed for storage/computing power.[133] Even selling the phone at a loss would not get them off the shelves, and it was discontinued in just over a year. This case was no fluke. Microsoft's Windows Phone shared the same fate for reasons of disadvantaged app availability.

If data behemoths can't even breach their own boundaries on account of each other, new players don't stand a chance. The Internet hierarchy operates in a Pareto distribution, which has grown too steep for anyone to climb. Options are to join it or restructure the hierarchy with a paradigm shift. Fighting this hierarchy head-on is a lost cause, and governments are learning that lesson the hard way.

Monopolistic Legalities

Antitrust violations in FAAMG mostly concern bundling, which is the selling of several products or services in a package but not separately. Platforms on the Internet hierarchy hold power strictly because of their ability to deliver these bundles, and it naturally raises antitrust concerns. Bundles in the last section are mutually beneficial for consumers and providers because they offer seamless interoperability for freemium services. They also leave doubt as to whether services succeed on merits derived from independent consumer judgment or automatic installation.[134] There are two central questions in the eyes of regulators: Is the bundle a separate or single product, and does it preclude customers from getting other 3rd-party versions?[135]

Microsoft was the pioneer company of the Internet age. It also paved the way for FAAMG by taking the brunt of every regulatory storm. Fear of bundling coercion could be thought to have started with Windows Media Player (WMP). Because Microsoft dominated the PC operating system market in the early 2000s, it could leverage manufacturers into a mandatory WMP preload on every Windows device. Microsoft gave the Windows distribution license exclusively to manufacturers that were preloading WMP.[136] Users could install other music apps but could not remove Microsoft's native music player.[137] The U.S. Department of Justice (DoJ) did not pursue the issue while the European Commission and E.U. courts pursued pro-competitive ramifications for monopolistic abuse of power.[138] In short, consequences from the European litigation war ignored efficiency gains of bundling, and the most significant loss was seen in consumer welfare.[139] Government interference made everyone angry because consumers liked the current state of Microsoft's products regardless of their monopolistic position.

Digital product bundling was just getting started. A later DoJ lawsuit found Microsoft in violation of the Sherman Act, mandating a company breakup for cutting exclusive deals to get its browser preloaded by manufacturers.[140] Ongoing litigation later reverted the decision in appeals court.[141] Microsoft's defense has always been that its varied service categories combine into a single unified product.[142] The argument against Microsoft states that there is independent demand for individual parts of product packages, which is monopolistic bundling. The nature of the Internet hierarchy is analogous to

Microsoft's early bundling attempts, just on a much grander scale. Microsoft could never shake charges as could FAAMG because it emerged before the data economy. High premiums made its dominance glaringly obvious, but today's freemium models get away with doing the same thing.

Google now leverages its operating system position to popularize its bundle. More than 90% of android device 3rd-party apps are downloaded through Google Play.[143] The European Commission condemned Google for its unlawful ties with Android OS and proprietary apps.[144] No palpable consequence ever came of it because every party involved would suffer from ramifications.

For the same reason people did not want government interference with Microsoft, no one is willing to lose Google's free services because of its monopolistic implications. This time around, the issue is more pressing because it doesn't just concern consumers. Entire businesses now depend on Google's freemium model.

Samsung already applies sovereignty in its decision to adopt Google's free bundle, but only because there are no other good options. To see how consumers and manufacturers would go astray without GMS, look at the Windows and Fire Phones. Google's "varied bundle as a unified product" argument works because, unlike the Microsoft era, there are now competitors of equal proportions. FAAMG is a pretty well-balanced oligopoly. Any damage to one company leaves room for another to grow.

Take a look at the pinch regulators are in when trying to combat Google's bundle. Apple and Microsoft's closed source operating systems are rivaled only by the open-source Android OS, which Google prefers. Disallowing bundles would force Google to make its own line closed-source and therefore support exclusionary software.[145]

These market realities provoked a unanimous FTC decision to discredit all antitrust complaints in Google's 2013 antitrust investigation.[146] The FTC has since remained relatively dormant on the issue.[147] Google's bundle paved a path that Microsoft never could by making a cornered market look like a gift in the public eye. Now every member of FAAMG can enjoy their walled gardens and bundles somewhat peacefully. Still, no regulatory victory for FAAMG will mark the end of their bureaucratic contention. Regulatory disputes in this sector will not have winners anyway because deep pockets on both sides will forestall any actionable resolution—for example, Apple V. Pepper is a "resolved" 2019 Supreme Court ruling against Apple, which merely opened doors to more lawsuits.

Governments have their only leverage over Big Tech removed by everyone's need for freemium models. Monopolies of the past were governable because they had simple revenue models, usually within a single industry. When the Standard Oil monopoly needed to be broken up by the federal government, it was split into different oil companies. Fair enough, but applying this to FAAMG leads everyone to an eternal set of crossroads.[148] How do you split a corporation that survives on data and control instead of revenue? Monopolistic subsidies are often unprofitable acquisitions and would not survive as standalone companies. Given their borderless influence, a proper dissolution of any tech titan would take inconceivable levels of global cooperation. Technology would continue to change too fast for the law to keep up. Government roles in this will continue to halt the innovation they desperately want to preserve.[149] If governments are to favor public welfare, they will continually be forced into complying with monopolies. Pursuing a litigation war would be a fool's errand on the part of governments.

Cognizable Market Domination

Internet behemoths did not succeed with luck or nefarious behavior. FAAMG services offer superior product interoperability, pricing, and peer-to-peer value. Tech giants have only each other left to compete with because they share the same openhanded principles. Their only crime has been putting customers before competitors and being too big—that is, their tactics for winning are completely cognizable. Academia is comfortable sharing this message, but the more popular media outlets won't share much optimistic news about FAAMG.

People should treat FAAMG just as they would any company representative. If someone offers you an excellent service for free, be skeptical but don't be afraid to thank them. If the skepticism prevails, then look for a trustworthy version of that service.

Maximum control being the winning strategy for FAAMG might imply a centralized organizational structure as the optimal choice. To an extent, this is true because of size. Advantages from platforms, data, and acquisitions are going to FAAMG chiefly because of their resources. Later portions of this book will show how decentralized economic models solve the resources problem. For now, we'll focus on the unavoidable difficulties that come along with growing centralization.

FAAMG operates in a multi-sided market, meaning they exist between dissimilar customer groups that depend on each other. These groups are usually retailers, advertisers, and users. For example, Amazon has sellers and buyers as distinct customers. Without one of them, the other becomes useless. All tech titans share this predicament, and it forces them to appeal to a variety of moving parts that they land in the center of. Disparate elements give them the protocol versatility to touch every industry, while competing networks can only hit one at a time. But this superiority becomes questionable when realizing that FAAMG can't divorce a protocol from its centralized hub.

Bundles make a good analogy for this. Apps are independent operations, but when offered in a bundle issued by a central authority, they become a point susceptible to attack. Data honeypots are FAAMG's most significant vulnerability with regards to centralized weak points. This problem draws an amount of privacy-related litigation threats comparable to that of antitrust. It was not discussed because no amount of regulation can address the core problem. Adding security requirements does not change the fact that centralized data architectures will eventually get hacked because they already solve an attacker's biggest challenge: knowing where to look.[150]

Resiliency also caps so long as isolated control points are on the network. Cloud service interruption that blocks data access has already occurred multiple times because of human error or natural disaster—single points of failure being the culprit in both cases. On February 28, 2017, Amazon's Simple Storage System forced applications in parts of the East Coast to lose functionality because of a minuscule coding error. Cloud outages, in general, occur pretty regularly and FAAMG's Internet is not built for resilience during many of Earth's possible black swan events. The trust factor in cloud service providers is essential to clients, and it will be limited provided that cloud data is centralized, regardless of how control over it shifts.[151]

Fixing the weak points of centralization in all tech titans will require a fundamental change in industry structure. But how can you change growing hierarchies that are so close to Pareto efficiency? A paradigm shift can change the rules of the game by creating a fresh market and new Pareto distribution to compete in. Orchestrators shape the structure of industries. Replacing network orchestrators with distributed equivalents is this fundamental shift. This topic is obscure because it is primarily a metaphor for a very technical revolution. The upcoming chapters will get technical about what Web3 parts are and are not part of an Internet paradigm shift. None of this is obvious because the blockchain world is not on track for this revolution.

Blockchain does not currently pose a threat to FAAMG. Centralized blockchain projects are winning at every turn. Ripple is the most successful fintech cryptocurrency because centralization makes it compatible with banking infrastructure. In the case of Facebook's Libra Coin, let's just say it's not for the purposes of distributing control. Coinbase and other exchanges are gatekeepers for cryptocurrency more so than FAAMG are gatekeepers for the Internet. Private blockchains are the leading choice for incumbent companies, and the vast majority of public blockchains are heavily centralized. The irony of these "decentralized" projects is that they came into being as attempts to gain control. This occurred without opposition because mainstream depictions of blockchain don't actually mean anything.

Is centralization or decentralization what expands influence? How is a blockchain decentralized if all of its biggest proponents use them as another monopolistic acquisition? Where does trust or transparency play into any of this? Infinite sets of questions like this can arise from the blockchain paradigm shift. None of them have straight answers. Two polar opposite answers can be accurate for different circumstances, but that truth doesn't sell very well, so everyone ended up telling the story that sounded best, and as a result, no one knows what's going on.

CHAPTER 4:

DISRUPTION AND DELUSION

Imagine explaining the Internet to the average American in 1995, when the user base was less than 1% of the world population.[152] Better yet, imagine you are one of the few innovators to understand TCP/IP in 1995. Attempting to spread the word, you define the Internet in the same way it was first formally agreed upon:

> "Internet" refers to the global information system that (i) is logically linked together by a globally unique address space based on the Internet Protocol (IP) or its subsequent extensions/follow-ons; (ii) is able to support communications using the Transmission Control Protocol/Internet Protocol (TCP/IP) suite or its subsequent extensions/follow-ons, and/or other IP-compatible protocols; and (iii) provides, uses or makes accessible, either publicly or privately, high level services layered on the communications and related infrastructure described herein.[153]

Considering the complexity of this premise, you would probably be ignored. How could the Internet's potential be realized with nothing similar ever having existed? Even the most basic ideas were incomprehensible: Amazon selling books how, exactly? Yahoo finding what information? Microsoft providing what services?[154] During this transitional period, innovators needed support, funding, users, and developers. Raising awareness required a terminology shift to something more publicly relatable.

Disruptive Vocabulary

Communicating ambitions for Internet technologies to a general audience was best accomplished by ignoring all logistics. Business models with a grand vision promising to "change the world" worked just fine, making the objective an excellent way to secure funding. Letting these buzzwords propagate among the general public for three years gave artificial credibility to tech startups by 1998. In October of 1999, the top 199 Internet stocks totaled a valuation of $450 billion, which created a sector that barely existed in 1995.[155] These companies collectively yielded a whopping negative $6.2 billion in profits that year, and the crash followed in 2000.[156]

Discussions of the dotcom bubble rarely give due consideration to the technology itself. Economists like to place blame on market manipulation and investor psychology, both of which reemerge unchanged in future market bubbles. Rhetoric replaces economics in all bubbles, making these discussions generally unproductive.[157] The more constructive question is this: Why was the Internet's spectacular success not shared with its original companies?

Retail investors, not institutional ones, fueled Internet stocks of the dotcom bubble.[158] The fundamental analysis from your average Joe or Jane was not adequate in predicting technology stock success. Everyone was hopping on the bandwagon of the next gold rush, without the first clue of what it was. In the spring of 1999, one in twelve Americans was in some stage of founding a business.[159] They all needed to attach a single understandable component of the Internet to their businesses. "Dotcom" was this label, an entry marker that allowed startups to be welcomed as investable contributors to the Internet.

The parallels to the 2018 cryptocurrency crash should be painfully obvious to anyone with 30 minutes of experience in the Cryptosphere. Cryptocurrency is that fruitless label, the isolated component used to simplify blockchain. The Bitcoin bubble was reminiscent of the dotcom bubble in that struggling companies associated themselves with a cryptocurrency in order to temporarily multiply valuations.[160]

Both blockchain and the Internet, at least in their first decades, are technologies best used as a supplement to brick-and-mortar businesses, not as the primary disruptor. In both bubbles, this unexciting truth was not compatible with the psychological temptation of quick money. In the years following, few tech companies survived, yet the Internet disrupted every major industry.

Another dismissed part of the dotcom narrative is how the Internet's lead contributors viewed the Internet as a radical attempt at decentralizing power by practically anonymous researchers and developers.[161] Sound familiar? It should, because it shares the same narrative as OSI, Napster-like protocols, and Bitcoin. It seems that every technology founded on principles of openness is either destroyed, centralized, or left in the shadow of private versions. Blockchain technology carries with it attributes like forced honesty through decentralization.

Internet technologies started with similar attributes that were made precarious by opposition from central authorities. Innovation does not inevitably coincide with benevolent progress. FAAMG's design developed the Internet but took away the opportunity to create some other arbitrary version. Collective narratives dictate how innovations are utilized and where developmental effort is spent. Pervasive delusion subtly directs the attention to blockchain developments of minuscule importance.

Without having a clear picture of how blockchain should change things, we will continue to make mistakes about how to prioritize its developments. Dotcoms didn't share the success of the Internet because their influx wasn't oriented for the Internet's purpose, but even the failed dotcoms had a great deal of influence on what the Internet eventually became.

The many crypto-obsessed projects are just repeating history. Unconventional practices that have become standard procedures in blockchain startups are often sneaky methods to hide their flaws. Unearthing these flaws remains taboo among the cryptocurrency community because it attacks a unique counterculture. What's more important than the feelings of cryptocurrency enthusiasts is how their message will disturb the possible arbitrary versions of Web3—prioritizing the ideal blockchain-based future calls for more objectivity in the way startups are viewed.

Failure at the Start(up)

Before people learn about blockchain, they first hear about Bitcoin, particularly that it is digital money, otherwise known as cryptocurrency. That is the famous story that everyone runs with. As you might expect, people and blockchain startups tend to use cryptocurrency as a currency, and this has its place, but their primary use case should have nothing to do with intrinsic value. Blockchains don't always need cryptocurrencies, but they do make convenient fundraising tools for startups.

Cryptocurrencies should be more commonly viewed as utility tokens used for buying network influence and computing power. Instead, companies use them to play some arbitrary and replaceable role in whatever business idea looks good.

The waning usefulness of cryptocurrency is best illustrated by the platform specialized in issuing them. Waves is a cryptocurrency startup and platform focusing on custom blockchain token operation.[162] Anyone can make a coin: I made a crypto in under ten minutes. The purpose here is primarily tokenization, which is representing physical assets with tokens. The value proposition of this is adding liquidity to things that would otherwise be difficult to convert into cash: for example, pieces of commercial real estate could be treated as tradable tokens. This simple concept landed Waves a spot in the top ten cryptocurrencies by market capitalization in June of 2017.[163]

Whoppercoin, Waves's only large-scale implementation, was used in Burger Kings across Russia, each coin redeemable for a Whopper. What resulted was nothing more than an inconvenient reward system that flopped within a few weeks.[164] Ironically, the sole value of each Waves-based token resided in the centralized authority that issued them—meaning that Whoppercoins would be useless as soon as Burger King said so.

This is a severe issue when applied to more extreme examples like real estate. The exception to a coin's worth being determined by its creators is when a complex platform is developed alongside it, where, inevitably, the utility is in the platform. Waves, one of the largest tokenization platforms, has made thousands of different tokens without any significant impact. The danger to the blockchain industry is not this failure itself, but the way news of general failures propagates.

The most obvious conclusion one might draw from this story is that tokenization doesn't work, but that conclusion doesn't follow. Tokenizing equity could be extraordinarily beneficial when applied to real-estate, company shares, or other physical value-bearing assets—just not for Whoppers. Using tokenization in a meaningful way requires jumping over complex technological and regulatory hurdles that publicly-funded startups like Waves are not capable of.

Every major use case for blockchain has an existing cryptocurrency to support it, often with a similar story. These destructive patterns create a stigma that stifles the involvement of reputable companies and governments. What remains is the assumption that countless failures point to a failed technology, when instead the blame should be on a flawed methodology underpinning a young industry. Recruiting the real drivers of innovation first requires shedding light on some uncomfortable truths about startups.

Talk that Doesn't Walk the Walk

The distinguishing features of blockchain are most commonly described with the words *transparency*, *trustlessness*, *decentralization*, and *security*. Although these buzzwords actually are misnomers, startups rarely advertise them as such. What gets better conveyed is a fog of hype, making the average consumer ignore the more complex side of the story.

Regardless of the features of a specific blockchain, the industry as a whole showed that these words don't properly apply to the entities issuing blockchain solutions. Company standards have become completely disassociated from these words and thus continually tarnish the reputation of blockchain technology.

Transparency (Versus Pseudo-Transparency)

Blockchain can come in forms ranging from entirely public to entirely private. Bitcoin is completely transparent about all transactions, but all transactions are between pseudonyms (anonymous addresses/identities that engage in public transactions). This sort of pseudo-transparency has the benefit of allowing everyone to share the same version of the truth while maintaining privacy.

Cryptocurrencies operate in a similar fashion, which adds some transparency to the startups issuing them, especially during their funding rounds or Initial Coin Offerings (ICOs). ERC20 (Ethereum-based) tokens have all ICO parameters immutably recorded and are viewable on any Ethereum blockchain explorer. Unit price, total supply, and amount purchased by each account are all public, with transactions arranged in a user-friendly, pseudo-transparent ledger.

Companies across industries have a lot to gain by running with this idea, but after the crowdfunding period, organizational transparency tends to fall by the wayside. ICOs usually receive payment in the cryptocurrency of the platform they are built on. Funds raised are put into a public account and generally cashed out for fiat currency. Following an ICO, company spending, income, and general fiscal health remain a mystery. Payments remaining on a startup's localized blockchain rarely show anything useful, especially with all account addresses being anonymous.

The vast majority of ICOs are not registered with the U.S. Securities and Exchange Commission (SEC). Market professionals avoid this obligation by labeling coins as currency-based products or utility tokens instead of securities, which require a license to sell.[165] Registering a security with the SEC requires a company business description, description of offered security, company management information, and financial statements, all of which are auditable. Registration statements are made public shortly after being filed for the sole purpose of investor protection.[166] These transparent features of the legacy system are often taken for granted and are seldom provided by blockchain startups.

The fact remains that the financials of cryptocurrency startups are far more private than that of traditional securities. Blockchain ledgers themselves provide an immutable truth about cryptocurrency specifications, but the overarching company could undermine that truth at its convenience.

The startup Coinmetrics digs for hard-to-find facts by analyzing blockchain data. Ripple, the fintech startup to replace SWIFT in synchronizing bank ledgers, low-balled its own quarterly escrow release by 200 million tokens (in XRP).[167] Coinmetrics also found inconsistencies in the XRP escrow release schedule, including an unaccounted for 55 million XRP.[168] Even with a universally transparent blockchain, the truth is still cryptic.

Transparency technically exists in all public blockchains, but its usefulness varies across applications. The optimal utility of transparency exists when there would otherwise be discrepancies or mistrust. Established organizations have the most to gain by publicizing finances and business practices with new technology. This perspective is unpopular as it would pull elements from the playbook of a stigmatized industry.

What remains is a misunderstood and underutilized feature of blockchain. At this point, the idea that blockchain is transparent and anonymous or public and private *at the same time* may seem paradoxical. This results from Blockchain's near perfectly-balanced anonymity and decentralization, which enables trust without leaders. It is a technological superpower for reasons made clear in the coming chapters.

Trustlessness (Versus Trustworthiness)

The word *trustlessness* has a counterintuitive definition in the cryptosphere: a lack of *need* for trust, not a lack of trust itself. A trustless system is a mechanism so foolproof that it will remain completely reliable even if most of its participants are untrustworthy. Trustlessness is used in this way throughout the rest of this book.

The trustless nature of Blockchain is boasted about in nearly every application, yet affiliated startups continually fail to deliver on this promise. Cryptocurrency-related fraud costs the public millions of dollars a day,[169] so what do we mean by trustless? In a truly trustless system, the underlying protocols are so reliable that it requires zero trusted entities to secure it, and even untrusted parties won't make network outcomes any less trustworthy. Like transparency, this principle only pertains to on-chain data, not the various endpoints that interact with the blockchain world. Endpoints refer to traditional Internet platforms that associate with distributed ledger technology (DLT). (For example, Binance is the largest cryptocurrency exchange, but the platform itself is a non-blockchain network endpoint, making it susceptible to hacks and stolen cryptocurrencies.) Dependency on endpoints may decrease, but they won't disappear unless a perfect Web3 is realized. Efforts are best spent determining which endpoints can be trusted.

The pervasive existence of cryptocurrency scams requires little explanation since they manipulate markets, not blockchains. The debunking in this book is reserved for unintentional lapses of trust that blame blockchain technology.

Bitcoin and many altcoins distinguish themselves from fiat currency by removing intermediaries from the exchange process, yet the most common exchange platforms are centralized and vulnerable. The Mt. Gox 2014 hack was responsible for a $400 million loss. The Bitfinex 2016 hack cost investors $70 million, and at least 15 other hacks each cost over $1 million in losses (all dollar values determined at the time of hack).[170]

Some of the few exchanges with a clean track record are Coinbase and Gemini. They also act as gatekeepers for the cryptosphere by supporting fiat-to-cryptocurrency conversion. This remarkable feature is not without its red tape-wrapped bank and government conglomeration. Although not the libertarian dream, it is trusted by many. Large, heavily regulated exchanges such as Coinbase attach data to verifiable identities through KYC. Without this, there can be no account recovery in the event of a cyberattack or loss of login credentials. Personally identifiable information also makes possible detection of money laundering, fraud, terrorist funding, and other financial crimes.[171]

Exchanges are just one example of the binding trade-off encountered in making endpoints trustworthy. Sacrificing decentralized anonymity for trust is also required in finance, supply chain, and IoT applications. Bitcoin maximalists oppose this idea because of the implications of trusting a centralized authority with personal data.

These conflicting ideologies tend to ignore the overlapping area that is trustlessness, where trust prevails in a system full of untrustworthy participants. Advances in blockchain technology can draw useful conclusions from data without revealing it, opening the door to a previously unimaginable middle-ground. Meaningful developments in this area are beginning to enable genuine trustlessness, but their success is thwarted by the two-front war created as organizations pick sides.

Security (Versus Cyberattack)

Moore's Law states that computing power will double every two years, making no rigid system safe for the 21st century. Even though vulnerabilities widely vary by blockchain, a brute-force attack can break any one of them. Because blockchains are purportedly unhackable, analysis of possible attacks is discussed ad nauseam in the research community. Quantum computing, for example, could potentially destroy blockchain, but that's not to say traditional systems are any more prepared. Quantum resistance is at least an active area of development for blockchain, and, more generally, security efforts will always require constant improvement for all computer systems, regardless of type.

Public blockchains tend to be much more secure than traditional database frameworks but are not unhackable. The more eminent, misconstrued, and solvable threats occur where blockchain connects to off-chain endpoints. The best way to summarize this is with an example of how blockchain would affect an average network endpoint.

In 2012, a group of Chinese hackers gained control of an American chemical company's servers via a phishing email. After months of gathering intellectual property, they managed to create a copycat product. They then disarranged the company's master production schedule (MPS), sabotaging distribution while offering their own products backed by newly acquired patents.[172] This is not a unique case; supply chain cybersecurity has grown so far beyond expectations that industry professionals are now underestimating their implementation costs by a factor of 10.[173] How would the beloved blockchain change the story for this chemical company?

Apparently, not by much. If the MPS were blockchain-based, the hack would still occur, and intellectual property would still be stolen. The MPS would have been immutable, meaning the company wouldn't have lost control of production.[174] This is far from an ideal solution. Researchers were led to this straightforward yet incomplete conclusion by analyzing bare-bones DLTs.

Cybersecurity concerns were not solved when distributing a company data honeypot. This should come as no surprise, but the research suggested that blockchain is an ineffective solution.

Unfortunately, many companies still take this unilateral approach to blockchain and are confused when solutions don't work. Notice that all vulnerabilities from the hack were on conventional Internet infrastructure. Throwing an MPS blockchain on top of that doesn't change things much. What that American chemical company needed was Web3. There is tremendous potential for blockchain to boost system security, but only tech companies are equipped to create such solutions. Brick-and-mortar corporations that throw their logistics on a blockchain are not part of the revolution.

Decentralization (Versus Centralization)

Establishing the criteria for what qualifies a system as decentralized requires a glimpse at Bitcoin's putative decentralization. Anonymity makes wealth distribution estimates difficult to verify, but the popular ballpark figure is 4% of people controlling 95% of bitcoin's supply, far more centralized than the current financial system.[175] Still, how bitcoins are distributed among holders means nothing for the network's consensus. It is the distribution of computing power shared by Bitcoin miners that is important for security. This too has been commercialized and centralized by a select few companies that have grown massive mining infrastructures.

Most other public blockchains function similarly in that consensus mechanisms (not currency distributions) dictate network influence and often become centralized. This issue directly conflicts with blockchain's other supposed immutability feature. "In code we trust" is the long-standing slogan that deems human intervention pointless for blockchains because they are so accurate that they never need fixing. This radical philosophy is flawless 99.99% of the time but is otherwise catastrophic.

In May of 2016, the startup slock.it proposed developing a decentralized autonomous organization (DAO) that would be self-sufficient in performing the business functions for crowdfunding various startups. Confusingly named The DAO, the project raised $150 million in a few weeks. Being made of multiple smart contracts, it used a split function so participants could exchange tokens and withdraw Ethereum when leaving The DAO. An attacker used this function while starting a new request before the previous one finished. During this time, pirated withdrawals were undetected.[176] This coding error amounted to more than $50 million in stolen funds.[177]

The Ethereum blockchain itself showed no flaws during the event. All transactions were consistent with the laws of code, just not the way developers intended. The Ethereum community was at a crossroads: Let the adversary off with stolen funds or band together and reverse the transaction with a hard fork. The latter path was chosen, splitting the blockchain into two identical versions, forcing all network nodes to adopt one or the other.

Most nodes accepted an update supporting the new blockchain. Ethereum Classic is that original blockchain and is maintained by a small group of miners to this day.[178] The Ethereum Foundation's decision proved that blockchain is not truly decentralized or immutable. More advanced developments will continually demand more precautions than initially anticipated, and blockchain-based trust needs a backup. The governance mechanisms examined in Chapter 5 offer the most novel approach but are very early stage and complex.

Regardless of how blockchains balance decentralization with immutability, it will be incredibly challenging to do well, and only the best blockchains will meet the challenge. Therein lies the central problem: Startups routinely bite off more than they can chew. For the same reason we don't want incipient energy companies trying their hand at hydrofracking, startups should not be leading the charge with blockchain's most advanced concepts.

Unproductive Extremes

Descriptions of the above failures are unidimensional. They are better seen as missteps, each having unique solutions that come into view after taking a step back. Creating more comprehensive solutions entails uprooting the existing software infrastructure and replacing it with a conglomeration of creative technologies like Dapps, ZKPs, DLTs, triple-blind identity verification, smart contracts, distributed computing, Proof of Existence, governance mechanisms, and DAOs. When decentralization is compromised, interim digital governments could be the distributed decision-makers. Because these winning solutions are perplexing and a bit slow out of the gate, they are often ignored by enthusiasts.

To that end, enthusiasts compensate for failures by raising the bar on ideas to the level of science fiction. Alex and Don Tapscott, renowned blockchain enthusiasts and the founders of the Blockchain Research Institute, repeatedly exemplify these unproductive extremes in their frequently cited book *Blockchain Revolution.*[179] Take this quote about meat supply chain tracking, for example:

> The food industry could store on the blockchain not just a number of every steer, but of every cut of meat, potentially linked to its DNA. Three-dimensional search abilities could enable comprehensive tracking of livestock and poultry so that users could link an animal's identity to its history. Using sophisticated (but relatively simple to use) DNA-based technologies and smart database management, even the largest meat producers could guarantee quality and safety.[180]

This concept has no explanation or citations in the surrounding paragraphs and brings with it commonly-ignored supply-chain-related complications. Assuming this sophisticated DNA-based technology exists, there would still need to be a means of relaying useful data to a blockchain, thus requiring an IoT sensor for every slab of meat. Even with flawless data produced from DNA-based animal identities, location and timestamp spoofing in measuring devices are still not preventable with an immutable ledger.

It's dangerous when enthusiasts paint the picture of a blockchain utopia using exciting ideas without weeding them first, which is very easy: When a blockchain use case sounds too good to be true, go on a treasure hunt. If you don't find pilots or technical requirements for a functioning product, it's probably not worth pursuing. The market, for the most part, doesn't know this. The grave danger in iconic (yet simplified) ideas occurs when they trickle down to the foundation of startups.

The consequences of faulty implementation are evident in energy demand response programs. Energy grids are becoming increasingly distributed given a rapid global increase in renewable energy sources (RES).[181] The centralized management of electricity distribution can no longer account for the growing number of distributed energy prosumers.[182] Current methods of incentivizing energy output onto the grid are Net Metering (NM) and Feed-in Tariff (FiT), both bound by a set of drawbacks.

NM has a cap on production, which precludes rewards for an annual electricity surplus and therefore discourages a decrease in energy consumption or the use of localized green energy. FiT operates with separate meters for consumption and production, with the value of output energy adjusted at the leisure of policymakers. This undermines investor confidence and does not allow for P2P energy transactions.

The crucial deficiency of both NM and FiT is a disregard for temporal data. Energy grids operate under stress during periods of low demand and resort to inefficient means of power production during peak load periods.[183] Renewable energy sources have the potential to provide a buffer on both an hourly and seasonal basis which would decrease the cost of electricity and reduce infrastructure maintenance requirements.

Dozens of cryptocurrencies claim to address these problems, with the leaders being Power Ledger, Greenpower, Wepower, each of which suffered approximately 97% drops from their all-time high prices.[184] [185] [186] [187] Across these startups, any proof of concept is illusory beyond press releases, and coming across a pilot program is like finding a needle in a haystack. Cryptocurrencies each have creative marketing schemes that artificially create investment value but contribute nothing at the protocol level.

NRGcoin is one of the most advanced energy grid solution concepts to date. Born out of academia, this project began with a mock city and simulated microgrid.[188] The virtual coin is an uninvestable utility token with a unit value equal to 1kWh of green energy. The Blockchain Climate Institute dedicated a chapter of their book to the concept: The NRGcoin mechanism uses gateway devices with current sensors in each home measuring imported and exported energy.[189] The temporal dimension reevaluates demand every 15 minutes.[190] Participants consume injected electricity with each kWh of green energy (1 NRGcoin) correlating to demand, making gray energy (not green energy) a secondary option.[191] Smart contracts facilitate payments in a real-time P2P automatically-executing energy market.

It is envisioned that NRGcoin will operate as a DAO running a public proof of stake consensus protocol. Blockchain is NRGcoin's only technology option because it facilitates transactions in a decentralized, transparent, and tamper-proof manner, whereas centralized alternatives offer none of the above.[192]

NRGcoin has partnered with gateway device providers but still has not seen large-scale implementation. This is not unique to NRGcoin, with most similar projects struggling to reach the mass market. Project lead Mihail Mihaylov has the following explanation:

> After several attempts at the market, we have concluded that currently the market is not yet ready for NRGcoin. At this point we sense that the concept is too advanced for most market players—they prefer easier and

more comprehensible/incremental improvements to the existing models…. Most other projects have an idea but no funding, so they need to do a lot of PR in order to get crowd/venture funding. Then they need to 'demonstrate results' to justify the funding, so they create more PR for this.[193]

There is little doubt that the NRGcoin concept or some variant will succeed in the coming years; there is cause for support, not opposition from utility companies. The hindrance created by poor projects crowding the energy space is not as detrimental when compared to blockchain use cases that threaten to demonetize Big Tech. Financial infrastructure, big data, and middlemen ordinarily defy the advanced equivalent of related blockchain solutions. As optimists keep taking shots in the dark, academics get tired of picking up the slack, and the result is more drastic than a time-to-market delay. With so many startups working on similar problems, great ones are getting lost in the shuffle.

Startups and Coopetition

Not only do the blockchain copycats of Netflix, Facebook, Google, or Amazon get the most attention with the least substance, they also immolate blockchain's reputation. Pumping legitimacy into blockchain's most fanciful stories has been taken to extremes such as buying slots on .edu domains.[194] Sensational ideas are being accepted on false authority, creating ideological echo chambers conducive only to wishful projections.[195] Unethical practices like these serve to magnify problems stemming from pervasive delusion.

At its best, startup culture has turned to unconventional, innovative methods that would otherwise be curbed by rigid corporate structures. Startups have encouraged creative exploration in decentralized technology and have given rise to previously unthinkable research. As for their role, when the harsh reality sinks in, cutting-edge blockchain startups might need help from the very organizations they mean to disrupt, which creates an apparent catch-22 because it requires reconciling a *decentralized* movement with *centralized* incumbents.

In other words, for a true paradigm shift, *coopetition* is needed, a term coined to capture the possibility of cooperative competition.

Blockchain is a powerful tool for increasing cooperative efficacy.[196] For a fully decentralized system to succeed, its creators often need to disassociate from their brainchild and forfeit rewards.[197] The best version of the future involves this humanitarian behavior, but it's not pragmatic for even the most selfless organizations. Altruistic motives certainly won't make many waves in the corporate world, so how can any real blockchain technology thrive in a capitalist society?

The real spirit of blockchain cannot be encapsulated in a startup. Instead, it must manifest in completely leaderless networks. Ironically, and as we'll see in the final chapter, another double-edged sword of the blockchain space is that the only projects capable of building sufficiently advanced networks are venture capital-backed startups. These projects usually function as nonprofit foundations that should not need to exist after building out their user-owned networks. Most of the innovation is then accomplished by the network community members while startups take a backseat. That's the real paradigm shift.

There's some good news and bad news about the world of blockchain startups. We'll start with the bad: The tendency of everything to centralize might overpower the blockchain movement's desire to decentralize—that is, the organizations that startups mean to disrupt can take control of networks. This can come in the form of companies building networks with private "blockchains" or wealthy entities taking control of a network's token supply, and thus governance rights. Startups centralize their creations by starting with an ambitious goal for a decentralized network and then gradually becoming more like a traditional business: securing funding, hiring employees, increasing revenue, and so on. All the while, the paradigm shift eludes us.

Now for the good news: It should be unsurprising that early attempts at leaderless organizations will fail their first time around, and so they must adopt familiar elements of centralized hierarchy as a temporary crutch. Early failures are okay because the larger changes will come gradually. Blockchain also doesn't have to take over everything to spread the benefits of decentralization successfully. Organizations always follow trends to and from decentralization based on what's strategic at the time.

Skype and Linux had to adopt a degree of centralization to monetize. Google's and Amazon's decentralized components put them on vastly better paths than that of their centralized competitors.[198] These Internet companies reluctantly hybridized for nothing but survival, and the byproducts were public-spirited. As blockchain creates a decentralized trust layer on digital organizations, companies will have to adapt toward a similar model for purely competitive reasons. Bringing decentralized protocols to market is slow and complicated, but the ongoing degradation of institutional trust is just buying the blockchain sphere more time and favorability. This, in one sense, is a very hopeful prospect.

Kicking Away the Ladder

If the blockchain industry moves in a direction that is aligned with its early vision, startups should play an increasingly futile role in its development. Anything less radical would not suffice as a replacement for FAAMG. The paradigm shift comes with user-owned platforms, where community members develop novel public Internet services, and everyone gets rewarded for network contributions through an integrated token economy.

We can't lose sight of the fact that current blockchain centralization should be a temporary crutch. The challenge of keeping leaderless organizations organized in a functional hierarchy is a pivotal part of keeping networks decentralized. The only known way to do this is with the right type of digital governance, which is no simple undertaking. Blockchain governance must deal with social questions about how to govern and technical questions about making pseudo-governments functional within a network.

Chapter 5 will cover these essential governance mechanisms in depth. The chapter is one of four (Chapters 5–8) geared toward the practicalities of a decentralized Internet movement. Chapters 9 and 10 dive directly into speculative topics regarding what leaderless digital hierarchies look like and which real projects succeed in creating them.

CHAPTER 5:

SOLVING THE GOVERNANCE PARADOX

The beautiful ways that the Internet has transformed our world always seem to coincide with very dark existential threats. Social networking sites, a fantastic avenue for borderless interaction, also reduce the need for people to think for themselves and are used to manipulate the masses. Internet technologies that should be a tool for governments to help their people preserve freedoms are being used for expanding totalitarianism and tyranny. Artificial intelligence, regardless of the context in which it is employed, will imply a reduction in the need for humans. Then there are the most cutting-edge technologies like designer babies, quantum computing, and digital consciousnesses whose ethical implications are far-reaching.

What's important about all the scary uses for technologies is how decisions will be made regarding their direction. Right now, it appears decisions are purely in the hands of those at the top of their respective dominance hierarchies. Top scientists and company executives govern FAAMGs' initiatives in quantum computing and artificial intelligence, for example. It always made sense to have creators in charge of their creations, but that no longer holds true as those creations become capable of initiating global catastrophe. There should be a way of distributing decision making for those decisions that carry worldly implications.

Luckily, practically all the innovation in science is attached to computing systems, which means they can involve larger communities in that decision-making process. It's not such a popular idea at present because we are still unfamiliar with trusted systems. That will likely change with time, but since we're talking about a foundation for digital governments, no technical details will be meaningful without their social aspect, particularly *hierarchy*, or the innate structure formed by groups that guides and will continue to guide decision making for all of humankind's collaborative endeavors.

The March to Fewer Hierarchies

Throughout history, humankind always used small sets of competing hierarchies. Whether it be tribes, feudal systems, organizations, or governments, they have always been geographically constrained to controlling only small domains. This dispersion of social groups allowed for a diversity of ideas and progress without interference from a global authority. This certainly did no favors for human advancement because it precluded the use of or diffusion of diverse ideas on any large scale.

Paradigm shifts like the printing press, steam engine, and the Internet closed gaps that helped fix the information-sharing problem, but with one caveat: larger hierarchies. These steps for humanity lessened the physical boundaries between hierarchies, reducing their overall number and increasing their average size. The upside of bigger hierarchical systems is greater opportunity for collaboration and overall efficiency for those inside them. The downside is steeper barriers to entry and tremendous exclusionary potential. When applying this to diverse ideas, it means fewer of them will see the light of day.

If you exclude the Earth's poles, the Internet removed all physical borders for corporate hierarchies, taking their size, particularly in FAAMG, to unprecedented heights. As the number of people inside them grows linearly, their size and relative centralization grow exponentially, following a Pareto distribution. Hierarchies now have millions of interconnected people, but all the decision-making power is concentrated in just a few leaders. It is usually okay to have authoritative leaders and groups, just not when they have millions of subjects.

Facebook's combined platforms, perhaps the world's supreme social hierarchy, consists of billions of people. On the bottom of that hierarchy is about 3 billion active users. You could think about placement in that hierarchy as the prestige of a given user profile relative to others, but this would be missing the bigger picture. In a much more real sense, the 0.002% of Facebook users who are also employees (June 2020)[199] hold more power in this supreme social hierarchy than the other 3 billion users combined. Of those employees, only a small fraction of them deal with the algorithms that dictate the experience of billions. You can find similar stories with all the members of FAAMG. The only leverage users have is the ability to stop using those platforms.

Problems with the overwhelming power of Internet company hierarchies are not meant to indicate issues with hierarchy itself. Every time humans collaborate in a group, they inevitably form a hierarchal dynamic. Evolutionarily speaking, human hierarchies are unofficial and naturally occurring for groups up to about 100. The problem is that, as the number increases, they begin to lose stability and must adopt formal rules, shared myths, and a certain degree of centralization to stay together. Even as we now have multi-billion-person hierarchies, the proportion of people responsible for controlling it is at a record low.

Modern hierarchies, particularly those of FAAMG, have become so large that they limit the use of diverse ideas by stringently controlling how they spread in the world. The expressed limitations of modern hierarchies should provide a reasonable argument for the existence of a global problem closely relating to blockchain's specialty function. I acknowledge that this historical contextualization has more at play than what I've distilled from it. Still, these are not particularly radical claims, and the full explanations would require a separate book.

At this point, it should be regarded as axiomatic that blockchain can add elements of transparency and decentralization to hierarchical systems when properly integrated. This enables trust and, in turn, encourages collaboration while preserving the efficiency of large hierarchies and the diversity of many small hierarchies. In other words, blockchain can get the best of both the centralized and decentralized worlds: diversity of novel ideas that can freely spread and be used on a global scale. Of course, some form of governance must replace corporate hierarchies, which is the gap that this chapter fills.

We now have a technology that can transparently distribute the power of multi-billion-person hierarchies. Governance is what blockchain is *really* designed for because it can combine the benefits of both decentralized and centralized systems. The idea is also incompatible with the conventional perspective that blockchain is intrinsically a tool to enable systems to operate without hierarchy.

The whole concept of blockchain combining with hierarchy may seem implausible at this point because there are so many failures to point to. There's also no compelling antidote to pervasive delusion at this point, as discussed in the last chapter—technologists seem to have no method for separating the wheat from the chaff when it comes to anything blockchain, hence the failed startups. Let me set the stage for finally solving the perplexing problem of mixing hierarchy with decentralization.

The Internet hierarchy explained in Chapter 3 is understood by few. It's an analogy describing the battle between FAAMG that seemingly leaves no room for other Internet players. A paradigm shift is the only way to topple this hierarchy and start anew. Assuming this is what's coming, Web3 is not meant to remove online hierarchies; it will just make their natural structure much flatter even as they grow to a gargantuan size.

Paradigm Shift Clarity

Some of the projects mentioned in this chapter are referred to as a paradigm shift because they essentially distribute computing. If this truly were the case, pervasive delusion from last chapter would turn out to be the visionary's fruition. In a much more real sense, projects aligned with the mainstream Web3 narrative are not even close to being part of a paradigm shift. The public's inability to look past this is caused by a misleading element in the Internet hierarchy analogy on a technological level, which is connected with how the Internet is already distributed.

In the 1990s, technology companies (especially Microsoft) envisioned a set of closed protocols underlying the Internet, but the open protocol standard won.[200] That's why Microsoft doesn't have an Internet monopoly right now. But even with FAAMG's control, we're technically using an open and decentralized Internet at the lowest-level protocols. As we further distribute systems using those same protocols, how exactly is that a paradigm shift, and how does it close the trust gap?

Let's think about how we pinpoint paradigm shifts. Electricity, for example, was responsible for a paradigm shift in human life, but what marked its starting point? Its existence, discovery, capture, or utilization? All of those are reasonable considerations and are themselves divisible into various subcategories. In Chapter 3, the printing press, steam engine, and Internet were described as paradigm shifts that closed the knowledge, distance, and communication gaps, respectively. Of course, these are foundational inventions, but their classification as paradigm shifts is not objectively correct. The printing press had hundreds of iterations spanning centuries that few remember.[201] The steam engine didn't directly close the distance gap. It enabled ships and trains to start to close the distance gap. Then the diesel engine and gas turbine further closed the distance gap more efficiently by allowing the invention of automobiles and planes. We call the steam engine a paradigm shift because it was the catalyst.

All of this is not meant to make subsequent inventions seem any less remarkable, but it doesn't make them all paradigm shifts either. Computers, TCP/IP, and participating nodes were all requisites for the Internet, which we now remember as the *single* paradigm shift in communication. FAAMG are all improvements to the Internet but not paradigm shifts themselves because they rely on existing infrastructure and don't create new ones.

We tend to put historical examples like the evolution of revolutionary inventions into simplified boxes. While we're in the midst of radical technological change, what seems to be coming out of thin air results from years of perpetual labor from nearly anonymous geniuses. It's no wonder the public ends up deluded.

Most blockchain initiatives are not paradigm shifts because they don't replace the Internet; they build on it. Blockchain's most common applications can't topple FAAMG's hierarchy because they share the same Internet real estate. An actual Internet paradigm shift would be some technology that can thrive without existing Internet infrastructure.

The trust gap still exists because, even with open protocols, trust is always concentrated in the hierarchical model of data collectors and certificate authorities (the reason a secure padlock icon is in the upper left of your web address bar).[202] Even the most notable "decentralized" startups have their blockchain nodes running on the FAAMG cloud. Real decentralized systems need to be built independently of pretty much anything (excluding telecommunication infrastructure): no owner, no cloud, no platform host, no parent organization. Thus far in this book, we've seen nothing that would pass as a paradigm shift.

Even with genuinely decentralized infrastructure, Web3 needs to take two more vital steps before qualifying as the paradigm shift to close the trust gap: solving blockchain's interoperability problem and the governance paradox. Chapter 10 will focus on the former. This chapter will focus on the latter.

Internet Governance

We don't think of FAAMG as governing entities, but maybe it's time we start. They are large organizations, fueled by the combined services of smaller entities, and to some extent, decide which of them succeed or fail. Their operations boil down to a series of decisions that are often automated and determine the fate of subsidiaries. The most obvious example of this and the starting point for decentralized systems is applications and web pages that are at the mercy of FAAMG. Small parties create services in the form of applications on FAAMG's cloud and accessible through FAAMG search engines. Developers pay for the cloud services, and FAAMG decides which ones are mischievous enough to censor. One can rightfully generalize FAAMG as the hub of Internet governance because they compose the Internet hierarchy's barriers to entry.

Blockchain technology offers an alternate route to climbing the Internet hierarchy. If a distributed set of computers can perform the same function as a centralized cloud server, then new Internet applications can be built on nothing but the Internet itself. This is already commonplace in circles of developers building decentralized applications (dapps). It's important to note that most dapps today still depend on the cloud though they all plan to change that as Web3 grows. This book assumes the word *dapp* refers to actual decentralized applications.

Dapps are increasingly popular because of the advantages they offer developers. Most notably, once a dapp is created, it does not need permission to run on an immutable network and becomes as permanent as the network itself. This movement toward a more decentralized Internet is what some refer to as a paradigm shift in computing.

As this decentralized infrastructure is being built, there exist two major problems that prevent adoption. The first is a lack of peer-to-peer value because the Internet hierarchy currently holds all of it. Acquiring more users is the countermeasure, but those solutions are nontechnical and outside the scope of this chapter. The more imminent problem is controversy regarding governance. How can a dapp contributing to terrorism or other criminal acts be shut down without undermining network immutability? The short answer is that it can't.

Instead of giving up, some of the world's brightest minds are conjuring up creative workarounds that are opening a floodgate of innovation in computer decision making. What is essentially being created is a proof of concept for transparent community-owned governments that adds elements of computer intelligence. Implementations that humbly begin by outlining the bounds of Internet conduct have analogous use cases that could scale to sizable governing bodies. Decentralized governance is conceivably blockchain's pinnacle use case.

Before diving deeper into the world of governance, we need to address the absence of an antidote to pervasive delusion. How can we know that what seems like a science fiction world of blockchain governance isn't just more recycled misinformation? A claim that governance is yet another killer use case for blockchain is the sort to leave skeptics with plenty of room to paint blockchain as a useless fad.

It's a fair case to make. We're talking about unproven systems recognized only by small bands of cryptographers. It's hard to know if these ideas are worth pursuing, just as all the inventions building on paradigm shifts were entirely forgettable in their early stages. A look back at the forgotten geniuses who built blockchain from nothing can provide a glimpse of unadulterated truth into its substantive purpose.

Let's play the blockchain skeptic for a bit, running with the idea that blockchain is a scam, tracing blockchain's roots through their eyes.

The Cypherpunk Ideal and the Blockchain Paradox

A favorite starting point for the typical blockchain cynic is Bitcoin. As they say, Bitcoin can never be a practical global currency and has no intrinsic value. The world doesn't even know where it came from because its creator(s) is/are anonymous, and the mainstream media's depiction of Bitcoin is increasingly divorced from reality. Though oversimplified, these are fair arguments. Here's what those claims are missing.

At its core, Bitcoin is the technological bedrock of an ideological revolution. Cryptography is the bigger picture. Archived communications dating back to the 1980s between Bitcoin's alleged creators and early developers (the Cypherpunks) describe many of their intentions.[203] The Cypherpunks wanted and still want a free and private Internet. They hold dearly the rights of free speech and the right to selectively reveal one's own personal attributes, both of which governments and corporations will not preserve on their own accord.[204] The methods in which to do this require writing and dispersing cryptography-related code which cannot be destroyed by established hierarchies.[205]

Recompiling deeper Cypherpunk principles requires some speculation, though some are concerted and reoccurring themes that few would dispute as a Cypherpunk ideal. Cypherpunks are anarchistic, at least for online matters. They are distrusting of governments and large corporate establishments. They also believe that their cryptographic software is reorienting civilization in a way that world leaders are too stupid to understand.[206]

This area of conversation is a breeding ground for unadorned conspiracy theories, so we won't speculate further without legitimate examples of Cypherpunk achievements. The most obvious example is the success of cryptocurrencies, of whom Cypherpunks are the leading beneficiaries. The other known example is WikiLeaks, a non-profit organization created by cypherpunks that makes leaked documents (mainly regarding government and corporate misbehavior) publicly available.[207] Of the millions of public records, one of the more famous ones resulted from the hacking of the Democratic National Committee email servers, which is posited to have impacted the swinging of the U.S. 2016 election and pressuring the FBI Director's removal.[208] More generally, WikiLeaks exposes illicit government actions and is alleged to execute Cypherpunk ambitions for the purposes of increasing distrust of governments.[209] An explicit example of the group's power was when

WikiLeaks donations were blocked by Visa, MasterCard, and PayPal, which was returned with each of their respective websites being taken down by some Jane Doe.[210]

Regardless of how one feels about Cypherpunk ethics, the group's technological achievements cannot be entirely denied. Underestimating the Cypherpunks has often been a mistake and will probably continue to be. Blockchain is perhaps their most significant achievement. The Cypherpunks often brag that their mission is being carried out under our noses but above our intellectual planes. At the very least, this would explain why there is no shortage of contradictory opinions about blockchain's societal function.

The broadest area of convergence for the Cypherpunk agenda and blockchain technology is decentralized systems. For the sake of simplicity, they are what we know as dapps, but they are theoretically capable of replicating any centralized system given enough network influence. Elections; electricity grids; supply chains; government fund collection and redistribution; corporate earning and spending; healthcare record keeping; and organizational data usage are a small fraction of what's managed by private software and is potentially replaceable with decentralized systems. Whether people know it or not, this is why blockchain is a big deal.

There's still a big problem with decentralized systems. When centralized software is used, the organization that uses it also governs it. Decentralized software needs to work independently of a governing organization, which has previously always been required for dispute resolution. In an extreme example, centralized systems can help recover a stolen identity because banks, governments, and credit unions have backups in place for when software systems fail end users. If decentralized software is exploited to attack end-users, there is no backup because it would follow the directive that "code is law."[211] Smart contracts are not sufficient in solving this problem because their makers will never be able to account for unknown unknowns, so code could never be perfect.

Many have been led to believe that this inherent limitation will prevent the acceptance of blockchain systems. Professor Vili of the Oxford Internet Institute explained this in 2016 as the blockchain paradox or Vili's Paradox.[212] With a background in both computer science and economic sociology, Vili posed an exceptionally astute argument in support of blockchain skeptics. It states that blockchain's revolutionary feature is the ability to replace 3rd parties with a more equitable distributed network. But distributed ledger protocols act as a 3rd party according to preset rules made by a centralized group of developers. In a sense, decentralized networks are just like centralized ones because, in both cases, their rules are set by their creators. The freedom offered by decentralized networks is illusory because all protocols always need governance, and governance always undermines decentralization. Hence the paradox.

In past circumstances, Cypherpunk technologies have been doubted and ignored, while their successes have continually exceeded expectations. Blockchain has been especially representative of this trend. Remember, blockchain governance is a challenge exclusively dealt with by blockchain developers, not their nontechnical counterparts. Ethereum Classic and Bitcoin Cash are examples of hard forks that weakened their networks because of developer disagreements. Indeed, the Cypherpunks and blockchain developers have always been aware of these dispute resolution limitations, yet they continue to support blockchain technologies. To put it simply, blockchain's depiction as a technology of ungovernability is wrong. Instead, *it's a technology about governance*.

Like the bitcoin maximalists, the blockchain skeptics have adopted a flawed ideology. The ongoing debate between both is really about decentralization versus centralization. The silver bullet for each side's argument lands us back at Vili's paradox, which gets to the core of this debate while avoiding the pitfalls of either side's pipe dream. Blockchain can get around this paradox by effectively combining centralized and decentralized elements. This newfound perspective bridges a gap in the fundamental determinant of blockchain's potential for development. For this reason, this chapter will approach governance mechanisms while bearing Vili's criticisms in mind.

Getting a deeper sense of how this paradox is evolving requires an in-depth look at current options in the realm of digital governance.

The Potential Mechanisms of Internet Governance

Governance is everywhere. It can be the enacting of written law. It can be a series of guidelines for organizational decision making. It's a vague term that refers to all sorts of things but needs meaning in the context of technology.

Governance is *the action or manner of governing*. Your mind is a governance mechanism in that it controls your actions. Luckily, your governance mechanism rapidly adapts through engagement with the external world. Community-based governance mechanisms such as local governments, by contrast, can't quickly adapt to change because they are bogged down by the need to satisfy disparate groups. The adaptability of governance mechanisms continues to degrade with increased scale. Trouble with governing something that gets too big is an age-old problem that needs reinventing for applications on the Internet. We will call this *Internet governance*.

Most of the work on Internet governance is nontechnical, focusing on the laws and guidelines for protocols.[213] This chapter focuses instead on the protocols themselves. Code could be written to enforce the same rules as written law, but with automatic enforcement. Adding enough complexity to a code, coupled with a democracy of online voters, creates an Internet/network governance mechanism. Moving forward, this is what the phrase *governance mechanism* will refer to.

Even though governance is ubiquitous, governance mechanisms struggle to get a foothold in any of their largest proponents. Governments are slow to change legislation and even slower to change their own methods of governance.[214]

Conceiving something as advanced as a governance mechanism for regulators is ludicrous because of how far behind they are on modernizing legislation. Corporations, on the other hand, are dynamic enough to experiment and innovate with governance mechanisms. The issue with the private sector's governance mechanisms is that it's impossible to determine whether they work.[215] Small-scale company trials are generally publicized, politicized, romanticized, and monetized, making them bad indicators of versatility. All this happens without companies revealing the raw technology.

Governments and corporations already govern quite comfortably because they have always done so. But understanding the need for new governance models becomes apparent when looking at previous iterations of them. In the last chapter, we established the dangers of modern hierarchies becoming too steep (especially those of the Internet). The dangers, at least in part, stem from oligopolistic governance tactics that intensify as hierarchies steepen.

The reason governance methods shift this way is simple, and it's a common theme inherent in hierarchies. The complexity of a hierarchy's governance increases in proportion to its size. Complex governance models are more rigid and minimally adaptable (e.g., the federal government). There are two ways to increase governance versatility: break it up into smaller versions (e.g., state and local governments), or put governing power into a smaller group of people (e.g., give the president/prime minister more power). Both options leave a void: the former a drop in efficiency and the latter a loss of freedom.

For FAAMG, efficiency and versatility are paramount. Breaking them up destroys their ability to innovate and is a poor choice. FAAMG compensates for its need to govern diverse global groups by concentrating power in a small minority of leaders, just like any conventional hierarchy. Decisions face less contradiction this way. Of course, the masses would be the potential beneficiaries of a FAAMG governance update.

To be clear, the consolidating-power and dispersing-power governance options we've been talking about are analogous to the spectrum extremes of the centralization versus decentralization debate. Hierarchies have a bend toward the centralized side while growing. Hence a steepening corporate Pareto distribution and a historical track record for ever-growing power in federal governments, while state and local governments shrink.

How different governance mechanisms fall on this spectrum is pretty determinable. Professor Zwitter of The University of Groningen categorized governance mechanisms concisely into three possible modes.[216] To keep this explanation simple, we will assume only three actors, with actors being participating nodes: governmental organizations, corporations, and societal actors (see Figure 4). Mode 1 is a centralized command and control hierarchy with the state having complete sovereignty over non-governmental organizations and with societal actors having little to no influence—sort of like a dictatorship.

Figure 4

Modes of Governance

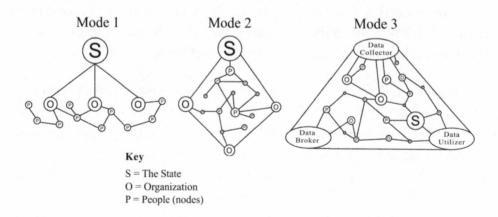

Key
S = The State
O = Organization
P = People (nodes)

Note. Circle size is proportional to network influence.

Mode 2 adds horizontal rulemaking where the state, corporations, and societal actors retain power in proportion to their place in the hierarchy but balance each other's influence by focusing on their immediate domains of influence. This is exemplified in how governments and organizations separate their operations into smaller, more targeted departments and are the most common governance mode today. For Modes 1 and 2, power tends to reside in roles or formal leadership positions in an organization.

Mode 3 primarily differs in that roles are not static, and thus power shifts are dynamic. It is the most decentralized option and has not been done on a large scale because it exists only in the digital domain, which has yet to be perfected. In Mode 3, power resides in changing relationships because every actor delegates based on incoming data and ever-changing social connections. This fluid power gives institutionalized actors limited control because formal roles are replaced by social network analysis.[217] The only known candidate for enabling this level of governance is blockchain technology.

This explanation of governance modes is awfully broad, especially that of Mode 3. An explanation of an organizational move toward decentralized governance is best captured in a hypothetical example. For this, we'll use Apple. Specifically, a possible shift from a Mode 1 and Mode 2 combination to full-blown Mode 3 governance.

Let's look at how a Mode 3 network governance mechanism would work with the Apple App Store. This example assumes that all the hoops developers jump through to get an app listed are non-existent (the next section is all about making this possible). We'll call this the i-Dapp Store for simplicity. Some responsibilities of the i-Dapp Store include blocking or removing nefarious applications, fairly ranking app listings, providing payment methods, hosting apps via distributed cloud, and securely managing user data. At present, Apple has full supremacy with all of these decisions and consumes a 30% commission on all sales. Their independent judgment could reasonably be called into question for most of these responsibilities.

Through the use of a governance mechanism, the i-Dapp Store would revamp its methods for rule creation and enforcement by removing all system ambiguity. The decision-makers at Apple would be replaced by a voting protocol where everyone could participate if they so choose. Each voter would have to establish their own reputation based on their network identity, areas of expertise, and stake in the network. Different qualifications for different specializations will determine the influence of each vote as it pertains to a given issue. Voters will have the effect of their past decisions factored into their reputation. This whole process is transparent.

When the Angry Birds creator gets ranked below Temple Run because the ranking algorithm is not recognizing rating ratio and customer satisfaction, anyone working with Angry Birds can propose a relevant change to the network. When an app that rewards anonymous bounty hunting is released, it would promptly be removed by a vote. If a Clash of Clans ended up stealing credit card information, the network could force it to pay reparations, almost as if there were a swift lawsuit without the baggage.

All these decisions are made in a meritocratic democracy. Changes to the governance model itself can be proposed and made in accordance with voter needs. The i-Dapp store is not a full-fledged Mode 3 governance model because there is no bilateral feedback with other institutions or even the rest of Apple.

Taking things further, Apple could be the founding organization. This is the part where blockchain enthusiasts halt. It initially seems contradictory to think that a decentralized tech could originate from a centralized corporation, but after recognizing its purpose in governance and not anarchy, this combination becomes reasonable. In practice, Apple could create the i-Dapp Store in just the same way centralized startups create decentralized platforms.

Once going down the rabbit hole of accepting centralized hosting of decentralized governance, there is no bottom. If Apple could successfully govern an app store, why couldn't they extend this model to other platforms?

What business decisions wouldn't be better made by democratized governance mechanisms? Why shouldn't this extend to public organizations and governments? The possibilities are endless. Of course, the giant leap of faith required for this whole chain of logic is getting Apple to create the i-Dapp Store—an idea the company would vehemently denounce.

More social and technical problems arise when unveiling some previously ignored layers of complexity. Governance Modes 1 through 3 are grand-scale governance models. Their three constituent parts are governments, organizations, and people, each with their own sub-governance models. Remember, as an example, something as small-scale as a human mind is an intricate governance mechanism. Each of those three actors (people, organizations, governments) have many pieces that need uniquely-tailored governance. Figure 5 is a condensed diagram of actor sub-components that use governance, each circle being one of them. You'll find the i-Dapp Store at the lowest level of organizational governance. For large-scale governance to work, all the pieces (inner circles) need to have some level of interoperability. Then all three agents must also regularly interact. It's quite a long road before this can be realized.

There is some encouraging news about governance mechanisms. The basic principles of each governance mode's methodology remain consistent regardless of scale. For this reason, decentralized governance can have success when applied top-down. For example, if a 3rd-party app developed an independent governance mechanism, it would only impact that app's users. If the Apple i-Dapp Store developed an independent governance mechanism, it would impact the users of every app in the store (just not with the same granularity as an app-specific governance mechanism). Theoretically, an Apple Inc. applied governance mechanism would accordingly grow massive influence.

Figure 5

Resolutions of Governance

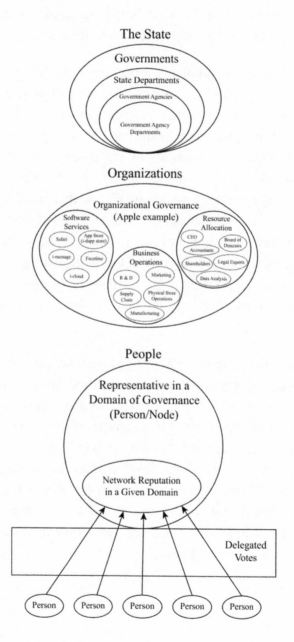

Now, getting an Apple or other Tech Titan to hop on board with this idea or a similar one is probably just a hopeful fantasy. Chapters 9 and 10 explore more realistic FAAMG scenarios. For now, the answer to those hypothetical questions from a social perspective is yes: Large-scale democratized governance mechanisms can potentially apply to organizations and governments.

As usual, getting an answer from the realm of technology is much more challenging. Legendary cryptographer Vitalik Buterin has been very vocal about the issues in blockchain governance. He is crystal clear about one thing: Blockchain as an algorithmic means to make all decisions without the flaw-ridden human mind is a preposterous concept.[218]

Buterin identifies three major problems for any decentralized network democracy[219]:

1. Voter turnout will be low because actors will have too small an influence and thus not enough incentive. This makes a fair voting system precarious and susceptible to bribery.

2. Governance mechanisms based on a token stake will create a plutocracy, leaving rich people with all the power.[220]

3. Voters will always vote based on self-interest—that is, if you have a stake in Bitcoin, you will want it to be a store of value and oppose changes that make it a more practical currency.

So long as these problems exist, the benefits of decentralization cannot hold because voters are basically acting in accordance with hierarchical motives. There are definitely solution options. All those problems have to do with voter incentives, which need to be intrinsic and not extrinsic to avoid the voter turnout, effort, and bribery issues.

A suitable governance mechanism needs good protocol randomness that will prevent one voter from knowing how another voted. Only after a vote concludes would a user decision become known, so there is no bandwagon fallacy with decisions. One tactic to prevent bribery might entail keeping specific voting decisions hidden but still visible to the algorithms that track them. In this way, voters could not be bribed and would only want to vote based on the merits of each proposal. To prevent the formation of a plutocracy, governance mechanisms need to prioritize merit more than the value of tokens staked.

Network governance needs to consider the competence of voter nodes. The popular method for this is rewarding voters for votes that align with the majority. This rewarding for "correct" decisions gives voters good reason to delegate votes to experts in some areas while having the option of acquiring voting power in their preferred domain of inquiry.

Of course, there are big problems with always favoring majority voters. After all, if the Internet had a governance mechanism right now and voted for moving to Web3 or staying with FAAMG, Web3 would lose because the majority doesn't understand Web3. More advanced proposals for governance would focus on ways to gauge the ethics of decisions and convert that into node reputation scores. There is plenty of user data to make this a reality, except these big data tactics will have transparent logic that is itself subject to network governance.

Algorithms could measure the efficacy of protocol changes over time, given their network effects. Having voted for protocol changes that positively impacted the network would improve your node reputation, network influence, and overall earnings. Having made bad decisions would have the opposite effect. In this way, a true idea meritocracy could emerge. Those who voted against a wrong decision would be rewarded and respected as authentic contrarians.

Buterin advocates for "multifactorial consensus" in governance mechanisms, where an ultimate decision is determined by the collective result of different diverse mechanisms.[221] In other words, an excellent governance mechanism will combine input from multiple independent sources to make decisions. Once this level of peer-to-peer trust is ensured in a network, the centralized actor roles become questionably trivial.[222] If this ideal became a reality, decentralized systems could match all the standards set by FAAMG services without the detriments of centralization.[223] As for the matter of how practical these solutions are, startups still remain the best indicators we have.

Exploring a Real-World Example: DFINITY Governance

DFINITY is one of many blockchain startups exploring blockchain governance. Aside from having an ingenious concept with the technology to back it up, DFINITY's governance is especially relevant because its full system closely resembles our i-Dapp Store hypothetical.

DFINITY is quick to point out flaws in the Internet monopoly, particularly with FAAMG's centralized cloud. The startup takes the perspective of today's web developers who have lost creative freedoms from mandatory use of complicated legacy IT stack components: databases, REST APIs, load balancers, firewalls, CDN's, browser extensions, usernames, passwords, and web servers.[224] To develop an application, you need to have an ongoing relationship with experts for every component to stay resistant to hacks and failures.[225] The majority of developer costs are wrapped up in this process.[226]

Developers are also forced into building software with FAAMG APIs, which automatically places them under Big Tech's guidelines.[227] What's more, shifts in Big Tech's motives could cause APIs to get revoked at any time, which demolishes the businesses of whoever depends on those APIs. That's why most tech startups consider "platform risk" as an existential threat to their business.[228] My top-down explanation for this has the startups failing because of a steep and crowded Internet hierarchy. DFINITY's bottom-up analogy views this power disparity as a result of startups "building on sand."[229]

To fix this, DFINITY begins with replacing or at least simplifying the legacy IT stack by creating "The Internet Computer," where you can build on just the Internet itself.[230] This is made possible with a data structure and a series of protocols that create something that resembles the next big generation in blockchain technology, hosted only by independent data centers instead of the FAAMG cloud. Data centers essentially share the same mathematical rules because they are formed by and run a protocol that makes The Internet Computer secure by default.[231] As a result, most of the IT stack is already built-in.

DFINITY does precisely as it claims to do. Developers are able to code websites, applications, or other Internet services without fear of mistreatment by platform proprietors. In this way, early-stage design for DFINITY and others is very similar to a dapp store. Just as the Apple App Store needs to be governed, DFINITY needs governance without the command-and-control hierarchy.

Guaranteeing honest and decentralized data centers is the first step—a feat that the legacy system has never achieved. All DFINITY independent servers acquire a Data Center Identity (DCIDs) through DFINITY's network governance mechanism or the Network Nervous System (NNS). In turn, the NNS makes decisions that support the network.

Like most of DFINITY's developments, NNS advancements are kept mostly under wraps. The following explanation describes the originally planned functionality of DFINITY's NNS. These reasons, combined with the rapidly changing nature of governance mechanisms, means some NNS concepts will be out of date.[232]

DFINITY's NNS uses "neurons" instead of nodes. Each neuron is capable of submitting proposals for network changes. Neurons vote on all accepted proposals to decide if it should be implemented. Votes are cast with influence proportional to the stake of native tokens (ICP) locked in any given neuron. Neurons are paid in proportion to the stake for the votes they participate in.

Voting could be manual or done automatically by delegating votes to other chosen neurons.[233] Most of the ICP token supply has been distributed to early supporters that claimed airdrops, early investors, and the foundation. Public markets will hopefully further decentralize the token supply by selling to latecomers who want to participate in governance.

Once this primary governance mechanism gets configured, adding elements of AI can be done fairly easily.[234] The idea is to add elements of distributed intelligence that study the results of decisions made. An AI would create a more probabilistic approach to decision making based on accruing data in the network. This is necessary to prevent situations where a demagogue gains the support and delegated votes of other neurons. A network AI would track all decisions and their impact, revealing poor decisions with their corresponding measurable failures. Eventually, the NNS will have many neurons joining to create a flexible brain for the Internet Computer, and each neuron having its quality or voter wisdom tracked by an honest AI.

DFINITY's governance is just one of many elements that make The Internet Computer exceedingly far ahead of the typical Web3 project, so much so that it may be unfair to put DFINITY in the Web3 category. It would probably be better to redefine the Web3 narrative to better align with DFINITY's plan for fixing the Big Tech oligopoly. What Bitcoin did for blockchain and what Ethereum did for the Web3 narrative, DFINITY is doing for the broader Internet. Chapter 10 covers DFINITY and The Internet Computer in greater depth.

The Many Flavors of Proto-Governance Mechanisms

In the crypto boom of late 2017, governance was barely a consideration for most startups. Now it seems you cannot find a cryptocurrency startup that doesn't mention "on-chain" governance on their website homepage. Governance has become a pervasive area of innovation in the blockchain space purely out of necessity. Every decentralized system needs some kind of oversight. With the many different decentralized systems, there's no one-size-fits-all governance mechanism, and that is okay.

Radically different needs from a diverse set of startups show how malleable network governance can be, and it is probably a step toward the multifactorial governance Buterin advocates. To be fair, most of these later proposals for blockchain governance are rudimentary, consisting only of voter groups with static influence. The startup Aragon even allows blockchain projects to make an on-chain governance system in five minutes, and it works like a charm but does not contribute to the more advanced versions we're interested in.[235] It is almost bizarre how far ahead of the curve DFINITY was with governance and other Internet Computer concepts. Many more blockchains have started to grasp the importance of governance.

Tezos, a leading cryptocurrency by market capitalization, has its most unique feature hinging on its ability to amend and adapt network design through distributed voting—that is, a governance mechanism.[236] Unlike most other top cryptocurrencies, Tezos is especially resilient because it can resolve network disputes without hard forks (splitting the network when disagreements occur).

Some groups might not trust a purely blockchain-based governance mechanism. In this case, a human pathway into network governance can merge with the blockchain version. Neo, a startup successful in dapp development, blockchain identity management, and in making a foundation layer for the "next-gen Internet," uses a combination of on-chain and off-chain governance for dispute resolution.[237]

Some enterprise applications prefer that centralized authorities make the decisions instead of a group of average Joes. It's a perfectly reasonable approach for those that don't need decentralization. Hedera Hashgraph, another startup aiming to build a trust layer on the Internet, provides similar software solutions with distributed voting. The difference is that they use 39 term-limited organizations and enterprises that serve as governing council nodes instead of individual stakeholders.[238] (A hashgraph, by the way, is basically a more efficient blockchain that does away with the chain of blocks idea, but please note that Hedera fans do not like this simplification.)

One of the biggest problems for different blockchains is interoperability, a feature they usually don't have. Some startups are making "bridges" between different blockchains. One tricky part of this concept is that there are different network rules on either side of each bridge because different blockchains follow different rules. For this, a governance mechanism is mandatory. Polkadot, possibly the most advanced proposal for blockchain interoperability, incorporates stakeholders and elected officials into their governance mechanism. Voters decide on proposals while an elected council of experts have the power to veto.[239]

Cosmos is another startup that allows individuals and enterprises to make and use their blockchains with sovereignty while maintaining interoperability with others. This collection of blockchains composes the Cosmos Hub. To allow concerted interactions between disparate blockchains, Cosmos uses a system of voters along with an amendable constitution for dispute resolution.[240]

Augur is a prediction market that takes an entirely different approach to solving probabilistic problems that loosely relates to governance. The concept is called the "wisdom of the crowd," where a large group of combined bets can be accurate predictors of global events. This completely unconventional approach to decision making created a potentially powerful data source that world leaders can use to shape policy.

It's important to note that all these governance examples are occurring irrespective of blockchain consensus. In most examples of blockchain governance, miners secure coin transactions, and voters approve protocol changes independent of one another. That doesn't mean governance doesn't have a role to play in blockchain consensus. Scalability issues with blockchain stem from every node having to agree on and replicate every transaction. When delegating this responsibility to only a few nodes to increase speed, centralization poses a risk to the consensus mechanism. Applying some of the above features of governance mechanisms makes picking delegates much safer. EOS is one of many startups that solves the scalability problem with a representative democracy style consensus: Token holders use a voting system to select the 21 block producers every 126 blocks.[241] Governance integrated consensus can keep a secure network without the need to reproduce and validate every transaction across thousands of nodes.

These governance mechanisms are still just raw decision-making machines, optimized to output the most favorable solutions. Governance mechanisms take many forms and can fill a diverse array of gaps in platform decision making. They also solve cryptocurrency's most widespread problem: having a purpose.

The last chapter showed how cryptocurrencies are often used to fund startups and not much else after that. Blockchain initiatives that make this mistake are then stuck building business models around useless coins. The equity model, as it is with stocks, does not work for network coins because blockchain systems should not have owners. Yet tokens are an integral part of every governance mechanism mentioned in this section.

Blockchain-based tokens are naturally a good fit for providing information about how a network is distributed. They are also a great way to delegate power without ownership. Tokens have value because their owners decide how the network evolves. Token owners will have the network's best interests in mind because the token's value rests on the success of its platform. Platform-specific tokens also make a fitting reward for those who make network contributions.

In this tokenization model, coins finally have a role that is conducive to network success. It is fair to say that owners, shareholders, and voters have just been replaced with token holders. The importance of this switch will be elaborated on in the next section when discussing classifications of governance. It is important to note that another essential token utility is buying compute power, just as Ethereum's ETH buys gas for computation.

Right now, network governance is still in an immature phase and is an underpublicized area in distributed ledger technologies. Its mostly theoretical framework and high complexity doesn't attract much attention at first glance. Conversely, organizational governance is a hot topic because the race towards automation can't happen without it. Most organizations are now turning toward conventional models for platform decisions. This looks like an unfavorable path given our move toward ever-increasing computer intelligence.

Vili's Paradox Again: Blockchain's Supposed Redundancy

Artificial Intelligence (AI), specifically Artificial Neural Networks (ANNs), are the foremost developments in machine decision making. ANNs are computing systems that resemble biological brains and are designed to become governance mechanisms, just like a human mind. Work on ANNs is extensive, and their applications in governance mechanisms surpass that of blockchain, unless of course, they worked together in some blockchain-based ANNs. This may make blockchain governance seem like a rather banal placeholder for the future ANNs of the world.

To see why this notion is mistaken, we arrive back at Vili's Paradox: Decentralized systems can't succeed because centralized elements will inevitably thrive in any potential scenario. Vili does acknowledge the utility of governance mechanisms, which brings us to his provocation:

> Once you address the problem of governance, you no longer need blockchain; you can just as well use conventional technology that assumes a trusted central party to enforce the rules, because you're already trusting somebody (or some organization/process) to make the rules. I call this blockchain's "governance paradox": once you master it, you no longer need it.[242]

By this logic, if DFINITY's governance mechanism became as trustworthy as blockchain consensus, there would be no need for the trust provided by a blockchain. Conventional systems could just apply that governance themselves. If ANN governance mechanisms are more advanced and trustworthy than ones based on blockchain voting, organizations could use those instead.

Except that on-chain and off-chain governance will always be fundamentally different because blockchain is the very thing that instills trust in a governance mechanism. If a sufficiently advanced ANN made all the decisions for an organization in a way similar to the network governance processes described throughout this chapter, that would not make it trustworthy. Conventional ANNs will always have private elements giving their creators disproportionately high levels of power. For governance to be trustworthy, all elements of the governance mechanism must be transparent from its inception, which is only possible by having all its logic on-chain. This includes having the ANN itself being under the control of network voters. We must distinguish trustworthy governance mechanisms from non-trustworthy ones because of how prevalent they will become.

The way FAAMG governs roughly shapes the modern Internet, and their decisions are questionable, to say the least. Being the kings of digital innovation, you would think their business decisions would also be partially automated. As far as the public knows, they run like a conventional organization at their highest levels of governance, with CEOs, boards of directors, and shareholders. It should be safe to say that hierarchies like FAAMG aren't interested in being governed by any system that distributes power. Traditional organizations similarly have owners and internal hierarchies, which leaves leaders with no motivation to democratize governance.

Even as ANNs develop to the point where their governing ability is too good to refuse, corporate adoption won't solve the governance problem. As Buterin warned, the concept of purely algorithmic governance without human intervention is just crazy. Off-chain governance for organizations will always be made with hierarchical motives baked into them. When human intervention is required, responsibility will fall to the same leaders that are meant to distribute power in the first place. Hierarchical organizations will always create corruptible governance mechanisms. Digital governance is not a unilateral problem to be solved but about appropriately employing the many possible solutions.

In every type of governance mechanism, there will be some displacement of trust. Off-chain versions place trust in established entities. This doesn't work because there is no such thing as an unbiased entity. Try to imagine an impartial entity using ANNs to resolve conflicts between FAAMG and governments. It's easy to see that no such entity could exist.

The on-chain versions of governance also require displacing of trust, but without the entity. That's why DFINITY or a similar model can't take the same path as the FAAMG oligopoly. The DFINITY Foundation does not make the rules or own the platform—the users do. The goal of DFINITY is to support the project to the point where the foundation has no reason to exist. On-chain governance models would resolve FAAMG and Government conflict not with entities, but with distributed pools of expert voters.

Both on-chain and off-chain governance mechanisms have trust displaced by some imperfect method of consensus. Differences between the two are depicted in Figure 6. Both types of governance still achieve consensus in a hierarchical manner. The most significant difference is that on-chain consensus has separate domains rather than one supreme group. Domains essentially flatten the hierarchy and add more granularity to decision making than larger hierarchies.

This granularity makes all on-chain positions in the system determined by voters rather than the appointees of a sitting leader, meaning that all low-level users have direct voting power, not just suggestive influence. The ever-changing nature of network governance allows for high fluidity of actor roles, so power is always shifting. A group of domain-specific hierarchies and the system that elects them are collectively what displaces the trust of some established entity. In this way, large hierarchies are composed of the collective effort of their constituent parts, and the multifactorial consensus Buterin advocates could be realized.

Figure 6

Classifications of Governance

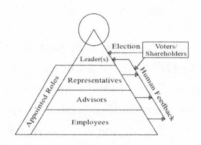

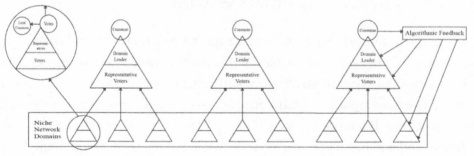

Technicalities aside, the idea of blockchain-integrated governance is relatively simple. Traditional methods of governance resort to hierarchical systems of leaders to represent individuals. There was never another choice before the digital age because tracking of every individual's input was impossible. When seamless individual connectivity and trust is added to the equation, the hierarchy could be granulated. It can turn networks into direct democracies, except the votes are for decisions instead of leaders. The way votes are delegated adds elements of meritocracy. This concept could not exist before blockchain technology because there would always be a potential lack of trust.

The Promise of Decentralized Autonomous Organizations

Properly combining governance and automation leads to self-sufficient technology. This is the idea behind one of blockchain's more flashy use cases: Decentralization Autonomous Organizations (DAOs). At their most advanced levels, DAOs are what they say they are: organizations that run themselves. Now let's take a step back to explain how we move from the original "chain of blocks" to completely automated companies.

Organizations, but more specifically technology companies, naturally look to automate things for efficiency reasons. Traditional software packages help with this but not without intermediaries. Blockchain was first noticed as a potential agent for removing intermediaries with the birth of Ethereum Smart Contracts. Smart contracts are pieces of software that execute automatically based on preset conditions and are now possible with many programming languages outside Ethereum's Solidity.

As the name suggests, one use case for a smart contract is as a contract: Multiple people, businesses, and machines could exchange value without the need for lawyers, accountants, notaries, bankers, or escrow services. But people get hung up on the idea of contracts, which is somewhat limiting. Code written on a distributed network has a special feature, whether it is a contract or not. Perhaps a better term is *autonomous software* because, once it's written in code, it isn't owned by anyone but will exist and execute as designed for anyone who uses it.[243] In this way, smart contracts/autonomous software could make apps, software services, and even entire businesses fully autonomous. The latter example would be a full-blown DAO.

Before we get to the stage of DAOs, there is much ground to cover. None of this works on conventional IT infrastructure, so reliable Internet Computers for building DAOs must be developed first. Platforms also need to have established blockchain-based identity management and financial services, which are problems for the next two chapters. Lastly, there needs to be a way to account for unknown unknowns—that is, some unforeseen circumstances that were not written as parameters in the smart contract. A bug such as this would again trigger the need for lawyers, accountants, and other 3rd-party moderators. To meet the autonomy requirement of a DAO, there needs to be a governance mechanism to resolve such disputes.

We are now familiar with both the functionality and need for governance mechanisms, which can pretty much be summed up as a path toward industry adoption of DAOs. But what does a DAO realistically look like? The term *decentralized autonomous organization* is just like the buzzwords *artificial intelligence, Internet of Things, quantum computing, hyper-automation,* and *blockchain* in the sense that it was coined before its associated phenomenon matures. DAOs must be described in the context of existing organizations, but any advanced DAO would be completely unrecognizable when compared to today's tech. With that in mind, an excerpt from the *Journal of Organization Design* offers a good starting point for understanding DAOs:

> Imagine working for a global business organization whose routine tasks are powered by a software protocol instead of being governed by managers and employees. Task assignments and rewards are randomized by the algorithm. Information is not channeled through a hierarchy but recorded transparently and securely on an immutable public ledger called "blockchain." Further, the organization decides on design and strategy changes through a democratic voting process involving a previously unseen class of stakeholders called "miners." Agreements need to be reached at the organizational level for any proposed protocol changes to be approved and activated.[244]

A relatable example that frequently shows up in the literature is a DAO similar to Uber: *Duber*. The current model consists of a ride-sharing app where users pay Uber, which later pays drivers after taking a cut. Uber takes responsibility for disputes and lawsuits in return for its earnings. This centralized corporation role that Uber plays is important because regulations can keep everyone playing by fair rules without a leading entity.

Now swap the Uber app with a Duber dapp on The Internet Computer. Aside from the Internet infrastructure benefits, this would charge riders less and pay drivers more because there's no profit-reaping parent company. Disputes would be resolved via a governance mechanism instead of lawsuits. Barring participation from network nodes, Duber would be completely autonomous and self-sustaining.

There's no need to stop at Uber. DAOs are equally applicable to Airbnb, Fiverr, Zoom, Spotify, and many FAAMG services. Some of the manufacturing aspects of FAAMG are a bit trickier to automate—more on that in Chapters 8 and 9. DAOs will start slowly, like any innovation, by replicating existing apps and software services, but interpreting them beyond the context of copycat technologies is a lost cause. The greater importance of DAOs will come from the new technological frontier that they unlock and the previously unimaginable creations that could now be built from a freer Internet.

This is right about where blockchain enthusiasts will stop talking about DAOs. The part we've ignored so far is that DAOs are not destined to succeed. Not even close. We haven't even seen a DAO hit any major market yet. Those that have tried are mostly remakes of existing online services. This strategy doesn't go very far because incumbent platforms already have all the peer-to-peer value. That is why if the perfect version of a Duber dapp were released tomorrow, no one would want or even be able to use it. Uber is currently valued at around 50 billion dollars not because its app is impressive, but because over 100 million people use it. The same goes for most social media platforms, websites, and other online services. Everyone wants to register with whichever one has the most users.

DAOs are not an inevitable part of our future. Decentralized copycats can't secure a future for the decentralized era. There are still plenty of ways that less transparent conventional technologies could govern autonomous systems. As far as I can tell, there are two possible ways, reflective of historical examples, that DAOs could be part of the future.

DAOs could initiate a true paradigm shift given the right architecture and governance, or they will have their logic privatized and implemented in traditional corporations. For example, the steam engine was indeed a paradigm shift, but its influence was dependent on the steel, oil, and railroad industries, which themselves were monopolies. The Internet, another real paradigm shift, needed FAAMG to become as great as it is. Autonomous organizations are a way for the private sector to advance and increase profits, and it won't require decentralization to occur. The ideals of the blockchain innovations are just as susceptible to privatization as paradigm shifts of the past. Although this analogy is not a perfect one, it is consistent with how technology evolves and gives a better direction than purely imaginative guessing.

Possibility 1 would be the creation of some unimaginable class of services that only work on decentralized infrastructure. Technologists speculate this as the probable outcome, but no notable examples exist. It could be the paradigm shift we've all been waiting for or a lost pipe dream. An example of this would be a self-governing Duber that beats Uber purely by being cheaper for users and better for drivers.

Possibility 2 would be incremental progress toward DAOs with enterprise-usable technology. Large companies will want to run autonomous software, and this could gradually lay the groundwork for a transition to hyper-automation. If a viable revenue model could be built around independently governed business operations, then DAOs could succeed alongside existing corporations—

Duber's best shot at success would be if Uber chose to merge with it. If some new class of services starts taking off with a DAO-like business model, conventional organizations will follow a similar path to stay competitive.

The acronym DAO is wrongfully used to describe the second scenario, which realistically drops the "decentralization." Public companies might pass them off as DAOs, but they will be more like semi-autonomous organizations with a few decision-making leaders.

The rest of this section will run with the assumption that DAOs merging with enterprise is realistic because real organizations are the only way to exemplify them in a relatable way, like with our hypothetical Duber. In a much more real sense, if enterprises become the leaders in autonomous software, DAOs will not be transparent, decentralized, or trustworthy. It would just be embedding the same principles from its centralized corporate hierarchy into a more advanced network.

The idea that DAOs will make organizations obsolete is not a consideration in this book. That would imply the fall of capitalism and traditional governments, and there is no developed evidence to suggest that such a scenario is even remotely likely. If the influence of information and communication technologies in the physical world continues to see rapid growth, I believe this will become a necessary conversation, and can only hope the Internet will be decentralized by then. Still, it is decades away and a useless pursuit at the time of this writing.

DAO implementers for possibilities 1 and 2 land on vastly different ends of an ideological spectrum: the first are contrarian developers and cryptographers, while the second are resourceful capitalists. Each would produce very different DAOs. If development of DAOs proceeds gradually, they won't start out completely decentralized and autonomous. Thus, different versions will land on all different parts of this spectrum. The lines separating DAOs and conventional autonomous systems might get blurred in just the same way that blockchain startups aren't necessarily based on blockchain. The word *blockchain* is also used continuously outside the context of Satoshi's chain-of-blocks idea. Since *decentralized* and *autonomous* are not the most objective characteristics, we need to define more intrinsic classifications of early-stage DAOs.

Transparency is a good candidate for this intrinsic principle. As DAOs evolve into something that we can't yet predict, they will probably continue to be composed of networks and governance mechanisms, both of which are nothing new. What's unique about *every* DAO's network and governance mechanism is transparency. Smart contracts, which outline the rules of any DAO, by their very nature cannot be hidden because the whole network shares them. In this way, a DAO's governance structure is intrinsically transparent.[245]

No matter how the characteristics of a DAO get twisted, no one should be able to escape this simple truth. If Apple creates an ANN that governs the Apple App Store and developers cannot see the algorithms, that's not a DAO. If Uber creates a Duber app and the users can't see where their money goes after paying for a ride, that's not a DAO. If Apple and Uber want to construct their governance mechanism nodes from boards of directors, government entities, and other centralized authorities, that's their prerogative, and it could still yield a DAO. If they hide any details of their decision-making process, then that system should not be considered a DAO.

Bear in mind that the idea of transparency being the qualifier for DAOs is a simplification, but an incredibly useful one nonetheless. The mentioned possibilities for DAOs of the future are speculative at best. Possibility 1 (relying on some arbitrary DAO to capture unimaginable success) is a Hail Mary. Possibility 2 (convincing established industries to integrate decentralized upgrades) requires a complete remake of traditional capitalistic revenue models. Because of this, transparency is not a random buzzword for attracting attention, but instead becomes an axiom as part of a meticulously calculated strategy.

Transparency is an increasingly important quality for businesses in the digital age. Fiscal transparency for organizations is a good starting point and has been proven to yield the best economic outcomes.[246] It's really rather simple: Make revenue and expense data available to scrutiny by everyone and rapid improvement will follow. Another form of transparency has to do with corporate governance, or the level of information disclosure between upper management and stakeholders. The amount of information disclosure between components of a corporate governance structure is a major determinant of institutional success.[247] Radical transparency in business operations is a further step which has a positive impact when taken.[248] Radical transparency has even been preached as an essential business principle by one of the world's most renowned investors.[249] The point is that general transparency as an idea and quality is becoming a big part of 21st century organizations. DAOs need to be leveraging this.

The bigger picture for DAOs, and what makes them contenders for "the final frontier" in blockchain technologies, is how their transparency could transform collaboration. The governance that has been discussed thus far takes place within systems. We saw how they could scale up from the individual level to subset services, then business departments, and eventually entire organizations. The big change in governance models as they increase in scale is how they interact with other mechanisms: Node governance connects to make departmental governance mechanisms, which collectively interact to compose the larger organizational governance. Figure 4 from earlier in this chapter classifies governance by the differences in how all the node, organizational, and governmental governance mechanisms interact. What we've been building up to is essentially types of "meta-governance," which could range from completely centralized to completely decentralized.

Figure 5 represents how the world is governed, and it is dependent on the style and influence of the constituent governance mechanisms: people, organizations, and governments. Relationships between these three parties is riddled with discrepancies and obscurity. Governments struggle most with enterprise funding and taxing decisions when they lack information about those enterprises. Governments don't know how to best moderate FAAMG's power because it's not always clear what that power is or how it's used. The election of officials is still subject to manipulation because voting is not transparent. Organizations must have their freedom and power limited by governments because there is not transparency in how it gets used.

In short, the world is still stuck using the Mode 2 governance in Figure 4. Applying DAOs and their deeply-ingrained transparency would move the world toward Mode 3 governance. Dispute resolution in this world would look like a pseudo-direct democracy, where the general population has direct influence in decisions and electing all representatives. Let's try to envision a resolution process for the FAAMG versus big government power disputes.

For this to become viable, it must be commonplace for organizations and governments to use network governance mechanisms that independently achieve consensus. FAAMG should first have delegate network nodes in the government consensus network and vice versa. Let's say Microsoft had used their consensus mechanism to set up the details for the LinkedIn acquisition. If United States Government independently voted this as anticompetitive, who would win? A decision of this prestige would be grounds for a nationwide, and perhaps worldwide, vote. Many organizations and perhaps even individual people would participate and have their voting power computed based on their network influence and relevance to the issue at hand. An even more optimal solution would be Microsoft agreeing to make all LinkedIn data publicly available upon the acquisition so it could not be leveraged for anticompetitive behavior.

Taking things further, if participating organizations run autonomous software, then they themselves could be DAOs. The advantages offered by AI and ANNs could extend to them because the same AI logic can be written on whatever Turing-complete programming language the DAO uses. Blockchain could offer much-needed transparency for AI development, making them complementary technologies. AI would be a tool for providing information while keeping humans in charge of final decisions.

As hard as this vision may be to develop, it would benefit everyone. With only the example we used, FAAMG and governments could have a way to avoid litigation war. The bottom line is that governments and corporations would become more honest for their own good. There should be plenty of motivation to make this world of interconnected DAOs a reality.

As mentioned before, it's not fair to be entirely optimistic about DAOs. Possibility 1 is unlikely because startups lack resources and blockchain is not necessarily a paradigm shift, and possibility 2 is probably just a gateway to centralized autonomous organizations. DAOs today are not a paradigm shift because there is a vast gap between what has been built and what the vision of a real DAO is. A decentralized Internet must come first, and that has yet to be achieved.

Entire blockchain-based revolutions must first occur in identity management, financial infrastructure, and manufacturing (Chapters 6, 7, and 8) before realistically considering a world of DAOs. Then they need an entirely new Internet infrastructure to deploy those solutions. Without those steps, FAAMG wins the battle for the Internet. The remainder of this book carves out a path toward growing decentralized Internet infrastructure into something that qualifies as a true paradigm shift.

CHAPTER 6:

IDENTITY

Legacy Systems

Identity management (IdM) hasn't undergone any serious innovation since it was capable of being deduced from paper documents. The Internet rose irrespective of any radical shift in tracking sensitive documentation. FAAMG is proof that entire brick-and-mortar industries can become digitized, but what is the digital equivalent of a passport, driver's license, or social security card? They don't exist because machines can't verify the authenticity of digital documents with the same degree of certainty as face-to-face verification with physical documents.[250]

IdM has yet to catch up with the way the Internet inadvertently changed industries. Most networks bring together the business logic of disparate entities, but identity does the opposite by forcing each entity to hold different customer credentials that cannot be shared. The sensitivity of identity-related data precludes any network approach, forcing centralized verification methods to remain intact and increasing fragmentation across organizations.[251] Furthermore, mimicking physical, personally identifiable information (PII) online carries with it a massive liability for any organization that touches it. Physical identity verification does not have the liability of a digital trail. Lack of trust between organizations forced the growth of barriers in IdM. Even spurts of technological innovation could not bridge the trust gap required to get organizations to use it.

This failure to advance with the times forces individuals to manage a distinct set of credentials for every organization they interact with—and it's the reason why you're probably managing over 100 online accounts with forgotten, shared, and repeated passwords.[252]

No one benefits from this. Users perform unnecessary work in proving who they are. Verifiers have to dedicate resources to secure this process. Both parties suffer from the risk of breaches, which is rapidly increasing on an annual basis.[253] [254] These inefficiencies are universally applicable to all the concepts discussed in this chapter. The particulars will be demonstrated on a practical basis toward the end of this chapter.

Quick Fixes

Fragmentation of human identities across the Internet has seen remediation attempts for no less than a decade with the concept of *re-centralization*. All the quick fixes reveal a whole slew of disregarded caveats for effective IdM. Password managers do this in their most basic form not by solving identity, but instead by removing one possibility for discrepancy (lost usernames and passwords). Aside from being vulnerable PII honeypots, they lack two major IdM components: *Identifiers* that can distinguish between users without discrepancy and *Attributes* or raw PII data to attach verifiable claims to an identifier.[255] In other words, usernames and passwords aren't of much utility outside the service they are generated in because they do not represent anything physical.

For a password manager, usernames serve as identifiers, and account information serves as attributes, but not anywhere outside of their designated service. Online identities could represent aliases or otherwise have an immaterial relationship with PII.[256] That makes even internally useful data generated on a single platform useless in relation to another one (at least for that individual user). An example of this would be keeping user preference settings uniform across platforms. It would be nice if you jumped from Facebook to YouTube and the accounts represented the same version of you. This cross-platform version of you should also not jeopardize your data. Data generated by a real identity could start to have its protection enforced because it would have become affixed to a person. This is a necessary step for making data sharing more transparent and preventing nefarious data usage. By the end of this chapter, it will become clear that making this possible starts with nailing IdM solutions.

Governments issue more discernible credentials, with ID numbers being identifiers and the information affiliated with that ID being attributes. With so many different versions of these IDs across governments, the increasingly borderless world has arrived no closer to a globally recognizable standard for PII.[257] Now energy is spent tweaking a legacy system that is ripe for a radical shift.

"Remediation of central governance" is one way: Make the issuers, relaying parties, and users more trustworthy,[258] possibly through making users more reliable in protecting their ID credentials or increasing the diversity of the identity provider's board.[259] Before the digital revolution, this unspecific solution category may have sufficed but now bears little relevance to IdMs unique predicament. The private sector knows more about our real identities than any government and can put it into IoT readable form. It's unclear whether "central governance" in IdM will have a stable meaning when we know FAAMG can at least intermittently serve as issuers, relaying parties, and verifiers. FAAMG certainly has the resources, motive, and highly tailored potentialities to solve IdM. But they haven't done so yet, and they keep trying, and they keep failing.

Attempts and Limited Success

Just because the Internet rose without an identity layer, it doesn't mean no one tried. In 1999, Microsoft's Passport was first introduced as a "single sign-on for web commerce" and later as an "internet-wide unified-login system."[260] Passport, serving as little more than an early password manager, failed as a standalone concept. Passport's centralized storage option would generate the data honeypots that in turn would attract hackers and preclude user ownership.[261] Windows 10 later added it to Windows Hello, expanding on it with multi-factor authentication features including biometric lock, password, and internal encrypted device key.[262]

CardSpace, Microsoft's successor to Passport, entered the scene in 2007 as the "Identity Metasystem."[263] This time the involvement of identity providers (IdPs) and relaying parties (RPs) made *identifiers* and *attributes* relevant in the form of Information Cards. IdPs are the authorities that issue identity information, and RPs are those that accept them for their own verification. Both of these entities can take the form of governments, credit unions, private businesses, etc. CardSpace implemented self-issued and managed cards controlled at the user's device level (not by Microsoft databases as in Passport).[264] Microsoft even decentralized the system with token-based authentication and public key infrastructure (PKI) for securing Information Cards.[265] CardSpace was discontinued for reasons that are not entirely clear. Being too early for user-centric identity, CardSpace probably failed to recruit enough IdPs and RPs because they were unaware of benefits or skeptical of system trustworthiness.

Microsoft's U-Prove followed in 2011 with two technical changes to the tokens. Proving attributes through tokens became more secure because issuance and presentation of associated data could no longer be linked to the tokens encoded key.[266] Furthermore, users had more control over PII disclosure by providing the minimum amount of data required for verification.[267] U-Prove seems now to only exist as an outdated and forgotten codebase.[268] Microsoft's IdM system evolution ended up converging on verification through certificate authorities without oversharing, which is the same theme consistent across IdM systems today.

Microsoft makes for a powerful example of IdM within FAAMG because it has one of the loosest associations with user data in the group. The remaining FAAMG members share comparably tortuous stories that eventually assembled IdM systems mirroring that same theme. Interestingly, these progressions proved increasing demand for distributed privacy and security completely independent of blockchain's rise. Google ID and Facebook Connect are examples of the current leaders in this arena, but systematic analysis of a platform-agnostic 3rd parties offers the broadest implications. OpenID single sign-on (SSO) solutions meet these criteria and are arguably the closest to becoming a standard.

Much of the world's online verification runs through the OpenID services/protocols, but its terminology cannot be more confusingly named. Security Assertion Markup Language (SAML) is the older but still prominent language in use for web-based applications.[269] SAML is XML-based, meaning it's used to make PII from documents machine-readable. OpenID Connect is the more recent deployment similarly purposed for user verification but tailored to simplify development on native/mobile applications compared to SAML.[270] It uses OAuth 2.0, a framework to support authentication protocol development while facilitating communication between JSON and HTTP (data transmitting/translating languages for various application/webpage formats).[271] Simply put, "OpenID Connect is the OAuth 2.0-based replacement for OpenID 2.0 (OpenID)."[272]

The OpenID umbrella and related languages cover the major tools available for connecting RPs and IdPs to users. OpenID has over one billion user accounts and is accepted by over 50,000 websites, including Facebook, Google, and Microsoft.[273] It allows app developers to authenticate their users across these applications without bearing responsibility for holding the user data themselves. It's why the Web has so many freely available applications and is safer to explore than in previous years. You've also probably never heard of it. OpenID is decentralized and so deeply embedded in solution architecture that you will never see it. It's almost a picture-perfect representation of all features that FAAMG IdM systems tried to emulate while remaining centralized. Now it composes the building blocks for FAAMG's own IdM solutions in a symbiotic relationship, combining the benefits of decentralized security with the efficiency of a centralized implementer. But giving FAAMG this decentralized

IdM underbelly is not enough for foolproofing the inherently malicious Internet.

OpenID Connect successfully addresses *most* attack vulnerabilities from its predecessors.[274] The next version will probably be released with fewer flaws, but even an impeccable version of OAuth will not fix root issues occurring at implementation. Since OAuth 2.0 is a development tool, not a standalone service, implementations not only waste resources by building separate systems for the same purpose but risk vulnerabilities in the code written for each deployment.[275] Although there exist many possibilities for an attack, two novel ones useful for analysis are IdP Confusion and Malicious Endpoint Attacks.[276] In both cases, the risk posed is unauthorized data access (usually by RPs), and users are generally unaware.[277] It's reasonable to assume that implementation will always lead to an increased number of vulnerabilities.[278]

Solutions for security flaws in IdM seem to come from the wrong angle by adding more services on top of SSO systems such as vulnerability scanners.[279] Even effective scanners will eventually reveal deficiencies and be forced into cyclical behavior—another quick fix through compounding another service layer. SSO needs fundamental change, not small tweaks.

Blockchain is the killer use case for this, but we are jumping the gun. Everything up to this point has been standard SSO technology with a few creative quirks. It is not anywhere close to verifying real human identity online. Good solutions don't exist online because systems haven't struck the right balance of sophistication and security. Private actors in general still can't agree on what combination of attributes qualifies as a legitimate identity.

Self-Sovereign Versus Federal Identity

The term *federal identity* is used in this section to mean PII credentials issued by a central authority. Usually this is a government, but privately issued/generated PII is also becoming increasingly relevant. A passport, driver's license, and social security card are some examples of federal identifiers.

Self-Sovereign Identity (SSI) is far more ambiguous because it exists only as a concept. The idea of SSI is driven by blockchain startups and can generally be explained as a set of self-owned and controlled personal attributes that compose a digital identity.

For example, an SSI in its simplest form might mirror some passport attributes—for example, name, height, weight, eye color—and a passport number might translate to a digital identifier (DID). The difference is in the issuance and ownership of that data. Instead of the government defining, owning, and controlling these attributes, you do. Unfortunately, being verified as Bob because you like to call yourself Bob doesn't get us very far. Every project combats this challenge through different methods of minimizing subjectivity. Once that baseline is set, more intimate (and allegedly useful) attributes can be added: "data from a social media account, a history of transactions on an e-commerce site, or attestations from friends or colleagues."[280] Essentially, intangible human features (the type of data discussed in "The Death of Privacy") is no longer off-limits with true SSI because they are protected by intrinsic user ownership.

This visionary concept is easier said than done but has proven useful when federal identity is not an option. Refugees without an identity have restored immutable PII attributes on blockchain and secured that relationship with biometric data.[281] Startups using blockchain and biometrics have communalized the distribution of funds to refugees and reduced national security risks in the process.[282] From a practical standpoint, SSI has not moved past this stage of replicating federally applicable PII for the few who need it. Beyond this, crossing borders (physical or virtual) is currently best authorized by a government-issued number, not a blockchain saying you're Bob because you self-identified as Bob.

Lack of intangible PII or demand for SSI are not valid justifications for its slow progress. Like most original ideas, it is tough to articulate a practical configuration when it's unlike anything that exists. SSI falls victim to this circumstance and is infrequently described without meaningless buzzwords. This is okay for its current stage, but the grander issue preventing subsequent development phases is the inability to skirt an already broken system. Online federal identity management needs to be rock solid before new versions can branch off.

SSI is highly sensitive compared to federal identity, and levels of security should increase proportionally before SSI implementation. Thus, federal identity needs to have blockchain level security before blockchain-based SSI receives legitimate consideration. IdM solutions in this chapter focus mostly on federal IdM solutions solely because they are apparent enough to provoke functional utility. If SSI works out its kinks, the main difference will just be the type of data behind DIDs. Advanced IdM developments in this chapter should converge on standardized DIDs and maintain broad applicability to SSI.

The Structural Components of Blockchain IdM

Legacy systems pose serious security risks, but potential threats are not appealing enough to shift a market toward radical change. Instead, efficiency (time and money) gains make for a better motivator of change. Whenever you register for a new service, lose your login credentials, or suffer from a security breach, both you and the destination service waste time and resources. Figures vary in each circumstance, so a specific example will later be given with the company SecureKey. Ideal Blockchain IdM systems reduce hassle for everyone by providing authentication without any parties withholding PII.[283]

Usually blockchain aims to remove middlemen, but the proper way of looking at IdM is as an attempt to add middlemen.[284] This is a peculiar case where adding more parties improves efficiency as long as they can interact seamlessly. We see this in companies that have some barrier that prevents interactions with others. Stores and customers always did everything themselves. Every store had to create physical stores for every geographical group of customers. Amazon delivery became an efficient middleman because the distance gap between stores and customers was always closed individually with every shopper experience. Although unconventional, it's the correct analogy given their never-existing identity middlemen in the private sector because companies could not outsource trust on behalf of their users. Blockchain is uniquely able to offer this trust and reduce liability by shielding both the middlemen and destination services from raw data.

In such a system, user data is indefinitely self-owned and controlled, making its use between organizations easily consented, executed, and verified.[285] Of course, the described characteristics are theoretical. One evaluation method for translating these to modern IdM equivalents is an analysis of seven design criteria as described in *A First Look at IdM Schemes on the Blockchain*:[286]

1. Release of information is at the user's consent.

2. Users can control the release of individual attributes for minimal disclosure.

3. Justifiable authority for PII access is provided by destination services.

4. Users control the visibility of all attributes in the network.

5. System interoperability with other IdM schemes.

6. Simple user experience.

7. Consistent functionality across different platforms.

Each of the above parameters lands on a spectrum when applied to real applications. Structural distinctions are what make these tradeoffs in IdM system design. Defining structures carries the assumption that system components and terminology are universally used even though they vary on a case by case basis. IdM systems connect three types of data on users, IdPs, and RPs: identity claims, proof, and attestations.[287] Identity claims would be a statement about you, proof would be the documentation/certification that verifies a claim, and attestations are proof of credential issuance by an authority.

Two fundamental IdM organizational structures are possible: top-down and bottom-up. Credential issuance that occurs by the system owner (central authority) is the top-down model, leading to a hierarchical structure.[288] Although federal identity is generally derived from top-down structures and SSI ideally represents the bottom-up approach, neither are synonymous.[289] Federal identity could be bottom-up if it relied on distributed protocols for generation, issuance, and storage. SSI would be top-down if it was generated, issued, controlled, and stored by FAAMG (although not still technically SSI it is the same new-age data arranged by a vastly different concept). IdM systems use a combination of these two organizational structures, demonstrating a need for features from both. Centralization currently provides the highest degree of PII authenticity, while decentralization gives users maximal freedom. The challenge for blockchain is enabling both.

Concepts that can be thought of as running analogously to this spectrum in startups are decentralized identity, SSI, and zero-knowledge proofs (ZKPs).[290] Most practical startups currently use strongly backed federal identity but give it consented release features and distributed storage—for example, decentralized identity—loosely relating to the top-down approach. With minimal reliance on centralized issuance and emphasis on user data ownership, SSI is closer to the bottom-up approach. About design criteria, SSI shines with "1" and "2" while decentralized identity's superior standardization currently excels in roles "5-7" and the remaining criteria seem to be an IdM tossup. ZKPs are a technology more than a system type but, applied to IdM as a concept, increase the functionality of "1-7" irrespective of organizational structure (within reason).

You know that green padlock in your address bar proving that your on an intended website (for example, not on a phishing site)? This is called an *extended validation certificate* (EV), and its beauty lies in ensuring authenticity in web interactions without PII exchange. It's made possible through public key infrastructure (PKI) and cryptography by extension. Websites give their public key to certificate authorities who sign it with a respected private key while returning an EV confirmed by a browser through HTTPS connections.[291] Unfortunately, there is still a centralized certificate authority that encounters the same drawbacks consistent with what's been redundantly discussed when placing trust in a single point of failure.[292] PKI technology is also too expensive and unscalable to extend to individual users by traditional means.[293]

ZKPs are the technology to perform these blind validation functions scalably. The technical process of ZKPs is outside of the scope of this chapter, but proof of its functionality will be evident in different projects. In an isolated use case example, a loan seeker needing to prove a certain credit score could have a credit bureau return "yes" or "no" to a bank while apportioning zero knowledge of other personal information. This method of analysis becomes benign when applied to other industry applications, such as creating objectively generated insurance and subscription rates.

ZKPs were first developed decades ago as single-purpose functions but have since become an expansive subset of algorithms playing a fundamental role in blockchain-based IdM.[294] Just as bitcoin is the original use case for a broader set of blockchain technologies, ZKPs are a narrowly-used technology that, when translated into a concept, becomes a metaphor for its grander significance.

The last structural element to be addressed is ecosystem convergence. Cross-blockchain interoperability is a whole other can of worms, but when applied to IdM, there are a few suitable options. Second layer (built with conventional Internet components that can talk with blockchains) IdM protocols is one option that allows data retrieval from multiple blockchains for the same system.[295] Bridges are another option for startups using larger open-source blockchains such as Corda and Hyperledger.[296] Second-layer protocols and bridge functionality are viewed favorably in the current ecosystem but are too restrictive to give way to a comprehensive global standard. Universal resolvers, most likely in the form of decentralized identifiers (DIDs), are the emerging standard breathing new life into the IdM scene.[297]

Before any IdM system becomes exceptionally efficient, official digital versions of identity need to exist. As formerly discussed, there is no digital equivalent of federal identity and the reason is lack of trust. Even issuing authorities have their power checked by others, hence why you need multiple forms of ID with various attestations. If all PII attributes are behind a single DID, what certificate authority can be trusted to issue one? The answer should be none whatsoever. Blockchain is useful for this because without it, DIDs couldn't be generated without third party interference. Just as Ethereum generates a public/private key pair for wallets without the Ethereum Foundation seeing them, blockchain DIDs could be created without an issuing entity.

Blockchain addresses can be considered DIDs once attributes become attached to them. The trouble with this simplicity is disparate DIDs with no reputation which makes a standard configuration hard to agree on. Once some agnostic form of DID is accepted, interoperability becomes attainable and the desired level of functionality will follow.

The World Wide Web Consortium (W3C) creates some emerging standards for IdM using DIDs and verifiable credentials.[298] All the attributes indicated in physical federal identity documents can be digitally translated to W3C verifiable credentials. Better yet, once these credentials are confirmed, they become tamper-evident and can be cryptographically verified.[299] For this reason, they could not be faked or changed like physical documents. DIDs are used to register verifiable credentials with distributed ledger technology, making attributes retrievable in affiliation with their owner.[300] Mechanisms for retrieval use unique data sets describing the DID subject (user) with biometric identifiers and cryptographic keys.[301] W3C designed these root IdM components to be easily linkable so SSI, federal, or otherwise configured schemes can have an interoperability bridge.[302]

That completes the overview of the consistent blockchain IdM concepts. Private companies have much to gain by getting this mode of operation right. The reusable identities proposed in this section would simplify KYC and AML compliance, supply chain management, asset traceability, exchange of datasets, insurance claims, and verification of certificates.[303]

Blockchain is by no stretch of the imagination the only technology working on IdM, but it is probably the best available to date. Unique identifiers, tamper-proofing of data, secure storage, secure endpoint communication, and trusted access management are crucial ingredients for all IdM systems.[304]

Three Startups: Uport, Sovrin, and ShoCard

Blockchain's relevance to IdM is best summarized by three of the most frequently cited startups: Uport, Sovrin, and ShoCard. Their different implementation strategies span across many of the configuration types previously discussed, making them the best example use cases. They are listed from most decentralized to most centralized.

Uport

Being built on Ethereum and using smart contract execution to perform functions, Uport is the most decentralized version of this IdM system trio. Fortunately, it functions with on-chain applications (dapps) as well as with conventional applications such as banking and email.[305] No central server is used for Uport, which gives users the most control and security. In an ideal world this works, but Uport can't offer proof of ownership for identities because of their loose ties to "real" identity.[306] This makes it easy for identity spoofing to punch holes in system integrity. The relative ease of making identities further disassociates them from "real" PII, and those with multiple Uport IDs have no way to link them.[307] Usability limitations from multiple identities make RPs unlikely to benefit from accepting Uport IDs.

Proof of identity ownership is held only with a user's private key which is held on their device.[308] If the device is lost, users must rely on a social recovery process. Once reliance falls to a social mechanism, trust is required in the process, and there is no guarantee of recovery.[309] Trustees responsible for social recovery also can collude, which jeopardizes user ID integrity.[310]

Because the private key represents full identity ownership, users can exclusively change attributes by changing data on InterPlanetary File System (storage layer).[311] This feature is a double-edged sword because users can minimally disclose information and selectively delete negative attributes (a bad credit score is an example) that may be important to RPs. Furthermore, user disclosure is based on unidirectional identifiers—for example, users can't verify the authenticity of RPs when revealing their identity.[312]

Uport is free to download and used as a SSO for services that accept it. Functionality is added to the system at the mercy of RPs. One successful example of this was in the Swiss city of Zug. The city government offered digital registration with only the Uport app, an online portal, and a quick visit to city hall.[313] The pilot primarily aimed to make minute simplifications such as borrowing a book without a library card with the hopes of more complex deployments down the road.[314] Uport's app put city-issued credentials on a blockchain, essentially acting as an SSO with superior security. Uport is fully capable of addressing the many limitations of traditional SSOs, but it remains to be seen if more comprehensive identity deployments are feasible.

Sovrin

Sovrin acknowledges that digitally-signed credentials, decentralized registration, discovery, and independently generated keys are IdM challenges that already have emerging standards thanks to the World Wide Web

Consortium (W3C) and Public Key Infrastructure (PKI).[315] Using these decentralized standards together with centralized systems is how Sovrin plans to bring usable identities to everyone. Their system is best described with the interaction between three segments: the client, agent, and ledger layers.[316] Clients are applications running on edge devices such as user phones and laptops. Agents can be thought of as cryptocurrency wallets—they are network endpoints that connect clients to the Sovrin ledger—which is the Sovrin Blockchain and data storage layer.[317] After attributes make it through clients and agents they are added to the ledger. Credential issuers and verifiers connect directly to the ledger to perform verification with on-chain data.

Unlike Uport, Sovrin leverages trusted institutions such as government institutions, banks, and credit unions, as specialized nodes (stewards).[318] On the user end, W3C DIDs standardize digital identities from PII attributes recognized by stewards. Through this system, users can choose what attributes they hold, where they can be shared (on-chain or on client servers), what agents can share data, and what attributes selected third parties can share.[319] Omnidirectional and unidirectional identifiers are enabled as well. This means RPs can publish an organizational identity and show senders where their PII will end up.[320] All these features equate to perhaps Sovrins biggest barrier to entry; a high complexity user experience.[321]

Sovrins use of existing IdM infrastructure gives its PII credentials superior validity but makes use of a permissioned (private) blockchain inevitable. Stewards are public entities that were already considered sufficiently trustworthy to achieve blockchain consensus.[322] The governing body for picking and regulating stewards is the Sovrin Foundation Board of Trustees, which follow a set of "laws" outlined in the Sovrin Governance Framework.[323] This permissioned approach has the benefits of efficient, cheap, and scalable consensus. Still, trust is derived from centralized entities (stewards) instead of the preferred binary code of law and user nodes.[324] The recovery process is based on the Sovrin Foundation Board of Trustees—again forfeiting the desired degree of objectivity with the involvement of centralized entities.[325]

Over time, a growing number of involved centralized entities will further disperse the "web of trust," making collusion unlikely.[326] Sovrin is not the ideal SSI system because federal identity is the only option for pragmatic verification at present. It does remain agnostic about whatever form of identity attributes become digitized, so this strategically leaves room for a SSI revolution. Sovrin's blockchain is specifically designed for identity and can be used to build other IdM protocols such as The Verifiable Organizations Network, another potential standard that would give organizations digital identities to secure web interactions.[327]

ShoCard

ShoCard is the most centralized of the blockchain IdM systems presented. The startup uses an app to generate ShoCardIDs for users by generating an asymmetric key pair from identity credentials scanned through a device camera.[328] After this initial certification process, additional attributes can be added through system interactions (for example, adding a savings account through a supported bank). Attributes are hashed and timestamped on the bitcoin blockchain when added to create an immutable identity record.[329]

Raw data is usually stored on the user's device because ShoCard does offer an encrypted storage option. Security is currently inadequate during PII data transfer between users and validators, which is done off-chain on centralized servers.[330] ShoCard doesn't use DIDs or any solution for converting paper credentials to digital versions. It uses hashed copies of federal identity documents. Hashes don't prove the authenticity of the document itself; instead, it just proves that it has not been tampered with since its original upload, comparable to the purpose of a proof-of-existence protocol.

ShoCardIDs rely on a centralized authority: For example, if ShoCard fails, the identities become unusable.[331] The type of documents used with ShoCardIDs (driver's license, passport, etc.) are also not necessary for most login credentials, making the app unattractive for low-value accounts like subscription-based site logins.[332] When used for verification, since attributes are rooted in physical documentation, the app is prone to oversharing: For example, if you send a digital driver's license to an RP to verify your name, you contribute far more information than that RP bargained for. For these reasons, ShoCard is very limited in features and a less than ideal startup candidate for IdM. ShoCard is unique in that it can serve as an SSO for services requiring legitimate credentials (not just a username and password as with most SSOs).

Two separate case studies have been conducted proving ShoCards commercial viability in the financial sector. In one example, the Bank of Aljazira used the ShoCard SDK with its bank app by combining government documents, biometrics, and bank credentials for verification.[333] This made it simple for the bank to register clients and comply with KYC requirements.[334] Another case study used ShoCard to verify a user's credit score via a credit app without ever revealing the actual score to the verifier.[335] This study proves ShoCard's utility in fulfilling discrete data proofs between apps.

Canadian IdM

Canada's geography makes in-person verification relatively burdensome and, as a result, the country's scales seem to have been tipped toward maximum IdM innovation. The Digital ID and Authentication Council of Canada (DIACC) is the leading organization combining a conglomerate of private and public institutions involved with IdM to fix online identity.[336] By its estimation, Canada loses at least $15 billion (1% of Canada's GDP) by not solving for digital identity.[337] DIACC also acknowledges that one of the consequences of inaction on this front is an increased presence of FAAMG in the lives of citizens.[338]

Of the many members of the DIACC consortium, one company standing out through its ingenious IdM solution proposal is SecureKey. (Note: This book is not in any way affiliated with SecureKey or any other projects mentioned). The system is discussed in depth because it comes the closest to an IdM system balancing the previously discussed tradeoffs. SecureKey melds the positive features of preceding startups into a comprehensive online identity that establishments have been craving. Furthermore, SecureKey uniquely managed to leave the realm of academia through its offering of a high-demand service.

Limitations discussed in the legacy system touched on a broader scope of identity issues. SecureKey demonstrates these problems with practical implications on an existing process. Destination services currently make the rules on what PII they need to verify users. This is a good thing that should be maintained; it's just really annoying for users. Major categories such as banks, utilities, social networking services, healthcare, commerce, and governments all have subcategories of entities that are destination services.[339] The fact that each one has different rules for verification is why it's not unlikely that you have over 200 sets of login credentials.[340] Options other than managing these login credentials yourself are limited to credential brokers. The problem here is the inevitable honest but curious brokers and the data honeypots they create, which solves the biggest problem for hackers: knowing where to look.[341]

Andre Boysen, Chief Identity Officer at SecureKey, delivered the following explanation. SecuryKey's blockchain uses the topology of a "public proof of a private secret" meaning it only holds hashes of PII, making attributes tamperproof.[342] It is built on Hyperledger Fabric as a permissioned blockchain run by trusted nodes that also hold PII (for example, credit bureaus, banks, phone carriers, and governmental organizations).[343] In this way, nodes can each send PII and verify its integrity without revealing the sending nodes themselves.

In practice, the process all happens on the verified.me app. From the user perspective, it takes less than five minutes to register with involved parties. Boysen's example used a bank, phone carrier, and credit bureau logins.[344]

Following login with those respective carriers, each of those trusted nodes cross-reference corresponding data, and the phone carrier verifies the phone number and sim card of the phone using the app.[345] All parties then verify the phone number and biometric data associated with the verified.me app login.[346] This is different from all the SSOs we've seen because almost all reputable forms of PII are now accessible through verified.me. It's also capable of registration for involved service providers, not just logins.

Rogers is used as the example phone service provider on the app.[347] If you want to buy a new phone, the transfer process currently takes about 45 minutes and costs Rogers $50.[348] Before transferring data to a new phone, Rogers needs confirmation that you are who you say you are from trusted institutions—for example, the nodes running SecureKey's blockchain.[349] With your consent through biometric verification, all that data can be safely transferred in two minutes and cost Rogers less than $5.[350]

Minimal disclosure and privacy are maintained throughout this process thanks to what SecureKey calls *triple-blind identity*.[351] PII receivers don't know exactly where it came from, PII senders can't tell where it's going, and SecurKey can't see any raw data, yet PII has its integrity ensured.[352] For the release of data, your phone and the destination service each hold keys which make the key pair required for the release of data.[353] Users control exactly what's released and curious users can view all data transfer details on the app.[354] Blockchain integration disallows PII duplication and keeps raw data off devices, so even if a device is stolen, identity remains secure, and recovery remains simple.[355] SecureKey's services are already being used by some of Canada's top banks and credit unions.[356]

Compared to Uport, SecureKey's use of real PII resolves the ID spoofing and alias' issue. Unidirectional verification is upgraded because verified.me users interact with their chosen institution. These institution based nodes presumably make recovery safer as well when compared to Uport's social recovery.[357] ShoCard's proclivity for oversharing, insecure PII transfer, and the limited PII authenticity derived from paper documents are all remedied by the demonstrated SecureKey solution.

In principle, SecureKey and Sovrin have the most in common with a few fundamental distinctions. SecureKey shows a clear superiority in terms of user simplicity. Sovrins recovery is also still dependent on the trustees of its foundation. Sovrin's economic model relies on the Sovrin Token which breeds a micropayment network between users, verifiers, and issuers for each of their respective proofs.[358] In relating to the phone registration example, SecureKey would just charge Rogers the $5, and Sovrin would expect Rogers to pay the user, credit bureau, and bank in Sovrin Tokens. Sovrins token-oriented economic model is an unnecessary added layer of complexity, but when the market becomes sufficiently advanced, this may become the standard for lowering costs and removing intermediaries.

SecureKey exquisitely represents blockchain's ability to facilitate a symbiotic collaboration with private companies and governments. This provides them with an inflated trust factor because of its illustrious partnerships, while projects like Sovrin are just starting to weave their "webs of trust." None of this is meant to say SecureKey is the ideal solution. One issue with leaving the realm of academia is settling for what's currently useful. Sovrin and similar projects are set up to welcome true SSI when it comes. That's why new IdM systems can be built on the Sovrin blockchain and DIDs are kept platform agnostic.

SecureKey hits a glass ceiling with SSI because user information is not attached to DIDs, and user PII control is limited to telling destination services when they can send data, not how they can use it themselves. This leaves the 2 billion humans without federal identity out of the equation. Beyond this, lack of data ownership won't be a severe issue until SSI systems add intangible PII. At this stage, SecureKey can't keep FAAMG from "stealing" user data. DIDs could push us to a point where self-generated data has enforceable ownership. We would then gain the leverage required to negotiate its use.

Future IdM Implications

The purpose of identity boils down to enabling trustless interactions. If you have a trusted friend named Dave, that trust was probably obtained through information from shared experiences. Upon first meeting Dave, you wouldn't readily engage in information/value transactions. Even though Dave is a trustworthy guy, you have no way to tell at first glance. In a nutshell, this is online IdM's problem.

When the Internet closed the communication gap, it made information/value transactions far more efficient without increasing trust in the transacting parties. Since we rely on centralized institutions to identify people, the logical solution is enabling more efficient and secure online transfer with those entities. This is the primary solution type that has been discussed. What if we could gather the kind of intimate information you get from Dave through social interactions? This data compiled into a comprehensive identity and reputation score would complete the SSI fundamentalist view.

This is not as far-fetched as it may seem. "The Death of Privacy" explored the ever-increasing human data collection. Mass data collection is done with purpose, and it's not going to stop, but how we chose to govern it is still up in the air. To show this is not far off: One just needs to look at China's social credit score program. The Chinese government has already classified citizens with social credit scores that gauge social integrity based on political activities, location history, purchase history, and interpersonal relationships.[359] This scoring system is comparable to the direction that social media is shaping Western democratic countries.[360] SSI virtually creates the most detailed version of the real you, and technology will not stop before realizing it. Putting all that data into a SSI might be the best way to protect it.

SSI can't have its practical implications dissected because no projects have reached the widespread adoption phase. FAAMG is the set of entities closest to doing this. They are at least capable of making private SSIs with a higher degree of accuracy than any other organization. Notice there is not much cited in this section because the idea that FAAMG controls identities does not exist in academia. It also should be reasonably indisputable at this point in the book. This forthright idea only becomes evident after arriving at it the hard way.

When and if SSI takes root in IdM, FAAMG will have everything to gain and everything to lose based on its market position. The outcome of an SSI revolution will land on a spectrum between two radical possibilities.

Data creation could be recognized as personal property attached to some form of DID. This includes digital data in any form. Humanitarian use cases for data would have consented release on a volunteer basis under the condition that their analytics practices and results remain transparent to the public. Private companies that monetize user data will have to bargain for its consented release. Humanity is a company already promoting this concept by attempting to enforce data ownership as the 31st human right.[361]

The more likely option would be the maintenance of centralized credential issuance. Governments would still issue federal identity, but it would be devalued as SSI becomes increasingly accurate. FAAMG would be the generator, issuer, and controller of SSI credentials. Of course, this criteria is FAAMG-sovereign and not self-sovereign, but it includes the desired level of PII intricacy. Blockchain is not the only technology possible for managing identity credentials. Advocates aren't taking into account the snowball effect SSI will have when coupled with the ideals of the growing data economy. This path is closer to what we are on track for and should scare us. Global opposition will be required to avoid this outcome.

Between utopian SSI and dystopian FAAMG-sovereign identity is an infinitely complex web of possibilities that cannot be predicted. Data helps the world solve problems in almost every way, and we do not want to ensure privacy at the expense of productivity. In principle, the only compromise to preserve user privacy and data analytics innovation is radical organizational transparency.

This paradoxical proposal does have a pragmatic approach for attainment. My31 could ideally enforce ownership of self-generated data. Sovrin-like systems can provide the technology to attach self-generated data to personal identifiers. SecureKey's strength is in blindly proving data authenticity in partnering with respected institutions. If FAAMG became clients of an IdM combining these respective features, each would induce the following changes: Users would have the option to store self-generated data and conceal it from its originating platform, data would be legally owned by the affiliated DID (end-user), and the corresponding platform could blindly authenticate data.

There is no technology platform for this, but it's not infeasible. Unlike data currently used in current IdM systems (federally-issued identity attributes), SSI from FAAMG or similar companies is not a big target for hackers. Social networking site data are most useful when collected on a large scale, which adds flexibility in storage options. Blockchain systems such as IPFS are good options. Federal identity is not as pressing an issue. Governments centrally storing social security numbers is okay because they can't be used for nefarious ambitions outside of identity theft. Psychometric data can contribute to nefarious motives, and, for this reason, FAAMG shouldn't be able to hold your personality profile.

Beyond Human Identities

Identity has thus far been discussed as a unidirectional relationship between users and destination services because only the destination services do the verifying. Organizations are usually centrally verified, similar to how humans are verified with federal identity. This comes in the form of a license to sell or practice as a service provider and consumer trust is implied by brand names, logos, company information, etc. Organizational identifiers beyond these features seldom exist because companies are too complex to compress into a comprehensive snapshot that would be conducive to interactions. As the purpose of identity becomes enhancing value transfers with things like reputation scores, its greatest utility would logically be in how it can apply to private institutions.

As an example, let's use American Eagle (AE) to show how this applies to identity. I trust AE as a brand name because they have business retail licenses which roughly equates to a chain store's federal identity. I also know AE sells great pants because of online reviews, a friend's recommendation, and my personal experience from previous purchases. This data set is less explicit and can't be encapsulated in a retail license, but technology is getting better at quantifying intangibles. Compile enough of this more subjective type of data, and you have an organization's SSI and reputation score predicated on user-centered reputation validation. Demand for this only goes up as business is further digitized. When applied to AE, if the company wants to sell more pants online, since customers can no longer see and feel the pants, the quality will need to be proven digitally.

Apply this concept to manufacturers, supply chains, and generic data generating entities—therein lies the same possibility. As already discussed, unique identifiers are often associated with IoT sensors and manufactured parts. All the data created by these mechanisms funnel back to the originating organization and are thus capable of creating reliable SSIs and reputation scores for the root entity. Governance mechanisms for distributed systems actually rely on this type of reputation scoring to adequately function.

This explanation is not meant to be an encouragement of the reputation score concept. It is meant to extrapolate a set of possibilities in SSI and demonstrate their broader implications.

FAAMG has enough data to pick industry winners and losers. Fortunately, they have restrictions on data usage that keep them from doing so. Successful Big Tech IdM systems would limit that restriction enforcement. If FAAMG managed this intimate and intricate data, the consequence would be reduced sovereignty in all identifiable entities.

When taken to these extremes, SSI has far-reaching implications for every other industry-specific chapter that follows. All the solutions that distributed systems offer depend on IdM not getting stuck under the thumb of centralized authorities. For organizational transparency to be practical, it needs reputation related data to transmit to the public through nonpartisan channels. Hopefully, the analogies in this section relay IdM's extensive potentialities.

IdM's Relevance to Web3

Web3 is all about adding trust to web interactions. If connections making the Internet are safe, people could do more things peer-to-peer, like directly exchanging assets, making contracts, and transmitting sensitive data. Dapps that enable these interactions cannot use the flaw-ridden username and password model for creating trust. Most startups that provide Web3 infrastructure also offer a blockchain ID that universally grants access to all dapps built with that infrastructure.

The blockchain ID for dapps works fine now, but it ignores the real problems with Web3 IdM. First, those blockchain IDs usually don't hold any PII that is useful in the non-blockchain world. It is primarily a way of saving where you left off with dapps and cryptocurrency wallets. Second is the bigger problem with having dozens of Web3 infrastructures, each with their own incompatible blockchain IDs. A separate blockchain ID needs to be issued for every Web3 architecture because it can't interoperate. This brings us right back to square one, with many incompatible and annoying login credentials for every Internet service.

Fixing this requires an IdM solution that standardizes the PII collection process, probably with elements from both federal identity and SSI. The solution would need to be blockchain-based: having completely transparent logic and secure data storage methods to make it trustworthy. Then all the Web3 architectures need to adopt that single standard instead of trying to each create their own. This is just one hurdle to jump for Web3 interoperability, and without it, we will continue to be annoyed with proving who we are for everything we do on the Internet.

CHAPTER 7

FINANCIAL INFRASTRUCTURE

Finance Makes No Sense

Bitcoin was built for the purpose of fixing (or replacing) financial infrastructure. Although this was blockchain's first use case, it's not the only or the best purpose for blockchain. Since bitcoin is the iconic use case for blockchain, it has been a vehicle for permeating the cryptoanarchic perspective. The popularity of adverse claims about governments and their currencies in the cryptosphere warrants a review of some crypto-anarchist's arguments.

Fiat currency can easily be mistaken as an artificial construct built by the elite to steal from the poor.[362] Skepticism can build some solid arguments for this idea of "fiat slavery" and other deviant conceptions that are still held by many.[363] Presumably, these ideas emerge between the cracks of the opaque and misunderstood components of the macroeconomic world. Fortunately, because of our newfound understanding of the Pareto Distribution, we cannot logically assign the blame of economic disparity to the fiat currency system. Let's now take the tinfoil hats off and dig down to the roots of these misconceptions.

On the surface, arguments between fiat and crypto enthusiasts continually return to the intrinsic value debate. It's actually quite comical, because neither has intrinsic value. Fiat's government backing doesn't mean anything because most fiat currency is not redeemable for a commodity.[364] Fiat currency and Bitcoin both have their value entirely held in shared myths. One well-founded cryptoanarchic argument against fiat currency has to do with the subjectivity of its parameters.

The United States National Debt at the end of the 2018 fiscal year was $21.6 trillion and climbing.[365] That's more than the U.S. gross domestic product (GDP) from the same year.[366] That debt is more than a quarter of the world's annual GDP.[367] It's also the equivalent of about four 2020 FAAMGs. This gets awfully confusing when considering that, as of 2020, only $1.75 trillion worth of federal reserve notes (physical bills) are in circulation.[368]

Inflation is equally enigmatic. The assumption (at least in the U.S.) is that the Federal Reserve prints money, which increases the supply and causes inflation as a result. But building on that $1.75 trillion is just a small fraction of what is required to meet inflationary demand. The Federal Reserve can't just increase some numbers in a master ledger, either. This is because inflation is haphazardly the effect of commercial bank lending.[369]

The logic for this can be shown in a simple analogy. Banks lend out money to most people in the U.S. at rates presumably higher than inflation so they can make a profit. For the sake of argument, let's say each loan charges 10% annually. Once a bank lends out $1,000 in 2020, it will be worth $1,100 in 2021. Since the world economy only grows about 2%-3% every year, this means $70-$80 dollars essentially came out of thin air and into the world economy.[370] This is even scarier because banks can lend around 10 times more than they have in reserves.[371] So if a bank has $1 billion in reserve, it could theoretically lend $10 billion at 10% annual interest. That would theoretically create another $1 billion out of thin air. Since not all money is held in the form of loan debt and not everyone pays their debt, the situation is not as drastic, but the money does get "made up" through inflation in ways that are impossible to trace.

This ability to loan at scale is a wonderful human invention for driving economic growth; it just accrues flaws when used immaturely and at times can undermine the integrity of fiat currencies. Of course, this is a gross oversimplification. There's an entire journal composed solely of similar analogies to flatten the learning curve for the general public.[372] Annual inflation doesn't have laws that could be encapsulated in a single summary. Determining inflation is generally based on heavy evaluations of markets, not by the state of a universal ledger or the claims of a government.[373] Still, combining loan debt inflation with equally baffling government printing behaviors makes the whole financial system feel a whole lot less legitimate.

Although the Internet closed the knowledge gap between the public and elite, some fiscal analyses go on behind closed doors and remain in locked boxes. The absence of information causes public comprehension cracks in the global economy's opaque components. The filling of unfamiliar cracks with conjecture is the only source of merit for crypto-anarchists. The nefarious fiat slavery perspective, though extreme, does serve a purpose by flaunting real deficiencies in the current system.

Since the entire finance sector is based on arcane principles, all ensuing markets are guessing games about something inherently binary. Fiat currency, the engine of this sector, should at least have stringent qualities. Instead, currency market fluctuations are nothing more than guesses about shared myths. Governments combat this with fixed exchange rates, which gives an artificial sense of stability by picking up the slack of devalued currencies. It's a valuable tool for short-term stability but leads to financial crises by masking objective evaluation of the world economy's underbelly.[374]

Cryptocurrency is advantageous because you can see all of its parameters. Total supply, inflation rates, and distribution between addresses are all public. Its value is not tied to politics but that's a trade-off with its own set of caveats.[375] Currency management and transactions are efficient and straightforward (at least in the more advanced cases). This slew of benefits can potentially extend to fiat with the right amount of effort.

All the above problems are fun to talk about. They are responsible for a lot of the buzz about cryptocurrency and might be productive undertakings decades from now. In principle, they presently resemble utopian ideologies and ignore all the practical limitations of blockchain. Blockchain alone is not ready to fix the world's meta-problems but proves itself to be a great stepping stone with the birth of decentralized finance. The discussion in this section is an exercise in avoiding the hysteria too many cryptocurrency enthusiasts adopt. These meta-problems will be revisited at the end of this chapter after the intricacies of fintech have been addressed.

A good starting point is with financial services, which essentially has three functions: offering credit (crowdfunding, business loans, and individual loans), asset management/financial advisory, and payment. This chapter will continually allude to services in these three categories. On top of each service is the data management component of fintech, which barely exists at present. Only 58% of organizations can record transactions across businesses, and that number drops to 53% with crossing jurisdictions.[376] Methods for transaction monitoring are still archaic and don't duly utilize available data. Efficient financial services that add advanced data management should be blockchain technology's foremost goal in financial infrastructure.

Banking

Banks have a tremendous history and legacy, which makes an honest conversation about their modern relevance hard to come by. Blockchain and distributed technologies have for the first time changed the game by offering financial services without financial institutions.[377] Modern payment processing, asset management, and loaning platforms have exposed the limitations of traditional banking methods. This is not to say that centralized banking will become obsolete. Centralized banks still hold tremendous power from long-standing trusted names, regulatory authority, existing customers, and, of course, working capital.

Consumers need to start asking what exactly they want from financial services. If it was just a matter of service features, than the steps required for replacing banks could fit in a brochure. Centralized banking composes the foundation of the global economy, and there is not much research measuring the consequences of removing them. Bear in mind that statement while reading this chapter. Blockchain enthusiasts can only make a strong argument for cryptocurrency's superiority over fiat currencies through univariate analysis of their features.

Banks uniquely balance the interests of private companies and governments in a proven relationship. Efficiency does not automatically supersede this reliable economic cohesion. Banking alternatives that are presented later should be viewed as technological means to improve banking or offer future options for decentralized finance, not ways to shift fintech toward private institutions. In short, don't be too quick to disregard banking because FAAMG are the most likely replacements, and we've already seen how they like to distribute wealth.

Banking ledgers all operate on the same principle as they did in the 16th century.[378] Every ledger is held centrally, and transactions between other ledgers must reflect that. When moving to e-ledgers, this double-entry bookkeeping style has been maintained. Updates in mobile banking have simply digitized the same paper logic and suffer major efficiency drawbacks as a result.[379]

Fedwire is the predominant technology used for sizeable B2B money transfers in the United States and is managed by the Federal Reserve. For this example, we only use the United States, but most countries have analogous systems that have not changed for over 100 years.[380] Banks, private companies, and government agencies building on top of Fedwire are forced to limit their distinctive features for ones consistent with this outdated infrastructure. The system processes trillions of dollars per day, but its expense and limited scalability make it useless outside of large (B2B) transactions.[381] Fedwire does not show regard for end users because it can't handle them. This responsibility is pushed off to smaller service providers.

There are now dozens of payment options for everyday customers. Credit cards, one of the most popular, make for an excellent example of residual wasted resources. While payment between banks and merchants is authorized instantly, what consumers don't see is the settlement process—for example, balancing the ledgers of merchants and banks—which can take days.[382] This double-entry bookkeeping is unnecessarily resource-intensive and expensive. A study involving over 100,000 European customers pegged the average expense for a 100 Euro credit card payment to be 2.80 Euros.[383] PayPal costs 1.67 Euros by the same token.[384] This is only a brief overview, but when traversing the traditional e-payment landscape, similar fees are incurred. Bitcoin already fixed the double-spend problem so money transactions could cost around as much as any raw data transfer (virtually free).

One of the issues with outdated financial infrastructure is the broader consequences that remain invisible to the developed world. As you read this, you probably don't care about Fedwire or credit card transaction fees because you don't see the cost. That's because banking economic models are designed to conceal it. They benefit by turning money held in existing accounts into assets through lending. Wealthy people are welcomed into the infrastructure for free because they offer working capital and make for reliable borrowers. This does not mean the cost doesn't exist; it is just reflected in interest rates and trickles down to consumers in almost every way imaginable.

Because of high financial infrastructure expenses, there is no incentive to admit poor people into the system. About 2 billion people still don't have access to a physical banking infrastructure.[385] This forces reliance on more expensive, burdensome, and unreliable ways of sending money.[386] Statistics can't represent the severity of this issue adequately, but that's over one-quarter of the world population cemented in poverty because they can't access capital. Banks do not have a moral obligation to tackle this problem, but blockchain and fintech solutions are solving it as a side effect.

Bank transaction related services so far have been the only topics of discussion in this section. The problem scope widens when analyzing how banking's previously strong foothold on asset management and loaning is slipping on account of dwindling trust.

Reckless banking decisions led the world into the 2008 financial crisis. Banks and investment banks were borrowing $30 to $40 of debt for every dollar they had to take advantage of a booming economy.[387] This "added capital" in the economy, lowered interest rates, and grew the demand for investments. Banks were not the only parties at fault, but lenders were the biggest culprit because loan defaults triggered the recession.[388]

In 2013, the two largest banks in Cyprus took a $13 billion (more than half the Cyprus GDP) bailout from the International Monetary Fund to avoid complete collapse.[389] In addition to the bailouts, the bank of Cyprus endured a bail-in where accounts were seized and used for restructuring.[390] Money missing from those accounts by the end of this is estimated between 6.5 and 13 billion dollars.[391] These events are a few of many that gave citizens reason to distrust banks.

Banks have a long history of privatizing gains while socializing losses. No one is on the side of banks in the 21st century, and people are ready for radical change to the financial system, whatever form that may take. Bitcoin was inspired by the 2008 banking bailouts, and Satoshi even referenced a related article in the genesis block.[392] Does this mean blockchain systems are smart enough to avoid and predict these circumstances better than banks? Absolutely not—we will come back to this later. In the end, public opinion of trust will determine winners in fintech, not necessarily facts.

It's not clear where the public stands in terms of what establishments they confide in. Interestingly, the public seems to be pretty split between FAAMG and banks in terms of trust preferences. A 2015 survey showed the levels of trust in various firms: Citibank was 37%, Google was 64%, and Amazon was 71%.[393] Even if this survey is a fluke, trends indicate that banking's trust and security advantage is dwindling and will no longer safeguard their market dominance from new-age competitors.[394]

Mobile banking is a big step in helping banks keep up with the times. In terms of features, mobile banking can compete with the same features of advanced fintech startups (barring low infrastructure expenses). Fintech more generally is becoming mobilized and their distinguishing feature is data utilization. Banks don't have the first clue of how to use data outside of fraud detection, risk management, and customer relations management.[395] Banks have gargantuan datasets that are too poorly structured for efficient analytics.[396]

Failure to adapt with big data is simply from lack of necessity—that is, banks don't focus on targeted advertising or retail. This fallacy won't necessarily destroy banks; it just allows FAAMG to profit more than banks by offering the same financial services for free. It also makes a transition to fiscal transparency oriented solutions doubtful. Banks have the resources to change this fate if they so choose, and blockchain is the best tool for it.

Blockchain is expected to save transaction processing and bookkeeping costs by 50-80%.[397] This is huge, specifically as it pertains to the trillions Fedwire processes daily. Blockchain integration with banks would also lead to perfect record keeping. Even a permissioned blockchain would improve data management, traceability, and economic upside for the implementer.[398] Couple this data structure with blockchain identities and digital signatures become enforceable. Online business contract approval, settlement, and even opening accounts can then become streamlined.[399] The formerly onerous KYC and AML compliance would become nearly automatic. Lastly and perhaps most importantly, blockchain applied to banking would avert economic crises by virtue of its transparency.[400]

Of course, all these benefits are hypothetical. Lack of logistics in this space makes this speculation hard to discern from reality. We will address the lack of practical functionality later.

Long gone are the days when savings account interest rates could ward off inflationary losses.[401] That may have been the bank's last irreplaceable point of leverage. A global fintech report estimating the probability of disruption in the space for various entities concluded the following: startups 75%, social media/internet platforms 55%, ICT and large tech companies 50%, E-retailers 43%, financial infrastructure companies 41%, and traditional financial institutions a measly 28%.[402] Banks are definitely moving too slow for fintech.

Centralized banking systems have been around since the 17th century, and they are just for the first time being challenged.[403] As exciting as this may seem, while consumers pick the winners of fintech, they should fear a disguised shift in centralization as opposed to the removal of it.

Fintechs

Financial technology (fintech) refers to innovative technologies in the financial services industry delivered to customers. Fintechs unofficially means financial technology companies and refers to the technology itself without an "s" on the end. This is all "fintech" and "fintechs" mean in the context of this chapter. Although there are many available FAAMG fintech services, this section will stick to startups. First, we need to understand why fintechs came to exist in the first place.

Every cycle of disruption starts with a paradigm shift and follows with the emergence of innovative techniques that accelerate disruption.[404] Centralized banking was a paradigm shift in economics, and efficiency tweaks like double-entry bookkeeping were developed as a consequence.[405] Mobile financial services are arguably the start of another disruptive cycle that started with investing and banking apps. As we know, mobile banking is convenient but costly and craves the innovative efficiency tweaks made available by fintechs. Decentralized transaction management (infinite entry bookkeeping), data management for predictive analytics, and smart lending contracts are the principal blockchain-based fintech contenders.

Information and communications technology (ICT) and identity are the only prerequisites for fintech involvement, not brick-and-mortar bank branches. Fortunately, ICT's global penetration is continually increasing and is intrinsically connected to the growth of fintech.[406] Since this industry is so new, growth predictions vary too widely to mean much. To put the current market size in perspective, Statista estimates the 2018 value of digital payments generated within fintechs at just over $3.5 trillion.[407] This does not include finance and lending services which have lower volume but are projected to see massive growth.[408] The value from digital payments has been generated almost entirely in China, making the potential for growth astronomical for the rest of the world.[409] With hundreds of fintech projects to chose from, only a few creating values in payment, asset management, and lending can be highlighted.

Payment services are the most pervasive use case in fintech. They are the most straightforward and highest demand of the three and therefore produce almost all the value in fintech. Take PlasmaPay, a fully functional "DLT-based ~~bank~~ account" capable of interacting with traditional financial infrastructure.[410] They offer dozens of currencies while complying with all the necessary regulations.[411] PlasmaPay is one of many blockchain-based "banks" with good services and scarcely any users.

These DLT "banks" are not a failure or a success, but a demonstration of how offering free capital storage and transfer is no longer unique. To the average consumer, PlasmaPay is just a sketchy new app that adds cryptocurrency functionality to banking apps. Technology is the easy part for payment services because they scale to infinity—that is, the world only needs one efficient payment network. Customer volume is what makes the difference for these startups. What this means for payment service startups is that being competitive at the very least requires offering something completely new or partnering with behemoths.

Traditional financial infrastructure can hide their payment service fees only because they thrive on asset management and lending. Startups in this arena have plenty of opportunities. Typical stock trading services charge on average $8.90 per trade, a $30.99 broker assistance fee, and a $32.50 account maintenance fee.[412] Robinhood is an online brokerage startup that charges virtually no fees for stock trading.[413] Robinhood proved that the brokerage overhead used to justify massive fees makes no economic sense. Removing middlemen made investments accessible to poor people with ICT access, and as a bonus, they support cryptocurrency trading. Robinhood's biggest hurdle, like payment networks, is gaining the trust of new users. Incumbent brokerages can no longer stay competitive without lowering or removing their fees.

Central banks similarly issue loans to compensate for their large operating expenses. P2P lending bypasses these middlemen costs by using blockchain as the trusted platform architecture. Circle and Lendoit are startups using smart contracts to enforce loans between individuals.[414] You can go lend money with return expectations based on credit/reputation systems right now.[415] Theoretically, returns are higher, rates are cheaper, and distributed protocol discrepancies are nearly impossible.

Ethereum, specifically ERC20 token sales, has favorably combined lending and crowdfunding in a robust protocol. Its only problem was limiting itself to cryptocurrencies. Equity token offerings could fill the void. Bitcoins, for example, could have bit-strings attached to create colored coins that cryptographically enforce ownership of anything.[416] Stigmas affiliated will cryptocurrency barred this idea from materializing but as the dust settles, cryptocurrencies could potentially offer transparent representations of stocks or any other asset.

This section is nowhere close to a comprehensive overview of fintechs. It does introduce some much-needed updates to the banking system that fintechs now offer. Blockchain is a proven asset for fintechs. Dual integration will yield a simplified ecosystem, higher security, increased speed, greater transparency, and lower cost of operation.[417] Of course, all of this means nothing without users. There are currently far more fintechs than is necessary, and the quality of their respective technologies will have hardly any bearing on success. The only antidote for marginalized fintech platforms comes from existing user bases, established reputations, and regulatory authorization—all of which are hopeless endeavors for most startups.

Marriage of the Middlemen

Fintechs and banks desperately need each other. Historically, incumbents that halt innovation to capitalize on present opportunities always suffer from long-term deterioration. Just look at IBM's decision to go all-in on the now obsolete mainframe technology. We know about these stories because crashing behemoths always make headlines. Startups receive false confidence because, as they replace incumbents, publicity never reaches the ones who fail. In actuality, brilliantly-constructed, pioneering startups get crushed when neglecting the power of incumbents.[418] Banks clearly can't keep up with the speed of fintechs' progress, but fintechs don't have enough resources at their disposal to reach markets like banks.

Cooperative competition (coopetition) will be the driving force for the convergence of banks and fintechs. Both sides are threatened by each other but are forced to collaborate for personal gain. Imagine Citibank partnered with PlasmaPay to bring efficient technology into a working bank. It would undoubtedly be a reluctant collaboration, as they both give up fundamental conventions but for the greater good. Upon successful implementation, every other bank would instead partner with an incipient rival than fall behind a primary competitor. Without this coopetition, no one will reap the benefits of innovation, and they will likely both perish.[419]

PSD2, or the European legal framework for financial transactions, has successfully encouraged and facilitated the merging of banks and fintechs.[420] Beyond this, publicly-released information makes successful collaborations near impossible to discern from fruitless partnerships.

Assuming fintechs and banks submit to the optimal version of ecosystem convergence, consumers will return to the original question posed early in the banking section: What exactly do we want from the financial services industry? What consumers get out of this arrangement is greatly improved efficiency, with all remaining drawbacks of centralized banking still intact. Besides, fintechs and banks are independently categorized as intermediaries, and their entanglement just leaves a bigger intermediary.[421] This combination of banks and fintechs seems to be a likely outcome and would land us back at square one, or pretty close to it.

FAAMG: The Perfect Candidates

What are the top three companies anticipated to have the largest global impact on retail payments in the coming years? You would probably think of banks, credit card companies, fintechs, or blockchain startups. Nope, think again. According to CGI Group, that ranking is led by Apple, Amazon, and Google (Facebook is ranked #7).[422] The basis for this is fascinating.

If you break down traditional financial services, banks are the service providers, fintechs implement new ideas and technology, and FAAMG are the network orchestrators.[423] Notice that the latter can do the job of each one before it but not vice versa—for example, FAAMG can make technology and offer it as a service, but fintechs and banks have a great deal of trouble being network orchestrators. Network orchestrators also have the most profit-reaping potential from fintech integration.[424] That's why online shopping, social media, and messaging all converge as complementary services and have a growing demand for cross-platform value exchange.[425] Since FAAMG controls these platforms, integrative payment methods have become top development priorities.[426]

Although this starts with attaching payments to Gmail or Facebook messages, it's not the market position they're after. Just adding payment features to existing FAAMG services severely constrains their potential. E-wallets are broadly applicable to payment and are FAAMG's more momentous ambition.[427] Because they are agnostic about different retail and P2P payments platforms, FAAMG's association with e-wallets will be the focal point of this section.

Banks do have one line of defense that FAAMG hasn't yet breached. E-wallets usually just handle the transmission of money, not holding and managing it, which is the more lucrative avenue.[428] FAAMG may graduate to this in the future, but they can currently enjoy dodging regulatory hurdles—it's the same kind of workaround Uber and Airbnb use to avoid licensing.[429]

For the first and only time in this book, the system for naming something has been kept simple. Apple Pay, Android Pay, Samsung Pay, Microsoft Pay, Amazon Pay, Facebook Pay, and Google Pay are some of the biggest e-wallets. The involved companies have various derivative payment services, but this list covers the main ones. Apple Pay will be the only digital wallet discussed because it has the highest market penetration, but those similar wallets indicate analogous trajectories.

Apple Pay

Apple Pay's 2014 release was fueled by hype. It planned to make credit cards obsolete and corner the mobile payments market. This wasn't just a public frenzy but a conglomeration with eager participation from the largest banks and credit card companies.[430] It also "failed" right out of the gate because user acceptance rates were so low. Apple Pay is still widely considered a failure and even the warning "shot heard round the world" for mobile payment,[431] but this notion is wrong. There is a reason all these FAAMG e-wallets continue to funnel resources into failing projects just to have them stick around.

Igor Pejic's *Blockchain Babel* is one of the very few sources that connects the dots between Big Tech and fintech. At the time of its writing, e-wallets were failing, and he suggested they would relentlessly persist while losing money and being considered a laughingstock by consumers.[432] What's in it for FAAMG?

It all comes back to data. "The Death of Privacy" referred to FAAMG's entire data collection and monetization process without payment data. It's easy to lose sight of the ultimate purpose, which is to convert data into money. Payment endpoints are the holy grail of consumer data. Banks and credit card companies have all this untapped potential, not in their vaults but on their ledgers. Since network orchestrators own the product and service outlets, they can translate this data into money better than anyone, and it's why they are going to dominate fintech.

FAAMG's slow start in fintech does not indicate a failure. Google Pay, Samsung Pay, and Apple pay are still a long way off from PayPal's market penetration, but trends reflect growth rates that will close the gap.[433] Apple Pay has been nearly doubling its number of users annually and as of September 2019 has 441 million.[434] Pejic was right; FAAMG is not giving up on payment services.

Potential FAAMG Leverage

Where FAAMG struggles most in the fintech space is in exciting the masses. It goes to show the minuscule significance technology differences play in fintech. The much more vital and challenging step for fintech is convincing users to sign up for yet another service. This area is another point of leverage for Big Tech. The barrier to entry for payment technologies is colossal, and FAAMG's favorite strategy is delaying profits to increase overall market share. Banks are the only other candidates for waiting out this storm, but they can't excite the masses. Banks provide a product that consumers seek out for a service in return. FAAMG gives users unexpected experiences with freemium default self-services, which is where the future of fintech is headed.[435]

Users and merchants will love this because e-wallets are free on their end (as opposed to the fee merchants pay for credit card transactions). All they care about is having the most used service. Once e-wallets get enough participants, they will enter a positive feedback loop and create a point of serenity for negotiations. FAAMG would become network gatekeepers, charging banks and credit card companies fees to serve their customers. At this point, you'll already be halfway to trusting FAAMG with your finances because you go through them to get to your bank. It ends up making traditional financial services look like unnecessary middlemen.

FAAMG should be ecstatic that everyone assumes their payment experiments have failed. They are very surreptitious about most blockchain and fintech developments.[436] This is likely a calculated maneuver because it hides the fact that fintech is becoming a barren wasteland for any non-FAAMG ventures. This all may seem far-fetched until we look at how an identical and independent circumstance already happened.

China is ahead of the rest of the world with mobile payments by far. Mobile payment is the norm there, and the whole country is pretty much covered by two services, Alipay and WeChat.[437] The national benefit has been significant, and it's only a matter of time before their respective equivalents reach the Western world. Just as a quick refresher, the five largest technology companies are FAAMG. Numbers six and seven are China's Alibaba and Tencent, the parent companies of Alipay and WeChat.[438] It's only sensible to reason that FAAMG is on track for global fintech domination.

Big Tech is more formidable in fintech than banks and fintechs combined. It has more resources, platforms to ease penetration, brand recognition, and the data-based incentive that competitors lack. For technologists, this should emphasize the need to support the best fintech through integration with the best companies and not be a reason to force competition.

Blockchain Fintechs

Cryptocurrencies are often presented as an all-in-one payment solution. Technologically, this is slightly true. You can send massive amounts of money anywhere in the world for a small transaction fee with cryptocurrencies. The problem is the massive barriers exchanges place between fiat currency and cryptocurrency. There is no head-on approach to tackle this problem because it's not a technology issue and would require collective action from governments, banks, and exchanges to solve.

Because of this, there is little evidence to suggest non-fiat cryptocurrencies as likely game-changers for payment. Fintechs can match or surpass the efficiency of cryptocurrency transactions and expand on their features. Cryptocurrency technology can be argued as a primary motivator for fintech innovation but not a prime mover. Banks have the robust reputation and market position that cryptocurrencies will never see. Cryptocurrencies also can't even merge with other fintechs without losing cornerstone features or tarnishing the reputation of the newly integrated system.

Central banks have considered issuing their own digital currencies as a supplement to transaction infrastructure. In a perfect world, this would allow banks to keep up with fintech without forfeiting supremacy. In actuality, these attempts lead to money laundering, privacy issues, legal issues, terrorist financing, and cyberattacks (this is true for both bank-backed coins and fiat-based stable-coins).[439] Cryptocurrency technology is not necessarily at fault, but at its unproven stage, flaws only get accentuated when clumped with banks. Banking's best bet is to prioritize mobile banking innovation without alternative virtual currencies.[440]

Cryptocurrency's failure in fintech is only a reflection of real attempts. The future of cryptocurrency is unpredictable and could still be relatively bright, especially as utility tokens or mediums for exchange. Cryptocurrency as the killer use case for currency is not a realistic perspective anymore. It was an excellent pilot use case for cryptocurrencies because humans already know how to quantify money. Digitization of assets, which humans have yet to standardize, is one essential utility for cryptocurrencies and tokens but ironically has little to do with currency. Blockchain has a more significant impact in fintech when assimilating with already stable representations of money.

RippleNet

RippleNet is possibly the most popular blockchain-based payment network in the world. Ripple is the private company with RippleNet as the primary service offering that currently involves over 300 financial institutions in more than 40 countries.[441] The network consists of two main parties: network users (small banks and payment providers) and network members (large banks and payment providers).[442] Most parties exclusively use RippleNet and less commonly use their native cryptocurrency. RippleNet's value proposition is the ability of network endpoints to interact through a standardized API that incorporates real-time payments, the ability to attach data (messages) to payments, and end-to-end visibility of transaction details.[443]

Ripple's popularity is in large part due to its famous cryptocurrency, XRP. It is sometimes used as a bridge currency in RippleNet and is known for its miraculous efficiency compared to early cryptocurrencies. In actuality, XRP is an unnecessary addition to RippleNet that owes its success to the efficiency of a permissioned blockchain.[444] Because of its affiliation with cryptocurrency, Ripple's community makes a big fuss about its centralization, which is actually the reason for its success. It's easier for a centralized system to adopt another centralized system, so validating nodes serving as centralized banks provide the necessary trust. After filtering out the hoopla, Ripple's only unique characteristic is its market position. The technology is no longer one of a kind, and the hundreds of partnerships is not a testament to the service utility. While partnership announcements are prevalent, the purpose or progress of such partnerships is scarcely specified.

One Pay

Ripple isn't just a standalone service but a base layer technology that can extend to other tailored solutions. Perhaps the name was just a pun made with the intention of producing a global ripple effect. One Pay is a blockchain-based program developed by Santander for international bank transfers and is already usable in five countries.[445] The technology is based on Ripple's xCurrent DLT (precursor to RippleNet) and allows for real-time processing that's much cheaper than conventional wire transfers.[446] The distinguishing feature for One Pay is the sender's ability to track the process while seeing all fees involved and the exact amount reaching the receiver.[447]

Corda

R3 is a blockchain company with its primary offering being Corda, an enterprise-grade DLT for financial services. Corda's ledger system is similarly purposed to replace the need for data duplication at each organization while eliminating discrepancies.[448] It also takes a network approach solution strategy, meaning that the standalone service is useless until multiple parties adopt and deploy it in a consortium. Since Corda is more of a set of building blocks than a rigid service, it can adapt to any organization and even have options to build Cordapps.[449] It is not technically a blockchain because the ledger does not use a chain of blocks, but the immutability and transparency features remain the same.[450] Many pilots have been done with the company, but as far as real industry impact is concerned, only time will tell.

Hyperledger Fabric

For international B2B trading, banks have used blockchain to facilitate trustworthy interactions. There is a need for intermediaries because sellers want upfront payment upon purchase and buyers want to finance products starting only after they receive it. Banks that use blockchain are helping to fix this mismatch. Over ten banks using Hyperledger Fabric have joined the we-trade consortium to complete this process.[451] The systems use preloaded smart contracts with event-based execution.[452] Banks advocate unknown parties and monitor the given events as outlined in a smart contract so interplay can occur blindly.

Batavia

Industrial purchases similarly face trust issues and traditionally combat them with excessive documentation. Between covering logistics, insurance, payment, foreign exchange, and financing, the process usually takes about seven days.[453] Batavia, a five-bank consortium project, takes the process down to an hour by digitizing these business interactions with IBM Blockchain.[454]

These are just a few of the more popular developments. Unlike other use cases, distinguishing the successes from failures in fintech is nearly impossible because of dubious practical reporting and oodles of useless information. Blockchain for fintech is pretty simple technology. It's just a fancy ledger, but the industry is so complex and unpredictable because thousands of startups are all attacking the same problems, and at the same time are forced to work together. This makes it very hard to separate the winners from the losers but all this collective effort is certainly giving blockchain fintech serious momentum. Ripple is a good analogy for this. The industry is like a flywheel, really hard to start, but once it gets moving, everyone catches on.[455]

Of course, most of this boils down to reducing those 1%–3% processing costs for mainstream transactions. While most are hung up on transaction efficiency, the greater potential for finance is generally overlooked. Blockchain's lesser-known applicability to finance is hiding in plain sight and already superbly demonstrated with regular cryptocurrencies.

Block Explorers

Block explorers are user interfaces that translate all blockchain transaction details into a nontechnical format. It's essentially a search engine for a blockchain. All reputable public blockchains have a block explorer. The one that will be discussed is etherscan.io or Ethereum's most popular block explorer. You can use it right now and see all the described features for yourself.

Every Ethereum transaction in history has the transaction hash, block number, timestamp, sender address, receiver address, amount sent, and incurred fee available on etherscan.io. Every ERC-20 token—every cryptocurrency made to be interoperable with the Ethereum network of which there are currently tens of thousands—can be viewed on Etherscan with those same details. When one clicks on a sender or receiver address, the whole transaction history of that node is available on a single web page. Furthermore, digital asset transactions from dapps offer the same details along with the raw code of the governing smart contract. The beauty of this is that all records are organized and identical across thousands of nodes that also have their information publicized.

Outside of block explorers, there is no system like this in the world, and it should be the selling point of fintech for businesses. Not only does it solve monetary transaction efficiency, but it could add total economic transparency to all financial services. This idea is not taken seriously because block explorers lack practical utility. Until access control mechanisms can make blockchain data partially private and pseudonyms represent authentic identities, the potential of block explorers won't be realized. We will revisit the importance of block explorers at the end of this chapter.

Problems with Blockchain Fintechs

Few dispute the relevance of blockchain in disrupting financial services, but I bet even fewer could explain why. The above examples poorly encompass the financial sector's blockchain-related progress because most hide specifics or only exist hypothetically. Academia has not approached blockchain solutions in fintech as it has in other industries, probably because the space is more business-oriented than technical. Speculative cryptocurrency startups do most of the work here, making the default source for information Cointelegraph or other crypto newsrooms. To avoid circulating misinformation, this section is forced to be vague with solution descriptions because relevant sources are rather nonspecific.

For instance, the most popular estimate for blockchain-based savings in the financial industry is $20 billion.[456] This came from a Coindesk article referring to an uncited Santander estimate that has no available public analysis. Estimates vary greatly, but this article is seemingly convenient to cite. R3 Corda and Hyperledger are referenced in nearly every broadly-focused explanation of blockchain and financial services. The honorable mentions include a brief description followed by the number of banks involved in each consortium. Sometimes the amount invested is estimated but is never consistent. After years of "progress," we have insufficient available data on the practicalities of the largest global fintech initiatives.

Because technology is no longer the problem, it's best to admit that we have no idea what blockchain is doing with fintech—only then can relevant analyses transcend the mainstream media idiocy and create something useful.

Despite this pervasive delusion, parallels across many blockchain-based fintech examples outline the foundational problems where solution approaches distinguish between technology options. The Society for Worldwide Interbank Financial Telecommunication (SWIFT) lists the remaining flawed characteristics preventing blockchain's benefit from manifesting: strong governance, data controls, regulatory compliance, standardization, identity framework, security, reliability, and scalability.[457]

As you'll notice, these big-picture topics constantly circulate throughout the book. They are also likely to become standardized outside of the fintech context and return as tailored solutions once proven dependable. The solution approaches taken can be either centralized or decentralized, hence the blockchain type debate. FAAMG and banks already have stable functionality, including these characteristics without blockchain. This makes centralized fintech the default mode of operation at the expense of transparency.

Public blockchain governance mechanisms, data controls, regulatory adequacy, and scalability are generally deplorable. This line of reasoning justifies the boring truth that no financial institution takes them seriously, and private blockchains rightfully boast interim superiority within fintech.[458]

Private blockchains force SWIFT's characteristic limitations to be addressed internally by each institution. Consortium blockchains must fulfill the same complex requirement but with multiple institutions simultaneously. Strong governance, data controls, standardization, security, and reliability all depend on a select few nodes, so they are "fixed" but to a lesser degree than decentralized options. Nick Szabo, legendary computer scientist, famously explains this:

> To remove vulnerability banks also have to remove individual human control and the individuals in charge or with root access. Banks naturally hate that loss to their power. But they don't have any choice if they want to gain the benefits of having an army of independent computers that rigorously, constantly and securely check each others' work.[459]

This is in reference to public blockchains, but since they aren't yet practical, fintech is turning to consortium blockchains as a compromise.

According to Ethereum co-founder Vitalik Buterin, there is a lack of public distinction between consortium blockchains and private blockchains. While private blockchains use one organization for a node, consortium blockchains have selected nodes from multiple organizations. In terms of features, there is little distinction between the two except slightly less centralization.[460] Essentially, consortium and private blockchains are almost interchangeable but antithetical to public blockchains. The remainder of this section will examine reasons for consortium blockchain's failure. The following sections will show restructuring options with more available features and a refined definition of consortium blockchains.

There is a considerable gap between consortium blockchains' theoretical capabilities and what the world's top consortium projects have come up with. Fintech has a unique implementation bottleneck because it's dominated by slow-moving incumbents. This limitation is not as applicable to the rapidly adapting fintechs, but there's less evidence to suggest startups will win in places where financial infrastructure is already developed.[461]

Only after fintechs and banks succumb to mutual collaboration can the gap start to close. This conception of a network approach with banks and fintechs is not controversial. It's not a particularly radical claim that technology companies need to work with incumbents, but it's also not apparent that they are taking action on this front. The hundreds of fintech "collaborations" doing absolutely nothing are just fulfilling these loosely defined criteria to satisfy a public image. The result is counterproductive press releases that engender pervasive delusion.

Even the simplest use cases in fintech require cross-functional collaboration. A properly delineated cooperative of this nature entails experimentation for a use case that actively includes all related parties, each of which is motivated by interdependent corporate strategies. R3 Corda, Hyperledger, and Ripple could all potentially meet this requirement but do not release the details regarding the inner workings of partnerships. One study summarized the inner workings of a leading bank with over 100,000 employees with interviews from participants in a pilot program creating blockchain-based representations of corporate bonds.[462] Results proved that startups were the best hires for building fintech in banking, and general blockchain use dramatically improved inter-organizational communication.[463] There was still no technological explanation, evaluation, or continuation of the actual pilot program, and this was the best example I could find.

Blockchain was useful for an unintended and intangible purpose: uniting disparate parties for constructive collaboration. The corporate bonds thing did not seem to be of crucial importance. Whichever blockchain and banking-related endeavor you find, after comparing them to similar attempts outside of banking, the verdict becomes crystal clear. Incumbents have no place pioneering blockchain innovations but their large, disorderly, error-ridden, and enshrouded databases need it to happen more than anyone.

As the aforementioned flawed characteristics of current blockchain technology get fixed, SWIFT suggests the following affordances will correspondingly emerge: disseminated trust in systems, efficient data broadcasting, complete transaction traceability, simplified reconciliation, and high resiliency.[464] Each of these exists in an ideal private/consortium blockchain deployment. You'll also notice that public blockchains are better suited for providing most (if not all) of these features and with more inclusivity, but they never get mentioned by bankers.

There doesn't seem to be any positive outcome here. In the 1990s, banks tried and failed an attempt at widespread inter-organizational transparency with the use of intranets.[465] Private blockchains are fundamentally efficient intranets with cryptographic auditability.[466] Consortium blockchains keep having their implementation avoided or botched by incumbents. Public blockchains offer all the potential solutions but are not taken seriously because they don't pragmatically satisfy convention.

Access Control Mechanisms

Public blockchains are not viable for two main reasons. First, anonymity makes KYC, AML, or any sort of regulatory compliance impossible because there is no central management. Attach blockchain identities to a public blockchain, and the problem takes a complete reversal.

Second, efficiency reduction is the other drawback that banks would endure when moving over to public blockchains. Year after year, blockchain technology gets better, and once we get over the complexity of their implementation, many options could exceed the efficiency of bank ledgers.

Access control mechanisms can solve both problems when applied to blockchain. The main challenge for blockchain-based access control systems is keeping identities private during the data-sharing process.[467] Triple-blind identity from the last chapter is the answer to this problem, but we haven't seen it applied to regular blockchains outside of identity management. In a perfect world, this stage in fintech would look like Etherscan's Block Explorer, except every address gets swapped for a decentralized identifier. Once the decentralized identifier became a part of regular blockchains, all intimate transaction details would remain open without any anonymity, which is a big problem and the reason blockchain addresses right now need to be pseudonymous. Access control mechanisms are the complementary solution option that no one in fintech is even acknowledging.

Since access control mechanisms do not yet exist in fintech blockchains, all upcoming explanations will correspond to the following rough definition: "An access control mechanism is a means of safeguarding the security by detecting and preventing unauthorized access and by permitting authorized access in an automated system."[468] Simply put, it is a mechanism for enforcing who could do what on a given platform. The section will wrap up in plain English what an access control mechanism looks like as it pertains to finance.

Conventional finance and general Internet services already have access controls. Blockchain-related services can add standard control mechanism features to second-layer (non-blockchain part) protocols, but this would be insufficient because of their many shortcomings. Namely, typical access control methods (1) have 3rd parties that can access system data, (2) have a single point of failure, (3) are notoriously hard to manage, and (4) are too inefficient to scale (especially PKI-based options).[469] Blockchain-based options are not only the perfect technologies to oust these issues, but under the right circumstances, they add an irrevocable trust element that has never been seen in access control.[470]

A general-purpose proof of concept (PoC) has already proven the potential for commercial viability of merging blockchain with an access control mechanism, specifically with Ethereum, where Solidity written smart contracts governed the parameters of access control.[471] The most profound result coming from this development was complete auditability. Full data traceability for those with access is one component of this, but even more important was transparency in the mechanism itself. This means a network orchestrator engaging in misbehavior by denying access to another entity has that smart contract tampering traceable back to the blue-penciler.[472] Both the data and the code that controls the data are transparent. It's also the depth of access control that we should be striving for.

Although just an isolated PoC, the concept has been verified across a dozen similar trials in various industries. A journal reviewing many blockchain and smart-contract related research studies found the primary consideration for applications was secure and efficient access control.[473] It also proceeded to demonstrate identity as the biggest hurdle for access control mechanisms.[474] Although this experimentation hasn't pervaded finance yet, it's application-specific utility is indicative of future congruity.

Devices in outer space very possibly have the utmost obligation for constructing robust access control, specifically in Space Situational Awareness (SSA) for preventing accidents and minimizing dangers from Earth-orbiting objects. This dire necessity gave rise to one of the most advanced PoC access control mechanisms. Currently, all the various SSA access control mechanisms fall victim to the same traditional system flaws: single points of failure, privacy issues, and performance bottlenecks.[475] SSA also requires an approach with multinational cooperation that doesn't sacrifice national security. A working prototype tackling this has been implemented on an Ethereum private blockchain.[476] It works by issuing "capability tokens" or tokens associated with a blockchain address that requests different levels of access.[477] Network service providers cross-reference requests for access control with the current permissions granted to that address by smart contracts. Upon approval, validating access rights then becomes enforceable with capability tokens.[478]

Of course, in this system, blockchain addresses are not anonymous. Very precise attributes are what make those addresses useful. The bulk of challenges in this prototype were identity-related and reflect the same theme that can't be overstated[479]: Access control's possibilities cannot emerge until immaculate identity solutions are realized.

After space satellites, self-driving cars (or vehicles in general) are perhaps the next most important devices with regard to enforceable access control because it would be very bad if someone hacked and took control of your car. Establishing communication channels for the Internet of Vehicles (IoV) is essential for taking autonomous driving to mass-market safely. The trouble arises from messily-designed attempts to utilize shared resources without sacrificing privacy altogether. A consortium blockchain simulation of this use case successfully allowed for trusted IoV resource sharing while ensuring privacy preservation.[480] Managing the data access/sharing based on node reputations made this possible.[481]

Traditional industries haven't caught on to this movement for a couple of reasons. First is the lack of available comprehensive blockchain-based solutions. Appreciable benefits can't even be revealed until there is an industry-winning access control mechanism that also integrates blockchain. Second, the push for this needs to be motivated by those overlooked potential benefits. Necessity is the mother of invention. If satellites and self-driving cars compartmentalized operational data in their originating organizations, collisions would result from the lack of sharing. If they opened up systems data to others, intellectual property would get stolen, and devices could get hacked. Most organizations don't make as ripe a target, and no catastrophe occurs when keeping data sharing to a minimum. That's why there are no blockchain access control pilots for bank ledgers.

What's still left separating the varied need for access control in IoV or space from conventional applications is the level of ICT penetration. The Internet is progressively advancing all industries because it closes the communication gap.

Whether internally or between organizations, this ICT advantage comes from increased resource sharing. The more data a business process exploits, the more efficient it becomes. This perpetual increase in data generation, sharing, and utilization is a proven innovation strategy that sees its humble beginnings enacted with driving automation and space object collaboration. That doesn't mean it will stop there. ICT will continue to advance industries that employ the resource sharing it enables. As data becomes a bigger part of conventional organizational models, the necessity for adequately managing it increases proportionally.

Finance has an inconspicuous but essential role in this, making it the perfect guinea pig for access control mechanisms. Fiscal transparency is a lush breeding ground for this use case because it is relatively simple, lower risk than other applications (no cataclysmic collisions or fatalities from implementation mishaps), and offers massive efficiency-reaping potential for those involved.

Financial institutions tend to wait around for an innovation to standardize before using it. This is fine because fintech isn't often a point of origin for far-reaching innovation. For financial transparency, there doesn't seem to be a way around the financial sector. Access control enabling fiscal transparency won't start with fintechs or any other outsourced technology. It will become possible only when imposed on large, top-down organizations solely by the force of competition.

Common Ground

Blockchain's integration with fintech will be "evolutionary, not revolutionary."[482] At the end of the day, all the blockchain hysteria in finance is about making payment more efficient—for example, taking those 1%-3% transaction costs from credit cards, PayPal, Fedwire, and others below 1%. That's the long and short of it. As exhilarating as this is, it's apparently not that simple because we still haven't seen sizable solutions.

On the other hand, monetary transactions are the Holy Grail of user data, and the finance industry is in the optimal position to harness it. Financial infrastructure is not the killer use case for blockchain. Finance, in general, is right up there in importance with identity management. Imagine looking through the eyes of a corporate financial consultant and being able to see the intricacies of money flow to every business unit, down through each division, and even to each endpoint of their respective departments. Traditionally, the pursuit of this data in large organizations is a wild goose chase. This technology would be a dream for consultants and a superpower for organizations. Etherscan and block explorers alike are hiding in plain sight as these whimsical database interfaces.

The tunnel vision that keeps us from seeing this future is from the sheer number of hoops left to jump through when looking toward the direction of transparency. This is in reference to the blockchain type debate, which does more harm than good and displays few signs of progress. As a quick refresher on the loose interpretation of blockchain types, private blockchains are held within an organization, consortium blockchains are private blockchains held within multiple organizations, and public blockchains are composed of many nodes, all with equal control and allow any new network participants. Each of those distinctions is based on who's in charge of consensus. Different consensus mechanisms underpin the technical arguments for each side of the blockchain type debate, which is really about transparency versus privacy. This technical divide alludes to there being only two characteristic options, which is wrong because methods of consensus are divorced from those characteristics. For example, private blockchains are completely transparent for those with full access (which could potentially be all parties), and a public blockchain's transparent aliases don't exactly fit the criteria for transparency. For a moment, let's view the type of blockchains mentioned in the upcoming examples with a grain of salt and instead focus on practicable transparency.

Building Transparency and DeFi

Access control can be a means to simulate the fundamental benefits of both public and private blockchains. One paper modeled a brilliant framework for blockchain-based access control of big data.[483] It functions with many organizations and thus serves the function of a consortium blockchain. This unique proposition separated the authorization architecture into two levels that could be managed by either a public or private blockchain.[484] Level 1 governs access permissions granted for cooperative engagements between organizations (called "clusters" in this network).[485] Level 2 strictly governs the access controls given to nodes within a given cluster.[486] Although any combination could be used, the proposed framework constructed level 1 as fully distributed and level 2 as fully permissioned.[487] Since the system preceded popularized blockchain identities, they relied on authorization tokens that granted entitlements for specific resources via smart contracts.[488]

In other words, if you were to apply this to a bank consortium blockchain, all the involved banks would collectively engage in a decentralized fashion. In contrast, individual banks maintain sovereign control of access permission and public release of data from their private ledgers. It can also be thought of as a sort of "meta-blockchain" where clusters act as public nodes in a host network but with each node hosting their own private databases. Applied to FAAMG's big data, this would be a tremendous step toward transparency. But there is a vast gap between testing and deployment, which is a stage this project never reached. It does offer the inkling of proof for the common ground occupied by both public and private blockchains in integrated systems.

The Financial Sector will look drastically different than it does today in the decades to come. Banks have lost their touch and will lose their competitive advantage with the dawn of a trusted Internet. Fintechs will probably continue to find niche areas ripe for innovation but will never be mature in broader markets like their incumbent counterparts. Banks' and fintech's refusal to collaborate will likely accelerate their mutual demise, but even joining forces would not be enough to hold their dominant position in the financial world. If every bank adopted Ripple's products in full, for example, this would be an excellent efficiency tweak for an inherently centralized system but would never lead to a paradigm shift.

FAAMG are dangerous contenders for replacing banks and fintechs for a few reasons. Any technology a fintech comes up with will probably be within reach of Big Tech. They have more resources than anyone to dump into research and development for financial services. FAAMG already has an easy way to reach markets because of their existing customer bases, which is often the most challenging part of growing financial services for newcomers. Perhaps the most crucial advantage of FAAMG is their unique incentive for entering the fintech arena. Payment endpoint data is their precious motivation because FAAMG could use it to learn everything about consumer habits and leverage that for other opportunities.

Barring government intervention, only one thing could stop FAAMG from further controlling finance: a paradigm shift. For finance, this can only mean providing trust in financial services in a decentralized fashion.

Defi is an umbrella term for coins and startups targeting the financial sector. It works by using blockchain in some way to provide financial services without intermediaries. It also changes more rapidly than is possible to keep up with. Solutions from this chapter serve as fundamental concepts and building blocks for the DeFi space but don't highlight specific projects because of their ever-changing and uncertain nature. One clear thing is that DeFi is here, and it doesn't need Web3 to start booming.

The Web3 described in Chapter 1 (the real Web3) depends on independent servers or hardware infrastructure being decentralized. The blockchain space isn't there yet because many blockchains use consensus nodes running on Amazon Web Services and Google Cloud. Ethereum, for example, has many, if not most of its nodes running on Big Tech's cloud. Decentralized web applications cannot be made when computational resources and data storage of the network is on centralized hardware infrastructure. Fortunately for DeFi, this isn't as severe an issue.

The goal of DeFi is to remove the need for intermediaries from financial services and return the excess resources to network users. They don't need to rework the Internet's infrastructure to do that because a public blockchain is a good enough foundation. Bitcoin, for example, removed the need for intermediaries in payment systems, even though all the apps and websites you use to send bitcoin are themselves centralized. Financial applications have gone far beyond this and have always been a test run preceding Web3's innovation because of their relative simplicity.

DeFi aims to disrupt the financial services industry by offering independent equivalents for every financial technology. The primary advantage of decentralized equivalents is the monetary incentives for users. The most obvious example is cross-border payments, which are already made practically free and instantaneous with cryptocurrencies like Stellar Lumens. Lending is another area that replaces the need for private and bank loans by giving users the ability to lend and earn to others in a completely peer-to-peer fashion that is enforced only with smart contracts. Another area for disruption is with exchanges, which are generally company-owned and charge high premiums. Decentralized exchanges have been built on Ethereum and similar platforms as ownerless and leaderless protocols that reduce fees and barriers to entry for trading. The DeFi equivalent of a bank account is simply a cryptocurrency wallet, and they are probably safer anyway.

These DeFi services still focus on cryptocurrencies, which is a problem for people looking for less volatile currency options. Stablecoins like Dai and USDC overcome this challenge by pegging their value to the U.S. Dollar. Users can earn passive income from trading fees by providing liquidity to decentralized exchanges to keep prices stable and accurate. Basically, in all these DeFi projects, everyday users do the job and earn profits that otherwise would be done with banks and financial service companies.

All the aforementioned DeFi solutions of this section are no longer speculation. You can find and participate in startups doing any of the above in a matter of minutes. There's a couple of things that keep DeFi projects from becoming mainstream. The first is that they will never integrate with incumbents like banks. Even if this were technologically feasible, it would be antithetical to the purpose of both banks and DeFi projects. The second is that the Internet is designed for incumbent financial services, making it hard to move anywhere else. Everyone somewhat trusts the security of a bank account and knows how to use them. DeFi services are in the opposite position.

Using DeFi starts with registering for a wallet that hooks up to other DeFi protocols and only holds cryptocurrency (not fiat currency). Most people don't trust or understand wallets, DeFi protocols, or cryptocurrencies. Government-backed entities insure none of these things in the event of system failures, and if you lose wallet keys, all your assets are gone forever. This is scary and discouraging enough to repel the vast majority of people.

The DeFi space looks like this because it is a makeshift version of what should be a default part of Web3. In other words, the current DeFi space lacks leverage in the Internet hierarchy. Most DeFi protocols are actually centralized—they have the backend logic running on the Big Tech Cloud, the website frontend is dependent on a similar centralized host, and connectivity with blockchain wallets is dependent on a browser extension. The most popular wallet for DeFi protocols is MetaMask, a browser extension that connects your cryptocurrency wallets to various websites. If you remember the Internet hierarchy, you will remember that extensions like MetaMask rank the lowest and are at the mercy of everyone else. If not using DeFi products in the browser, the only other option is getting their app through one of the mainstream app stores. Websites and apps are just one step up on the Internet hierarchy, placing the most popular DeFi applications at the mercy of Big Tech in more ways than one.

This doesn't mean Big Tech will block everything DeFi—the public outcry would be too great. The biggest consequence of a monopolized Internet on DeFi right now is that it is really annoying to take part in because extra steps must be taken to enter DeFi's makeshift Web3, and there are minimal network effects in that browser extension-based Web3. This all gives FAAMG serious leverage. Just as FAAMG implements their equivalents of any successful product below them on the Internet hierarchy, FAAMG could provide their own wallet connectivity and DeFi products if they wanted to. DeFi isn't even decentralized right now, and so FAAMG is not blocked from entering it. The FAAMG versions will of course be restructured to benefit themselves, which is the risk we take when having low standards for the decentralized part of DeFi. This proposition should be quite scary because, if it became mainstream to have a cryptocurrency wallet automatically synced up to your FAAMG accounts, imagine how hard it would be to move DeFi users to an actual Web3.

If the Internet follows a path of restructuring that is decentralized and aligned with blockchain's most fundamental principles, DeFi will become an inevitably successful part of it. DeFi projects will be easier to use and trust because they will be synced to your real identity, secured by cryptography, and enforced by a fault-tolerant protocol, with no required login credentials or browser extensions. In essence, financial services would be automatically embedded in the Internet.

Of course, these wishful projections will require a move toward a Web3 that isn't repurposed to suit the desires of incumbents. The threat of centralization in DeFi is a genuine risk because it is easier to make a tokenomics model that benefits a single entity than one that fairly compensates everyone in a distributed network. DeFi, like many other applications for decentralized technology, generally has its success hinging on its underlying infrastructure, hence this book's ongoing focus on Web3. Should we see a transition toward a decentralized Internet, DeFi will slowly but surely take away FAAMG's role in disrupting financial infrastructure.

CHAPTER 8:

SUPPLY CHAIN AND MANUFACTURING

Arguments that move from the flashy use cases of the digital world to projecting blockchain's potential in the physical world may at first appear hollow. Sit tight, because this is only a result of under-representation. Blockchain's potential in industrial applications supersedes its importance in finance and identity management (when evaluated as isolated circumstances). Unlike finance and identity, industrial integration with blockchain is somewhat tangible—case studies can engage all the senses instead of being purely theoretical solutions somewhere in cyberspace. They're also the most involved use cases we've seen and the least likely to be realized.

Blockchain identities, specifically for machines, are prerequisites for practical blockchain solutions in manufacturing and supply chains. Blockchain payment networks are also an integral part of the Industrial Internet of Things (IIoT). To keep this chapter targeted, it is assumed that solutions from the previous two chapters have already been established. Chief use cases for blockchain in manufacturing and supply chain are as follows: easing paperwork processing, identification of counterfeit products, facilitation of origin tracking, and operationalization of the Internet of Things.

Top-Down Decentralization

Before delving into the details of each use case, the surrounding enterprise circumstances need some review. Consider a distributed system that perfectly meshed with supply chain and manufacturing processes to create transparent provenance tracking of products. This hypothetical ideal assumes blockchain identities for all IoT devices and a dapp that facilitates their interactions. We will call this theoretical solution the Industrial Internet of Things Dapp (IIoT

Dapp). As we'll soon see, existing solutions are not far off from the IIoT Dapp, but even a perfect version of this doesn't automatically progress innovation.

The first implementer of IIoT Dapp would be in for a rude awakening. Take a pharmaceutical company that covers the whole production and distribution line of its products as an example. The software of IIoT would be most useful if combined with hardware for all products. A particularly sensitive drug, for example, needs to be kept within a temperature range, exposed to minimal vibrations, out of direct sunlight, and delivered in a specific time frame, all of which are device measurable factors. The company installs sensors that are compatible with the IIoT Dapp along the whole delivery and distribution network and are capable of tracking every batch. Furthermore, original potency and further testing would need to be ensured. Documents containing these details would be hashed on a blockchain with the digital signature of liable chemists, and raw device data would be included on a blockchain to further prove authenticity.

The astronomical expense associated with initiating this system would be the least of the company's worries. How many of those drugs do you think would be delivered without an error being reported by a sensor? It'd probably be very few. Most consumers probably wouldn't care about or understand the transparency offered through IIoT Dapp. Those who did use the dapp would gain a bargaining chip for refunds or lawsuits every time something went wrong. What if the company had a bad batch because the ingredients they received from the Congo rainforest came from bogus plants? How are they to prove that? Even a completely honest pharmaceutical company would be demolished at first. Perhaps the worst impact of all this would be the warning cast toward Big Pharma, making future attempts at transparency seem ludicrous.

These are only initial drawbacks, and though severe, the rest of this chapter will argue that they are minuscule compared to the overarching benefits of organizational transparency. To understand why, let's shift this example to the automotive industry, which requires an ongoing relationship between its customers and manufacturers. The IIoT Dapp would similarly provide detailed provenance tracking and continued monitoring of car operation with each car's computer system. Assuming the IIoT Dapp exists, its industry implications can be summarized with three possible scenarios.

Scenario 1: No car manufacturer would ever deploy it themselves because the initial drawbacks would be too drastic. Accurate provenance tracking is also extraordinarily difficult for something as complicated as a car, even with the perfect dapp. This is by far the most likely outcome and it's why blockchain is probably destined for failure in the industrial sector.

Scenario 2: Startups can drive this movement. Maybe a startup's dapp would be used as a tool for consulting, and many startups are working on just this. Unfortunately, it's highly unlikely because making any difference would require radically shifting the mode of operation of many parties along an entire supply chain. That's hardly practical for any startup. Since manufacturing and supply chain deal with the physical and not digital world, startups can't infinitely scale their technology like in other industries.

Scenario 3: A seasoned industrial gargantuan could serve as the sole creator and implementer of such a solution. The only ones with the power to implement these solutions properly are those with profuse resources. In the long term, implementers of scenario 3 would dominate on account of an improved reputation, and others would be forced to do the same.

We will use the car company Toyota for this purely illustrative example. Pretend Toyota goes through the entire process of making their cars traceable, down to each of the major components. The suppliers from which Toyota gets raw materials will have their components mentioned on the IIoT Dapp. In the future, suppliers might do the same for the raw material collection and refinement process. Toyota's assembly line will have sensors and detailed documentation on each process with the liable component makers using digital signatures to validate their work. Machines that create car components and the car components themselves will have an associated digital identifier (blockchain identity). Toyota's implementation costs for this endeavor are in the billions and take several years for completion.

What Toyota gets in return is data, which is more valuable than money or time in the long term. Toyota and its customers will see the history of a whole car. When the check engine light comes on, the problem diagnosis will be broadcasted on a blockchain. If covered by a warranty, Toyota can send mechanics to fix the problem before the owner has a chance to worry about it, which can be outlined in the smart contract for the car's original purchase. If not, the car can request maintenance itself and pay via smart contracts. This is not AI; it's just preexisting conditions set by a manufacturer being executed in code. Better yet, every customer would know how reliable each of Toyota's cars are. Toyota also knows the frequency of problems occurring in cars across the globe and in what component. Factory adjustments can be made perpetually based on real-time data from every Toyota in the world. Customers will trust Toyota more than any car company, and Toyota's manufacturing-related decisions will be exponentially more economical than their competitors.

Once this works, every car company will get intense pressure to do the same or fail to compete. At this point, the necessity of radical industrial transparency will go from inconceivable to blatantly obvious. In fact, rival companies might insist on data sharing and cooperative competition (coopetition) just to keep up with Toyota. The ripple effect of this would be massive, but it must start with a gargantuan, not startups. As we've seen in Chapter 4, startups already tarnished the reputation of cryptocurrency. Supply chain and manufacturer provenance tracking is far from inevitable. Startups mustn't drive blockchain's industrial applications to the same reputational fate as cryptocurrency.

Do these sound like outlandish goals with outcomes too good to be true? Maybe they should. I mean, how could Toyota be convinced of this radical approach when there's little proof of its commercial success? I would argue that top-down decentralization is the principle that made Toyota the world's largest car company, and the IIoT Dapp idea fosters that principle with a technology update. Let's provide some historical context for that statement.

The assembly line is responsible for the commercialization of industrially produced products, including cars. In the 1980s, this was the standard methodology for car manufacturers, and it naturally leads to very rigid corporate hierarchies. Toyota and General Motors (GM) are the best examples of distinctions between management approaches as depicted in Brafman's *The Starfish And The Spider*. The unique part of Toyota's assembly lines were team-oriented work environments that flattened the corporate hierarchy. Anyone could stop all factory operations if they saw a quality assurance issue. The lowest status workers had better access to upper management and were encouraged to recommend changes concerning their part in the assembly line. 100% of proposals were implemented and only reverted by another proposal.[489] The result was and continues to be an ever-improving manufacturing process and a better finished product.

GM did a test run allowing Toyota to take over management for the same employees in GM's worst-performing factory.[490] Three years after starting this joint venture, GM's worst factory became its best factory, becoming an estimated 60% more efficient than the average GM factory.[491]

The reason for this is more granularity in available manufacturing-related information. As an organization grows, it becomes harder to track the small details of operations and even harder to make changes to them. The most successful organizations leave room for adaptability while growing. At the time, no Toyota employee knew more about the "front lower outer driver passenger side ball joint" than the guy that installed it. Now it's not a person who installs the part, but a machine. Across all these working machines is valuable data that has yet to see full utilization. A Toyota IIoT Dapp would be in the business of maximizing production data granularity and bringing that same distributed collaboration principle into the modern age. Just as GM and other car companies learned to follow in Toyota's footsteps, this time around would be no different.

As remarkable as this whole Toyota idea seems, related technologies to enable an IIoT Dapp are not yet sufficiently advanced to enact it. Blockchain applications start with financial applications, which need a strong foundational layer in identity. Notice, identity is a reasonably targeted area where startups alone were able to suffice in driving innovation. Financial infrastructure is more complex, and as we saw in the last chapter, innovation in finance uses the combined efforts of startups and incumbents. In manufacturing and supply chain, startups are too small to penetrate this market and FAAMG has no direct involvement. This puts the driving force for innovation solely in the hands of incumbent manufacturers. In essence, large organizations like Toyota need to be persuaded to decentralize from the top down.

Trade Finance

The Industrial Internet of Things (IIoT) and its derivatives will later be discussed in depth. For now, IIoT refers to an interconnected industrial framework of machines and devices that collaborate on a shared network platform.[492] It's comparable to the 1995 definition of the Internet in the sense that it's axiomatic and worth coining before it can be fully understood or quantified. IIoT will take off independent of distributed ledger technology. Blockchain doesn't have any direct influence on IoT device functionality. Blockchain's primary offering to IIoT and the concept of this whole chapter revolves around data utilization.

The last chapter argued that blockchain could streamline monetary transaction processing between parties of all types (P2P and B2B). Major preconditions for the success of financial solutions were blockchain identities for both people and organizations. Essentially, all financial solutions do is make data transfers better. They can only do this when identity data is transferred too. This is a broad generalization built up over the last two chapters. Still, at their core, those solutions accomplished (or can accomplish) a restoration of trust, which expanded the flow of data transactions.

The simplest use case for blockchain in supply chain and manufacturing is trade finance, which refers to the same financial solutions from the previous chapter but along supply chains. The buying and selling of goods on any scale is met with a payment that's facilitated by a 3rd-party financial institution.[493] Supply chains (which manufacturers are in the middle of) multiply the number of intermediaries with every step along the chain. For this reason, a blockchain-based update to the financial infrastructure legacy system is viewed with tremendous optimism by the vast majority of companies in trade finance.[494]

The much-needed efficiency update in supply chain and manufacturing is heavily dependent on the success of financial infrastructure in doing the same. The last chapter's demonstrated financial infrastructure solutions are the foundation layer that this chapter's solutions will build on. Although manufacturing and fintech conceptually have nothing to do with one another, the technological and social underpinnings that connect these two industries are abundantly clear.

Technologically speaking, trade finance is blockchain's simplest use case, and it merely consists of streamlining inefficient data transaction processing.[495] Problems with supply chain and manufacturing stem from poor data transaction and processing methods. What most separates financial and supply chain blockchain solutions is how they are used, not the technology itself.

In terms of social implications, financial infrastructure needs to be the catalyst to establish blockchain's reputation in trade finance. As we saw in the last chapter, behemoths will probably lead any fintech revolution until decentralized alternatives take over. This also holds true for industrial applications. Without a blockchain-based step in trade finance, behemoths won't take the leap to manufacturing's more complex data-based solutions.

This argument for blockchain in finance, manufacturing, and supply chain as being complementary use cases, though essential, is tough to make. To see why this conclusion isn't obvious, let's look at two examples. Suppose a car manufacturer finds that the service life of a transmission from one of its models has been cut in half compared to models from previous years. Finding the root of the problem requires collecting data from newly sold cars, the transmission manufacturer, and the producers of the raw materials used to construct each transmission. As a separate scenario, suppose a bank wants to make its international wire transfer cost less than $20 and take less than three days.

An in-depth look into each of these examples reveals that both problems are about data. A low-quality raw material for a transmission component could be the culprit for our manufacturer, and a legacy system that doesn't establish inter-bank trust could be the bank's culprit. Both problems are alleviated with data transparency across involved organizations. Blockchain's ability to enable trusted exchange of information between organizations is an analogous solution for both the bank and the manufacturer.

Manufacturing and trade finance are also inextricably linked during blockchain integration by the nature of developing platforms. Applications being created to improve manufacturing/supply chain processes also incorporate payments. It's only sensible that data exchanging applications have a payment method to coincide with each data transaction. As we'll see, the pinnacle use case of these applications is allowing for self-sufficient machinery. This consists of machines using their own diagnostics software to request service maintenance, order parts, and, more generally, fix themselves. When machines have their own blockchain identifiers and wallets, they can pay for these operations without human intervention.

Other propositions suggest a performance-dependent pay-as-you-go model for manufactured goods to mitigate risk for consumers.[496] Even the centralized IIoT platforms are emerging with functionality for currency and general data transfer between providers and consumers, but their biggest problem is lack of users, which is contributed to by lack of trust in data storage and transfer within each platform.[497] Centralized models generally suffer from issues regarding reliability, security, scalability, a single point of failure, and the possibility of data manipulation.[498] Both centralized and decentralized IIoT applications need value transaction functionality to compete, and blockchain is the ideal enabling technology. It is also the best-known way to alleviate the issues associated with centralized models.

Just as fintech applications are useless until a growing user base generates peer-to-peer value, manufacturing/supply chain applications are useless until there exist enough parties to create business-to-business value. Decentralized models struggle to get off the ground because they start with zero users, no reputation, and no organizational backing. Centralized models struggle from technical specifications that limit trust.

Even if you're convinced of the connection between these finance and manufacturing examples, they may still seem futile. Besides, all the manufacturing/supply chain-related blockchain solutions to be discussed are being built independent of trade finance. Most upcoming examples are also devoid of any marked industry success. The last chapter's blockchain fintech startups were the same, evidently having little to no success. Fintech startups stood a chance but only through partnerships with banks. FAAMG had by far the most profit-reaping potential from internally developed fintech solutions.

The trend is toward higher degrees of success with bigger organizations, particularly those with a foothold in the sector being changed. The industrial sector doesn't have its version of FAAMG. Combine this lack of industry leaders with the fact that manufacturing and supply chain have the most complex operations of any non-technical industry, the probability of success for all the solutions about to be discussed are relatively slim.

Transparency and Traceability

The difference between blockchain solutions in fintech and manufacturing/supply chain can be summarized as the difference between transparency and traceability. Transparency is revealing critical business logic that is already known and is the central principle underlying this book.[499] Financial information makes for a good example. Banks always have all their transaction data stored on various ledgers. Revealing this, whether it be to other banks, governmental organizations, shareholders, customers, or the general public, uses various optional levels of transparency.

Our car manufacturer can exhibit the same transparency with its balance sheet and incorporate further business logic into public documents. For the defective transmission example, this would mean revealing how many cars have the issue, possible causes, and changes to be made as best the company is aware. These transparent car manufacturer features can be revealed in SEC filings, press releases, recalls, owner manuals, and other company filings. Traceability takes transparency much further. Traceability requires all the significant data-points across a multi-organizational network to be maintained and revealed.[500]

Various levels of organizational transparency have been possible since the birth of organizations. The challenge with transparency is verifying its authenticity. A Toyota press release and a Santander financial statement derived from traditional ledgers cannot make their point of origin known. It could be transparent but flawed data, which is not helpful. Blockchains enable trust in that transparent data because its point of origin is traceable. What constitutes transparency is highly debatable because of these organizational intricacies, so we refer to transparency as a cluster with different levels rather than a definitive quality. For the purposes of this book, perfect transparency is revealing everything you know, while perfect traceability is knowing everything and also revealing it.

Traceability needs to offer up extremely high levels of transparency while keeping data secure and trusted. It's quite the paradox. Doing this, as we'll see, requires tremendous additional resources to existing processes. It can apply to many industries, but since the use case most directly applies to material things, manufacturing and supply chain applications will be the only examples covered in this chapter.

Transparency is still extraordinarily useful by itself but has been discussed ad nauseam. The following sections will discount typical transparency-related solutions and explore the technological limits of traceability-based options. They will be mostly impractical until levels of transparency similar to what's been depicted in previous chapters are realized.

Overwhelming Complexity

Recall the description in Chapter 3 of how the grocery industry shifted. As a quick refresher, mom-and-pop shops basically were replaced by enormous chain stores, and heavy competition squeezed profit margins down to about 1%. Consumers now have access to dozens of competing brand options for each of the same products instead of being limited to the previously unreliable and redundant options of local grocers. This was made possible through data utilization and predictive analytics. That's why store chains can buy the same amount of avocados as they will sell in the same window of their shelf life. Manufacturers evolved in the same way, except it's as if the avocados are constructed from the materials of many different parties, each with their respective supply chain and demand prediction management.

Manufacturing process flows for mom and pop shops were relatively linear: raw material producers → raw material suppliers → sub-manufacturer → manufacturer → distributors → retailers (mom-and-pop) → consumers. Parties before the manufacturer perform what is referred to as upstream activities: material suppliers, component makers, and sub-assembly providers respectively. Parties after the manufacturer perform what is referred to as downstream activities: distributors, wholesalers, and retailers. These are the six supply chain components (consumers don't count) that the relevant literature and this chapter continually allude to. Proofs of concept tend to use this six-part model, which is really just a skeleton that excludes the many smaller entities involved with supply chains.

The described process flow increases in length with the increasingly steep corporate Pareto distribution. Disparate business goals and multidisciplinary collaboration converged under the same roofs. A diverse production ecosystem makes previously linear supply lines cross one another in a sort of web. Increasingly complex relationships between these suppliers allow for a tremendous opportunity with diverse materials and parts, but documentation-processing efficiency decreases with more complexity.

To understand how the upstream and downstream interactions got so contorted, we will use wristwatches as a simple manufacturing example. Generally, a wristwatch's sole function is telling time. Sure, there were plenty of unique watches, but until recent decades, consumers didn't get to choose between every model in existence. A linear supply chain and manufacturing process flow for working wristwatches was simple because the consumer choice was limited to options provided by the local retailer. The extent to which a select wristwatch model spread to the consumer was restrained by the supply chain of its mother company.

The personal luxury goods explosion coincides with the growth of the Internet.[501] This has reflected the leading watch makers like The Swatch Group, Movado, and Fossil Group, which all saw substantial growth in the last two decades. Now every watch you could imagine, every buckle shape, strap color, case material, and general style, is accessible to anyone with access to the Internet. You could sometimes buy each of those desired parts by itself too. The Internet similarly transformed all manufacturing processes by updating New Age consumerism to favor unlimited consumer choice. Shipping is now so efficient that supply chain boundaries disappeared. Manufacturers and supply chains can stay competitive only by catering to this ideal.

In essence, we've created omnicustomers who demand omnichannels: Customers can request any part, from any point in the supply chain, at any time.[502] This wouldn't be so inefficient if process flows were linear, but the increased number of intricacies within consumer products doesn't sustain this. Wristwatches having an increasingly diverse set of component styles causes their whole supply chain to broaden exponentially. For the sake of example, let's assume a single wristwatch contains ten materials. The manufacturer uses those ten materials to make ten different watch models. So far, we're conservatively up to 100 combinations. But manufacturers don't usually produce those 100 combinations from the ten materials they have on hand. They outsource this to upstream parties: One sub-assembly provider might construct the casing, one component maker might specialize in casing parts, and the material supplier might refine the stainless steel suitable for one casing style. These are the three upstream components, but you'll notice that meeting demand requires doubling or tripling the number of parties for each upstream step (roughly speaking) when accounting for the other wristwatch parts.[503] That means for every manufacturer there are about three subassembly providers, five to ten component makers, and over a dozen material suppliers.

Radical changes seen in manufacturing and supply chain over recent decades have been progressive and well-founded. Restrictions they place on operating efficiency are the points of contention. So far we've seen the physical manufacturing process flow but not its preceding documentation process flow. It runs somewhat analogous to the last process flow: orders placed via purchase order with detailed product specifications → the supplier adds it to a pile of incoming requests, compares the pile against their own inventory, and sends an invoice to a warehouse to obtain necessary supplies → warehouse ships supplies which are documented via a bill of lading → manufacturer can now make product and place a distribution order → shipping services delivers products downstream.[504] This is just the bare bones example for a condensed physical process flow. In practice, this structure is more like a web than a line.

Each step of that documentation process flow is a data transfer that runs the risk of being accidentally authored.[505] Omnicustomers have made features of accuracy and trust in those transactions more crucial than ever. Flexible preferences coincide with decreased trust in supply chains because many new, less tested channels are being created to accommodate growing consumer demands. Direct communication and visibility from two different points now take longer than movement along the physical supply chain.[506] What happens if someone increases the quantity of their order or unexpectedly cancels? These valued consumer options force suppliers to tolerate losses from mishaps. Demand management methods have not caught up with the increased strain put on supply chains.[507]

But all of this talk has been restricted to upstream process flows. Downstream process flows have less to do with this chapter because they are relatively efficient. There's an inconspicuous rationale for this efficiency gap. Increasing complexity driven by flexible consumer demands has kept pace with both retailers and manufacturers.[508] A reasonable estimate puts three wholesalers for every manufacturer and multiple retailers for every wholesaler, so structural intricacies are largely the same for both upstream and downstream operations. Engineering is excluded from the downstream process, which contributes to its relative simplicity, but this doesn't explain the whole story because upstream/downstream distinctions have become the most pronounced in recent decades. Ecommerce is the essential variable of this timeframe because it made every website, IoT device, online account, and physical store a potential downstream omnicustomer.

Data flow rates are the major bottleneck for upstream and downstream physical process flows. Augmenting trust and efficiency in data pipelines is the way to widen the bottleneck. We've only seen this done with downstream operations by putting multiple components under the same roof (that is, centralizing supply chains). Amazon mastered this by becoming a wholesaler, retailer, and delivering agent in no particular industry. Data exchanges between Amazon's operational segments are handled internally and beneficial for all parties. The trust issue is resolved because all actions are taken for the benefit of a common company. This brilliant methodology's unmatched efficiency is promoting expansion further upstream.

The downside to this reliance on centralization is a steepening corporate Pareto distribution. Until multiparty transparency and efficiency enable seamless data communications, omnicustomers will only bolster mega-organization supremacy.

Excessive Documentation and Wasted Data

The increasing complexity of supply chains is well understood and is being addressed in many ways. Documenting everything is one approach that comes as close to organizational transparency as is possible through traditional means. It also wastes resources because the data often sits in locked boxes or is too poorly managed to analyze. Since the industrial revolution, machines have been replacing jobs, and organizations have been filling them by creating more documentation to manage.

Trends toward increased documentation are not slowing because it is how organizations combat lack of trust. About 200 billion dollars was lost to counterfeiting from international U.S. trade in 2005.[509] The indirect expense from this can be found in shipping companies, which now spend more on documentation costs than physical transportation costs.[510] At a certain point, the problem can no longer be attributed to a lack of documentation but instead a lack of authenticity in that documentation. Technology offering accurate record-keeping has not grown in acceptance at a rate consistent with general record keeping.

ERP Software

Managing supply chain documentation (data) is done with enterprise resource planning software (ERP). ERP is a broad categorization for software that connect islands of data from project management, finance, and manufacturing systems. One common standard is SAP-ERP. It works by taking point of sale data and performing analytics that adjusts operations within vendors, sales departments, inventories, human resource departments, and production processes. Every major supply chain relies on some form of ERP for automated decisions. It is not as well known as the island software like Microsoft's suite because ERP mostly exists behind the scenes of large organizations.

Entire books are dedicated to various ERPs. Customer relationship management, financial services management, supply chain management, human resources management, production planning, or production scheduling are all categories under ERP that compose a few of many related acronyms.[511] Luckily, the functionality details are not as relevant to this book as what remains consistent among all of them, which is their system architecture. ERP breaks down into a database layer, application layer, and presentation layer.[512] The latter layers serve to extract data from the database to formulate useful insights.

ERPs are prevented from adapting with advancements in the data economy because of their centralized database layers. Wireless communication between centralized databases leaves architecture flaws for attackers to exploit.[513] All manufacturing-related devices are made available to hackers once connected to an Internet database.[514] Whenever centralizing the software involved with manufacturing processes, the threat of cyberattacks becomes imminent. For cybersecurity reasons, collaborative data analytics adds complex technology layers as a barrier to entry, leaving smaller-scale operational data out of the equation.

Currently, the database layer is insufficient because a lack of trust between isolated participants restrains necessary communications.[515] Blockchain add-ons and alternatives target the database layer only, with the benefits being increased traceability and trust.[516]

To explain why the ERP databases need an upgrade, let's use an example. Distributors update database ledgers based on outgoing orders. Suppliers update the ledger based on what's been received. What happens when some of the product has been lost in transit or one party makes a data entry error? Nothing happens unless the mistake is severe enough to warrant a nightmarish backtracking process.[517] Avoiding these mishaps requires a method for authenticating data that is not susceptible to human error.

Solutions of this nature are highly practical. One study configured a payback period of 4.1 years for a business adding blockchain to existing ERPs and less than one year when implemented through a consortium.[518] Results-oriented implementations of this type are still in the incubation phase.

Cloud Manufacturing

Part of what makes a database layer update for ERPs important is how the manufacturing parts of supply chains have changed in the last two decades. Cloud Manufacturing (CM) embodies some of the relevant industry shifts: "CM can be defined as a manufacturing paradigm that utilizes cloud computing and IoT to transfer the manufacturing resources and capabilities into the cloud environment as services which provide anything that is required by the customers and users."[519] The term was coined to describe an evolutionary transition in manufacturing that new technologies made inevitable.[520] Ubiquitous device computing scales with IoT and RFID technologies. In manufacturing, this means using real-time machine performance data to diagnose and maintain equipment remotely.[521] Its implications extend data-driven decision making to nearly every domain of industrial production.

CM is the manufacturing industry's only choice for logistics that is conducive to omnicustomers because it implements analytics complicated enough to track rapidly fluctuating consumer demands. It also makes the document process flow more extensive, necessitating a radical shift in how it is managed.

Supply chain and manufacturing have been clumped in a single chapter because their relevance to blockchain solutions is at the database layer. ERP and CM are really about data mining and processing. Software using manufacturing intelligence impacts a factory more than any single machine could.

There is an important caveat, though: Even completely tangible industries have their biggest efficiency bottlenecks caused by poor data management. Industries outside of the scope of this book likely have major inefficiencies with root causes of the same nature. Once a foundation has been laid in the connecting industries (identity and finance), blockchain-related data-based solutions can build up from there. Most other industries should shift attention toward data solutions, which is also where blockchain's contribution is most relevant.

Architecture Solutions

Classification of architecture for a logistics-related system boils down to its database layer. ERP and CM architectures rely on centralized models because their data layers are closed. Even though both systems operate with real-time data between disparate parties, they exclude potentially useful data from smaller sources. Decentralized alternatives increase the accessibility of data from small parties, similar to a supply chain that can track and trace real-time changes to every single customer order.[522] The challenge with an open database architecture is keeping critical business logic safe.

Limited data communication in the industrial sphere is a widely known issue. Anyone who acknowledges the growing prominence of Industry 4.0 (autonomizing production and logistics) must also acknowledge the need for secure data exchange as much as the need for IoT sensors.[523] Industrial Data Space (IDS) is perhaps a growing standard for improving data exchange, particularly in manufacturing and supply chain.[524] It's not a single cloud platform but instead a compilation of connecting platforms that establish the sort of data sovereignty we saw with self-sovereign identity, but for businesses.[525] The landscape for architecture options ranges from fully centralized data lakes to fully decentralized blockchains, depending on each application and owner preference.[526] In the peer-to-peer approach, business logic does not need to get disclosed, and sensitive data stays private.[527] Basically, blockchain makes the data trustworthy and IDS makes it shareable.

IDS is one emerging standard and proof of concept born out of a reputable company (Fraunhofer). At present, it's a broadly applicable architecture and concept that has yet to be widely implemented within a niche utility. Although IDS is possibly the best indicator of the trajectory of industrial logistics, it's not the best system to use when learning the makeup of supply chain and manufacturing-related blockchain systems. A more fundamental system architecture that more closely relates to this chapter's goals will be explained instead of IDS. Then industry examples using related innovations will be analyzed.

The article "Toward a Blockchain Cloud Manufacturing System as a Peer to Peer Distributed Network Platform" offers a comprehensive and heavily-cited approach to solving the industrial logistics data problem. The concept is based on a system architecture's usage in a simulation with 15 manufacturers and 32 customers.[528] Below is the abridged summary of the Blockchain Cloud Manufacturing (BCmfg) architecture components:[529]

> *Resource layer*: physical machine hardware and the software that runs it and collects its data. Example: robotic and other manufacturing-related machines
>
> *Perception layer*: connects the resource layer to main networks. Example: IoT devices and adapters

Manufacturing service provider layer: hashes and converts perception layer data into blocks. Example: blockchain clients and factory control systems.

Infrastructure layer: developer-based consortium that encourages collaboration with cloud manufacturing providers through distributed interactions with other parties and securely storing data. Example: proof of work mining, algorithms managing user and service provider information requests and receipts, and general cloud manufacturing components.

Application layer: end-user software and interfaces. Example: conventional ERPs and related management software with newly integrated blockchain wallets

The proposed system is not an attempted replacement for any application layer software but a tool that adds functionality to each. Cloud manufacturing is a compilation of many software bundles with an architecture closely resembling that of BCmfg. The beneficial difference with blockchain is the indirect communication that's provided for by the manufacturing service provider layer.[530] In conventional supply chain and manufacturing process flows, data is created and sent along the chain from party to party. As data propagates, it is slow to update or verify and is withheld if sensitive. BCmfg stores hashed data on a public blockchain cloud. Access is only granted to those with a key, so sensitive data could be strategically utilized. Data acquisition from the resource and perception layer is autonomous and automatically updating because it does not travel through multiple parties. Authenticity and origin tracing is made simple and would be unequivocal with the addition of blockchain-based device identities. The protocol basically "knows" everything, but participants extracting data only know that it is trusted without knowing sensitive details of the sender.[531]

The collaborative potential from this BCmfg is astronomical, but the simulation only tests its efficacy in service-oriented manufacturing. In this system, manufacturer data indicates what resources are available as customers post their needs. Once the data is tabulated, finding the best match can be done algorithmically. It exemplifies the ability to process data even at the lowest level of the process flow: individual customers. The BCmfg consumer and service provider relationship is moderated with smart contracts and tracked on a block explorer that grants interface access to both parties.[532]

Ineffectual supply chain webs would no longer struggle because collaboration would scale independent of business relationships. This makes trust optional when sharing data, making this trustless approach the best way to accommodate omnicustomers.

Architecture Benefits

A generic architecture doesn't demonstrate changes induced on the factory floor. Let's jump back to The Swatch Group for an example and assume they manufacture a signature watch model that makes up half their sales. The Swatch Group releases a new watch this year, and to their surprise, demand explodes for this new watch that has not yet had its manufacturing process perfected. The factory floor is now faced with some difficult decisions. Not knowing how demand will change, engineers will have to decide if resources should be reallocated to the new watch or stick with mass production of the signature Swatch Watch. These are both high-risk scenarios, each of which will result in reduced sales if demand for both watches isn't met.

Although this is not so severe in the case of watches, it equally applies to all manufacturers limited by space, materials, and equipment. A more extreme example is Ford and GM's transition to building ventilators instead of cars for the COVID-19 pandemic.[533] How can these companies decide resource allocation strategies for revamping entire factories when demand changes drastically by the hour? Perhaps the biggest problem here is self-contained prediction analytics. Customers need a way to communicate with manufacturers in a secure way to protect their data-sensitive interests.[534] Ford and GM cannot freely share data and make decisions jointly because they have personal interests that are in direct conflict with each other and their customers.

Blockchain is not a silver bullet for the constant seesawing demand, but it does enable a more appropriate response to these situations. "A Framework for Enabling Order Management Process in a Decentralized Production Network Based on The Blockchain Technology" demonstrates this in a simulation similar to BCmfg's by using smart contracts as the decision-makers. It builds on BCmfg by updating not only payment data but also the manufacturer's production abilities/capacities over time.[535] Manufacturers only upload accurate data because it sets the parameters for which customer orders are accepted. Data uploaded would indicate a company's capacity limitations, at which point customers would bid to have their order requests prioritized.[536] There is no more guessing what to prioritize because it becomes a deterministic decision-making process. This decentralized production network is designed to include many manufacturers that cooperatively compete to meet omnichannel demands. Since Ethereum smart contracts dictate what parties are involved in the production and delivery of products, all delivery data is labeled publicly, which automatically accomplishes the first step in supply chain transparency.[537]

These smart contract integrated systems are just providing a line for direct communication between customers and a service-providing machine. Consumers often don't need the decision-makers in the middle because the machines coupled with smart contracts make decisions better than any human could.

3D printing services are a perfect example of why this trend is important. If you were to build a digital prototype for a part or invention, all of your intellectual property for that novel device would be contained in a single CAD file. To access a 3D printer without buying one, you must submit that CAD file to a service provider. All you need is the 3D printer and a payment method. Service price could be calculated and executed with a smart contract relatively quickly (just factor time to print and materials used). No one needs intellectual property except the machine itself. This same system has already been proposed and enacted on a small scale.[538] With it, inventors don't need to risk losing the rights to their inventions when outsourcing a 3D printing service.

Arguments against this type of automation commonly regard the quality of service. For the 3D printer example, the data indicates that removing the human facilitator improves services across the board. In general, there are improvements in reliability, delivery speed, and general usefulness when the service providers are just unaccompanied machines utilizing incoming data.[539] A 3D printing service platform without a middleman also leaves more room for collaborative intervention between consumers. We've seen this collaborative relationship organically grow and improve overall services.[540]

When viewing the scope of related service providers, a blockchain architecture makes data reliable and available. What follows is the realization that machines combined with smart contracts only need relevant data to replace human tasks. This ultimately ends up looking like the IIoT Dapp, where machines not only provide services on their own, but perform their own maintenance and order their own replacements.[541] The first manufacturer to develop and deploy a dapp like this would disrupt the industry.

It is important to give a brief mention of the ethical aspect of this automation strategy. Concerns regarding the loss of jobs and artificial intelligence development are well-founded. Both cases are also going to grow in the industrial sector, independent of distributed technologies. Blockchain architecture is perhaps the addition that can make these advancements honest. To see where this might be applicable, let's look at the electric car company Tesla.

The company is very possibly the most efficient data-collecting car company. Their self-driving fleet essentially crowdsources driver data from all their drivers to improve its software.[542] Car software updates are delivered to owners "over-the-air."[543] All this innovation happening under our noses is still hidden so trade secrets are not stolen. We can't replicate Tesla's self-driving technology just from owning the car. This extended so far as to involve actually hiding hardware in a mass-market vehicle. For example, supercharging capability was added in early Tesla models before the company announced it, and no one realized what was in their cars. Tesla's manufacturing processes are another blatant example of the expanding influence of artificial intelligence and advanced data science in manufacturing.

All these examples were, for the most part, in the consumer's best interest. They also come very close to the efficiency upgrades proposed in this chapter for generic manufacturers. Tesla, as a company, is also extremely limited in what they can release because much of it is valuable intellectual property that can be stolen. The necessity for change elevates as technologies break new boundaries, especially in artificial intelligence. Elon Musk, Tesla's CEO, has also proposed Neuralink—a chip that gets implanted in your brain with the ultimate goal of merging the human brain with artificial intelligence. Do we want hidden technological features for that brain chip as they're being installed as we had in the Tesla cars?

None of the single solutions mentioned can turn Tesla into a transparent company. Some places to start are provenance tracking, BCmfg-like data collection, and data utilization involving distributed consensus. Technologists not only need these trust mechanisms to win over customers, but humanity needs them to preclude nefarious corporate agendas.

Supply Chain Industry Examples

With so many companies having launched a blockchain initiative, it's hard to tell which are legitimate. It's even harder to find specific details about each initiative. Thus, this book prioritizes academic references over company ones, but here are some of the most notable company examples.

Likely the most frequently cited example of blockchain in supply chain and manufacturing is in the shipping and technology giants, Maersk Lines and IBM. Shipping a single container with Maersk requires over 200 communications, which could be replaced by putting those data communications on a Hyperledger Blockchain.[544] Anticipated benefits are expected to be tremendous and are frequently repeated in both parties' press releases, but there are few more details than that.[545]

Some more brief examples are Intel integrating with a blockchain-based seafood supply chain. El Maouchi TRADE created a transparent blockchain for customers to participate in the supply chain of their orders and Walmart for tracking pork loads to recover recalls quickly and easily.[546] Again, it's anybody's guess how these work at a deep level or affect their parent companies.

Finding a good example of how this works in practice requires delving back into the startup world. There are dozens of blockchain startups involved in supply chain, but Provenance uniquely has successful cases with coherent technical explanations. They integrate blockchain tracking abilities into independent companies that aim to improve product traceability. Much of their initiative has been with food, where ethical farmers can prove the authenticity of meat products by appending time-dependent data points to a blockchain that customers could see.[547] Provenance systems strive for the ideal of what blockchain enthusiasts imagine for consumer product transparency. Unfortunately, even the details of Provenance are fuzzy, which will make them our example for the next section's chopping block.

Notice the industry examples are few and focus on supply chain far more than manufacturing examples as they relate to blockchain technologies. Blockchain enthusiasts also rave about supply chain disruption while manufacturing solutions barely make any mention. The fundamental reason is supply chain solutions have been made to seem comparatively simple by startup initiatives. In reality, depictions of blockchain in supply chain have been flawed since their beginnings, and solution attempts chasing this ideal were doomed from the start. Perpetual failure with small-scale testing has since prevented the industry giants (ones qualified for creating solutions) from deploying related technologies.

Untold Fallacies

Industry solutions in the preceding section have a common theme: They each tackle supply chain problems with blockchain in place of IoT era technologies. This mistake has misled implementers and surrounding institutions as a result. Here's why.

Maersk and other shipping companies have used blockchain as an alternative to excessive documentation. This is totally sensible and important but not revolutionary. Replacing the 200 communications required to ship a container with a distributed access database is a long overdue progression, not a revolution. Trouble comes with other promises of supply chain traceability that doesn't transition from methods based on paper logic. Contrary to popular belief, even documentation (order notifications, receipts, trade agreements, etc.) converted to blockchain form can never reliably indicate the condition of a product that is in transit.[548]

A challenging example for this section is hypothetically tracking an organic chicken from farm to store and proving its authenticity. To do this, we need to know the chicken's lifestyle and that it was not swapped with any other chicken. It's a tricky problem but highly relevant because many blockchain initiatives focus on this exact challenge with various foods. It should be evident at this point that more documentation won't help the chickens very much, so we'll move straight to the IoT era options.

The first is a typical barcode or QR code that directs a customer to data about the product. You've probably done this to get price information. The blockchain company Provenance uses this same principle in their case studies but swaps price information with the companies product information, which is on a blockchain.[549]

There are a few issues with this QR code strategy. The biggest is the authenticity of the actual on-chain information. Public blockchains generally require a consensus mechanism that ensures accuracy based on math. Provenance blockchain deems accurate information to be anything uploaded from the providing party/company and does not incorporate a rigorous consensus mechanism. When scanning a package of chicken, you are looking at documentation that was uploaded by Grassroots Farmers Cooperative. It is all paper logic. No data is included from a scanner monitoring conditions of the live chickens, a tracker showing the type of feed used, a digital signature of the butcher, IoT temperature sensor data during shipment, or device-produced time stamping for any of the preceding data points. This approach essentially clarifies a company's own unchecked guarantee for its products.

Another problem with Provenance is that their resulting barcodes are made of paper. Anyone who has a computer could easily clone the barcode on a package.[550] I can go copy one of Provenance's barcodes and put it on every piece of poultry at my local Costco. I can do the same to "prove" that a box of Wheaties is an organic chicken. The moral of this story is that whenever we meld paper logic with blockchain technology, the outcome tends to be aimless (the exception to that is contractual agreements and proof of existence type use cases).

One technology that is cheaply stepping away from paper logic is Radio Frequency Identification (RFID) technologies. RFID is a chip or tag with information encoded in it. The chips use one-way communication, which means they are device-readable when in range but cannot receive new information from consumer devices. In supply chain, each embedded RFID tag assigns an electronic product code to its corresponding product. With an electronic product code, parties along the supply chain can have accurate data about what they're receiving and add data to the RFID tag about their own role.[551] Once the RFID reaches its retail destination, the issue of cloning is all too real because anyone with a reader can make counterfeit versions.[552] In short, RFID has a similar function as barcodes but it is easier for multiple parties to work with and is somewhat harder to clone. RFID use cases have little to do with blockchain, but just as is the case for barcodes, their encoded data can refer to information on a blockchain. This is hardly sufficient for our goal of tracking organic chickens.

Chickens and all other products that endure production changes throughout their supply chain are classified as modifiable goods. Any information regarding post-manufacturer modification is inaccessible to QR codes and RFID.[553] That's not to say that startups using this are not great pilots for static objects. Everledger, for example, tracks diamonds with document proof of existence for transfers from miners, unrefined pictures at each stage, and the digital signatures of diamond cutters all on a blockchain.[554] It's an alluring first attempt at supply chain solutions even though its blockchain doesn't do any favors for the already unverifiable paper logic it uploads. A more advanced example in the works comes from the Origyn Project, which makes blockchain-based digital twins of luxury watches, verifiable with just a phone camera and its native machine learning algorithms.

These examples only begin to introduce the range of methods available for making supply chain traceability realistic. Still, a chicken breast is just not distinct enough to ensure that a picture, the butcher's digital signature, or a digital twin matches a given breast. This example might seem silly, but in practice, modifiable goods are much more common. It won't be practical to prove organic farm animals' conditions until IoT infrastructure has penetrated the food industry. IoT has only begun seriously developing in manufacturing, which is the starting point for more legitimate proposals for traceability.

IoT sensors are a broad categorization of technologies that allow monitoring of modifiable conditions and are ubiquitous in industrial applications. They also rarely provide data that is accessible outside of their immediate facility. Few are benefiting from this IoT sensor data, and blockchain startups are rarely integrating them with supply chain for a few reasons.

IoT sensors are far more expensive than RFID. Remember that startups in this arena are acting as consultants to existing companies. Their most popular starting point is usually small farmers, and it's not economically viable to place sensors all around the chickens we eat. Bigger examples, like car manufacturers, have a plethora of IoT sensors readily available. This is no help to a startup like Provenance, which couldn't convince a giant to participate or handle its complexity.

So why can't a giant like Toyota use its already omnipresent IoT infrastructure to make a transparent supply chain? Aside from the fact that Toyota doesn't control every part of its infinitely complex supply chain, IoT sensors still have their problems. While they can effectively measure essential variables like temperatures, gaseous conditions, vibrations, etc., once that data is broadcasted on an IoT network, there is no proof of where it came from.[555] In other words, I could have an IoT sensor reading data from an ice bath in Guam and have it's outgoing data correspond to that of my "American cryogenic-made nanochip." With conventional IoT standards, there would be no way to prove or disprove that sensor's authenticity. This ongoing issue is called *location spoofing*, and the next section will demonstrate why DLT's are its top solution prospect.

Blockchain startups still stuck using paper logic are the same ones claiming to be ideal solutions for supply chain. They get the most attention because it is easy for clients, investors, and the general public to understand. Untold fallacies like RFID cloning and location spoofing are blatantly ignored on company websites. The trifling efficacy of paper logic in proving product authenticity is omitted from most related concept designs.

If the entirety of supply chain and blockchain-related startups could be compressed in one sentence, it would be this: Startups are making unchecked projections of physical goods into digital representations, which is useless when any post-production processing takes place.[556] The next section will depict a method for converting already prominent technologies into digital representations of the physical goods themselves, which is much more likely to achieve transparency-related goals.

IoT devices are uniquely adaptable enough to make a meaningful difference in supply chain transparency. With industry giants holding the already existing IoT infrastructure, they are the only options for driving impactful change. If this were to be applied to a car battery, a startup would add a barcode that refers to product information on a blockchain. Ideally, a digital representation (perhaps a token) of that battery and all its constituent parts that proves ownership as it transfers along a supply chain would be used instead. The Toyotas of the world need to pioneer these radical shifts in supply chain. Prices of IoT devices are rapidly declining, which will potentially reduce the barrier to entry enough for small farmers to fix our organic chicken problem,[557] but not before the more capable industry giants pave the way by solving device flaws.

Searching for Transparent Solutions

Much of the untold fallacies of supply chain solutions revolve around the double-spend problem. Any data that "proves" the authenticity of something while being susceptible to forgery cannot reliably prove anything. Blockchain solved this paradox with money but translating the concept to nonmonetary data is not as simple.

Making product supply chain data transparent, at least in part, requires a digital representation of formal product ownership that cannot be copied. We'll look at some options for doing this with the major three technologies at play: barcodes, RFID tags, and IoT sensors.

Barcodes

Barcodes are projections of the data that are projections of the product. It's rigid paper logic with no straightforward ways to encrypt or modify its data. It is lines on paper that can always be duplicated, which creates more problems than it solves.

RFID Tags

RFID tags have more freedom with the data that gets implanted. One approach encrypts the data within the tags that only authorized parties can decrypt via a secret sharing scheme.[558] Aside from a vexing procedure for data access, this approach only provides a snapshot of one supply chain party's data instead of the whole chain. It's unclear how this extends to customers, and it doesn't create a digital representation corresponding to product ownership. The private nature of this encryption scheme is best suited only for cutting-edge developments with highly sensitive intellectual property.

Another option for RFID tags is digitally attaching them with a protocol enabling proof of ownership.[559] The concept is fairly involved with most of the complexity in distributing the power of those who can authorize ownership transfers—that is, only the designated manufacturer can sell a newly created product, only a shipping service is reliable in delegating its transfer, and only a credible vendor can facilitate its transition to consumers. There should not be much need to delve into the details of how this is achieved because distributed consensus with protocol trustees composes the active mechanism at the grassroots of leading identity and financial blockchain solutions from previous chapters.

Whatever technique IdM manages to issue, validate, and share identity credentials will probably be similarly applied to sharing credentials for product ownership. The primary benefit of RFID tags with this type of protocol is that product data is affiliated with its owner's blockchain wallet. Product transactions are completed with Ethereum's solidity smart contracts in conjunction with programmable tools.[560] The transparency of a blockchain makes any cloned tags virtually meaningless because they are visibly irreconcilable with their real owner.[561] It's quite a clever workaround for supply chain data's double-spend paradox.

The above solution works wonders at preventing counterfeiters. A prospective buyer could discern a fraudulent vendor that carried a cloned RFID tag because they would have no proof of ownership.[562] Unfortunately, this system is still not ideal for mass-market applications because alternate problems arose as the corollary of design trade-offs made to invalidate duplicate tag data. As a vendor, the way to cheat this protocol is to buy a real product and swap its tag with a counterfeit. This isn't too serious because it ordinarily requires offloading the "real" product as if it were "fake" and has little economic justification.[563] Protocol, overall hardware, and computing expense for smart contracts end up being about $1 per product (this assumes a transaction between six parties),[564] so feasibility is justifiable for expensive products. This works okay because cheap products have no incentives for counterfeits. There are a few more minor logistical kinks that need to be ironed out, like user-friendliness. Thorough protocols like this haven't figured out how to compete with the simplicity of scanning a barcode and viewing a website as Provenance does.

RFID tags and blockchain alone don't make the jump to mass-market products. The above model only makes economic sense with a combination of luxury goods and a sophisticated set of consumers and vendors. Added hardware (an RFID tag) creates a bottleneck because its embedded data is hard to read or change. Proof of ownership on a blockchain is the real meat and potatoes of the preceding provenance tracking system, while RFID merely contains the paper logic that enables its transactions. In essence, it's a tokenization system without the name.

Tokenized Traceability

A necessary advancement to the preceding supply chain tracking systems entails moving one step closer to Bitcoin's solution to the double-spend problem, particularly through the use of Non-Fungible Tokens (NFTs). As a refresher, NFTs are indivisible tokens that cannot be duplicated and can represent something physical when endorsed by its creator(s). This works because the entire history of each NFT is on the blockchain, which acts as a master copy.

Suppose Toyota sold me a car along with an NFT that represented it (and regulatory bodies accepted this), then holding that token would prove my ownership. You would be able to see and copy the raw token data, but there's no way to implant a duplicate on the master copy; thus, you couldn't formally own the car unless I sent you the token. This concept is crucial to making traceability mainstream because it adds value for manufacturers, not just customers.

A novel approach that proves the viability of tokenized traceability is outlined in the paper "Tracing Manufacturing Processes Using Blockchain-Based Token Compositions," based on a simulation of the manufacture and delivery of edge-glued wood. This seemingly random use case is instrumental because its specificity allows an end-to-end solution that speaks for itself, while generalized simulations only work in theory. Edge-glued wood sales also relate to the management of omnichannels in that it's like following a recipe: Manufacturers are always balancing different ratios of raw materials with fluctuating consumer demand.[565] When idealizing this into a Web interface as is done here, simulation efficacy increases with the number of parties that join because they just add NFT (product) data to supply chain management software. Although it's application-specific, variants of this system could be made broadly applicable in the manufacturing sphere thanks to the design concept's relative simplicity.

 The simulation/prototype starts with representing parties involved with the production and sale of edge-glued wood: customers, logistics/retailers (shipping service and hardware stores), sawmill/factory, and resource suppliers (glue plant and forester).[566] The supply chain is set in motion when the customer places an order, at which point the request information trickles down through each subsequent party. This resembles the same inefficiencies of manufacturing/supply chain processes discussed previously—namely, the transfer of information takes too long, manufacturer's aren't good at keeping track of where all the raw materials are in the supply chain, and inventory holdups make production slow to meet demand shifts.

NFTs change this by providing a real-time picture of what resources are available and where they are in the supply chain. In the edge-glued wood simulation, whenever a raw material batch or finished product batch is created, it gets a token minted by its creator to represent it.[567] All connected members of the supply chain can see the records of tokens, and once the batch leaves the supply chain, the token data is no longer relevant to analytics software.[568] This tokenization method is the crux of this prototype's originality. Transactions are conducted with a web app user interface and underlying smart contracts.[569] Other intricacies regarding how blockchain enables data certification and transfer are repetitive, so they will be left out.

The direct benefit here is simple. Without this system, if I place an order for a particular batch of edge-glued wood, the sawmill will be notified by the retail store, the glue factory will be notified by the sawmill, and so on. With this system, my newly placed order immediately notifies the glue factory and all other involved parties of each product's real-time demand. This operational tweak becomes more constructive as the technology scales. For example, let's say when I order edge-glued wood, I have 5 wood type choices (coming from the forester), 5 glue choices (coming from the glue factory), and 5 wood shape choices (produced by the sawmill). Let's also assume two of each business type (two foresters, glue factories, and sawmills), and each only has enough resources to offer 3 out of the 5 options at a time. If competing parties did not collaborate, and there was one of each business type in the supply chain, then only 27 out of 125 product types would be available to customers. Adding more parties of the same business type is a challenge because it's nearly impossible to split a customer base fairly.

Complete transparency is one element of the edge-glued wood example. Not only can customers see product history, but collaborating businesses can see each other's activity. When an order is placed through the web-app, it could be filled agnostic of company and solely based on the availability of each production line. Splitting a customer base is possible here because negotiated terms for splitting demand shifts can be written into the algorithm that delegates orders. Any misbehavior would be blatantly obvious. This radical transparency may not be conducive to all companies (such as cutting edge technology companies that would give up a competitive advantage by releasing business logic). Still, in the vast majority of cases, the benefits of transparency's collaborative advantage outweigh the costs.[570]

There's still the problem of catering to consumers that the edge-glued wood example doesn't address. Their setup is convenient for manufacturer analytics and fails to consider relevant issues in the post supply chain. Customers can see the information associated with their token/product on the blockchain, but the data has the same rigidity issue as similar RFID tracking systems. Product data should be dynamic and change with the product itself, not based on what the manufacturer decides to upload.

The first solution in this section (RFID architecture) focused on consumers' right to see their product's life-cycle, which continues through the post supply chain. The second example (edge-glued wood) focused on benefiting the supply chain parties by enabling collaborative data sharing. Both use transparency as the governing principle, but each is limited by the amount of data they can digitally record. Edge-glued wood could use tokens corresponding to data consisting of "product images, expiration dates, disposal instructions, manuals, documentation of defects, and many other factors," and product batch specifications like "items, weight, volume, or size."[571] There is no special hardware involved here, and data is only as trustworthy as the third party that uploads it.

IoT Devices

All preceding solutions solved the software side of things but didn't profoundly relate to the physical world. The absence of IoT sensors means that data on these application-specific blockchains come from humans instead of machines. Therefore both solutions are susceptible to human error and lack the impenetrable trust that supply chains need to improve. Not much specific work has been done on this because the IoT device industry is still young and expensive.

As IoT devices become more prominent, their application in supply chain and blockchain solutions are relatively straightforward. Instead of a glue factory worker taking a picture of finished glue, the glue machine itself uploads the circumstances under which a batch of glue was made. In the sawmill, the machine that cuts and shapes the wood will produce and deliver more useful data more efficiently and more reliably than anyone who takes part in operating that machine. Authenticity issues stemming from IoT sensor spoofing can be addressed by a separate blockchain-based Proof of Location protocol. The startup Foam and others are developing a hardware environment for just this purpose.[572]

Small startups and academic works compose most information about blockchain's role in manufacturing and supply chain. Identity and financial infrastructure applications started the same way. This time, the activation energy for innovation is higher because it requires a massive existing hardware infrastructure. Because of these combined factors, use cases for blockchain in the industrial sphere hardly get any recognition. Use cases of this type were actually serious considerations before hype-driven blockchain projects started popping up like mushrooms.

The 2016 book *Bitcoin and Cryptocurrency Technologies: A Comprehensive Introduction* was released by Princeton University Press and authored by five academics. Ideas related to tokenization flourish throughout this book. The work demonstrates how a bitcoin alone can be colored (have a bit string attached to it), making it unique and capable of representing any asset (for example, company stocks, physical property, or car ownership).[573] Keep in mind that this book depicts the few altcoins that existed at the time as frivolous extensions to Bitcoin with little future potential.[574] Now cryptocurrency can mean anything (or nothing) but is hardly ever used to represent equity in an asset.

The book goes further in demonstrating how this would work for automobiles. A wearable device or key fob is the piece of hardware that gives you access to your car. Unfortunately, if someone else gets access to that key fob, they can also access the car. If asymmetric key cryptography was implemented to associate the device to the car, ownership would be enforceable by just the key fob data.[575] This means the car ownership can be transferred on the blockchain to different devices/key fobs (there is no need for physical exchange of the devices).[576] A seller's device would be incompatible with a car immediately after selling it to the new owner. Cryptographically secured car ownership would also extend up the supply chain because possession transfers of the car throughout the manufacturing process would also be tracked.[577] This would make supply chain traceability occur almost naturally. If that blockchain data received legal recognition, then the paperwork involved in a car sale would be a thing of the past. This simple application of coupling raw blockchain cryptography to wearable devices creates a foundation for tracking *both* pre- and post-supply chain.

As far as I can tell, ideas of this sort are dying out. Some of the reputable startups left working with IoT devices in supply chain and manufacturing are Slock.it and Chronicled, but there are few details about their progress.[578][579] The lost momentum doesn't have any bearing on the real potential of solutions discussed in this section. Opportunities are growing with the number of IoT sensors. Small-scale trials show that proper implementation benefits everyone: Raw material suppliers, manufacturers, the transporters in between, and the customer at the end all stand to have a better experience when tracking involves operational data on a blockchain.

The reason for related solutions being unlikely to manifest is representative of other large industry-specific applications. Chapters 6–8 all target a specific industry, each with solutions that become increasingly complex. Identity is reasonably targeted, and blockchain startups alone are successful in driving innovation. Banks, fintechs, blockchain startups, and tech titans all have their respective services that leave no clear industry standard. Manufacturing and supply chain may have the most potential for blockchain integration. Still, incumbents remain stagnant, and any worthwhile undertaking in the industrial sector is too big for a startup to succeed. The energy, healthcare, and real estate sectors deserve chapters of their own but share this same story: They are too complicated for startups to penetrate without help. Moving past this, at the very least, requires the financial and identity applications to standardize blockchain solutions in order to captivate the interest of large companies.

There are encouraging signs that these solutions are just going to take a long time instead of being failures. The car key fob/colored bitcoins idea was proposed in 2016 and has remained technologically similar to today's NFTs. For reasons beyond me, it took until mid-2020 for people to start getting excited about using NFTs. Perhaps these complex logistics and IoT solutions aren't failing but are just slowly crawling from the incubation phase to the mass market. Right now, it's time to take a more realistic look at how these solutions are likely to impact supply chain and manufacturing companies.

FAAMG's Role or Lack Thereof

There are four major areas where blockchain can improve supply chain and manufacturing. Each was covered sequentially throughout this chapter: easing paperwork processing, identification of counterfeit products, facilitation of origin tracking, and operationalization of the Internet of things. Each of those applications is more complex than the last, making them like four stepping stones to building an ideal system. They are also consecutively less likely to manifest in large-scale industrial applications because each step needs to be technologically proven before moving to the next step. There is a strong argument to suggest all four categories have a significant ability to produce value, but only the easing paperwork processing category is likely to succeed.[580] This is because DLTs are a simple to apply and clear money-saving set of technologies already being implemented by giants. That's how Maersk and IBM are attempting to reduce their hundreds of logistics-related communications required to ship one container.

This solution is not impeded by the incompatibility of platforms and involves only the mild technical shift of uploading documentation on a public ledger instead of individually transferring documents. The remaining steps (identification of counterfeit products, facilitation of origin tracking, and operationalization of the Internet of things) show little evidence to suggest any successful future. Right now, we're not even finished with step one.

FAAMG had a clear role to play in industries from previous chapters. Typically, FAAMG's incentive to innovate blockchain solutions is the opportunity for more control. For industries that don't have a tremendous reliance on digitization, FAAMG's role is harder to nail down. The energy, health care, real estate, supply chain, and manufacturing industries all use SaaS running on the cloud servers of technology giants.

Let's take a specific example. If you are a manufacturer today, you are also part of a supply chain, likely managing operations with many software packages, and use some ERP as your central logistics management tool. You are also probably hosting that software and related data on either a Google, Amazon, or Microsoft cloud platform. The movement toward cloud manufacturing encourages more reliance on these cloud services and is responsible for the emergence of a centralized communication network paradigm.[581] Any data that you add to the cloud is your intellectual property, meaning it cannot be republished but can be viewed by its possessor and/or government agencies that request it.[582] The terms and conditions for each company do not clarify how that cloud data gets used.

This is not a position that FAAMG and other software companies want to interrupt. You, as the manufacturer, probably don't care about those details because they will scarcely ever affect you. The collective impact on manufacturers is significant because their governing software is intuitively centralized, which leaves no room for consideration of decentralized options.

Blockchain solutions of the SaaS type are based on a peer-to-peer model. Solutions of this chapter revolve around the principle of distributed logistics and data sharing. It's too early to predict how blockchain logistics SaaS will interact with legacy software services, but if developments in other industries are any indication, it's hard to find reasons for existing SaaS providers to be happy about this. The BCmfc concept and IIoT Dapp discussed earlier would ideally be hosted across a network of disparate computers, not a server in a Google facility. This would reward contributors but not a single governing entity or parent company.

In most cases, siloed data could not be leveraged by its possessor because it would be readily available to all network participants. At first, this would not dramatically change the SaaS business model because IIoT Dapp and BCmfc architecture is designed as an extension to ERP and other logistics software, not a replacement. Changes start at the database layer of software architectures. It's too early to evaluate decentralized options as a replacement for old software beyond the database layer, but its use as an add-on would open the door for that option. Solutions relating to the ideals of this chapter are ordinarily bad for the maintenance of the Internet hierarchy and leave FAAMG with no incentive to participate.[583]

Who's left to break ground in the area where blockchain and manufacturing meet are the Toyotas of the world. We've seen this done before in the pre-IoT era. Toyota saw wild successes because it decentralized and consumed data from the most modest people and places in their factories. Others like GM followed Toyota's lead to keep up. In manufacturing, people and places are increasingly being swapped with machines and IoT devices. Toyota and others should adapt their operations to uphold their principle of top-down decentralization. The extent to which changes are made will match the breadth of its ripple effect.

As for the supply chains, demand for multidisciplinary manufacturing collaboration has woven an infinitely complex supply web instead of a series of supply chains to appease omnicustomers. Replacing physical documentation with transparent data sharing is the way to do this without sacrificing efficiency. The first supply chain that gets everyone on board to participate will reap considerable advantages and leave competitors with no choice but to follow. Toyota, for example, would collect extra data about car parts/raw materials before making a car and extra data about car performance post supply chain. Visibility of this data for consumers would yield unparalleled trust. If no one followed this trend, you would be skeptical about buying any car that wasn't a Toyota.

This chapter covered a diverse array of topics and solution prospects, none of which were able to be deeply examined. Potential applications for these solutions are so broad that every attempt seems to pop out with something original, making it impossible to nail down a single one without neglecting others. The largest commonality across all examples is recognizing peer-to-peer (P2P) logistics for data-based operation management as superior to centralized options.[584] All things considered, the probability of industry adoption of P2P in manufacturing and supply chain is relatively low.

FAAMG took the backseat in this chapter for economic reasons. The P2P approach disallows FAAMG from gaining platform dominance and decreases the need for its cloud services. P2P services' chance of widespread adoption being low is unfortunate because it's our chance to reduce reliance on the

Internet oligopoly in the material realm. Should these solutions succeed, FAAMG's economic disadvantage in this arena is subject to change. We saw P2P platforms like Brave and Steemit flip legacy economic models on their heads. It's possible that even P2P platform facilitators will find ways to profit.

All solutions thus far have been building up to the way they could change how FAAMG interacts with the world. We've seen blockchain being used by startups, academics, large corporations, and technology companies alike. Many ambitious ideas from these participants are loosely aimed at replacing/improving FAAMG services. Very few to none of those cases created something that FAAMG couldn't. If these solutions manifest into something resembling the blockchain revolution that enthusiasts predict, there is no way FAAMG will take it lying down.

CHAPTER 9:

AN IDEALIZED FAAMG

People are growing tired of FAAMG. Just as any novel drug takes decades to understand, the long-term effects of Internet service usage are just beginning to be understood. We know social media usage is linked with depression, anxiety, and suicide. We know that user interfaces are intentionally created to act as addictive dopamine simulators. And we know that everything landing on our screens while surfing the web has an inherent bias because the Internet's core business model is advertising. No one disputes these effects, which have become trendy topics.

The most popular media piece on this issue has been Netflix's *The Social Dilemma*. Although the documentary was a great awareness tool for Big Tech problems, it didn't offer any actionable solutions. Many of us are eager for a way out of the FAAMG customer trap that doesn't jeopardize all of our accrued data and freemium features, but there is no available option.

Even if we did have a perfect decentralized FAAMG replica, there would still be a long path toward adoption. The public is clearly aware of social media's dangers, but Facebook is still growing, a situation that can be explained with a drug analogy. Just as *The Social Dilemma* pointed out that the drugs and technology industries are the only ones that refer to their customers as *users*, there are many other parallels as well. Both industries feed off addictive behavior, cannot be controlled by governments, and make money in proportion to how damaging their products are.

This might help explain why everyone is still using social media. With most drugs, it takes a couple of decades of research to get an idea of how they work. Even then, there is rarely a clear picture of a drug's long-term effect on the human brain. Social media could be thought of as the most massive neuropsychological experiment of all time, and one that can be explained quite simply. Let's see what happens when we make three billion people subject to unlimited inputs from the other three billion based on a set of rules. Furthermore, let's observe the impact on the masses as we periodically change these rules.

Despite the results we already have from this experiment, they don't seem to be enough to motivate any counteraction. I'd bet 99% of people who viewed *The Social Dilemma* returned to their social media feeds and other FAAMG services the very day after watching. Perhaps this is because we don't have enough results from this mass experiment. Most neuropsychological research relating to Internet use is about people who were gradually integrated into the world of FAAMG during adulthood. There is no data on how those born into a prospering Web2 will be affected during adulthood. There are inklings of proof that FAAMG's powers undermine democracy, but there is no quantifiable evidence of its destabilizing effect. Maybe in time, a clearer picture of the Internet's long-term effects will motivate efforts to change it.

People are often confused about why I hate new technology while also being obsessed with it. Frankly, I'm puzzled by those who see it differently. Technology is quite literally a superpower, and most choose to use it for the stupidest things.

It is easier to get a group to rally around a problem than a solution. That's why you will scarcely find solution proposals to these very real problems in our popular media. The present book claims that Web3 is one of the solutions, so it is crucial to provide a clear vision for what decentralized FAAMG services could look like.

The next sections will run through ideal versions of decentralized FAAMG copycats, but this is a sort of promissory note that (1) provides goals for the parent companies that are not entirely realistic at present, and (2) does not consider the many peripheral tech companies outside of FAAMG that contribute to the same problems. And the most significant consideration is that successful FAAMG copycats are misaligned with Web3's goal. Web3 should be a brand-new infrastructure that creates currently unimaginable things.

Since I can't merely conjure up creative visions for novel Web3 services, we're stuck using FAAMG as a model for the possibilities of decentralization. All that said, these idealized company visions do not need to wait for a new wave of technology to change. All the technological tools required to make these changes are already available.

Brief Mention of the Cloud

The Cloud is all the processes that happen on the web that don't happen on your devices. It is cyberspace, but more literally, it is servers that hold the Internet's data and perform computations so that you could do stuff with data that is not stored locally on your device. Big Tech owns the Cloud, putting it in the perfect position to own the other parts of the Internet. Amazon Web Services, Microsoft Azure, and Google Cloud are the most notable service providers. They will not be mentioned elsewhere in this chapter because they all share a common, idealized version.

An idealized version of the Cloud is one that does not exist. Big Tech owns the Cloud because our computers didn't trust each other during the early Internet, and so we entrusted large companies with securing connections between private networks. This heavily-centralized Cloud causes massive wealth and power disparities for tech companies and everyday users.

The blockchain revolution is about connecting computers through indeterminately secure methods so they don't need to trust anything else. This should make the Cloud obsolete, or at least make the Cloud decentralized by default. Although there are many ways to replace the Cloud, the next chapter is about one possible—and perhaps best—way of creating the decentralized Internet's storage and compute infrastructure.

Tough decisions about the upcoming idealized FAAMG examples will pass on that responsibility to a governance mechanism. The Idealized Governance section will explain the process of arriving at such decisions.

Idealized Facebook

As we know, Facebook works by using past behavior to influence future behavior. This model for social media keeps users locked in an insular sphere of influence. This is the world's largest violation of privacy with respect to the collective community mind concept from Chapter 2. A decentralized Facebook is an important model for the rest of the tech world because Facebook is the king of social networking sites (SNS).

The first step is completely removing advertisements. Some blockchain enthusiasts would call this radical and prefer an ad model that pays back users, but there is just no reason for it in 2020. If attention can be bought, content will flow with a bias aligned with wealthy entities. Web3 SNSs should not have ads, ever.

The no ads proposal raises two questions: (1) How does the platform make money? (2) How can companies advertise products? We will start with the second.

Advertising can come in any form, and it has evolved to be more targeted and less annoying. Facebook's targeting is so effective because it specializes in delivering ads about stuff that you love. The least annoying ads now are native pieces of sponsored content. Blogs, SNS posts, vlogs, and so on can still be sponsored by companies. Advertisers could also provide native content themselves under a company account. Since all this content would be attached to a SNS identity and reputation score, salesy or disingenuous content will suffer decreased visibility. The benefit is "adspace" being distributed across thousands of content creators instead of being dictated by a single entity that always picks the highest bidder. This looks similar to Facebook and Instagram, except no content is favored by search algorithms, and the rules for SNS reputations and content visibility are transparent and changeable with a governance mechanism instead of a CEO.

An economic model for the platform that rewards its contributors could be achieved in many ways, but the most common one would be with SNS tokenomics. A decentralized Facebook would issue a platform token that contributes to network influence. Steemit has proven this can sustainably work on SNSs. With such a system, upvotes/likes actually pay the creator. The amount an upvote is worth is dependent on the associated user's token holding and reputation. A preset percentage of these token proceeds are allocated to a pool for developers and other contributions that maintain the network. A governance mechanism will determine the allocation percentages and other rewards system parameters.

When it comes to the question of a decentralized Facebook's data management, the answer is more subjective because there are many valid approaches. In one sense, since nefarious advertising can't exist on any large scale in such a platform, user data can be seen in a completely different light. All data could be transparent and available to everyone, while user accounts reserve a right to be anonymous. Of course, transparent SNS data could be used on secondary markets in ways that some network participants would not want to permit. An option that offers more privacy would be keeping user account data private by default and accessible only to chosen platform users. The hybrid version of this might broadcast blog posts to a public ledger but keep likes, dislikes, and other clicking activity encrypted. Analytics for all that clicking data is still necessary to determine what content is shown. For this, multi-party computation or having private data on a public blockchain could derive useful insights from encrypted data without ever revealing raw data.[585]

Many data structures can achieve the customized levels of data sovereignty that users deserve. The bottom line is preserving the user's ability to decide what happens with their data. Regardless of data structure type, for this idealized decentralized Facebook to work, nodes must be independent entities (users instead of organizations), and all protocol processes must be transparent.

Now comes the more dicey territory of determining what algorithms should generate user feeds and keyword search results. The short answer is a governance mechanism, but this immediately sprouts new problems that social media users might already foresee, such as online trolls or shaming mobs that might conspire to destroy individual reputations for the wrong reasons. Suppose an evolutionary psychologist spreads the word about their peer-reviewed and scientifically accurate research on this decentralized Facebook, but those findings happen to be politically incorrect. Thousands of people downvote the post and leave nasty comments but have no authority in that field. How is a SNS to deal with this?

This example should highlight the importance of multifactorial consensus with domain experts, as explained in Chapter 5. The upcoming Idealized Governance will offer an even more direct way to minimize bias in reputation scoring systems. Still, in short, it will put more weight on the upvoting/commenting from people within the field of evolutionary psychology.

A final step for some decentralized version of Facebook guarantees the permanence of the building blocks that others rely on. An API must provide guarantees about their rules so games and other applications that connect to SNSs won't risk their business models being destroyed. Content creators must have guarantees written in code that their posts will persist for a lifetime or other timeframe so they won't risk losing personal data. A decentralized Facebook would basically need to guarantee the permanence of their new rules. The market will be what decides if this is to be upheld, and a sound network governance system is the way to flexibly maintain it.

Idealized Amazon

Amazon is a wonderful company that brought e-commerce directly to consumers. Doing that required bridging gaps between every industry, and today it is a kind of superpower. We have seen this power used for good as Amazon kept e-store profit margins razor-thin while growing market share and outperforming every competitor. This process simultaneously encroached upon every industry's supply chain web, and in some cases, the entire industry itself.

Amazon, for example, was the one glaringly obvious option for profitably publishing this book. They manufacture books cheaper than anyone, they dominate all methods for reach, they are better at handling distribution than anyone, and they never go out of stock. Amazon's algorithms favor profitability and likely give preferential treatment to their own books (this is speculation on my part, but the truth is not public). I have so much to lose by stepping outside of Amazon's publishing services, and thus have little choice besides giving Amazon 40-60% of all this book's profits. Unsurprisingly, the future of publishing companies and bookstores looks bleak from every angle, except for Amazon Publishing, which has seen an explosion in growth over recent years.

Amazon makes economies of scale out of every industry it touches, making everything remarkably cheap and efficient. An ideal version of Amazon keeps manufacturing and transport operations commercialized to not interrupt any logistics processes. If anticompetitive abuses were to come out of that, governments and the public could deal with it as they always have with brick-and-mortar monopolies. Amazon's tech platform and data monopolies remaining untouched by regulation is what necessitates Web3 solutions.

The solution is an Amazon DAO that replaces the Amazon website and all its offshoots. Once you convince an entity as big as Amazon to pursue this, the technological steps are relatively simple. Replace the database infrastructure and developer tools that create amazon.com with a blockchain and open-source developer tools. Then use a governance mechanism to decide on all future protocol changes.

This idea and process is a reoccurring theme in this book, and it should require little explanation. Many mentioned infrastructure solutions are capable of decentralizing Amazon. This book has the space for a deep dive into one such topology that will be reserved for the next and last chapter.

Amazon's store would be an ecommerce DAO copycat, and Amazon Music, Video, Drive, etc., would be dapps. Retailers would reap substantial benefits while barely noticing a change in user experience.

Amazon DAO would first and foremost have transparent search algorithms. The governance mechanism would determine how products, movies, music, and other content is found. Since participants in governance don't make sales commissions, their only incentive would be tailoring the site's algorithms toward an optimized user experience. This same philosophy extends to advertising, which is permitted to whatever extent the governance mechanism sees fit. Profits from ads could be in the form of a platform token or traditional currency and returned to a rewards pool that pays platform hosts, governance participants, and network contributors. Subscription-based services for music and video streaming would work mostly the same, except more profits would go to the content creators because the DAO would take a much smaller cut than the corporation.

Our idealized Amazon went through the typical steps for idealized FAAMG: Decentralize the platforms and make the algorithms transparent. Amazon's data is the more unique and subtle asset that makes them so dangerous. Chapter 3 briefly mentioned how this works with headphones. Amazon knows the prices, features, and consumer behaviors for thousands of headphone types. They know the probability that a consumer will buy headphones based on their combined features and overall price. They know the best shapes, sizes, colors, and features to put in front of people for all products. The headphones with the most desirable price-to-feature ratio are the ones Amazon puts in front of you.

All this data gives Amazon world-class market research for every product you could think of. This data could be used to create the most competitive version of any product Amazon decides to make. Amazon Basics uses consumer data to craft immaculate products while controlling the system for production, advertisement, and delivery. This is undoubtedly a great convenience for consumers in the interim, but how is anyone else to compete?

A perfect Amazon DAO would make all market data transparent, which is much different than a decentralized Facebook. That is because SNS data is sensitive, and shopping data could easily be pseudonymous and not violate privacy. Just like a bitcoin wallet, e-commerce identities could be disassociated from a shopper's personally identifiable information. Then all their searches, clicks, and purchases could be a matter of public record without damaging privacy. Every datapoint would be arbitrary, making behavioral microtargeting impossible, but complete enough to produce macro insights. This would level the playing field for entrepreneurs, giving them equal access to market data and a fair shot at filling gaps for buyers.

All the shipping and manufacturing-related logistics would still be taken care of by Amazon company services. For the time being, this is outside of the realm of technologies, and the time-tested corporate hierarchy is the best approach. In the coming decades, as IoT grows, there will be similar concerns about data monopolies in logistics. When machines and self-driving vehicles are handling Amazon company services, there may be a renewed need for an extension of Amazon DAO that loosely relates to the last chapter's IIoT Dapp concept. More on how to decentralize a FAAMG manufacturing process in the next section.

Idealized Apple

Apple, as a large company, is hyper-focused on reducing liabilities. The company claims to be dedicated to environmental sustainability and data privacy. Most of the ways Apple drives capital growth is not replaceable with blockchain, but an idealized Apple would put its money where its mouth is when claiming a commitment to ethics, particularly through using blockchain technologies to provide transparency and traceability.

Apple product models are overall few in number, comparatively speaking. This makes device traceability practical and would start with representing iPhones as non-fungible tokens (NFTs). In the factory where an iPhone is created, an NFT would be minted by the manufacturer and tied to a device serial number or other identifiable characteristics on the physical phone. At each step of an iPhone batch's delivery, a device transfer would coincide with a NFT transfer. Once in the retail store, consumers who buy the phone also receive the NFT in a public/private key wallet.

This NFT transfer process becomes useful when implementing a self-sovereign identity (SSI). Instead of Apple IDs, idealized Apple products would opt for blockchain identities. In Chapter 6, these identities included federal and/or personal attributes: biometric data, bank account logins, federally issued identity documents, or social media profile data. In every circumstance, that SSI data would be owned and viewable only by the user. Apple and Telcom companies could never see the SSI.

When purchasing an iPhone, the buyer sets up an SSI in minutes. The NFT transfer takes place seamlessly without the buyer needing knowledge of it. The NFT wallet keys are held and accessible within that SSI.

Some incredible efficiency gains would go on behind the scenes as an idealized Apple used product NFTs. One benefit is the elimination of legacy tracking systems. With NFT transfers being on a transparent blockchain, there are no discrepancies about what supply chain party held iPhones at what time. Supply chain logistics just got massively simplified. Furthermore, customers could see their device's history from its birth if supply chain parties use recognizable wallet addresses. Measuring the environmental impact and ethical implications of a given product's production would become feasible.

An iPhone NFT adds functionality for users. A stolen phone is disabled without Apple or Samsung's help because the NFT enforces ownership, and a thief's SSI would not have one. iPhone ownership transfer becomes easy too, requiring only a token transfer, which also makes registration and setup seamless.

As an idealized Apple grew this concept, it would extend NFTs to all device component makers. Logistics tracking for Apple's supply chain managers would become transparent. Tracking an entire product lifecycle would be done with even more granularity. Newly acquired data would improve Apple's ability to strategize and adapt when finding component flaws, just as an idealized Toyota from the last chapter improved manufacturing decisions based on post supply chain data. This concept might very well extend to manufacturing process data from factory IoT sensors.

Apple's production methods don't have a nefarious agenda at present. It is targeted here because Apple is in an ideal position to make the changes. Having relatively few product types makes the switch approachable. Traceable iPhones would give consumers all the more reason to trust and purchase them. Competing phones with hidden production methods would appear substandard by comparison. It would also be the push other manufacturers need to start investing in blockchain solutions.

As for the matter of software, the case for fixing Apple is a lost cause. Ideally, Apple would move its closed and watered-down version of Linux and to the fully open Linux Operating System. In most cases, this is a requirement for privacy-preserving SSIs and data ownership enforcement being provided by Apple. The company would move toward DAO or dapp versions of its music app, podcast app, Safari browser, and app store. All of this, however, is pretty much a fairy tale because it would strip away all the advantages of Apple hardware. Apple doesn't just recruit a cult-like following because their devices are stylish, but because of the convenience and exclusivity of their preloaded applications.

Apple is unique because it became unbelievably successful in rejecting the trend toward openness. Steve Jobs envisioned a company of computers that were completely closed end-to-end. Apple products would have very few versions of each product that were only compatible with other Apple products and that you could not upgrade or alter. The idea seemed insane to engineers in the late 90s but turned out to work wonders for the company. Apple's empire thrives because its closed systems can produce the highest quality without introducing tradeoffs tied to cross-platform compatibility or putting confusing decisions in front of customers. A rapid shift toward openness would ruin everything Apple is about.

This poses a tricky problem for blockchain maximalists but is an opportunity to solidify a moderate perspective. Not every system needs to be decentralized. Apple creates amazing hardware and software because of its centralization, and the company rarely abuses its monopolistic position on the Internet. Apple devices have preloaded apps, but users generally can download any application.

If Apple is to be centralized in a nonthreatening way, there are a few notable changes to be made. Apple should democratize its ability to censor apps and other content as well as the algorithms that determine what 3rd-party content gets found. A single company should not be able to dictate what apps or online content is okay for people to access. There must also be more guarantees about user data protection and privacy. Perhaps this starts with putting all personal data on a decentralized database instead of iCloud. This is especially important if there is to be SSI, which cannot be held in an Apple-owned database.

If Web3 is to create an open Internet, Apple could keep its i-product bundles so long as they do not impede the user's free choice. Apple does not use their market position to mistreat others, so the market should decide between decentralized and centralized products and services. As decentralized versions of Apple Apps become cheaper, safer, ad-free, and more profitable for creators, Apple will no longer hold an advantageous position in software from centralization.

The issue of preloading is still tricky. Physical devices are the apex of Chapter 3's Internet hierarchy. If Apple can preload apps, then the rules would probably extend to the rest of FAAMG. This is a massive problem because no one with an Apple product bothers to download 3rd-party versions of Apple apps. Making preloading illegal comes at a huge cost to consumers because removing pre-downloaded apps makes devices complicated. Device preloading will continue to place barriers between users and Web3 unless FAAMG builds idealized services themselves.

Idealized Microsoft

We've seen throughout this book that Microsoft was always ahead of the curve with early Internet technologies. Thankfully, every anticompetitive move they made was halted by governments. Microsoft could have been a monopoly of all, but "cyber blockades" throughout the 1990s and 2000s gave room for the rest of FAAMG to create the Internet's oligopoly.

Now Microsoft is a jack of all trades, monopoly of none. It has a foothold in social networking with LinkedIn and GitHub. They have a diverse hardware line, but not one that could overshadow the many hardware giants. They have an independent operating system, app store, browser, and search engine, all of which are inferior in market share to the Google and Apple equivalents. Microsoft splits its earnings somewhat equally across these segments.

An idealized Microsoft follows the footsteps of the other idealized domain monopolies. Microsoft's LinkedIn and GitHub should decentralize their platform logic and data storage. Microsoft should add the supply chain solutions of an ideal Apple for their hardware lines. Their apps and software services should be converted to dapps and DAOs, but will more likely be replaced by them.

One area where Microsoft can boast superiority over FAAMG is in software-as-a-service (SaaS). We've all probably used Microsoft Office, Excel, and PowerPoint because they are the industry standards. They also have dozens of similar application-specific SaaS offerings. An idealized Microsoft would just make these services free and take them off the centralized Cloud, but this is not a viable shift for the company.

Nonetheless, Microsoft's SaaS position is harmless. It does not take control of other Internet services, and it doesn't keep customers captive. The only downside is the high expense. Free copycat versions of Microsoft SaaS are a dime a dozen in both centralized and decentralized forms. As soon as consumers are willing to make the free switch to a less common and less familiar alternative, they can.

The lessons embedded in Microsoft's history are invaluable. They are a demonstration of how the balance of powers shifted over the past 20 years. In the 2000s, Microsoft was nearly dismantled by the European and American governments for preloading Windows Media Player and Internet Explorer on devices. In 2020, FAAMG gets a slap on the wrist for supervising all political discourse.

Idealized Google

Google is a unique member of FAAMG because it is viewed most fondly by the public, but its tactics are just a more subtle version of FAAMG's least liked member, Facebook. Both companies' competitive advantages come from knowing more about you than competitors do and using that to filter the information you access.

Social media doesn't surprise us with these tactics. They are, in one sense, less dangerous because, well, we would at least hope people aren't doing serious research on Facebook. Conversely, Google Search is everyone's starting point for research. Who you are and where you are in the world determines the results you get with Google. The ripple effects of this are dizzying. Imagine how much bias from the Internet's search algorithms is reflected in this book, for example. (As a side note, I have only ever spent time on social media for inquiries relating to this book's topic—excluding a week-long fling with Facebook when I was fifteen years old—and use DuckDuckGo Search or academic databases for deep research.)

Creating an idealized Google starts with adding transparency to Google Search. All the algorithms should be made open source at first to revamp bias. This would extend to YouTube and all Google apps that decide what 3rd-party content consumers see. Whatever baseline set of algorithms are implemented would be controlled by a governance mechanism that decides on all later changes. Censorship and determining what are considered bad actors are all to be controlled by that governance mechanism.

Switching to transparent algorithms is possible for Google because it wouldn't interrupt its advertising revenue streams. Google AdWords, AdSense, and YouTube ads could work just the same to cover operational expenses. Since an independent community determines the algorithms, there wouldn't be any ad-driven ulterior motives. If they become greedy or annoying with advertising, it would provide the necessary nudge to get users to choose decentralized versions of Google services. This switch would increase Google's trust, which would grant them a better reputation, better standing with regulators, and more loyal users.

Google does have much to lose by making such a radical move. One thing is the competitive advantage it reaps from having top-secret algorithms. Another is the power it holds over the public by withholding the sole ability to censor and tweak search results at will. Perhaps the biggest downside for Google would be a worse overall user experience. If the algorithms for search and feed were made ethically, they would be far less addictive. We should consider this a worthwhile tradeoff.

Any idealized version of the remaining Google services would be ruinous to its monopolistic position. An ideal situation for Web3 would be a ban on Google preloading app bundles on 3rd-party devices, which would include no default browsers or search engines. This would not only ruin Google's market dominance but would damage hardware companies that rely on Google's Mobile Application Distribution Agreement (MADA). Consumers would also suffer significantly from the lost convenience of prepackaged apps.

The same tricky problem of app preloading is seen with Apple devices as well. They are not necessarily abusive, but they also don't give consumers a chance to decide what apps are best. There seems to be no way around the Internet hierarchy here. How can we get the masses to download a decentralized version of a dapp store if the Apple and Google app stores are already right on their screens?

A few fanciful ideas would get around the app preloading problem. In a perfect world, dapps would be so great that Samsung and other hardware giants would prefer to preload them instead of Google's bundle. The last and most unlikely possibility is Google decentralizing itself, but we'll entertain this idea to see what decentralized copycats of Google services look like.

Google has gotten rid of its cloud services and built its applications on a blockchain hosted by independent data centers. All these dapps have open-source codebases with no hidden logic. Those that make copycats fail to capture users because of Google's superior network effects. Google Maps cannot collect location data because users can see and control everything that happens to the data they generate. Google Play prioritizes dapps in the store by rules the people could see and change. Google Photos and Drive are cryptographically secured in a blockchain and accessible only by you and your blockchain identity. Google Pay is just a cryptocurrency wallet that has credentials only held by users. Chrome and Google Search operate with the same principles. The open-source code that creates these Internet services is mutable and under the control of a user-centric governance mechanism.

Google still preloads all these dapps with MADA so users still keep a feature-packed smartphone right out of the box. Google does not advertise on any of these dapps because they use a micropayment system to drive profits. Actions online could incur micropayment to support whatever work Google does for maintaining the apps—for example, one-tenth of a penny to send a Gmail—which also destroys the economics of spam as a side effect.

The default state of Google apps and services would prohibit the collection of user data. Since this hinders the user's experience, especially at the browser and search engine level, the user has toggles in settings for data collection permissions. Toggles are granular enough to describe exactly what is collected and what Google can use it for. Collected data is either transparent or placed in a data marketplace, depending on the type. In this way, private entities can buy data, and users that provided it get paid a portion of the proceeds.

Besides this being utterly antithetical to the purpose of Google, what's even more problematic is how little sense the idea of a corporation makes in this setting. An idealized Google does not need Alphabet Inc. (Google's parent company). All these idealized versions of FAAMG inadvertently mitigate or eliminate the need for a company.

Idealized Governance

Methods of governance have been error-prone and susceptible to severe abuses since their birth. Even though the world seems to have agreed on democracy as being the best style of government humans have developed, the democratic systems in place today are fundamentally similar and fall victim to the same flaws as ancient governments. The upcoming proposal for idealized digital governance is not a suggested replacement for governments but rather a system for making network decisions that affect a collective. It can apply anywhere that this criterion is met.

The beauty of digitizing governmental decision-making is increased transparency and information processing speed. The former is now possible thanks to blockchain technology. It is implied that the idealized governance mechanism of this section is built on blockchain infrastructure like what's described in Chapter 5. The latter, information processing, is already how all decisions are made. In all governments, leaders make decisions based on the information they independently receive and think about, just as they should. Conflict always arises when trying to coordinate all the independent decisions into a single coherent one. Whose votes count and for how much? How do we compile up the results into one coherent decision? The logistics involved with arriving at and enforcing answers to these questions is done best with computers.

When processing everyone's input for network decisions, there is a tremendous opportunity for including more voters and tweaking their influence based on any number of factors. The result is a maximally inclusive system of government that does not face logistical challenges.

Designing and encoding the logic for such a system is not any more straightforward than traditional methods; it is quite the opposite. Every design tweak in a governance mechanism comes with an equitable tradeoff, so there is no such thing as ideal governance. Every system of digital governance will uncover unanticipated flaws upon implementation. That is why each governance mechanism must itself be mutable through the same processes and rules it uses to change other network protocols.

The next sections represent one idea for a governance mechanism that solves Vili's paradox through Mode 3 governance (concepts from Chapter 5). Such a challenge deserves an entire technical whitepaper, but in an effort to keep things concise, the rationale for each design tradeoff will be kept to a minimum.

All the parameters and percentages are just suggestions that will most definitely require tweaks. These are just my ideas, and you should challenge and adjust them to create your own version of idealized governance. Hundreds of people will need to work on this concept's skeleton before a production-ready concept is created. The beauty of a suitable governance mechanism is that it can adapt according to the recommendations and contributions of its supporters.

One definite truth coming from the below design is the extreme lengths that must be taken to keep power decentralized. All the design intricacies that may seem excessive are essential tradeoffs that keep entities from gaming the system.

Distributed Intelligence

Governments have a tough time distributing power while maintaining order. Most government systems have to give a large majority of power to a minority elite to stay decisive. Democracy gets around this by distributing power to the masses, which introduces a new and ongoing problem: the average person is not qualified to make informed decisions about policy, nor do they have any reason to. Involving more people leads to more division and more deadlock than finalized decisions.

This oversimplification does not account for the different types of democracy, which come in roughly three forms: representative (the people elect leaders), participatory (the people can influence the decisions of leaders), and direct (the people vote for all decisions). Each type has its own set of problems: Representative democracy often degrades the distribution of power with a minority elite, participatory democracy is ambiguous and prone to logistical failures, and direct democracy leaves policy at the mercy of public opinion. An ideal governance mechanism combines elements of all three.

Distributed intelligence is what can combine the best elements of each without compromising. It does this by granting everyone the right to vote on every decision while giving more power to the informed experts in the given category of that decision. Digitizing this process gives everyone the ability to vote on policy like a direct democracy, easily coordinate with leaders for decisions like a participatory democracy, and choose expert leaders based on past decisions like a representative democracy.

Improvement Proposals and Incentives

A network governance process starts with an improvement proposal, which anyone could propose for a fee. Any number of methods could be used to keep only legitimate proposals, but the simplest is probably a council or board of elected members that check only for technical kinks. If a proposal for a protocol or algorithm change does what it intends to, it goes to a vote. Those with errors are blocked. Council members are not allowed to reject proposals for reasons outside of technical mistakes.

To account for bad councilmembers, anyone can report the misbehavior of a councilmember. A threshold for complaints, let's say 10, is cause for impeachment, which sends the case to the entire network for a vote. Other council members could also impeach them if they are not pulling their weight, and the rest of the network would carry out the final vote. Presumably, this would be an infrequent case because the council will be a team of engineers with little incentive to reject proposals. The rewards, election, and reputation of council members are details that could be ironed out on a case by case basis. If voting volume became too high, a consensus mechanism could randomly assign the votes for each proposal to a smaller fraction of the voter population, but for now we'll assume every voter votes on every proposal.

The council also checks the presentation and description of each proposal because voters will probably only view a brief description before voting. The underlying code will always be public, but most people will not look at it, so the council must ensure the description of the proposal's function is aligned with the code's actual function. We won't spend more time on this issue because the council is just a glorified network spam filter.

Once approved by the council, proposals are sent to the network for a vote that is completed inside of three days. A 60% majority vote is required to approve the change. Otherwise, it is denied and could be proposed again with adjustments.

Blockchain networks generally keep a rewards pool of tokens that accrue from transaction fees and token inflation. The governance mechanism pulls from this pool according to preset conditions to reward those who participate in the governance process.

Proposers are charged a fee that is not refunded if the improvement proposal is rejected. If the proposal is approved, the proposer receives a hefty reward. Council members are paid in tokens to hold their seats, and the number of seats is dynamic to meet the demand for the volume of proposals.

The largest expense for the token rewards pool will be actual voters, the real meat and potatoes of any governance mechanism.

Voting Power

Voters are the lifeblood of governance. Anyone could become a voter, and at a technical level, they are just cryptocurrency wallets with some extra functionality. Voters do not just get a single vote but get voting power based on several factors. Voting power is just a way of making a vote divisible so it could be used for different things.

Three factors will determine voting power: reputation score, stake, and lock-in time. Reputation score is not a popularity contest and will be explained in more detail later. Stake is the amount of value-bearing network tokens held by that voter. Lock-in time is how long the stake is mandated to be held in the voter's wallet. Larger stakes with longer lock-in times are favored because they encourage the decisions that are in the network's long-term interest.

The exact way voting power generation is divided between these factors is easy to code, but the mathematics don't translate well in writing, so we'll assume it's split three ways, with each factor having a linear relationship with voting power.

For each proposal, voting power will be split, approximately one-half going toward a direct vote on the proposal or "the sovereign vote," and approximately one-half being delegated to a chosen domain of experts or "the domain vote." Rewards are distributed in proportion to how much voting power is cast, so when voters miss a vote, they are not paid.

The sovereign vote could be delegated to any other voter or cast directly on a proposal. It does not affect voter reputation, but final decisions are broadcast to the network. Since proposals will probably occur daily, the popular course will be delegating this voting power to someone who is paying attention to proposals daily, in which case you would keep 80% of the rewards for delegated votes. The other 20% would go to the person who voted on your behalf.

The domain vote is used to pick a domain that decides where that voting power goes. The establishment and function of domains will be explained in a later section, but for now, they are just a group of chosen field-specific experts. This could be delegated under the same conditions as the sovereign vote. Domain vote impacts reputation score: If you vote for the cryptographer domain to decide on a social problem or vice versa, your network reputation will suffer as a result. Since this will be mostly easy decisions with a large impact on voters, it encourages these decisions to be made independently.

That is all the voters need to understand to get started. They should never have to care about how the rest works, but we will look under the hood at some of the crucial design decisions that keep voting power distributed.

Rationale

Most blockchain governance mechanisms stick to a popular vote and reward voters who voted with the majority. The design decision behind the sovereign vote intentionally detaches rewards from the vote cast. This is essential to keep a free election because without it, voters would guess what everyone believes to earn incentives rather than vote for what they believe. A design philosophy of governance should not penalize contrarians.

The ability to delegate sovereign votes is essential because it gives everyone a reason to participate in governance, even if they don't have time to track every proposal. Rewards received from using others' delegated voting power also give the enthusiastic network participant a reason to grow a following, stay up to date on project initiatives, and make the best decisions possible for those entrusting them with voting power. These votes do not directly impact reputation but are made public after the vote's completion to keep a historical record. This way, voters can ensure a voter's claims align with their actions before delegating them, which will become even more relevant when we discuss domain leaders.

A balanced system of governance cannot leave everything to a popular vote. There needs to a means for adding distributed intelligence into the equation. Domains add this element by temporarily giving disproportionately high amounts of voting power to experts in the category of a given proposal.

This works by putting the populace's domain votes in the hands of experts, so, in essence, your domain vote is a decision about what category a proposal should be in. Reputation will be improved if you voted with the majority and will be damaged if you didn't.

For example, suppose there is a proposal about a change in blockchain block size. There are two domains you might think are qualified to make the decision: one full of cryptographers and one full of sociologists. After some thought, you prefer that the sociologists make the decision because block size is partially about the broader implications of blockchain scalability, so you use your delegate vote to send voting power to that domain.

The proposal is probably more related to cryptography, and so the network voted 70% for the cryptographer domain and 30% for the sociologist domain. Your voting power still went to the sociologists, but your voter reputation decreased as a result of voting against the network. The damage to reputation would still be much worse if the vote were 99% in favor of the cryptographers because that would imply an obvious choice was avoided because of personal bias. If the vote were about determining misbehavior, it would probably flip to serve the sociologists more than the cryptographers. Reputation goes up proportionally when voting with the network on these types of issues.

Again, outlining these processes well is a problem for math, not words. It is more realistic that this process would have 10 or 20 domains, and voters would want to have picked the most popular ones. The idea is giving dynamic field-specific voter reputation. Representative democracy usually resorts to two-party systems even though either side is only right about half the time. A better idea has 20 parties, each cumulatively making about 1/20th of all the decisions. Building domains that are only called upon for relevant decisions is approaching that ideal.

Domain Anatomy

"Domain" is a fictitious word meaning a conglomerate of field-specific expert voters in cyberspace. If domains had to be compared to an existing concept, they might be thought of as digitized political parties.

Any voter can create a domain or join an existing one. The tradeoff is that it completely removes their domain voting rights, so they are reduced to half their original voting power. These domains have a relatively simple existence: they have a title, brief description, and members.

The incentive for joining a domain is the potential to get more voting power, which equals a larger stake and a larger reward. The domain puts delegated voting power into a pool for each proposal. Each domain leader owns a piece of this pool. Proportions of ownership of the pool are decided by the members, each voting for other members inside that domain. Let's call this pool *voting power*, which can be thought of as being swapped with domain voting power when becoming a part of a domain.

Every domain leader has an equal proportion of pool voting power. They cannot vote for themselves, and they do not earn rewards for using it. When joining a domain, voters must allocate all this pool ownership power to others in whatever proportions they like. Each member owns the amount of the pool that has been decided by other members. Whenever a domain leader casts a vote, they redirect their part of the pool's voting power.

There is, of course, a sweet spot to be found here as a voter. If you create or join a small domain that no one delegates voting power to, you just threw away domain voting power for no reason. If you join a domain with a massive voting pool, you might not have the support to get noticed, and if no domain leader allocates their pool voting power to you, then you don't earn any rewards for voting in that domain because you won't own part of the pool. The goal is to have researchers, PhDs, and enthusiasts connecting proof of their expertise and values through connected social accounts.

Becoming a popular domain leader is a great way to get otherwise unobtained voting power and earn greater rewards. They vote just as they would any other voter except there is no ability to delegate, so missing a vote is lost voting power that would be subsumed by the rest of the domain members that did vote.

There can be a reputation score for domain leaders but a purely social one for voting records that does not impact voting power. The incentive here is that everyone has a vested interest in making good decisions because they care about their domain's reputation. They could also see the impacts that they themselves make. This differs from traditional voting methods, where participants never know their impact.

Striking a Balance

The balance between domain voting power and sovereign voting power can be struck by equalizing incentives—that is, the rewards pool gives an equal amount of rewards to each. If too many people become domain leaders, there will be a higher percentage of sovereign voting power with far fewer people. It works both ways where sovereign votes will always control more than 50% (assuming that everyone casts their sovereign votes), but if that goes above 60% or 70% from an influx of domain leaders, it becomes less profitable to do so because there is less domain voting power to go around. This incentivizes a constant balance between the number of domain leaders and the number of regular voter participants.

Once keeping a roughly 55/45 balance of the entire network's sovereign/domain voting power, there is still a risk of monopolizing voting power within each type, which calls for some constraints.

Since any amount of sovereign voting power could be delegated to anyone, each voter has a 5% cap on the amount of voting power assigned to them. This means once 5% of all the sovereign voting power or 2.5–3% of the total voting power is delegated to a single person, their wallet will be locked so no one else could delegate to them. This keeps the sovereign voting power distributed.

Keeping power distributed around and within domains is slightly more involved. The risk here is one domain becoming so powerful because everyone is motivated to vote for the most popular one. If there were two domains, one liberal and one conservative, they would each get half the voting power each time and recreate the two-party system that desperately needs reform.

Fixing large domains requires a cap on their voting power over a specified time interval. We would opt for a 20% maximum of the total domain voting power during each one-week period (calculated based on the last week's total voting power). So if a bunch of proposals came out on the first day of the week and everyone's domain votes went to one domain, that domain would not be locked, and voters would not be able to vote for it until the end of the week.

In this way, no domain pool becomes too powerful, and it leaves room for multiple domains to flourish. Even though there can be an infinite number of domains, there will probably only be 10 or 20 popular ones. This is a manageable amount for voters to keep track of while being sufficiently decentralized.

Domain themselves are at risk of being monopolized by one popular leader. Preventing this is done in the same way. Domain leaders can only own a maximum of 20% of the domain pool. This not only keeps power distributed but leaves room for multiple domain leaders to be noticed. This rule can only apply to popular domains that have a large amount of voting power. Small domains will be exempt from this rule until they have a certain amount of voting power.

To demonstrate these rules in action, we'll walk through how a voter can max out their overall voting power. First, a voter must obtain sovereign voting power, either with a high reputation, stake, and lock in time, or having others delegate their sovereign votes to them until they hit 5% of the total supply of sovereign voting power or 2.5-3% of the total voting power. Then they must join the largest domain, which is one that has 20% of the total domain voting power. With enough other domain leaders delegating pooled voting power to them, they can earn up to 20% of that domain's pool. This gives them a total of 4% of all the domain voting power. In total, this voter has a maximum total of 6.5% of all the voting power. As unforeseen power imbalances or general problems appear, new or adjusted parameters can be made accordingly through the proposal process.

Computing Results

Any change to the network could be made through this proposed governance system. Let's do a full walkthrough of the process as if it were used to accept or deny Bitcoin Improvement Proposals (BIPs).

You write a proposal for the long-debated bitcoin block size debate. It includes the code that would change as a result of an approved proposal and a description. The current block size of 1MB is too small to handle the data capacity and must be increased to prevent backlogged transactions. The BIP first goes to council members for review. If legitimate, the proposal moves to the rest of the network for the voting process.

Participants receive the proposal on a dapp with the option to approve, deny, or delegate for sovereign votes. For the domain voting power, participants receive all the options for which domain to delegate to. They will have three days to act on this.

Domain leaders receive the proposal with the option to approve or deny it and also cast their votes inside of three days. Since this is a complex and technical proposal, voters are most likely to delegate their voting power to bitcoin developers and a technology-focused domain.

At the end of the three days, the BIP is approved or denied according to how the most voting power was allocated. The appeal process is done simply by making another proposal.

The result is a simple yes or no, depending on where more voting power ends up at the end of the three days. It is accepted as the best decision because it uses multifactorial consensus, or inputs from many disparate sources to compute a result.

The block size debate is used as an example to demonstrate the need for governance. Right now, opposing views on the issue forced the network to hard fork, or split into other versions of Bitcoin because the nodes won't agree on a solution. This method of governance can apply to all networks to keep them united.

Future Integrations

Idealized governance is going to involve many people and lots of resources. Therefore, only essential decisions about large infrastructures will use it. The many smaller blockchains applications that build on those infrastructures will need their own governance. Polkadot and Dfinity work this way, having very complex infrastructures ruled by a governance mechanism, but the parachains and subnetworks that people will build on them need their own small-scale governance.

In Polkadot and Dfinity, applications built on top of them can create their own governance mechanisms that play by the rules of the "meta-governance" mechanism. The trend will move toward this, with many applications that need governance being able to customize their own model. If a decentralized Uber is built on Dfinity, a simple voting system of stakeholders can decide how to set prices, how much to pay drivers, etc. Having good meta-governance allows the people that build applications like a decentralized Uber to rest assured that their apps infrastructure can't be controlled or manipulated by anyone.

Chapter 5 mentioned a proposal for AI integration with governance. As AI gets better at quantifying the long-term impact of proposals on the network, it can be used to influence voter reputation. Those that voted against the crowd but turned out to be right could be rewarded for this. It remains to be seen how AI could do this, but in any case, the Artificial Neural Network responsible for this would have to have to be open and have its logic also under the control of that governance mechanism. When using reputation scores, users should withhold the right to be anonymous.

Idealized governance is still far off. We still have a very archaic way of governing that makes this complex governance strategy entirely inaccessible for current power structures. That is why this movement must start with decentralized networks' success. People can then become interested in creating something radical like dynamic hierarchies because they are most conducive to their Internet services. Only after the coordination required to put this in place finally works, then evidence of its benefits will become undeniable. Once a solid foundation is laid for decentralized network governance, the places where it remains applicable to corporate and national systems of government will only grow.

Idealized Money

People will always decide on what they assign value to, and blockchain should not change that. Whether it be debt-backed fiat, bitcoin, gold coins, equity in the form of stock, raw commodities, or monopoly money, whatever people put their faith in could work. Blockchain's job is only to make trustworthy digital representations of money, regardless of type. The bonus feature of trustworthy digital money is its ability to be completely transparent or completely private, depending on need.

The 2010 Haiti earthquake was a devastating event that highlights an uncommonly mentioned shortcoming of today's digital money. Supposedly, about half a billion dollars of United States relief funding disappeared from the

American Red Cross and is alleged to appear as expenses in the Clinton Foundation.[586] Let me be clear in saying I have no clue which parts of this statement are real and not. This is just something that has been recycled on the legacy media and blogs thousands of times, seemingly without an origin. Perhaps that's the problem.

There's no reason that in 2020 public entities shouldn't be publicly tracking their finances. Cryptocurrency provides that as a default, but with anonymous addresses instead of known entities. If entities such as the American Red Cross and its subdivisions attached their identities to cryptocurrency wallet addresses, the confusion around tracking money would be gone instantly. People who donated money to the American Red Cross could follow its entire history and see where the money ended up. The question of how much money went to employee salaries versus Haitian victims would have a definitive answer.

Of course, cryptocurrency is not an ideal form of money right now because it is not as stable or widely accepted as fiat currency. One popular concept that has not yet been adopted is a Central Bank Digital Currency (CBDC) or a government-backed and centralized blockchain-based token.[587] This could add transparency in certain areas where it can be useful: For example, government stimulus money could be distributed more efficiently and must be spent by a specific date to encourage economic growth best. Tax dollars could and should be transparent in how they are spent to a point as well. Imagine you could follow the lifecycle of a dollar that was taken out of your paycheck. It would surely push governments to be more careful with spending.

Ideally, governance processes would take part in this too. CBDC could apply to taxes by using a system of voting on how that money gets spent. This would make taxation more like a democratic process than thievery. Every tax dollar would have its lifecycle traceable down to the department it landed in and what expense it was used for. All the measures of inflation and total/circulating supply could be public, which would make things like the wealth gap, national debt, and inflation from lending a whole lot less enigmatic.

Since any CBDC would be centralized, it could have some of blockchain's fancy database features, but none of them would be enforceable. If revealing a currency's total supply or the way taxes got spent was not in the interest of a government, centralized blockchains could not guarantee transparency as a feature. Decentralized blockchains and cryptocurrencies are of paramount importance because they cannot have those wonderful features removed.

Ideally, a CBDC would use a decentralized architecture and governance mechanism, but that is impossible to achieve without undermining the power of governments. The only way around this by using nongovernmental cryptocurrencies for things that necessitate transparency.

One practical version of idealized money merely is as Internet money. Right now, cryptocurrencies are confusing and fueled mostly by investors that plan on cashing out into fiat currencies. If Web3 succeeds in decentralizing the Internet, then governments will lose jurisdiction there, and people will opt for the method of value transfer that is native to the networks they use. It would become a seamless part of the user experience. Cryptocurrencies and government currencies should have no trouble coexisting like this.

Contagion Effects

All the idealized examples we've seen in this chapter were described in the context of existing companies and governments. The Web3 world doesn't recognize these as appropriate comparisons because it is predicated on the development of new architecture independent of companies and governments. Although this is true, legacy entities will not disappear, nor will they remain untouched by a global movement toward decentralization. Suggesting that economies should start anew and disregard all existing power structures is damaging to the blockchain space. Instead, this topic should be an area where fundamentalists from both centralized and decentralized spheres are eager to find areas of compromise.

The utility of getting large entities turned on to blockchain solutions is straightforward. If Facebook and Google started seeking ways to decentralize their logic, tech companies would follow in their footsteps as they always have. If Apple started making traceable iPhones and MacBooks, other hardware companies would be forced to do the same to stay competitive. If Amazon made all its online services into dapps and DAOs, it would gain a higher market share on account of increased trust. If the American Red Cross started publicly tracking all its expenses, the charity would attract more donors. If America implemented a voting and tracking system for all tax dollars, we would be praised on the world stage and other countries would follow. Maybe the most effective catalyst for global decentralization starts with its largest entities.

Conversely, if smaller entities reap the benefits of decentralization first, it will only serve as a threat to the larger ones. If Samsung decided to preload dapps onto phones instead of Google's bundle and marketed it as the first line of blockchain-based devices, it would rattle the whole FAAMG oligopoly. A social media startup implementing transparent logic, private storage, and a tokenomics model that rewards users would finally have enough reason to get Facebook users to switch.

I don't anticipate that many companies will be eager to decentralize themselves because those changes are expensive and can't promise significant returns. Right now, it is only a unique class of unproven startups working on these possibilities. That and the relatively high complexity of decentralized systems is making adoption slow. As the blockchain space grows, it should be viewed not only as an isolated revolution but also as a way to motivate the spread of decentralized tools to already mainstream technologies.

Before that can happen, Web3 needs to start delivering on its many promises. Of the thousands of blockchain startups, it's likely only a select few become mainstream. We are at a point in blockchain's evolution, where it is no longer constructive to tout the endless use cases for the technology. The wild experimentation phase is coming to an end. Thought leaders have seen the many experiments' results and now must pick the best decentralized building blocks for the Internet's trust layer.

CHAPTER 10

THE INTERNET COMPUTER

Last chapter's idealized Web3 versions of FAAMG are entirely hypothetical. Evidence of the fact that Web3 is perhaps a failed pipedream is in all the ways Big Tech nonetheless continues to prosper.

Most of the solutions mentioned throughout this book are about specific blockchains doing certain interesting things, but none of those have seen mass adoption. That's because each of those flashy use cases are more like puzzle pieces, with the completed puzzle being a blockchain-like Internet, one that is decentralized, trustworthy, secure by default, private for the individual, and transparent for the collective. The individual pieces are virtually useless without the whole puzzle, but no one has put them together.

Modern blockchains that upgrade speed, scalability, governance, and simplicity from previous generations are essential puzzle pieces, but interoperability is the glue needed to hold the puzzle together. None solve the problem of connecting disparate blockchains, and maybe no one ever will.

This book spent a lot of time covering Web3 but always with blockchain as the conceptual model. Chapter 1 outlined the Web3 vision as blockchain technology replacing the cloud, followed by decentralized developer tools using that infrastructure to replace FAAMG. This book, just like all the literature for all the use cases, uses blockchain as a conceptual model through which to view the decentralized computing revolution. The trouble is that the fancy data structure has almost nothing to do with the trustworthy and decentralized network computations.

The Crypto Puzzle Piece

The crypto world is so tethered to the idea of data-centric blockchains that it is beginning to look more like an attempt to preserve tradition instead of a paradigm shift. Real blockchains have inherent limitations that the blockchain maximalists are trying to overcome by mixing and matching all different standards with a structure archaic enough to be still considered blockchain technology.

This book has advocated taking on the FAAMG oligopoly, and such an undertaking leaves little room for error. In 2009, a chain of blocks happened to be the best structural choice for cryptographers to make a decentralized and independent currency system. There's no rule saying that a chain of blocks is the best way to build a decentralized and independent Internet in 2021. The evidence today seems to indicate that blockchains are having the opposite of their intended effect.

Flipside Crypto is a data science company that studies the inner workings of cryptocurrency projects and their blockchains to extract raw truths about their operations. The company sums up its findings with a good rule of thumb called the 0.1%–0.9%–99% rule of blockchains: About 0.1% of blockchains hold true to Satoshi's vision by being fully liberated decentralized networks, 0.9% of blockchains are still trying to reach this ideal, and 99% of blockchains inevitably become like businesses, having employees, revenue, and investors to report to.[588]

Cryptocurrency startups often recreate the environments they were originally dead set on getting away from. Furthermore, these ventures go uncriticized because they are done under the flag of the now meaningless word *blockchain*. The road to decentralization is paved with hypocrisy.

I sometimes wonder what all the antiestablishment computer geeks would be doing today if Bitcoin was never invented. There would be far fewer people involved because the lack of money would have always kept the movement from being exciting. But I also bet there would be a lot less misinformation surrounding these systems. Most people wouldn't care, but those who did would probably just think of decentralized networks as collections of advanced computer science tools and cryptographic protocols.

Blockchain is no longer about chains of blocks. If Big Tech companies want to act as though they are progressive, they could just sprinkle in some private blockchains and centralized cryptos into their services, which might appear genuine but would only accentuate the problem of Internet monopolization. Blockchain is about decentralization, transparency, privacy, openness, and trust in computer systems. Who cares what structure we use to get these characteristics? Maybe blockchain supporters should swallow their pride when something non-blockchain comes along that can offer those same characteristics.

It is still wonderful that Bitcoin's blockchain captured the world's attention. Extracting the value decentralized systems have to offer is so challenging that it needs a coordinated global effort to fix or replace Big Tech. It doesn't look like many projects are succeeding in decentralizing the Internet, but there are a few on the right track. This chapter will focus on the few technologies that exist as fundamental parts of a Web3 legitimate enough to compete on Big Tech's turf.

Evolution of Protocols

Chapter 1 discussed OSI and TCP/IP, the two competing protocol standards for what would become known as the Internet. The story of how they came to make the Internet is very telling of blockchain's trajectory.

OSI was the obvious choice in the early 1980s. It remained intensely committed to openness and completeness but was complicated and clunky. Only corporate endeavors were sophisticated enough to make OSI networks, and their full customizability made each network design unique to match the many different use cases.

These "open" networks turned out to be very exclusive. Their complexity made them unusable outside of the company that made it. Their uniqueness made connecting to other systems difficult. Having a completely open set of network building blocks was nice in theory but wasn't mature enough to be accessible to the masses.

TCP/IP is a simpler load-it-and-go type of stack that anyone can use. It is the model of how computers transfer data, and even today you will only hear about OSI when learning how TCP/IP managed to simplify it. Now all other Internet services make their building blocks or less fundamental protocols on top of IP.

While OSI tried to give everyone network building blocks, TCP/IP left room for the market to decide what prearranged building blocks everyone would use. These can now be roughly summarized as FAAMG's developer tools.

In the OSI and TCP/IP race, but also more generally in everything that has to do with networks, you will find this common theme: The benefits of open and decentralized systems come at the cost of much higher complexity.

Today's blockchains are like OSI: super-complicated with fancy new concepts and lingo that boast a commitment to openness and completeness. Their engineers are always excited to share all the technological feats that make their protocol different. New consensus mechanisms, block arrangements, and other loopholes that make computers do cool things together are forcibly shared with any potential supporters that will listen. Both OSI and Web3 infrastructures failed to tailor themselves toward layman users.

All this boils down to blockchain not being able to compete at the same level as FAAMG, which crypto enthusiasts tend to think is okay, but if the space can't be made free and simple like the legacy Internet, then what's the point of all this?

The science fiction author Arthur C. Clarke said, "Any sufficiently advanced technology is indistinguishable from magic." I would take this quote further by saying that, for any sufficiently advanced technology to reach mass adoption, it must be indistinguishable from magic. OSI was not magical because anyone who wanted to build with it needed to learn how it worked. TCP/IP is closer to being magic to us because it works even after removing many of OSI's layers and most web developers have no idea how. In the early 2000s, building a network required some knowledge of TCP/IP, but today's proprietary platforms fill all the gaps. Using or building on the Internet today is basically magic. You can do anything on the Internet with only the knowledge of how to use FAAMG services, yet no one has a clue about how FAAMG works. FAAMG services are basically magic.

Blockchain does not seem like magic at all to the casual observer. Cryptocurrencies have long numerical keys that cannot be lost, are accessible mostly through sketchy websites, are confusing and risky to transact without prior knowledge, and offer no utility for newcomers outside of speculative investment opportunities. The only ones who join this movement are those interested in technology.

Blockchain technologies need to appear more like magic. Users should have their identities verified without login credentials and never know how it works. Cryptocurrency wallets should appear safer and simpler than bank accounts to everybody, not just cryptographers. Using blockchain in businesses (or to make a business) should work just like it does with any other Software-as-a-Service. There should only be a select few ample options for blockchain identities, wallets, and software services, so everyone knows their choices, not thousands of copycat projects that makes picking one a distressing choice for users.

The need is for another fundamental protocol. This differs from Chapter 1's Web3, which sat on blockchain. Web3 would be everything on the Internet that goes through the protocol(s). Although the word "protocol" could be considered as ambiguous as "blockchain," since there will not be one blockchain for Web3 or one way to connect all the blockchains, "protocol" is the most appropriate term for the topic.

But what exactly is a protocol? Well, it might be thought of as rules for how computers can interact. The fundamental ones should make systems work where applicable without users ever knowing of their existence. The future of blockchain and Web3 hinges on the arbitrary few projects that can make such a protocol.

Blockchain Hubs

One problem with blockchain technology is the current paradigm of creating a new blockchain for every entrepreneurial idea without any emphasis on compatibility. Building applications with those very many incompatible blockchains is a repeat of OSI's mistake. A protocol that solves blockchain interoperability is the magic fix that this space desperately needs.

For an interoperability protocol to be worthwhile on a platform of blockchains, it must already be extremely secure, somewhat committed to decentralization, fast, capable of scaling, and able to support applications as ambitious as FAAMG's. Throughout the book, we've seen blockchains with all these abilities but none that also fix interoperability. For this reason, we'll now focus mainly on the interoperability aspect of two projects that are trying to combine every characteristic a blockchain should have.

Cosmos and Polkadot are the two largest blockchain projects currently tackling the interoperability problem. These are both fantastically advanced blockchain infrastructures that can be used to code blockchain versions of FAAMG services right now. Still, this chapter focuses only on how they might conjoin the whole blockchain and cryptocurrency world. The hub approach makes blockchains specifically designed to connect other blockchains. A hub in the context of this section is one of these blockchains.

Cosmos

The Interchain Foundation's Cosmos is a blockchain infrastructure platform that tries to make it simple for individuals or businesses to build customized blockchains. These range from fully private to fully public and use prepackaged bundles of code that are plug-and-play modules for various blockchain features. Like many of the top blockchain infrastructures, the goal is to allow developers and entrepreneurs to focus on their application logic while all the magic blockchain stuff gets taken care of automatically. But none of this is particularly unique to Cosmos. The much grander goal is for its Inter-Blockchain Communication Protocol (IBC) to connect all blockchains, Cosmos-built or otherwise.

Cosmos-specific chains can, for all intents and purposes, interoperate. Cosmos is also nowhere close to being the standard place everyone builds blockchains. That's where IBC comes in. Theoretically, any blockchain that is sovereign and has fast finality can be compatible with IBC.[589]

It works by using hubs, or specialized blockchains, that relay coded logic and cryptographic proofs of interactions between chains. Eventually, this will yield what Cosmos calls the Internet of Blockchains. It sounds like the perfect fix for interoperability, but like any protocol that claims to fix any buzzword, it is not without its caveats.

IBC is not a single, neat protocol that works for all blockchains at once. It instead pulls fancy cryptography tricks to jury-rig connections between disparate blockchains, which can only be done one blockchain at a time. It is also still in the early development phases and has yet to be used publicly. The first allegedly successful implementation occurred with the cryptocurrency Zcash, a privacy token that should soon work on Cosmos blockchains.

Zcash (ZEC) makes for a good example of how this would work. If 10 ZEC were transferred to Cosmos, no ZEC would exist on Cosmos. Instead, IBC would create a cryptographic proof or promise that the Zcash blockchain froze those 10 ZEC, and a new cryptocurrency that represents those 10 ZEC would be minted for use on Cosmos.[590]

There are a few problems with this approach. Detaching assets from their native blockchains opens the door to more unanswered questions. It is becoming commonplace in DeFi to make digital representations of other cryptocurrencies, most notably with wrapped Bitcoin and Ethereum. This allows representations of Bitcoin and Ethereum transactions to occur on other blockchains but degrades the utility of the real blockchains. If ZEC can be used on Cosmos blockchains, what is the point of the Zcash blockchain?

The more technical concerns come along with more chains being added to this mix. If IBC connected Litecoin and Zcash, and ZEC representations started spawning on the Litecoin blockchain, the ZEC's security now depends on the Zcash blockchain, the Cosmos hub, the Litecoin blockchain, and all connecting protocols. If one of those components fails, so do all the others.

More IBC connection means more complexity for developers and users. The interoperability use case starts with cryptocurrencies but replicating a representation of smart contract logic on multiple chains is even more convoluted. The essential function of interoperability is scaling applications seamlessly across different blockchain platforms. Although it is theoretically possible with IBC, even given years of grueling development, it will never produce the desired simplicity of Web3's vision.

In terms of pure building blocks for simple blockchains, Cosmos is on par with other leading platforms. Intra-blockchain interoperability of the Cosmos ecosystem is still great. The problem is that not every blockchain is going to run on Cosmos.

To its credit, Cosmos has the highest commitment to openness and inclusiveness of all the Interoperability solutions in this chapter. Anyone can build on Cosmos. Any blockchain that connects to IBC can be completely sovereign, handling its own consensus and governance. Modules and tools used to build Cosmos blockchains are available to everyone, and community members can make more tools that anyone can use. IBC does not force commitments or restrictions relating to Cosmos-specific blockchains. There will always be significant utility in the Cosmos ecosystem, even if it can't marry the whole blockchain world.

The Internet of Blockchains vision is a wonderful one, but there is not nearly enough evidence to suggest that it is practical. Incessant commitment to openness and decentralization is what makes the ideal IBC protocol almost impossible.

Polkadot

The Web3 Foundation's Polkadot is a blockchain infrastructure platform. Ethereum co-founder Gavin Wood created it to address the scalability and interoperability challenges of current blockchains. It starts with one blockchain that has consensus and governance mechanisms called the *relay chain*. It is like a hub in that it connects many blockchains, but it does so differently from Cosmos hubs. From that relay chain, people can build their own blockchains that share its security in what the network calls parachains. Polkadot can currently host about 100 parachains, but future generations will allow parachains to become relay chains, essentially allowing the network to host an infinite number of blockchains. Each parachain can be built by anyone that reserves a slot and benefits from functionality as expansive as Ethereum's blockchain but with full interoperability with all other parachains through the relay chain. That's Polkadot in a nutshell.

Interoperability within parachains is relatively seamless. They are quite literally parallelizable chains because the actual blockchain-centric part of them is shared with all the other parachains via the relay chain.[591] Being made of the same stuff, message passing and smart contract execution propagate results through multiple chains. No more cryptographic locks that detach and replicate coded logic from one chain to the next.

The one caveat is that as the network grows, it is not known how secure and simple interoperability will be. Messages pass from parachain to parachain through a relay chain. As parachains become relay chains, a tree-like structure will form. Depending on where two interacting parachains are in that structure will determine how many different chains messages must pass through. Polkadot has not created any 2nd-order relay chains at the time of this writing, which leaves some unanswered questions about a future with thousands of Polkadot parachains: Will the main relay chain be able to handle all these requests? How can parachains trust the security of multiple 2nd-order relay chains for their transactions? On what chain is the official transaction timestamp generated? How does this complicate things for users and developers? Luckily, the need to answers these questions is still a long way off for the Polkadot project.

Interoperability between Polkadot and other blockchains is even more distant. The plan is to make "bridges" to other large blockchains such as Bitcoin and Ethereum. There are a few proposals for making these bridges,[592] but we have no idea how those details will change as a finished product develops or how long it will take. Many projects are trying to create some interoperability that resembles bridges, but few seem hopeful at this point. Polkadot's early goal of supporting Ethereum interoperability kept design philosophies aligned with Ethereum's own, so if anyone is in the right position to be making Ethereum bridges, it's Polkadot.

Interoperability between Polkadot and legacy systems is not particularly unique. One criticism of even the best Web3 platforms is that generic Internet services, including most of FAAMG's, have no need for a traditional blockchain. Eventually, Polkadot blockchains will look like any other website or application and will use whatever Oracle standard exists when transferring data from blockchain to non-blockchain worlds.

Polkadot is not attempting to take on Big Tech because its network-maintaining nodes run on the cloud. It's not clear where all nodes are, but the standard approach for participating in the Polkadot Network is setting up with a virtual private server (not your hardware), which carries the threat of centralization,[593] and in some cases, uses Big Tech's Cloud (Microsoft Azure).[594] This is the antithesis of the Web3 goal because it not only gives FAAMG the ability to attack Polkadot but grows Big Tech's profits and power as the network adds thousands of cloud-based parachains.

Polkadot is an innovative step for the blockchain world. Its scalability, simplicity, usability, functionality, and popularity surpass Cosmo's in most respects. It is a completely open-source project, but that doesn't make it open per se. Polkadot was intentionally created to be less open by design than Cosmos because it limits interoperability to non-sovereign blockchains.[595] If you want to build a parachain, you cannot pick your own consensus mechanism or customize blockchain features that don't work on Polkadot's network. Parachains are forced to share the security of the one relay chain and pay for that security. To be IBC compatible, you can make a blockchain by whatever rules and security measures you want. IBC is also theoretically capable of connecting to Polkadot, and Polkadot has pledged support for IBC, but a productive connection between the two is still science fiction.

Polkadot secures its relay chain in a decentralized way, but it is still one chain that rules and charges all other parachains. In that respect, it is centralized to make interoperable and straightforward blockchains a reality.

The Lost Promise of Interoperability

Many more notable projects focus on interoperability that won't fit in this chapter, namely Interledger, Cardano, and ICON. The DeFi world also is working on a bunch of neat interoperability tricks to make crypto payments/transactions work anywhere. Still, none are a radical shift from what we've seen in Web3 solutions. Another increasingly popular option is 2nd-layer protocols: Putting a little bit of an application's logic on a blockchain and keeping the rest on traditional infrastructure. This manages to work around the limitations of current blockchains but is just kicking the can down the road when it comes to the goal of decreasing FAAMG's influence. To the best of my knowledge, no existing proposal has a groundbreaking way to connect all blockchains and probably never will.

Innovations in information and communications technology always faced this problem. You can draw plenty of parallels between the blockchain and Web2 worlds, for example. Facebook is entirely "interoperable" with itself because you can view and interact with any other Facebook page. Facebook is kind of interoperable with other platforms because you can post a Facebook link on LinkedIn and vice versa, find Facebook via Google Search, and interoperate with other applications according to the rules of Facebook's APIs.

The Internet is made of big platforms that use fancy tools to interoperate where needed. So even though we don't think of today's Internet as lacking interoperability, it does every bit as much as some theoretical Internet of blockchains. It's just that decentralized systems are always more complex than centralized ones, and so must be their interoperability solutions.

Conventional system interoperability appears seamless on the Internet because only a few companies control such systems. Most of this supposed interoperability is really just intra-platform compatibility. If everyone were using thousands of different app stores, browsers, email accounts, search engines, and streaming services, the Internet would be a burdensome place to do anything you normally do. Web3 works the same way and will have to follow the same trend as the legacy Web by selecting only a few big winners.

Some might resist the notion that only a few infrastructure platforms can succeed in Web3. Chapter 3 showed how this is a natural and inevitable progression that follows the Pareto distribution. The more important and beautiful thing about this time around is that the winners can, for the first time, be unowned. It could be like if FAAMG was owned and managed by its hundreds of millions of users and existed only to benefit those users. Web3 would be better off if those resisting the rise of a few winners switched their efforts toward ensuring the winners uphold decentralization as a core value.

Composability Instead of Interoperability

Web3 either needs a protocol that connects blockchains or one blockchain-related protocol that everyone agrees to use. The former doesn't seem to be working, especially if we are talking about all blockchains rather than a select few. The latter comes at the cost of being limited to the features and functionality of one protocol. Composability is the design philosophy of providing the most building blocks for creating systems while staying in one interoperable ecosystem. This is the goal of Polkadot, but if composability is the trend of Web3, then the one biggest project will win, which brings us to Ethereum.

Ethereum has done more blockchain, token, and decentralized application development than any other project. With Ethereum having the lion's share of users and developers, building elsewhere leaves you somewhat alienated from the largest decentralized ecosystem around. Minus a few logistical kinks, Ethereum has more features and functionality than anyone. Ethereum's vision is to be a world computer, so can it alone build Web3?

It may be too early to tell. The Ethereum blockchain is still very inefficient. Even the simplest of transactions can cost up to a few dollars in fees.

Computation for using any decentralized application is expensive. Ethereum doesn't scale well because every transaction is replicated across all nodes. This is a massive problem because the bigger it gets, the slower the network becomes. Poor scalability was typical for all blockchains when Ethereum was first developed because the standard approach prioritized unparalleled security through inefficient means.

It is also extremely difficult to code securely on the Ethereum blockchain, and code bugs can be multi-million-dollar mistakes. Stanford professor Dan Boneh demonstrates this perfectly as every one of his classes' final exams includes a program written in Ethereum's solidity language. Students are asked to find the five errors, and every year students collectively find ten.[596] Ethereum today is also not the perfect picture of security. Security limitations are not unique to Ethereum, but if they are to be the one project Web3 is dependent on, there needs to be even higher security, which includes resistance against quantum computers.

So Ethereum still needs serious fixing, but the project can now pick from all the very best solutions that have been discovered since its inception. Ethereum 2.0 is the next evolution of the network and is planned to increase simplicity, security (quantum resistance), participation (moving off the cloud and onto home computers), speed, and performance.[597] It may be what the blockchain world has been waiting for and will take at least until 2022 for the public launch.

Ethereum 2.0 will come in three stages: the Beacon Chain, shard chains, and docking.[598] The Beacon Chain moves consensus from Proof of Work to Proof of Stake, which is markedly more efficient and scalable. Sharding will break the Ethereum blockchain into 64 separate but interconnected blockchains that are called *shards*. This is done to split the database portion of the blockchain to make participation require less data storage, but this does not split code execution, which will in all likelihood still occur on the current Ethereum blockchain that in turn will become one of 64 shards.[599]

The Beacon Chain is essential to all the shards because it coordinates interactions and chooses shard validators with a verifiable random function.[600] This randomness is essential for securing Proof of Stake consensus because it will make it extraordinarily unlikely for a collusion attack to happen on a shard if no one can predict who will validate what shard. The Ethereum everyone uses today will not see any of these changes until the docking phase, where the Ethereum main net connects to the Beacon Chain and becomes one of 64 shards.

There's still tremendous uncertainty surrounding Ethereum 2.0. Everyone has an opinion, but there is no agreement about how well this will work, how long it will take to implement, and depending on whom you ask, what the plan's details even are. There is still no known way to scale computation, which will remain unchanged by shard chains.

There are basically two schools of thought on this. One says the whole blockchain space is built around Ethereum, and some of the smartest people in the world are committed to making it work. As time passes, there will be more innovation than anywhere else because it has the highest composability and the longest history. No one can compete with this.

The other says that Ethereum is a historically significant technology that is not capable of evolving. It's like starting a digital revolution with a subpar foundation that everyone compensates for by building innovative fragments. The challenge now is piecing all those fragments back together to fit with an ever-changing core. Dependance on any single blockchain regardless of circumstances is also problematic because that blockchain becomes a single point of failure for Web3.

Ethereum is exceptionally committed to openness and decentralization, but ironically that's what decreases its availability. Yes, anyone can build on Ethereum, but it is not cheap or simple. Developers also must give up so much by moving to a smaller blockchain infrastructure platform.

None of the platforms of this chapter can be considered a fundamental protocol that brings blockchain-level trust to everything on the Internet. This book should produce at least one practical version of this that isn't purely theoretical and doesn't have deal-breaking tradeoffs. I have only found one that can elevate the blockchain world to the level of Big Tech.

DFINITY and the Internet Computer

(Disclaimer: DFINITY has a bigger part in this chapter than what should correspond to its size and popularity. In essence, I am speculating that its solution is the best available for fusing blockchain's principles with the legacy Internet and taking on Big Tech. I am biased in the sense that I spent far longer researching DFINITY than other projects and am an active community member. I have no affiliation with and have never received any form of compensation from the DFINITY Foundation or related organizations.)

It's difficult to phrase this section without doing a disservice to the Internet Computer vision because DFINITY keeps trade secrets quite close at the time of this writing, and the rabbit holes run much deeper than any startup I've come across. In other words, what I understand about the Internet Computer project is only what the public understands, which can fit in a thimble and be thrown away without changing much of the overall picture. The reason for DFINITY's strategic decision to keep the project's inner workings a secret will be discussed later. With that in mind, this chapter is forced to stick to a surface level overview.

The DFINITY Foundation is a not-for-profit organization based in Zurich, Switzerland, that oversees research centers in Palo Alto, San Francisco, Tokyo, and Zurich, as well as remote teams around the world. Its mission is to build the Internet Computer, which extends the functionality of the Internet from a network that connects billions of people (via TCP/IP protocols) to a public compute platform that empowers millions of developers and entrepreneurs (via the Internet Computer Protocol, or ICP).

> The Internet Computer is a public blockchain network so powerful that it can natively host hyperscale open Internet services, pan-industry platforms, DeFi systems, secure enterprise systems, websites, and all of humanity's software logic and data in smart contracts. It is created by independent data centers worldwide for running the *Internet Computer Protocol* (ICP).[601]

This describes transforming today's public Internet into the first blockchain computer that runs at Web speed with unbounded capacity. It is undoubtedly the most ambitious mission we've seen in a startup discussed in this book. The claim is essentially to create a more advanced but decentralized version of the Internet entirely outside Big Tech's jurisdiction. If we are to assume that no other lone blockchain project can take on Big Tech, then the most important part of this book is describing how a Big Tech versus Internet Computer battle would play out.

The upcoming section is an Internet Computer overview. The rest of the chapter circles back to the Big Tech versus Internet Computer question.

Chain Key Technology

While traditional blockchain projects are in a one-dimensional competition to build faster and more reliable consensus mechanisms, DFINITY has invented and applied "Chain Key Technology" to the Internet Computer, which allows anyone to verify correctness by applying a simple "chain key" (akin to a public key) to interactions, no longer requiring the need to make blocks of transactions available for download so that interactions can be validated.

It is important to note that Chain Key Technology is a combination of dozens of computer science breakthroughs, such as Random Beacon, Probabilistic Slot Consensus, Advanced Consensus Mechanism, Network Nervous System, and subnets, that allow the Internet Computer to be the first blockchain computer that runs at Web speed with unbounded capacity.

Chain Key Technology allows the Internet Computer to finalize transactions that modify the state of smart contracts (i.e., update data hosted in cyberspace) in 1–2 seconds. While this is an enormous improvement compared to Bitcoin and Ethereum, it is still insufficient to allow blockchain developers to construct competitive user experiences for which responses must be provided in milliseconds. As a result, the Internet Computer splits smart contract function execution into two different types: "update calls" and "query calls." Update calls are those we are already familiar with and take 1–2 seconds to finalize their execution, while query calls behave differently because any changes they make to the state (i.e., the memory pages of a developer's WebAssembly canisters) are discarded after execution. Essentially, this allows query calls to execute in milliseconds "on the edge."

For example, in the case of an open version of Reddit running on the Internet Computer, when a user browses the forum, customized views of the hosted content would be formulated and served into their web browser by the execution of query calls, which run in milliseconds on a nearby node, providing a fantastic user experience. But when a user wishes to occasionally make a post or provide a tip of tokens to the author of a post, this would involve update calls, which would take 1–2 seconds, an acceptable delay, which could also be hidden by optimistic execution in the manner of a one-click payment that assumes the credit card will work.

Capacity

The Internet Computer boasts potential for unlimited storage and computing capacity that expands with network demand. This is unheard of for any blockchain, which calls for some explanation. The Internet Computer constantly scales out its computing capacity by inducting new node machines into its network such that it never runs out, allowing the pricing of resources used by smart contracts to be closely derived from the underlying cost of the hardware involved in providing them. This works very differently than traditional blockchains, where the compute capacity available to hosted smart contracts is finite, and remains so no matter how much additional hardware is added to their networks, requiring them to auction their finite capacity to whoever will pay the most using "transaction fee markets"—which is why transactions on Ethereum can cost tens of dollars to run, while comparable computation on the Internet Computer cost only fractions of a cent.

Because the cost of computation on the Internet Computer can be made approximately constant, this makes it far easier to manage the resources needed to run systems and services, whose operational costs become much more predictable. But the provision of computing resources at constant cost is only part of what is needed. On the Internet Computer, smart contracts must be pre-charged with cycles to provide them with fuel that pays down computing resources at the moment of consumption, which occurs in the future. This means that cycles should also have constant value so that the number of cycles placed inside smart contracts predicts the amount of computation that they can actually pay for.

This point strikes at the core of what DFINITY is doing: appearing like a familiar computing platform for Internet services on the outside but having fundamentally different technology on the inside. This is a design to compete on the same grounds as FAAMG, not with other blockchain startups. So why can't every blockchain project make simple and decentralized Internet services without the blockchain bloat?

In the Web3 diagram from Chapter 1, the lowest layer was a data structure with developer tools resting on top of it. The legacy Internet functions with code running locally or in a virtual machine while referring to some external database. Most Web3 models do something like swap the database with a blockchain to add trust from the bottom up. The problem is that ten years after the birth of blockchain, we still don't have an efficient or simple standard for a fancy database-style blockchain. Maybe the problem is copying the legacy Internet's structure when Web3 should be completely original.

The Internet Computer holds all its logic and data in "WebAssembly Canisters," an evolution of smart contracts, as well as host a limitless quantity of canisters and canister data, one of the many reasons it's revolutionary. Another reason it's revolutionary is that it uses software, such as a web browser or an app on a phone, to interact directly with canisters. There are no intermediaries, which makes the Internet Computer very different from a traditional blockchain like Ethereum, where you need to run a website from a server or from a cloud service like AWS to create an interface. The Internet Computer provides an end-to-end solution, allowing one to build anything from traditional websites and enterprise systems to DeFi, pan-industry platforms, and hyperscale open Internet services without dependencies on legacy IT. You don't need proprietary cloud services, databases, firewalls, CDNs, and so on.

The developer of the future builds simply by writing abstract logic, using any programming language that compiles to WebAssembly, such as Motoko, Rust, or AssemblyScript, into cyberspace and directly onto the public Internet via the Internet Computer. In a decade, public cyberspace could host a substantial chunk of humankind's backend software and data, and developers and users could be free from legacy IT.

To grasp the novelty of this approach, we need an example of its use. DFINITY launched an open version of TikTok called CanCan, complete with a reward system for users and content creators. The entire backend of the app was written in less than 1,000 lines of code,[602] [603] when TikTok is thought to be in the millions.[604] All the storage and computation for users and developers happens exclusively in canisters (i.e., cyberspace without databases). The slots for CanCan videos rest inside the variables of canister code.

All this data and computation lives more literally on residential servers, that is, instead of the server farms controlled by Big Tech, individual and small business owned independent data centers around the world. The Internet Computer is created by the ICP protocol, which runs over TCP/IP and weaves together the computing capacity of special machines. Anyone can participate, which is how the Internet Computer can be kept decentralized. Developers, not users, pay for the storage and computation that canisters use.

We know that the Internet Computer can support inexpensive software development with high performance. During the Sodium Launch Event, the company uploaded gigabytes of data within about a second and then used its makeshift search engine, BigMap, to find it. This example should defy everything we thought we knew about blockchains. We unfortunately don't yet know how the Internet Computer's data structure can store so much while keeping such fast lookup times.

From what we know so far, the Internet Computer seems to combine the best features of linked lists, distributed hash tables, binary search trees, and bloom filters.[605] Blockchains were previously explained as fancy databases that developer tools rest on top of to mirror the legacy IT stack. No conceptual data structure can similarly be mapped onto ICP or the canister model because, as far as we know, there is none.

Simplicity

In Chapter 1, we saw all the hoops Alice needed to jump through to make a successful app. Instead of just worrying about her application logic, Alice needed to mix in a bunch of legacy IT components—such as a Big Tech cloud service, database system, memcached, filesystem, firewalls, middleware, DNS services, CDNs, and so on and on—to stay competitive. From the 1980s through the early 2000s, the dominant Internet services were built on open protocols that the Internet community controlled. However, since IP only provides a global network and not a computing platform, from the mid-2000s to the present, trust in open protocols was replaced by trust in corporate management teams.

As companies like Google, Twitter, and Facebook built software and services that surpassed the capabilities of open protocols, users migrated to these more sophisticated platforms.[606] But their code was proprietary, and their governing principles could change on a whim. ICP builds on IP to extend the public Internet's functionality to include a decentralized computing platform, an alternative to the legacy IT stack. This means databases, middleware, REST APIs, load balancers, firewalls, content delivery networks, browser extensions, usernames, passwords, and web servers are all gone.[607] The Internet Computer's structure has no reason to include those components, and that means Alice wouldn't have to worry about any of them—she just needs to write code in any language that compiles to WebAssembly and deploy her canister(s) directly to the public Internet via Internet Computer Protocol.

Developers who want to deploy open Internet services can do so in an effortless way. It starts with programming the app, which can be done in any language that shares compatibility with WebAssembly (a growing global standard for connecting different programming languages). Right now, this includes Rust, AssemblyScript, and Motoko, a language built for the Internet Computer by Andreas Rossberg, co-creator of WebAssembly. Motoko is a modern language designed to be approachable for developers who have a basic familiarity with JavaScript, Rust, Swift, TypeScript, C#, or Java. By design, Motoko helps developers write safer and more efficient code, compiles quickly, and links with WebAssembly modules written in other languages. It also enables developers to write sequential code through multiple canisters.

Code compiled into a WebAssembly module is ready to deploy onto the Internet Computer network and communicate asynchronously across other canisters. Most importantly, Motoko is one of many innovations that will help make the Internet Computer a compelling alternative to today's legacy IT stack. Ultimately, Motoko is optimized for both WebAssembly and the Internet Computer, while being much simpler and less susceptible to bugs and vulnerabilities that are all too common in languages such as Ethereum's Solidity. That code is then uploaded to the Internet Computer via a canister. An app's canister can also pull any public data or function from other canisters, which in some cases will act as permanent APIs. Supporting the app's front end is also a default part of the Internet Computer, which was never the case with Web3 apps. Ethereum dapps, for example, typically use Amazon Web Services to host their websites. This is a demonstratable failure on the part of Web3 that should be made a thing of the past.

To developers, it is just coding and deploying without extra steps. You can learn Motoko right now and build open Internet services. There are no permissions necessary, no exclusivity, no platform risk, and no censorship outside of what's permitted by the governance mechanism.

Governance Again

As we saw in Chapter 5, the Internet Computer's governance concept is well ahead of its time. Unfortunately, all the public information on it still rests on a few outdated blog posts written by Dominic Williams, Founder and Chief Scientist at DFINITY. The governance mechanism is expected to launch with the concept intact, but proof of success in practice will have to wait for the utility token launch. It is also theoretically dynamic enough to evolve itself into something closer to the last chapter's Idealized Governance.

Internet Computer governance should essentially turn the rules of the new Internet into a liquid democracy. It will be a grand experiment in comparing how decentralized governance of an open Internet compares to that of a closed Internet controlled by a handful of mega monopolies. The importance of getting this right can't be understated for reasons that will become clear presently.

In terms of performance, security, capacity, simplicity, and governance, the Internet Computer has the best Web3 solution proposed that we've seen. It could be the magic protocol we've been waiting for, so simple yet so complex that it appears indistinguishable from magic. The trouble is that such proposals are still backed only by the words of their creators, not raw code available to the public. For now, this is speculation based on the credibility and integrity of the DFINITY team. There is still plenty of room for unanticipated problems on the path toward dethroning Big Tech.

The Internet Computer Versus Big Tech

It's hard to pinpoint how a battle between Big Tech and Web3 would play out, especially since Web3 is such an ill-defined term. If we are to assume that the Internet Computer is the perfect embodiment of the Web3 paradigm, that provides a more concrete reference point.

This book covered a vast expanse of perspectives on Internet-related topics that span ideas from the early cypherpunk to the FAAMG executive. It's all for nothing if they can't be used to make sense of the present and help shape the future. This section outlines the fork in the road that lies ahead.

An Internet Computer Victory

Blockchain infrastructures, no matter how technologically sound and feature-rich, will still need interoperability or composability to reach mass adoption. We've seen why projects such as Ethereum, Polkadot, and Cosmos are not up to the task.

DFINITY has an optimistic proposition for the blockchain world. Since composability is limited for Ethereum because of scaling problems, and interoperability isn't possible for Polkadot and Cosmos because there are too many blockchains, there is no reason the Internet Computer can't get the best of both worlds. The Internet Computer can run Ethereum smart contract logic and frontends inside canisters. Why not leave Ethereum as the sediment layer for DeFi but put all the resource-intensive parts on the Internet Computer? People who build natively on the Internet Computer will have a web of interoperable *subnets*, which is analogous in principle to Polkadot's network of parachains. Interoperability with external blockchains can be reserved only for the absolute best with bridges like in Cosmos' vision. Interoperability and composability doesn't need to be an either/or thing anymore. You can have your cake and eat it too.

The interoperability portion of this still needs to change with time, and it will likely happen alongside whatever becomes the industry standard. Composability is a more imminent goal that also has people scratching their heads. How can one blockchain project capture the network effects of something as big as Ethereum? Even then, how does that make the jump to FAAMG-level network effects?

Blockchain development today is severely limiting. As an Ethereum dapp developer, for example, your job is to use a bunch of computer science tricks to minimize the amount of data that will go on the blockchain. Creativity falls by the wayside because the game is about making otherwise simple tasks work in really complex ways by adding blockchain. DFINITY's goal is to make otherwise complicated tasks really simple with the help of a decentralized computing architecture.

The only way to understand why all the innovation will flock to something like the Internet Computer is by looking at it from an entrepreneur's perspective. Imagine that's you. You don't respect that Uber as a company takes billions of dollars from riders and drivers just because they have ownership of an app. Let's look at your options if you want to build a more inclusive ride-sharing app that replaces Uber.

The first is the conventional route. Build an app, hosted by the cloud, accessible through all the major app stores, with payment methods hooked up to legacy fintech. The development will be expensive because implementing security measures and platform hosting will cost a small fortune. You're going to need a good development team, legal team, and marketing team at the very least. Your goal of keeping things cheap for users and drivers is in the dump because operating expenses are so high. The next step, raising money, is impossible at this point. No venture capitalist is going to want to go anywhere near you. Using low prices and good incentives while going against a monopoly on proprietary infrastructure is the perfect recipe for disaster.

Okay, so the probability of success of a ride-sharing app through conventional channels is zero. Onward.

Unless there is a non-Internet way to facilitate ride-sharing, the only alternative infrastructure to build on is Web3. You first look to Ethereum to build a decentralized Uber or "Duber." Now the development side of things will be overly complicated, much more than with legacy IT options. It will require a competent team of blockchain developers and web developers. For funding, you launch a token with the platform that gives users and drivers governance rights and special privileges. Duber features will be kept to the bare minimum because they would otherwise cause tremendous computational expense. By the time Duber is built out, it will be of little use to anyone because transactions could end up being more expensive than the rides. If Duber went viral, the entire network of all Ethereum dapps would become extremely slow and expensive. Building an Ethereum-based Duber or any dapp that can attract millions of users ends up being terrible for the grander ecosystem.

How about the alternative Web3 infrastructures? How about Polkadot, Cosmos, and the countless other dapp development platforms? You know Duber doesn't need a blockchain, and attaching one will make everything harder, but with no other choice, you go through with it. It's a complicated process, but if you follow the same steps as with Ethereum and pick the right infrastructure alternative, the result is a Duber with slower speed and more expense-related complications.

Then there is the accessibility problem. It's a bit like the predicament of Chapter 1 Alice in the 1990s. The infrastructure might be complete enough to build out a fantastic application, but if it is not the popular infrastructure, no one will find out about Duber. It will only be accessible to those who have a registered blockchain identity with that infrastructure, know how to buy and transfer coins, and are familiar with the burdensome parts of using early-stage dapps. You just cut your addressable market down by 99%. This goes right back to the desperate need for composability, which is only somewhat existent on Ethereum right now.

So far, the future for your Duber idea and really the whole Web3 space is looking quite bleak. I've seen this Duber idea cited in academia and mentioned by prominent leaders repeatedly over the years, and yet no one has done it. People rightfully wonder why blockchain has been around for more than a decade but still has next to no adoption, and this Duber example shows why: Entrepreneurs still don't have the right tools. This is okay, and there is no sign of a plateau in blockchain innovation. It's just a complex paradigm shift that takes a lot of failures before getting it right. As a reminder, let's look at the blockchain-like features Duber *does* need in the first place.

The original goal was making a cheaper Uber that charges less and gives its riders and drivers part ownership in the platform. For this, the platform must be decentralized and secure so drivers and riders trust it. It also needs a token for governance, a possible payment medium, a rewards system for early adopters, and funding. Those features are enough for a solid strategy that can beat Uber. Knowing that you can leverage the Internet Computer to get these blockchain-like features without the blockchain baggage, you go through with the Duber idea.

Since you're a good programmer and development on the Internet Computer is comparatively simple, you build the proof of concept yourself. It's a beta Uber clone without all the bells and whistles. Since you choose to build with ICP, Duber is accessible right in the browser and does not require users to get key pairs or tokens. Then you mint one billion Duber governance tokens and sell them on the open market for funding. You hire some employees to develop the platform further and start recruiting drivers and riders in your area. As a bonus, those early drivers and riders get free Duber tokens for participating, essentially granting them part ownership of Duber. A small fee can be taken off rider transactions to pay for computation and the governance mechanism that upholds Duber, but since operating costs are comparatively low, almost the entirety of the driver-rider exchange is kept by involved parties.

Done right, this will make the first drivers and riders rich, and everyone will want to ride Duber for the extra tokens. Even without that incentive, the low overhead and lack of corporate greed will make a Duber economic model superior to Uber. Judging by Uber's market capitalization, there's $100 billion worth of value here.

There's no stopping this. Any industry that is heavily profiting from a digital platform monopoly is going to be at risk. Open versions of Fiverr, Airbnb, Twitter, and Spotify have the same opportunity. These are just the copycats. Once novel open Internet services and pan-industry platforms become available, the potential of a blockchain Internet can finally be realized.

A Big Tech Victory

Knowing what we know about the Internet Computer, something isn't adding up. Market sentiment hasn't generated valuations that reflect superiority over Polkadot, for example, or a crumb of a crumb of FAAMG's valuation. Think about how premature every visionary claim about ICP must be if the platform and project token have not even been released. No one, including industry competitors, are acknowledging the Internet Computer. What's going on here?

Can I, after years of searching for solutions to Big Tech tyranny, be so delusional that I'm willing to pick one enticing project as *the* answer just to believe in a bright future? Let's get back to the tone of ruthless pragmatism and look at all the forces that can drive DFINITY towards failure.

FAAMG executives will still scoff at DFINITY at this stage. The Internet Computer could still be a colossal flop entirely on its own. As far as the public is concerned, the Internet Computer could be nothing like what the DFINITY Foundation promised. Their public launch is two years late and counting (as of

January 2021). Updates regarding the Internet Computer's functionality or the team's progress is sparse at best. In this way, the community's trust in DFINITY is utterly reliant on the team's words, which is the opposite of what the cryptosphere stands for. The counter to this is that the DFINITY Foundation is a nonprofit packed with close to 150 of the world's best cryptographers, distributed systems, and programming language experts, who are staking their enormously valuable reputations on the success of the Internet Computer.

On a more realistic note, the Internet Computer might not end up being as independent or convenient as we expect. There is not supposed to be any usernames or passwords for any Internet Computer open Internet service, but it's still unclear what blockchain identities will replace it. We don't even know where you will access it. Will there be an Internet Computer dapp store through some portal? Will Internet Computer-based websites be as easy to access as regular websites? Will they be as easy to build? There might need to be a dapp that makes it easy to build Internet Computer-based websites without programming knowledge. Can you use the Apple App Store to find that dapp and Google Search to find those websites? If yes, then the Internet Computer is less independent; if no, then the Internet Computer is less convenient.

Maybe these limitations are okay. The Internet Computer paradigm shift comes from taking power away from Big Tech's cloud services and platforms. But is this an Internet paradigm shift?

Let's review Chapter 3's Internet hierarchy concept: Device manufacturers control the browsers and app stores; the browsers control the extensions and search engines; and the app stores and search engines control the visibility of Internet services. The Internet Computer's open Internet services still fall at the bottom of the hierarchy. It remains to be seen if something can replace app stores/search engines/browsers.

A lot of uncertain things must go right for DFINITY before it can even think about competing with Big Tech. The developer experience has to be as seamless and versatile as the DFINITY Foundation claims. Then the best tech entrepreneurs have to decide to build their services on the Internet Computer. Open Internet services that are completely novel, leverage the Internet Computer's unique features, and have high-demand use cases need to be created with high availability. Community support needs to be strong enough to fund these endeavors, and user support needs to be large enough to stimulate network effects without FAAMG's help. That's a lot of maybes.

Let's assume that the Internet Computer is as described by the DFINITY Foundation and it overcomes all the challenges mentioned above. Imagine open Internet services competing with Big Tech are on the rise: an "open Facebook" with fancy tokenomics enticing enough to get users to leave Facebook and start a social media account from scratch, as well as a network of Internet Computer websites and internal search engines that make Google Search a less common way to explore the web. As ICP starts eating away at FAAMG services, what could tech titans do to stop it?

Could Big Tech Make an Internet Computer?

One option would be for FAAMG to build their own Internet Computer. When starting this book, I was under the impression that anything these tiny Web3 startups can muster up, Big Tech would be able to replicate with ease as soon as it felt like it. In asking questions about the threat of FAAMG, no one had a good explanation. The closest to the truth we get is that FAAMG doesn't care about Web3 solutions because they are mostly useless and contradict corporate motives. But if the Internet Computer goes as planned, this excuse no longer works to protect Web3 from leviathan competitors.

DFINITY founder Dominic Williams offered me a brief meeting to discuss this. To avoid getting the same fruitless answers that I have become so accustomed to, I started by pressing him with all the details, leaving no way out of the question: FAAMG has trillions, and you have millions. FAAMG has all the data, users, and servers while DFINITY has nothing. FAAMG has enormously powerful people who can hire anyone for whatever pay they want. The Internet has a cyclical history of proprietors crushing decentralized platforms. How can the Internet Computer compete with this?

At the time, I knew Dominic as nothing more than the creator of a famous video game and the face of DFINITY. I was expecting to hear, well, something I've already heard before, so I could rule out DFINITY as a run-of-the-mill project and move on. I basically listed out all the reasons DFINITY would fail, and he sat there eating lunch in what appeared like complete boredom, more amused by his salad than my words.

When he finally spoke, his tone went from calm and reactionless to frustrated, and I barely got a word in for the rest of the meeting. He kindly, but firmly explained why none of those claims threaten the Internet Computer or even come close. From what I could gather, his frustration was with the rest of the Web3 world, which did not have answers to these questions or the ability to understand what DFINITY was doing.

I later learned that Dominic exhibits every characteristic you might expect to find in a genius (except the nerdy demeanor) and has been working toward decentralized computation solutions before FAAMG even existed. I've come to learn in the months thereafter why he was completely right.

FAAMG can never build an Internet Computer for a multitude of reasons. First of all, those companies know nothing about decentralized technology. It took decades of failures for the space to learn what works and what doesn't. Another Dominic Williams would never agree to work for FAAMG. Getting 150 world-class cryptographers and distributed systems experts to incessantly work on one problem for years as DFINITY did is another requirement FAAMG would not follow through on.

Even if they did, it would be more of a PR stunt than an Internet Computer because any version of a FAAMG Internet Computer would have corporate motives baked into it, which would immediately void benefits from decentralization. It'd be the Web3 equivalent of company-sponsored "innovation" with "private blockchains." Even after the years it would take to build, no one would support it. Everyone would build on the real Internet Computer because it's where the real paradigm shift will be. It would be quite flattering if FAAMG tried to beat DFINITY at its own game, but it would never happen because FAAMG would never win.

Could Big Tech Break the Internet Computer?

If you can't make it, why not break it? If open Internet services on the Internet Computer started taking Big Tech users, couldn't the FAAMG oligopoly do what they do best and just crush the Internet Computer? Let's see what that would require.

After DFINITY became public enemy number one, the most practical option for FAAMG would be leveraging the Internet hierarchy to decrease the visibility of Internet Computer platforms, with search engines neglecting open Internet services, app stores blocking dapps, terms and conditions disallowing tokenized platforms, that kind of thing. Not only would these tactics be super-illegal, but they would also accelerate a shift toward an open Internet as people chose search engines and app stores with better access.

FAAMG's other option is to break the Internet Computer more literally. Finding a flaw in system cryptography is always a possibility, although an extremely improbable one. Another scary proposition has to do with FAAMG's quantum computers. If these computers live up to the hype, they might be able to crack the code, break the Internet Computer's security guarantees (via Chain Key Technology), and destroy the Internet Computer. It is also fair to say that if quantum computers start breaking pre-quantum cryptography, nothing about any part of the Internet is safe, including Bitcoin and Ethereum. Quantum resistance seems to be an evolutionary step for cryptography, and DFINITY has stated that it will become a focus of the team post-launch.

In almost every respect, the Internet Computer was stubbornly designed to be more robust than anything else. Nuclear attacks, solar flares, quantum computing, and every other black swan event you can think of is better prepared for by the Internet Computer than FAAMG's Internet. Big Tech can't break the Internet Computer.

How DFINITY Loses

If the Internet Computer is as described, the most realistic way that it fails is if no one uses it. ICP is an incredible technological feat for the 21st century but will remain completely useless until people employ it to build amazing things. FAAMG still has all the peer-to-peer value, and it will take a long time for those network effects to transfer, if they ever do. As of this moment, there is nothing for FAAMG users to switch to. It all has yet to be built.

This open Internet wave is also a hypercompetitive arena with many players. As soon as one of the many infrastructure platforms starts getting all the developer building blocks, or composability, it will generate a positive feedback loop making it *the* development platform. I can only hope this happens on the best dapp development platform because, as we saw with Ethereum, it is tough to reverse once that feedback loop gets started. Supposing the Internet Computer is the best, it is not exactly easy for entrepreneurs to arrive at that conclusion when every Web3 platform is touting grandiose claims about its own blockchain revolution.

Better the Devil You Know

This book has dedicated a disproportionately large amount of space to governance mechanisms considering that they are barely in use today. Still, governance is the final frontier for blockchain that will make or break the free Internet. This is what keeps me up at night (literally), yet I've never seen the problem publicly addressed because it is an exceedingly early-stage idea.

This topic is equally applicable to all blockchain infrastructure platforms, but let's assume the Internet Computer is Web3's dark horse since we're already familiar with its governance. Why should we think the Internet Computer will be ruled fairly? Has any ideological revolution that rose to power to fix the tyranny of an old system ever gone on to build a utopia? How do things usually go when trying out a new system of governance for the first time? Are we to think the Internet Computer will be Elysian Fields in cyberspace? Of course not.

As a reminder, FAAMG is not evil, their existence has been net positive, and you can still do pretty much anything on the Internet. The major problem with Big Tech is the amount of power it holds and how it leverages that power. ICP or any open Internet protocol/infrastructure that becomes the standard can be considerably more powerful than FAAMG.

The way the Internet Computer governs is inherently hierarchal. All open Internet services, pan-industry platforms, DeFi solutions, and so on built on the Internet Computer can implement their own governance with one important caveat: The Internet Computer's Network Nervous System (NNS), an algorithmic governance system, can override decisions of open Internet service governance. This meta-governance style is still the best way to operate an entire Internet layer, as it prevents abuses at the application layer, but corrupting it would mean corrupting the entire Internet Computer ecosystem.

This is a high-risk play for the world. At least with today's closed Internet, there is always an alternative to abusive proprietors. For government censorship, you can use a VPN. For FAAMG censorship, you can use or create a different platform. These checks through competition keep monopolistic abuse from going completely off the rails.

A world computer would not have these checks. If you think search engine and social network algorithms manipulate the public, think about all "open" equivalents that are impossible to sue under the supreme control of the Internet

Computer's governance. Any victim of a potentially authoritarian governance mechanism has no other choice but to resort to a now inferior legacy Internet. This could massively tip the world's balance of power.

I acknowledge that industry leaders will dismiss this idea as a ludicrous interpretation of blockchain governance. They will say the purpose of decentralization is to avoid this problem—a true Puritan response. No collective ever does expect the new and improved system to fall into patterns of the old, but here's how it can happen.

If you look deep enough at anything "decentralized," you will find that it is not. We've discussed the technical ways decentralization can be undermined ad nauseam in this book. Those problems are somewhat objective and addressable with system design tradeoffs, but the subjective side of this can corrupt even perfectly decentralized governance. The Internet Computer's governance, the Network Nervous System, will be ruled by utility token holders. Even if tokens are accessible to all on open markets, early supporters, especially wealthy ones, will buy before the token price skyrockets and will hold the lion's share of network influence.

This is a great thing, at first: Early supporters who know what's best for the network use that knowledge to make early technical decisions. But if the Internet Computer's ambitions go as planned, the critical decisions will become much softer: whom to censor, how to handle activity whose legality is dependent on geographic boundaries, and what algorithms should dictate search engine and social media results. Making fair decisions in these areas requires a whole new level of decentralization.

DFINITY's early community shares a similar value system. That's what brings them together. But in time, the Internet Computer's success could force the whole world into using it, incumbent innovators included. We are living in a world where every decision becomes politicized, and every political decision becomes polarizing. If group identities form on the Network Nervous System, and the Internet Computer controls the spread of information, those groups will disperse and form into fewer but larger groups. Once more than half of the Network Nervous System associates itself with one group identity, it is not decentralized. That group can outvote everyone and make the Internet Computer into an echo chamber for group advocacy. Remember, the Internet Computer has no responsibility to governments, corporations, or anything else. Nothing can stop it.

I hope the populace is ready to start making all its own decisions. There is no hard-and-fast solution to this. The last chapter's idealized governance concept was twenty or so field-specific groups with various voting power caps to keep the many group identities from ever combining. This is not in the cards for the Network Nervous System, or at least has never been acknowledged by its creators. It would be great if twenty disparate and competing but equally capable ICPs came about without interoperability challenges, but that won't happen either.

Widespread awareness about the threat of a corrupted governance mechanism is the only real fix. This entails that the associated foundations and early leaders remove themselves from it over time. Early investors and venture capital holders must slowly sell off their tokens. As with everything decentralized, Dominic Williams and the other faces of DFINITY should altogether remove their voices and voting power from the project within twenty years. And you should buy tokens and start voting, especially if you have a different value system than what is being reflected by the Network Nervous System.

The Internet Computer's Purpose

Application-specific blockchain solutions are plentiful throughout this book, but none have seen mass adoption. They took a backseat in this chapter to make way for infrastructure platforms. It's time for the two to meet.

There is a lot of misinformation in the blockchain world and plenty of failures to point to over the last decade. Most initiatives mentioned in this book will fail, but at their core is something exceptional. The concepts of these initiatives are lovely, and those failures in execution were valuable lessons.

Each was primarily pulled from experiments in academia and incubation-phase startups. There was no other way to see what worked and what didn't. It was an elementary school playground, and now we are entering the big leagues.

Those failed ideas still stand. Everyone who took their shots at improving identity management, financial infrastructure, and supply chains were starting from scratch. Now the opportunity for these massive undertakings is greater than ever with the Internet Computer. The last decade of blockchain experimentation is about to start paying off.

Broader issues relating to the data economy are solved almost by default with Internet Computer architecture. All of the data relating to you will either be encrypted or accessible to other parties based on smart contract logic. This means if system transparency is enforced by NNS where applicable, which should include all platforms where you create personal data, the harsh elements of FAAMG's data manipulation and behavioral microtargeting no longer make technical sense. If the Internet Computer community chooses to prioritize this functionality in what gets built, surveillance capitalism can be replaced with more benevolent economic models in one fell swoop.

The Future

It is still wholly justifiable to be cautious of any vision for a future that dethrones Big Tech. As far as I can tell, the whole blockchain space is still far too immature to be dealing with problems of such magnitude. The Internet Computer appears to be an exception, but this chapter's depiction of it is forced to be optimistic because their project details are not specific enough to extract flaws. As DFINITY releases more information and the practicalities of its tech begin to sink in, the Internet Computer will, in all likelihood, be forced to diverge from the Web3 ideal and settle for something more practicable.

Assuming the Internet Computer or similar project becomes a wild success, the Internet is not absolved from the past dilemmas. Addictive platforms and algorithmic bias can still exist in a more extreme form. One primary goal of tokenization is to increase the addictiveness of platforms, and algorithms will still be subject to their creators' bias. The Internet hierarchy is not going away; it's just being restructured. Again, the benefit of the blockchain Internet is early people's ability to shape what's hopefully a more benevolent version, which is otherwise impossible in today's monopolistic landscape.

It will probably be around twenty years before the winner of a blockchain versus Big Tech war can be declared. That leaves a lot of time for things to change. Perhaps the Internet Computer will fail, and whatever drove its failure will be a valuable lesson. All the technological innovation from DFINITY can be adopted into an improved attempt at taking on Big Tech. Perhaps whatever paradigm follows blockchain will arrive and change everything. Maybe some yet to be conceived magical protocol will be a FAAMG killer.

There are some claims surrounding this story that I can make with confidence. One is that demand for alternatives to Big Tech monopolies is high and not going away. Another is that social and political change can no longer produce real solutions for mega-monopolies. The only optimistic outlook I can find for the Internet's future is found in a hyperspecialized and precarious corner of the blockchain world.

Beyond Blockchain

The problems this book speaks to often fall on deaf ears. I think this is because numbers are a terrible way to elicit empathy in humans, and any summary of the data economy must be grounded in purely objective reasoning. To demonstrate, let's try to quantify the magnitude of the data economy's threat to human autonomy.

In Chapter 2, we saw the extent of the threat to democracy, a gateway for independent decision-making. The Cambridge Analytica (CA) Scandal was highlighted because it was the only behavioral microtargeting incident that the public seemed to care about. But the facts tell a much more chilling story than the media narrative.

CA's tactics were used hundreds of times before the 2016 presidential election, and they continue to be used long after. Despite public backlash and constant government retaliation attempts, Big Tech came out the other side of this stronger than ever. The CA Scandal occurred more than four years ago and seems to have been completely forgotten. It had a moment in the sun only while it was politically convenient, and perhaps that's fine because CA itself was not a big deal, but the much bigger picture that it represented was never acknowledged.

The whole scandal amounted to a service worth $6 million, and if we are to assume that the FTC is correct in saying that CA is just a small-scale reflection of Facebook's own tactics, [608] then using Facebook revenue as a proxy should indicate that related problems today are about 13,000 times more prominent per year. Of course, this money is for influencing human decisions that are less sensitive than ones having to do with presidential elections, but if changing your vote is an inconsequential part of the big picture, it should make you question what decisions are your own.

Netflix's *The Great Hack* was all about the CA scandal, and it did a fantastic job of pulling an emotional reaction from the audience. Unfortunately, it did so through ambiguous claims about how technology spies on you, the crying of CA whistleblowers, fruitless clips from the testimony of "bad guys," severe accusations completely devoid of hard evidence, and, of course, heart-wrenching and ominous music throughout. Details or proof about grander microtargeting was absent.

No one, including me, can decipher the truth from the core representation of problems in our data economy. If we can't get anywhere close to the true story of a very cut-and-dried case, imagine how elusive the truth is about the inner workings of FAAMG. Stories by journalists spread misinformation (the parts of FAAMG they don't understand) through the channels designed to spread misinformation (FAAMG platforms). Is this the game we must play now to make a change?

It appears the size of an issue in the public eye is proportional to how much anger and fear it can generate. The noise surrounding social problems is at an all-time high, but most people today live with more comforts, food variety, and safety than any king from more than 500 years ago. Imagine if we could adequately calibrate the emotional response to world problems. Would you be able to get the details right or separate the big from the small? I certainly couldn't, but if the data economy is responsible for humanity's inability to quantify world problems, wouldn't that make it the biggest problem?

What's scary is the trend: Nothing is moving away from digitization. Surveillance capitalism is already omnipresent, and we are only at the dawn of IoT. The switch from mobile computers to virtual reality will only make people more affected by digital surroundings. Hyper-automation is the assumed direction of machine improvement. The rise of nanotechnology is not exactly a calming movement. No one is getting less worried about artificial intelligence year after year. Adding elements of all these innovations to a brain chip is a legitimate plan for the 21st century. Quantum computers powerful enough to make simulations of consciousness is another.

All these speculative technologies will have an enduring relationship with information and communication technologies. Blockchain is not an answer to everything, but it can be thought of as a fork in the road for the Internet. One direction is the continuation of a downward spiral. The other is an opportunity to democratize ethical frameworks for humanity's technological feats.

NOTES

[1]. Nakamoto, S. (2009). Bitcoin: A Peer-to-Peer Electronic Cash System. Cryptography Mailing list at https://metzdowd.com.

[2]. Narayanan, A., Bonneau, J., Felten, E., Miller, A., & Goldfeder, S. (2016). Forward. *Bitcoin and Cryptocurrency Technologies: A Comprehensive Introduction*. Princeton: Princeton University Press.

[3]. Narayanan, A., Bonneau, J., Felten, E., Miller, A., & Goldfeder, S. (2016). Forward. *Bitcoin and Cryptocurrency Technologies: A Comprehensive Introduction*. Princeton: Princeton University Press.

[4]. Russell, A. L. (2013, July 30). OSI: The Internet that Wasn't. Retrieved from https://spectrum.ieee.org/tech-history/cyberspace/osi-the-internet-that-wasnt

[5]. Watts, A. (1989). *The Book on The Taboo of Knowing Who You are*. New York: Vintage Books.

[6]. Chopra, R. (July 24, 2019). *In re Facebook, Inc.* Commission File No. 1823109 (p. 8). Washington D.C.: Federal Trade Commission.

[7]. Mineo, L. (August 25, 2017). *On Internet Privacy, Be Very Afraid*. Retrieved from https://today.law.harvard.edu/internet-privacy-afraid/

[8]. Rubinstein, I. S., G. T. Nojeim, & R. D. Lee. (May 2014). Systematic Government Access to Personal Data: A Comparative Analysis. *International Data Privacy Law*, *4*(2), 96–119, https://doi.org/10.1093/idpl/ipu004

[9]. Rubinstein, I. S., G. T. Nojeim, & R. D. Lee. (May 2014). Systematic Government Access to Personal Data: A Comparative Analysis. *International Data Privacy Law*, *4*(2), 96–119, https://doi.org/10.1093/idpl/ipu004

[10]. Mulligan, S. P., Freeman, W. C., & Linebaugh, C. D. (2019). *Data Protection Law: An Overview*. Congressional Research Service. Retrieved from https://fas.org/sgp/crs/misc/R45631.pdf

[11]. Maris, E., Libert, T., & Henrichsen, J. (15AD). *Tracking Sex: The Implications of Widespread Sexual Data Leakage and Tracking on Porn Websites*. Retrieved from https://arxiv.org/pdf/1907.06520.pdf

[12]. Covenant Eyes: Internet Accountability and Filtering. (2015). *Porn Stats: 250 Facts, Quotes, and Statistics about Pornography*. Retrieved from https://www.bevillandassociates.com/wp-content/uploads/2015/05/2015-porn-stats-covenant-eyes-1.pdf

[13]. Rubinstein, I. S., G. T. Nojeim, & R. D. Lee. (May 2014). Systematic Government Access to Personal Data: A Comparative Analysis. *International Data Privacy Law*, *4*(2), 96–119, https://doi.org/10.1093/idpl/ipu004

[14]. Written Statement to the United States Senate Committee on the Judiciary in the Matter of Cambridge Analytica and Other Related Issues. Christopher Wylie Testimony, 16 May, 2018. Retrieved From https://www.judiciary.senate.gov/imo/media/doc/05-16-18%20Wylie%20Testimony.pdf

[15]. Ward, K. (2018). Social Networks, the 2016 US Presidential Election, and Kantian Ethics: Applying the Categorical Imperative to Cambridge Analytica's Behavioral Microtargeting. *Journal of Media Ethics*, *33*(3), 133–148. doi: 10.1080/23736992.2018.1477047

[16]. Nix, A. (2016, September 27). *The Power of Big Data and Phycographics in The Electoral Process*. Retrieved from https://youtu.be/n8Dd5aVXLCc

[17]. Nix, A. (2016, September 27). *The Power of Big Data and Phycographics in The Electoral Process*. Retrieved from https://youtu.be/n8Dd5aVXLCc

[18]. Magee, T. (2019, July 30). What is Cambridge Analytica? A History of the Firm Behind the Facebook Data Scandal. Retrieved from https://www.techworld.com/data/what-is-cambridge-analytica-3674029/

[19]. Eckersley, S. Investigation into the Use of Data Analytics in Political Campaigns: Investigation Update (November 6, 2018). Retrieved from https://ico.org.uk/media/action-weve-taken/2260271/investigation-into-the-use-of-data-analytics-in-political-campaigns-final-20181105.pdf

[20]. Chopra, R. (July 24, 2019). *In re Facebook, Inc.* Commission File No. 1823109 (p. 8). Washington D.C.: Federal Trade Commission.

[21]. Ward, K. (2018). Social Networks, the 2016 US Presidential Election, and Kantian Ethics: Applying the Categorical Imperative to Cambridge Analytica's Behavioral Microtargeting. *Journal of Media Ethics*, *33*(3), 133–148. doi: 10.1080/23736992.2018.1477047

[22]. Mad Men to Math Men: Alexander Nix Interview with WebSummit. (2018, March 20). Retrieved from https://youtu.be/L6PWrsr-44E.

[23]. Laterza, V. (2018). Cambridge Analytica, Independent Research and the National Interest. *Anthropology Today*, *34*(3), 1–2. doi: 10.1111/1467-8322.12430

[24]. Briant, E. L. (2018, May 4). As Cambridge Analytica and SCL Elections Shut Down, SCL Group's Defence Work Needs Real Scrutiny. Retrieved from https://www.opendemocracy.net/en/opendemocracyuk/as-cambridge-analytica-and-scl-elections-shut-down-scl-groups-defence-work-needs-re/.

[25]. Alexander Nix, Former Cambridge Analytica CEO, Testifies to "Fake News" Inquiry. (2018, June 6). Retrieved from https://youtu.be/SqKU0gqY7oo.

[26]. Mad Men to Math Men: Alexander Nix Interview with WebSummit. (2018, March 20). Retrieved from https://youtu.be/L6PWrsr-44E.

[27]. Ward, K. (2018). Social Networks, the 2016 US Presidential Election, and Kantian Ethics: Applying the Categorical Imperative to Cambridge Analytica's Behavioral Microtargeting. Journal of Media Ethics, 33(3), 133–148. doi: 10.1080/23736992.2018.1477047

[28]. Ward, K. (2018). Social Networks, the 2016 US Presidential Election, and Kantian Ethics: Applying the Categorical Imperative to Cambridge Analytica's Behavioral Microtargeting. Journal of Media Ethics, 33(3), 133–148. doi: 10.1080/23736992.2018.1477047

[29]. Chopra, R. (July 24, 2019). *In re Facebook, Inc.* Commission File No. 1823109 (p. 8). Washington D.C.: Federal Trade Commission.

[30]. Williams, E., & Yerby, J. (n.d.).. *Google and Facebook Data Retention and Location Tracking Through Forensic Cloud Analysis*. Association for Information Systems Electronic Library (AISeL). Retrieved from https://aisel.aisnet.org/sais2019/3

[31]. Chopra, R. (July 24, 2019). *In re Facebook, Inc.* Commission File No. 1823109 (p. 8). Washington D.C.: Federal Trade Commission.

[32]. Chopra, R. (July 24, 2019). *In re Facebook, Inc.* Commission File No. 1823109 (p. 8). Washington D.C.: Federal Trade Commission.

[33]. Williams, E., & Yerby, J. (n.d.).. Google and Facebook Data Retention and Location Tracking Through Forensic Cloud Analysis. Association for Information Systems Electronic Library (AISeL). Retrieved from https://aisel.aisnet.org/sais2019/3

[34]. Williams, E., & Yerby, J. (n.d.).. Google and Facebook Data Retention and Location Tracking Through Forensic Cloud Analysis. Association for Information Systems Electronic Library (AISeL). Retrieved from https://aisel.aisnet.org/sais2019/3

[35]. Laterza, V. (2018). Cambridge Analytica, Independent Research and the National Interest. *Anthropology Today*, *34*(3), 1–2. doi: 10.1111/1467-8322.12430

[36]. Apple Privacy. (n.d.). Retrieved from https://www.apple.com/privacy/.

[37]. Zuckerberg, M. (2019, March 6). A Privacy-Focused Vision for Social Networking. Retrieved from https://www.facebook.com/notes/mark-zuckerberg/a-privacy-focused-vision-for-social-networking/10156700570096634/.

[38]. Privacy Policy: Privacy & Terms. (2019, October 15). Retrieved from https://policies.google.com/privacy?hl=en-US#whycollect.

[39]. Google Privacy Policy: Privacy & Terms. (2019, October 15). Retrieved from https://policies.google.com/privacy?hl=en-US#whycollect.

[40]. Ingram, H., & Reed, A. (2016). Lessons from History for Counter-Terrorism Strategic Communications. *Terrorism and Counter-Terrorism Studies*. doi: 10.19165/2016.2.04

[41]. Cotton, Jess. Why Socrates Hated Democracy. *The Book of Life*, 27 Feb. 2019, https://www.theschooloflife.com/thebookoflife/why-socrates-hated-democracy/.

[42]. Green , H. (n.d.). The Internet of Things in the Cognitive Era. *IBM Watson IoT*. Retrieved from https://www.ibm.com/downloads/cas/V6ZB5L4P

[43]. Isaak, J., & Hanna, M. J. (2018). User Data Privacy: Facebook, Cambridge Analytica, and Privacy Protection. *IEEE Computer Society*, *51*(8), 56–59. doi: 10.1109/mc.2018.3191268

[44]. Bahga, A., & Madisetti, V. (2017). *Blockchain Applications: A Hands-On Approach* (pp. 46-48). Erscheinungsort nicht ermittelbar: Verlag nicht ermittelbar

[45]. Gubbi, J., Buyya, R., Marusic, S., & Palaniswami, M. (2013). Internet of Things (IoT): A Vision, Architectural Elements, and Future Directions. *Future Generation Computer Systems*, *29*(7), 1645–1660. doi: 10.1016/j.future.2013.01.010

[46]. Green , H. (n.d.). The Internet of Things in the Cognitive Era. *IBM Watson IoT*. Retrieved from https://www.ibm.com/downloads/cas/V6ZB5L4P

[47]. Vermesan, O., Bröring, A., Tragos, E., Serrano, M., Bacciu, D. et al. (2017) Internet of Robotic Things: Converging Sensing/Actuating, Hypoconnectivity, Artificial Intelligence and IoT Platforms. In O. Vermesan, J. Bacquet (eds.), *Cognitive Hyperconnected Digital Transformation: Internet of Things Intelligence Evolution* (pp. 97-155). River Publishers.

[48]. Biswas, K., & Muthukkumarasamy, V. (2016). Securing Smart Cities Using Blockchain Technology. *2016 IEEE 18th International Conference on High Performance Computing and Communications; IEEE 14th International Conference on Smart City; IEEE 2nd International Conference on Data Science and Systems (HPCC/SmartCity/DSS)*. doi: 10.1109/hpcc-smartcity-dss.2016.0198

[49]. Biswas, K., & Muthukkumarasamy, V. (2016). Securing Smart Cities Using Blockchain Technology. *2016 IEEE 18th International Conference on High Performance Computing and Communications; IEEE 14th International Conference on Smart City; IEEE 2nd International Conference on Data Science and Systems (HPCC/SmartCity/DSS)*. doi: 10.1109/hpcc-smartcity-dss.2016.0198

[50]. Gottwalt, F., & Karduck, A. P. (2017). Securing Smart Cities: A Big Data Challenge. *Information Innovation Technology in Smart Cities*, 183–197. doi: 10.1007/978-981-10-1741-4_13

[51]. Chauhan, S., Agarwal, N., & Kar, A. K. (2016). Addressing Big Data Challenges in Smart Cities: A Systematic Literature Review. *Info*, *18*(4), 73–90. doi: 10.1108/info-03-2016-0012

[52]. Ismail, A. (2016). Utilizing Big Data Analytics as a Solution for Smart Cities. *2016 3rd MEC International Conference on Big Data and Smart City (ICBDSC)*. doi: 10.1109/icbdsc.2016.7460348

[53]. Gottwalt, F., & Karduck, A. P. (2017). Securing Smart Cities: A Big Data Challenge. Information Innovation Technology in Smart Cities, 183–197. doi: 10.1007/978-981-10-1741-4_13

[54]. Wood, L. (2020). Big Data Analytics Industry Report 2020: Rapidly Increasing Volume & Complexity of Data, Cloud Computing Traffic, and Adoption of IoT & AI are Driving Growth. *Research and Markets*. doi:https://www.globenewswire.com/news-release/2020/03/02/1993369/0/en/Big-Data-Analytics-Industry-Report-2020-Rapidly-Increasing-Volume-Complexity-of-Data-Cloud-Computing-Traffic-and-Adoption-of-IoT-AI-are-Driving-Growth.html

[55]. Liang, Fan, & Das, Vishnupriya & Kostyuk, Nadiya & Hussain, Muzammil. (2018). Constructing a Data-Driven Society: China's Social Credit System as a State Surveillance Infrastructure. *Policy and Internet*, *10*. 10.1002/poi3.183.

[56]. Mozur, P., & Krolik, A. (2019, December 18). A Surveillance Net Blankets China's Cities, Giving Police Vast Powers. Retrieved from https://www.nytimes.com/2019/12/17/technology/china-surveillance.html

[57]. UCI Department of Statistics. (2020). Data Scientist Ranked Top U.S. Job by Glassdoor. *Donald Bren School of Information & Computer Sciences*. doi:https://www.stat.uci.edu/slider/data-scientist-ranked-top-u-s-job-by-glassdoor/#:~:text=On%20both%20Glassdoor%20lists%2C%20data,good%20sign%20for%20job%20seekers.

[58]. Linn, L. A., & Koo, M. B. (n.d.). Blockchain for Health Data and Its Potential Use in Health IT and Health Care Related Research. *Office of the National Coordinator for Health Information Technology*. Retrieved from https://www.healthit.gov/sites/default/files/11-74-ablockchainforhealthcare.pdf

[59]. Azaria, A., Ekblaw, A., Vieira, T., & Lippman, A. (2016). MedRec: Using Blockchain for Medical Data Access and Permission Management. *2016 2nd International Conference on Open and Big Data (OBD)*. doi: 10.1109/obd.2016.11

[60]. Azaria, A., Ekblaw, A., Vieira, T., & Lippman, A. (2016). MedRec: Using Blockchain for Medical Data Access and Permission Management. *2016 2nd International Conference on Open and Big Data (OBD)*. doi: 10.1109/obd.2016.11

[61]. Azaria, A., Ekblaw, A., Vieira, T., & Lippman, A. (2016). MedRec: Using Blockchain for Medical Data Access and Permission Management. *2016 2nd International Conference on Open and Big Data (OBD)*. doi: 10.1109/obd.2016.11

[62]. "IPFS Documentation." *How IPFS Works*. Protocol Labs, https://docs.ipfs.io/introduction/how-ipfs-works/.

[63]. Greenspan, Gideon. "Blockchains vs Centralized Databases." *Open Source Blockchain Platform*, Multichain Enterprise, 3 Mar. 2016, https://www.multichain.com/blog/2016/03/blockchains-vs-centralized-databases/.

[64]. Tosh, D. K., Shetty, S., Liang, X., Kamhoua, C. A., Kwiat, K. A., & Njilla, L. (2017). Security Implications of Blockchain Cloud with Analysis of Block Withholding Attack. *2017 17th IEEE/ACM International Symposium on Cluster, Cloud and Grid Computing (CCGRID)*. doi: 10.1109/ccgrid.2017.111

[65]. Liang, X., Shetty, S., Tosh, D., Kamhoua, C., Kwiat, K., & Njilla, L. (2017). ProvChain: A Blockchain-Based Data Provenance Architecture in Cloud Environment with Enhanced Privacy and Availability. *2017 17th IEEE/ACM International Symposium on Cluster, Cloud and Grid Computing (CCGRID)*. doi: 10.1109/ccgrid.2017.8

[66]. Liang, X., Shetty, S., Tosh, D., Kamhoua, C., Kwiat, K., & Njilla, L. (2017). ProvChain: A Blockchain-Based Data Provenance Architecture in Cloud Environment with Enhanced

Privacy and Availability. *2017 17th IEEE/ACM International Symposium on Cluster, Cloud and Grid Computing (CCGRID)*. doi: 10.1109/ccgrid.2017.8

[67]. Guin, U., Cui, P., & Skjellum, A. (2018). Ensuring Proof-of-Authenticity of IoT Edge Devices Using Blockchain Technology. *2018 IEEE International Conference on Internet of Things (IThings) and IEEE Green Computing and Communications (GreenCom) and IEEE Cyber, Physical and Social Computing (CPSCom) and IEEE Smart Data (SmartData)*. doi: 10.1109/cybermatics_2018.2018.00193

[68]. Guin, U., Cui, P., & Skjellum, A. (2018). Ensuring Proof-of-Authenticity of IoT Edge Devices Using Blockchain Technology. *2018 IEEE International Conference on Internet of Things (IThings) and IEEE Green Computing and Communications (GreenCom) and IEEE Cyber, Physical and Social Computing (CPSCom) and IEEE Smart Data (SmartData)*. doi: 10.1109/cybermatics_2018.2018.00193

[69]. Xu, Q., Aung, K. M. M., Zhu, Y., & Yong, K. L. (2017). A Blockchain-Based Storage System for Data Analytics in the Internet of Things. *New Advances in the Internet of Things Studies in Computational Intelligence*, 119–138. doi: 10.1007/978-3-319-58190-3_8

[70].. Xu, Q., Aung, K. M. M., Zhu, Y., & Yong, K. L. (2017). A Blockchain-Based Storage System for Data Analytics in the Internet of Things. *New Advances in the Internet of Things Studies in Computational Intelligence*, 119–138. doi: 10.1007/978-3-319-58190-3_8

[71]. Zyskind, G., Nathan, O., & Pentland, A. (2018). Enigma: Decentralized Computation Platform with Guaranteed Privacy. *Enigma Developer Portal*. doi: 10.7551/mitpress/11636.003.0018

[72]. Shrier, A. A., Chang, A., Diakun-thibault, N., Forni, L., Landa, F., Mayo, J., & Riezen, R. V. (n.d.). Blockchain and Health IT: Algorithms, Privacy, and Data. *Project PharmOrchard of MIT's Experimental Learning "MIT Fintech: Future Commerce"*. Retrieved from https://www.healthit.gov/sites/default/files/1-78-blockchainandhealthitalgorithmsprivacydata_whitepaper.pdf

[73]. Enigma Project. (2017, December 18). Why Enigma's Privacy Protocol Will Power Our Decentralized Future. Retrieved from https://blog.enigma.co/why-enigmas-privacy-protocol-will-power-our-decentralized-future-aedb8c9ee2f6.

74. Wang, Y., Kung, L., & Byrd, T. A. (2018). Big data analytics: Understanding its capabilities and potential benefits for healthcare organizations. *Technological Forecasting and Social Change, 126*, 3–13. doi: 10.1016/j.techfore.2015.12.019

75. Sterling, G. (2019, June 17). Almost 70% of Digital Ad Spending Going to Google, Facebook, Amazon, Says Analyst Firm. Retrieved from https://marketingland.com/almost-70-of-digital-ad-spending-going-to-google-facebook-amazon-says-analyst-firm-262565.

76. Brave Team. (n.d.). Basic Attention Token (BAT) Blockchain Based Digital Advertising [White Paper]. *Basic Attention Token*. Retrieved from https://basicattentiontoken.org/BasicAttentionTokenWhitePaper-4.pdf

77. C. Nguyen, Personal Communication, January 5, 2019.

78. C. Nguyen, Personal Communication, January 5, 2019.

79. Brave Team. (n.d.). Basic Attention Token (BAT) Blockchain Based Digital Advertising [White Paper]. *Basic Attention Token*. Retrieved from https://basicattentiontoken.org/BasicAttentionTokenWhitePaper-4.pdf

80. Steemit Frequently Asked Questions. (n.d.). Retrieved from https://steemit.com/faq.html#What_is_the_Steem_blockchain.

81. Steemit Frequently Asked Questions. (n.d.). Retrieved from https://steemit.com/faq.html#What_is_the_Steem_blockchain.

82. Steem Team. (2017). Steem: An Incentivized, Blockchain-Based, Public Content Platform. [White Paper]. Steemit Inc. Retrieved From https://steem.com/SteemWhitePaper.pdf

83. Steem Team. (2017). A Protocol for Enabling Smart, Social Currency for Publishers and Content Businesses Across the Internet [Blue Paper]. Steemit Inc. Retrieved From https://steem.com/steem-bluepaper.pdf

84. Segalin, C., Celli, F., Polonio, L., Kosinski, M., Stillwell, D., Sebe, N., … Lepri, B. (2017). What your Facebook Profile Picture Reveals about your Personality. *Proceedings of the 2017 ACM on Multimedia Conference - MM 17*. doi: 10.1145/3123266.3123331

[85]. Harari, Y. N. (2019). *Sapiens: a brief history of humankind*. London: Vintage. (Pt. I)

[86]. Harari, Y. N. (2019). *Sapiens: a brief history of humankind*. London: Vintage. (Pt. I)

[87]. Harari, Y. N. (2019). *Sapiens: a brief history of humankind*. London: Vintage. (Pt. I)

[88]. Jordan Peterson on Wealth Concentration & Normal vs Pareto Distributions. (2017, June 17). Retrieved from https://youtu.be/CsRLVZTYpGo.

[89]. Jordan Peterson on Wealth Concentration & Normal vs Pareto Distributions. (2017, June 17). Retrieved from https://youtu.be/CsRLVZTYpGo.

[90]. Davies, J., Sandstrom, S., Shorrocks, A., & Wolff, E. N. (n.d.). The Global Distribution of Household Wealth. *United Nations University*. Retrieved from https://www.wider.unu.edu/publication/global-distribution-household-wealth

[91]. Stone, C., Trisi, D., Shermon, A., & Taylor, R. (2019). A Guide to Statistics on Historical Trends in Income Inequality. *Center on Budget and Privacy Priorities*. Retrieved from https://www.cbpp.org/research/poverty-and-inequality/a-guide-to-statistics-on-historical-trends-in-income-inequality

[92]. Disfold.com. (2020, September 29). Top 30 Largest US Companies in the S&P 500 Index 2020. Retrieved October 30, 2020, from https://disfold.com/top-us-companies-sp500/

[93]. Etwaru, R. (2017). *Blockchain: Trust Companies: Every company is at Risk of Being Disrupted by a Trusted Version of Itself*. Indianapolis, IN: Dog Ear Publishing.

[94]. Levinson, M. (2012). *The Great A & P and the Struggle for Small Business in America*. New York: Hill and Wang.

[95]. Parker, R. E., Whaples, R. (2013). Chapter 33: Retail Innovations in Economic History—The Rise of Mass-Market Merchandisers. *Routledge Handbook of Major Events in Economic History*. Abingdon: Routledge.

[96]. Kramer, A. (2019, October 15). These 10 Companies Make a Lot of the Food We Buy: Here's How We Made Them Better. *Oxfam*. Retrieved from

https://www.oxfamamerica.org/explore/stories/these-10-companies-make-a-lot-of-the-food-we-buy-heres-how-we-made-them-better/.

97. Grocery Store Chains Net Profit, Food Retailing Industry Speaks. (2017, October). Food Marketing Institute. Retrieved from https://www.fmi.org/our-research/supermarket-facts/grocery-store-chains-net-profit

98. Anderson, G. Did Amazon Fail Fast or Fail Fresh with Grocery Delivery? (2017, November 16). *Retail Wire*. Retrieved from https://www.forbes.com/sites/retailwire/2017/11/16/did-amazon-fail-fast-or-fail-fresh-with-grocery-delivery/.

99. Chace, Z. (2011, November 15). Why Amazon Loses Money on Every Kindle Fire. Retrieved from https://www.npr.org/sections/money/2011/11/16/142310104/why-amazon-loses-money-on-every-kindle-fire.

100. Winkler, R. (2015, February 25). YouTube: 1 Billion Viewers, No Profit. *Wall Street Journal* . Retrieved from https://www.wsj.com/articles/viewers-dont-add-up-to-profit-for-youtube-1424897967

101. Tassi, P. (2014, August 11). Why It's Perfectly Fine If Microsoft Has Lost Money on Xbox One [Updated]. *Forbes*. Retrieved from https://www.forbes.com/sites/insertcoin/2014/08/11/why-its-perfectly-fine-if-microsoft-has-lost-400m-on-xbox-one/#17da1bf56662

102. Pejic, I. (2019). Chapter 4, Data Behemoths Are Coming. *Blockchain Babel: The Crypto Craze and the Challenge To Business*. London: Kogan Page.

103. Amazon.com Announces Fourth Quarter Sales up 20% to $72.4 Billion. (2019, January 31). *Business Wire: A Berkshire Hathaway Company*. Retrieved from https://www.businesswire.com/news/home/20190131005900/en/Amazon.com-Announces-Fourth-Quarter-Sales-20-72.4

104. Cloud Infrastructure Spend Grows 46% In Q4 2018 to Exceed US$80 Billion for Full Year. (2019, February 5). *Canayls*. Retrieved from https://www.canalys.com/static/press_release/2019/pr20190204.pdf

[105]. Fuchs, C., & Sevignani, S. (2013). What Is Digital Labour? What Is Digital Work? What's Their Difference? And Why Do These Questions Matter for Understanding Social Media? *TripleC: Communication, Capitalism & Critique. Open Access Journal for a Global Sustainable Information Society*, *11*(2), 237–293. doi: 10.31269/vol11iss2pp237-293

[106]. Galloway, S. (2017). *The Four: the Hidden DNA of the Tech Giants* (p.6). Portfolio/Penguin Pub Group.

[107]. Hannu Saarijärvi, Hannu Kuusela, P. K. Kannan, Gauri Kulkarni & Timo Rintamäki (2016). Unlocking the Transformative Potential of Customer Data in Retailing. *The International Review of Retail, Distribution and Consumer Research, 26*(3), 225-241, DOI: 10.1080/09593969.2015.1105846

[108]. Kumar, S. (2008). A Study of the Supermarket Industry and Its Growing Logistics Capabilities. *International Journal of Retail & Distribution Management*, *36*(3), 192-211. https://doi.org/10.1108/09590550810859150

[109]. Kumar, S. (2008). A Study of the Supermarket Industry and Its Growing Logistics Capabilities. *International Journal of Retail & Distribution Management*, *36*(3), 192-211. https://doi.org/10.1108/09590550810859150

[110]. Amazon Privacy Notice. (2017). Retrieved from https://www.amazon.com/gp/help/customer/display.html/ref=ap_footer_privacy_notice?ie=UTF8&nodeId=468496&pop-up=1.

[111]. Turner, M. (2017). Amazon Brand Registry Benefits. Retrieved from https://brandservices.amazon.com/benefits.

[112]. Galloway, S. (2017). *The Four: the Hidden DNA of the Tech Giants* (p.6). Portfolio/Penguin Pub Group.

[113]. Hamida, C., & Landi, A. (2018). The Lack of Decentralization of Data: Barriers, Exclusivity, and Monopoly in Open Data. *SSRN Electronic Journal*. doi: 10.2139/ssrn.3266881

[114]. Krastev, I. (n.d.). Does More Transparency Mean More Trust? Retrieved from https://www.opengovpartnership.org/trust/does-more-transparency-mean-more-trust/.

[115]. Open Knowledge Foundation, Open Global Data Index. (2015). Retrieved from https://index.okfn.org/place/.

[116]. World Wide Web Foundation. (2019). The Open Data Barometer. Retrieved from https://opendatabarometer.org/?_year=2017&indicator=ODB.

[117]. Hamida, C., & Landi, A. (2018). The Lack of Decentralization of Data: Barriers, Exclusivity, and Monopoly in Open Data. *SSRN Electronic Journal*. doi: 10.2139/ssrn.3266881

[118]. Kahn, L. M. (2018). Sources of Tech Platform Power. *Georgetown Law Technology Review*, 330–331. Retrieved from https://georgetownlawtechreview.org/wp-content/uploads/2018/07/2.2-Khan-pp-225-34.pdf

[119]. Google Security Blog. (2019, June 12). Improving Security and Privacy for Extensions Users. Retrieved from https://security.googleblog.com/2019/06/improving-security-and-privacy-for.html.

[120]. Leswing, K. (2019, September 29). Apple makes Billions from Google's Dominance in Search—and It's a Bigger Business than iCloud or Apple Music. *Business Insider*. Retrieved from https://www.businessinsider.com/aapl-share-price-google-pays-apple-9-billion-annually-tac-goldman-2018-9

[121]. Edelman, B. (2017). Google, Mobile and Competition: The Current State of Play. *CPI Antitrust Chronicle*, 1–2. Retrieved from https://www.benedelman.org/publications/cpi-edelman-google-mobile-2017.pdf

[122]. Edelman, B. (2017). Google, Mobile and Competition: The Current State of Play. *CPI Antitrust Chronicle*, 1–2. Retrieved from https://www.benedelman.org/publications/cpi-edelman-google-mobile-2017.pdf

[123]. Clement, J. (2019, October 9). App Stores: Number of Apps in Leading App Stores 2019. Retrieved from https://www.statista.com/statistics/276623/number-of-apps-available-in-leading-app-stores/.

[124]. Landau, T. (2010, February 16). Rejected by Apple. Retrieved from https://www.macobserver.com/tmo/article/rejected_by_apple.

[125]. Weber, H. (2013, July 25). Treehouse Branches Out to the iPad with a New App. Retrieved from https://thenextweb.com/apps/2013/07/25/tech-education-startup-treehouse-branches-out-to-the-ipad/.

[126]. Google Play Console Help. (2018). Service Fees: Play Console Help. Retrieved from https://support.google.com/googleplay/android-developer/answer/112622?hl=en.

[127]. Wasserman, J. (2019). Apple v. Pepper: Applying the Indirect Purchaser Rule to Online Platforms. *Duke Journal of Constitutional Law & Public Policy, Vol. 14*, 149–151. Retrieved from
https://scholarship.law.duke.edu/cgi/viewcontent.cgi?article=1177&context=djclpp_sidebar

[128]. Wells, G., & Seetharaman, D. (2019, September 24). Snap Detailed Facebook's Aggressive Tactics in "Project Voldemort" Dossier. *The Wall Street Journal*. Retrieved from https://www.wsj.com/articles/snap-detailed-facebooks-aggressive-tactics-in-project-voldemort-dossier-11569236404

[129]. Wells, G., & Seetharaman, D. (2019, September 24). Snap Detailed Facebook's Aggressive Tactics in "Project Voldemort" Dossier. *The Wall Street Journal*. Retrieved from https://www.wsj.com/articles/snap-detailed-facebooks-aggressive-tactics-in-project-voldemort-dossier-11569236404

[130]. King, R. (2016, September 29). Salesforce.com to Press Regulators to Block Microsoft-LinkedIn Deal. *The Wall Street Journal*. Retrieved from https://www.wsj.com/articles/salesforce-com-to-press-regulators-to-block-microsoft-linkedin-deal-1475178870

[131]. Lina M. Khan. (2016). Amazon's Antitrust Paradox, *Yale Law* Journal, *126*, 185-187. Retrieved from https://digitalcommons.law.yale.edu/ylj/vol126/iss3/3

[132]. Edelman, B. (2017). Google, Mobile and Competition: The Current State of Play. *CPI Antitrust Chronicle*. Retrieved from https://www.benedelman.org/publications/cpi-edelman-google-mobile-2017.pdf

[133]. Edelman, B. (2017). Google, Mobile and Competition: The Current State of Play. *CPI Antitrust Chronicle*. Retrieved from https://www.benedelman.org/publications/cpi-edelman-google-mobile-2017.pdf

[134]. Clark, T. (2017). Google v. Commissioner: A Comparison of European Unions and United States Antitrust Law. *Seton Hall Law Review, 47,* 1026–1027. Retrieved from https://scholarship.shu.edu/cgi/viewcontent.cgi?article=1607&context=shlr

[135]. Clark, T. (2017). Google v. Commissioner: A Comparison of European Unions and United States Antitrust Law. *Seton Hall Law Review*, 47, 1026–1027. Retrieved from https://scholarship.shu.edu/cgi/viewcontent.cgi?article=1607&context=shlr

[136]. Clark, T. (2017). Google v. Commissioner: A Comparison of European Unions and United States Antitrust Law. *Seton Hall Law Review*, 47, 1026–1027. Retrieved from https://scholarship.shu.edu/cgi/viewcontent.cgi?article=1607&context=shlr

[137]. Clark, T. (2017). Google v. Commissioner: A Comparison of European Unions and United States Antitrust Law. *Seton Hall Law Review, 47,* 1026–1027. Retrieved from https://scholarship.shu.edu/cgi/viewcontent.cgi?article=1607&context=shlr

[138]. Clark, T. (2017). Google v. Commissioner: A Comparison of European Unions and United States Antitrust Law. *Seton Hall Law Review, 47,* 1026–1027. Retrieved from https://scholarship.shu.edu/cgi/viewcontent.cgi?article=1607&context=shlr

[139]. Clark, T. (2017). Google v. Commissioner: A Comparison of European Unions and United States Antitrust Law. *Seton Hall Law Review, 47,* 1026–1027. Retrieved from https://scholarship.shu.edu/cgi/viewcontent.cgi?article=1607&context=shlr

[140]. Lamoreaux, N. R. (2019). The Problem of Bigness: From Standard Oil to Google. *Journal of Economic Perspectives*, *33*(3), 111. doi: 10.1257/jep.33.3.94

[141]. Lamoreaux, N. R. (2019). The Problem of Bigness: From Standard Oil to Google. *Journal of Economic Perspectives*, *33*(3), 111. doi: 10.1257/jep.33.3.94

[142]. Baseman, K. C., Warren-Boulton, F. R., & Woroch, G. A. (2000). Microsoft Plays Hardball: The Use of Exclusionary Pricing and Technical Incompatibility to Maintain Monopoly Power in Markets for Operating System Software. *SSRN Electronic Journal*. doi: 10.2139/ssrn.241988

[143]. Clark, T. (2017). Google v. Commissioner: A Comparison of European Unions and United States Antitrust Law. *Seton Hall Law Review, 47,* 1026–1027. Retrieved from https://scholarship.shu.edu/cgi/viewcontent.cgi?article=1607&context=shlr

[144]. Clark, T. (2017). Google v. Commissioner: A Comparison of European Unions and United States Antitrust Law. *Seton Hall Law Review, 47,* 1026–1027. Retrieved from https://scholarship.shu.edu/cgi/viewcontent.cgi?article=1607&context=shlr

[145]. Clark, T. (2017). Google v. Commissioner: A Comparison of European Unions and United States Antitrust Law. *Seton Hall Law Review, 47,* 1026–1027. Retrieved from https://scholarship.shu.edu/cgi/viewcontent.cgi?article=1607&context=shlr

[146]. Manne, G. A., & Rinehart, W. (n.d.). The Market Realities that Undermined the FTC's Antitrust Case Against Google. *Harvard Journal of Law & Technology*. Retrieved from https://jolt.law.harvard.edu/assets/misc/ManneRinehart.pdf

[147]. Google. (2017, October 19). Retrieved from https://www.ftc.gov/about-ftc/foia/frequently-requested-records/google.

[148]. Lamoreaux, N. R. (2019). The Problem of Bigness: From Standard Oil to Google. *Journal of Economic Perspectives*, *33*(3). doi: 10.1257/jep.33.3.94

[149]. Haucap, J. (2015). Competition and Antitrust In Internet markets. DICE Discussion Paper, No. 199. *Handbook on the Economics of the Internet* (pp. 15–21). doi: 10.4337/9780857939852.00017

[150]. Gilder, G. (2018). *Life after Google*. 168-169. Regnery Publishing..

[151]. Srinivasan, S. (2014). Building Trust in Cloud Computing: Challenges in the Midst of Outages. *Proceedings of the 2014 InSITE Conference*. doi: 10.28945/2018

[152]. Murphy, J., & Roser, M. (2015, July 14). Internet. Retrieved from https://ourworldindata.org/internet

[153]. Leiner, B. M., Cerf, V. G., Clark, D. D., Kahn, R. E., Lynch, D. C., Postel, J., … Wolff, S. (1997). Brief History of the Internet. Retrieved from https://www.internetsociety.org/internet/history-internet/brief-history-internet/

154. (n.d.). Dot-Com Bubble Timeline. Retrieved from https://worldhistoryproject.org/topics/dot-com-bubble

155. McCullough, B. (2018, December 4). An Eye-Opening Look at the Dot-Com Bubble of 2000—and How It Shapes Our Lives Today. Retrieved from https://ideas.ted.com/an-eye-opening-look-at-the-dot-com-bubble-of-2000-and-how-it-shapes-our-lives-today/

156. McCullough, B. (2018, December 4). An Eye-Opening Look at the Dot-Com Bubble of 2000—and How It Shapes Our Lives Today. Retrieved from https://ideas.ted.com/an-eye-opening-look-at-the-dot-com-bubble-of-2000-and-how-it-shapes-our-lives-today/

157. Goodnight, G. T., & Green, S. (2010). Rhetoric, Risk, and Markets: The Dot-Com Bubble. *QOfek, E., & Richardson, M. (2001). DotCom Mania: The Rise and Fall of Internet Stock Prices, 32–33. DOI: 10.3386/w8630uarterly Journal of Speech*, 96(2), 131–132. DOI: 10.1080/00335631003796669

158. Ofek, E., & Richardson, M. (2001). DotCom Mania: The Rise and Fall of Internet Stock Prices, 32–33. doi: 10.3386/w8630

159. McCullough, B. (2018, December 4). An Eye-Opening Look at the Dot-Com Bubble of 2000—and How It Shapes Our Lives Today. Retrieved from https://ideas.ted.com/an-eye-opening-look-at-the-dot-com-bubble-of-2000-and-how-it-shapes-our-lives-today/

160. Leath, J. L. (2019). Is Bitcoin Reminiscent of Past Bubbles? *University of Tennessee at Chattanooga UTC Scholar*, 36–36.

161. Werbach, K. (2018). *The Blockchain and the New Architecture of Trust* (pp. 228-29). Cambridge, MA: The MIT Press.

162. Waves Platform. (2016, April 1). WAVES Whitepaper. Retrieved from https://blog.wavesplatform.com/waves-whitepaper-164dd6ca6a23

163. (n.d.). Historical Snapshot: June 04, 2017. Retrieved from https://coinmarketcap.com/historical/20170604/

[164]. (2018, December 14). Whatever Happened to Burger King's Own Official Concurrency? Retrieved from https://cryptonewsreview.com/whatever-happened-to-burger-kings-own-official-cryptocurrency/

[165]. Clayton, J. Www.researchgate.net. SEC.gov, 11 Dec. 2017, https://www.researchgate.net/publication/334194583_Initial_Coin_Offering_Mercato_Regolamentazione_e_Performance_Di_Breve_e_Medio-Lungo_Termine.

[166]. Registration Under the Securities Act of 1933. (2011, September 2). SEC Emblem, https://www.sec.gov/fast-answers/answersregis33htm.html.

[167]. Coinmetrics team, C. M. (2019, May 24). An On-Chain Analysis of Ripple's Escrow System. Retrieved from https://coinmetrics.io/an-on-chain-analysis-of-ripples-escrow-system/

[168]. Coinmetrics team, C. M. (2019, May 24). An On-Chain Analysis of Ripple's Escrow System. Retrieved from https://coinmetrics.io/an-on-chain-analysis-of-ripples-escrow-system/

[169]. Baum, S. C. (2018). University Honors Program Thesis. Retrieved from https://digitalcommons.georgiasouthern.edu/cgi/viewcontent.cgi?article=1432&context=honors-theses

[170]. Werbach, K. (2018). *The Blockchain and the New Architecture of Trust* (p. 130). Cambridge, MA: The MIT Press.

[171]. (2019, January 31). Coinbase User Agreement. Retrieved from https://www.coinbase.com/legal/user_agreement

[172]. Melnyk, Steven A., et al. Blockchain Is Vastly Overrated; Supply Chain Cybersecurity Is Vastly Underrated. (May 2019). Supply Chain 24 7, https://www.supplychain247.com/article/blockchain_is_overrated_supply_chain_cybersecurity_is_underrated.

[173]. Melnyk, S. A., Peters, C., Spruill, J., & Sullivan, K. W. (2018). Implementing Cybersecurity in DoD Supply Chains White Paper Manufacturing Division Survey Results. Retrieved from http://www.ndia.org/-/media/sites/ndia/divisions/manufacturing/documents/cybersecurity-in-dod-supply-chains.ashx?la=en

174. Melnyk, Steven A., et al. Blockchain Is Vastly Overrated; Supply Chain Cybersecurity Is Vastly Underrated. (May 2019). Supply Chain 24 7, https://www.supplychain247.com/article/blockchain_is_overrated_supply_chain_cybersecurity_is_underrated.

175. (18AD, September 18). This Chart Reveals the Centralization of Bitcoin Wealth. Retrieved from https://howmuch.net/articles/bitcoin-wealth-distribution

176. (2016). The DAO Chronology of a Daring Heist and Its Resolution. *Deloitte*. Retrieved from https://www2.deloitte.com/content/dam/Deloitte/de/Documents/Innovation/Deloitte_Blockchain_Institute_Whitepaper_The_DAO.pdf

177. (2016). The DAO Chronology of a Daring Heist and Its Resolution. *Deloitte*. Retrieved from https://www2.deloitte.com/content/dam/Deloitte/de/Documents/Innovation/Deloitte_Blockchain_Institute_Whitepaper_The_DAO.pdf

178. Werbach, K. (2018). *The Blockchain and the New Architecture of Trust*. (pp. 67-69). Cambridge, MA: The MIT Press.

179. Homepage. Alex Tapscott, http://www.alextapscott.com/.

180. Tapscott, D., & Tapscott, A. (2018). *Blockchain Revolution: How the Technology Behind Bitcoin and Other Cryptocurrencies Is Changing the World* (p. 139). Toronto, Canada: Penguin.

181. Energy Technology Systems Analysis Programme (2013). *Renewable Integration In Power Grids*. Retrieved from https://iea-etsap.org/E-TechDS/PDF/E15_Ren_integr_FINAL_Dec2013_GSOK.pdf

182. Pop, C., Cioara, T., Antal, M., Anghel, I., Salomie, I., & Bertoncini, M. (2018). Blockchain Based Decentralized Management of Demand Response Programs in Smart Energy Grids. *Sensors*, *18*(2), 162. doi: 10.3390/s18010162

183. Marke, A., Sylvester, B., Macinante, J., & Klauser, S. (2018). Chapter 9. *Transforming Climate Finance and Green Investment with Blockchains*. London: Academic Press.

184. Energy Cryptocurrencies. (n.d.). Retrieved September 13, 2019, from https://cryptoslate.com/cryptos/energy/

185. Power Ledger (POWR) Price, Charts, Market Cap, and Other Metrics. (n.d.). Retrieved September 13, 2019, from https://coinmarketcap.com/currencies/power-ledger/

186. GreenPower (GRN) Price, Charts, Market Cap, and Other Metrics. (n.d.). Retrieved September 13, 2019, from https://coinmarketcap.com/currencies/greenpower/

187. Restart Energy MWAT (MWAT) Price, Charts, Market Cap, and Other Metrics. (n.d.). Retrieved September 13, 2019, from https://coinmarketcap.com/currencies/restart-energy-mwat/

188. Mihaylov, M., Razo-Zapata, I., Rădulescu, R., Jurado, S., Avellana, N., & Nowé, A. (2016). Smart Grid Demonstration Platform for Renewable Energy Exchange. *Advances in Practical Applications of Scalable Multi-Agent Systems. The PAAMS Collection Lecture Notes in Computer Science*. doi: 10.1007/978-3-319-39324-7_30

189. Marke, A., Sylvester, B., Macinante, J., & Klauser, S. (2018). Chapter 9. *Transforming Climate Finance and Green Investment with Blockchains*. London: Academic Press.

190. Marke, A., Sylvester, B., Macinante, J., & Klauser, S. (2018). Chapter 9. *Transforming Climate Finance and Green Investment with Blockchains*. London: Academic Press.

191. Marke, A., Sylvester, B., Macinante, J., & Klauser, S. (2018). Chapter 9. *Transforming Climate Finance and Green Investment with Blockchains*. London: Academic Press.

192. Marke, A., Sylvester, B., Macinante, J., & Klauser, S. (2018). Chapter 9. *Transforming Climate Finance and Green Investment with Blockchains*. London: Academic Press.

193. M. Mihaylov (personal communication, September 10, 2019).

194. Kinsey, D. (2019). *The Blockchain Code: Decrypt The Jungle of Complexity to Win the Crypto-Anarchy Game* (pp.. 164-165). Independently published.

195. Kinsey, D. (2019). *The Blockchain Code: Decrypt The Jungle of Complexity to Win the Crypto-Anarchy Game* (p. 180). Independently published.

[196] Nair, M., & Sutter, D. (2018). Independent. *The Blockchain and Increasing Cooperative Efficacy*. Retrieved from https://www.independent.org/pdf/tir/tir_22_4_03_nair.pdf

[197]. Brafman, O., & Beckstrom, R. A. (2006). *The Starfish and the Spider: The Unstoppable Power of Leaderless Organizations* (pp. 128-129). London: Portfolio.

[198]. Brafman, O., & Beckstrom, R. A. (2006). *The Starfish and the Spider: The Unstoppable Power of Leaderless Organizations* (pp. 128-129). London: Portfolio.

[199.] Market.us. (2020, August 4). Facebook Statistics and Facts. Retrieved from https://market.us/statistics/social-media/facebook/

[200]. The DFINITY Foundation. (2017). Evolution of the Internet. Retrieved from https://DFINITY.org/evolution-of-the-Internet/

[201]. American Printing History Association. (2015). History of Printing Timeline. Retrieved from https://printinghistory.org/timeline/

[202]. Werbach, K. (2018). The Blockchain and the New Architecture of Trust. Cambridge, MA: MIT Press. (P. 232)

[203]. Kinsey, D. (2019). *The Blockchain Code: Decrypt The Jungle of Complexity to Win the Crypto-Anarchy Game* (p. 180). Independently published.

[204]. Hughes, E. (1993, March 9). A Cypherpunk's Manifesto. Retrieved from https://www.activism.net/cypherpunk/manifesto.html

[205]. Hughes, E. (1993, March 9). A Cypherpunk's Manifesto. Retrieved from https://www.activism.net/cypherpunk/manifesto.html

[206]. Kinsey, D. (2019). *The Blockchain Code: Decrypt The Jungle of Complexity to Win the Crypto-Anarchy Game* (pp. 224-225). Independently published.

[207]. https://wikileaks.org/

[208]. Kinsey, D. (2019). *The Blockchain Code: Decrypt The Jungle of Complexity to Win the Crypto-Anarchy Game* (pp. 224-225). Independently published.

209. Kinsey, D. (2019). *The Blockchain Code: Decrypt The Jungle of Complexity to Win the Crypto-Anarchy Game* (pp. 217-227). Independently published.

210. Unknown. (2011, October 24). WikiLeaks: Banking Blockade and Donations Campaign. Retrieved from https://wikileaks.org/IMG/pdf/WikiLeaks-Banking-Blockade-Information-Pack.pdf

211. Lessig, L. (2012, February 29). Code Is Law. Retrieved from https://harvardmagazine.com/2000/01/code-is-law-html

212. Lehdonvirta, V. (2016, November 21). The Blockchain Paradox: Why Distributed Ledger Technologies May Do Little to Transform The Economy. Retrieved from https://www.oii.ox.ac.uk/blog/the-blockchain-paradox-why-distributed-ledger-technologies-may-do-little-to-transform-the-economy/

213. Mathiason, J., Mueller, M., Klein, H., Holitscher, M., & McKnight, L. (2004). Internet Governance: The State of Play. The Internet Governance Project. doi:https://www.internetgovernance.org/wp-content/uploads/mainreport-final.pdf

214. Abramowicz, M. B. (2019). The Very Brief History of Decentralized Blockchain Governance. SSRN Electronic Journal. doi:10.2139/ssrn.3366613

215. Abramowicz, M. B. (2019). The Very Brief History of Decentralized Blockchain Governance. SSRN Electronic Journal. doi:10.2139/ssrn.3366613

216. Zwitter A and Hazenberg J (2020) Decentralized Network Governance: Blockchain Technology and the Future of Regulation. Front. Blockchain 3:12. doi: 10.3389/fbloc.2020.00012

217. Zwitter A and Hazenberg J (2020) Decentralized Network Governance: Blockchain Technology and the Future of Regulation. Front. Blockchain 3:12. doi: 10.3389/fbloc.2020.00012

218. Buterin, V. (2019, May 30). Notes on Blockchain Governance. Retrieved from https://hackernoon.com/notes-on-blockchain-governance-ob65o3pod

219. Buterin, V. (2019, May 30). Notes on Blockchain Governance. Retrieved from https://hackernoon.com/notes-on-blockchain-governance-ob65o3pod

220. Buterin, V. (2017). Governance, Part 2: Plutocracy Is Still Bad. Retrieved from https://vitalik.ca/general/2018/03/28/plutocracy.html

221. Buterin, V. (2019, May 30). Notes on Blockchain Governance. Retrieved from https://hackernoon.com/notes-on-blockchain-governance-ob65o3pod

222. Seidel, Marc-David. (2018). Questioning Centralized Organizations in a Time of Distributed Trust. *Journal of Management Inquiry*, *27*, 40-44. 10.1177/1056492617734942.

223. Seidel, Marc-David. (2018). Questioning Centralized Organizations in a Time of Distributed Trust. *Journal of Management Inquiry*, *27*, 40-44. 10.1177/1056492617734942.

224. Williams, D., & Jones, S. (2020, April 03). DFINITY: Vision for a Simplified IT Stack. Retrieved from https://youtu.be/hiZ-EPwG9uQ

225. The DFINITY Foundation. (2019). How Does the Internet Computer Make Things Better? Retrieved from https://DFINITY.org/faq/how-does-the-Internet-computer-make-things-better

226. The DFINITY Foundation. (2019). How Does the Internet Computer Make Things Better? Retrieved from https://DFINITY.org/faq/how-does-the-Internet-computer-make-things-better

227. The DFINITY Foundation. (2019). How Can the Internet Computer Undo the Monopolization of the Internet? Retrieved from https://DFINITY.org/faq/how-can-the-Internet-computer-undo-the-monopolization-of-the-Internet

228. The DFINITY Foundation. (2019). How Can the Internet Computer Undo the Monopolization of the Internet? Retrieved from https://DFINITY.org/faq/how-can-the-Internet-computer-undo-the-monopolization-of-the-Internet

229. The DFINITY Foundation. (2019). How Can the Internet Computer Undo the Monopolization of the Internet? Retrieved from https://DFINITY.org/faq/how-can-the-Internet-computer-undo-the-monopolization-of-the-Internet

230. DFINITY Foundation: Internet Computer. (n.d.). Retrieved from https://DFINITY.org/

[231]. The DFINITY Foundation. (2019). How Does the Internet Computer Host Tamperproof Systems? Retrieved from https://DFINITY.org/faq/how-does-the-Internet-computer-host-tamperproof-systems

[232]. Polkadot and DFINITY. (n.d.). · Polkadot Wiki. Retrieved from https://wiki.polkadot.network/docs/en/learn-comparisons-DFINITY

[233]. Williams, D. (2020, July 31). The DFINITY "Blockchain Nervous System." Retrieved from https://medium.com/DFINITY/the-DFINITY-blockchain-nervous-system-a5dd1783288e

[234]. Williams, D. (2020, July 31). Future Governance? Integrating Traditional AI Technology into the Blockchain Nervous System. Retrieved from https://medium.com/DFINITY/future-governance-integrating-traditional-ai-technology-into-the-blockchain-nervous-system-825ababf9d9

[235]. Next-level Communities Run on Aragon. (n.d.). Retrieved from https://aragon.org/

[236]. Bernardo B., Cauderlier R., Hu Z., Pesin B., Tesson J. (2020) Mi-Cho-Coq, a Framework for Certifying Tezos Smart Contracts. In: Sekerinski E. et al. (eds) *Formal Methods*. FM 2019 International Workshops. *Lecture Notes in Computer Science, 12232*. Springer, https://doi.org/10.1007/978-3-030-54994-7_28

[237]. Neo-Project. (n.d.). Neo Documentation (Governance Mechanism Section). Retrieved November 30, 2020, from https://docs.neo.org/docs/en-us/basic/whitepaper.html

[238]. Baird, L., Harmon, M., & Madsen, P. (2017).: The Trust Layer of the Internet. Hedera: A Public Hashgraph Network & Governing Council. Retrieved from https://hedera.com/hh-whitepaper-v2.0-17Sep19.pdf P. 20

[239]. Polkadot Team. (2020, May 20). A Walkthrough of Polkadot's Governance. Retrieved from https://polkadot.network/a-walkthrough-of-polkadots-governance/

[240]. Kwon, J., & Buchman, E. (n.d.). Cosmos Whitepaper. Retrieved from https://cosmos.network/resources/whitepaper

[241]. Xu, B., Luthra, D., Cole, Z., & Blakely, N. (2018). EOS: An Architectural, Performance, and Economic Analysis. doi:https://blog.bitmex.com/wp-content/uploads/2018/11/eos-test-report.pdf Section IV.E

[242]. Lehdonvirta, V. (2016). The blockchain Paradox: Why Distributed Ledger Technologies May Do Little to Transform The Economy. Retrieved from https://www.oii.ox.ac.uk/blog/the-blockchain-paradox-why-distributed-ledger-technologies-may-do-little-to-transform-the-economy/

[243]. The DFINITY Foundation. (2020). Rebooting the Internet: A Conversation with Chris Dixon and Dominic Williams. Retrieved from https://youtu.be/dALucsAgAwE

[244]. Hsieh, Y., Vergne, J., Anderson, P., Lakhani, K., & Reitzig, M. (2019). Correction to: Bitcoin and the Rise of Decentralized Autonomous Organizations. *Journal of Organization Design*, *8*(1). doi:10.1186/s41469-019-0041-1

[245]. Kondova, G., & Barba, R. (2019). Governance of Decentralized Autonomous Organizations. *Journal of Modern Accounting and Auditing*, *15*(8). doi:10.17265/1548-6583/2019.08.003

[246]. Hameed, F. (2005). Fiscal Transparency and Economic Outcomes. *IMF Working Papers*, *5*(225), 1. doi:10.5089/9781451862447.001

[247]. Millar, C. C., Eldomiaty, T. I., Choi, C. J., & Hilton, B. (2005). Corporate Governance and Institutional Transparency in Emerging Markets. *Journal of Business Ethics*, *59*(1-2), 163-174. doi:10.1007/s10551-005-3412-1

[248]. Birchall, C. (2014). Radical Transparency? *Cultural Studies ↔ Critical Methodologies*, *14*(1), 77-88. doi:10.1177/1532708613517442

[249]. Dalio, R. (2017). Principles: Life and Work. Simon and Schuster.

[250]. Sovrin™: A Protocol and Token for SelfSovereign Identity and Decentralized Trust. (2018). *A White Paper from the Sovrin Foundation, Version 1.0*. Retrieved from https://sovrin.org/wp-content/uploads/Sovrin-Protocol-and-Token-White-Paper.pdf (P. 4)

251. Kassem, J. A., Sayeed, S., Marco-Gisbert, H., Pervez, Z., & Dahal, K. (2019). DNS-IdM: A Blockchain Identity Management System to Secure Personal Data Sharing in a Network. *Applied Sciences*, *9*(15), 2953. doi: 10.3390/app9152953

252. Schalit, E. (2015). Digital Indifference in the Workplace. Dashlane. Retrieved from https://blog.dashlane.com/wp-content/uploads/2015/09/report_passwordsharing_US-1.pdf

253. *Itrc Breach Statistics 2005-2016*. (2016). Identity Theft Resource Center. Retrieved from https://www.idtheftcenter.org/images/breach/Overview2005to2016Finalv2.pdf

254. *2018 End of Year Data Breach Report*. (n. d.) Identity Theft Resource Center. Retrieved From https://www.idtheftcenter.org/wp-content/uploads/2019/02/ITRC_2018-End-of-Year-Aftermath_FINAL_V2_combinedWEB.pdf

255. Dunphy, P., & Petitcolas, F. A. (2018). A First Look at Identity Management Schemes on the Blockchain. *IEEE Security & Privacy*, *16*(4), 20–29. doi: 10.1109/msp.2018.3111247

256. Lyons, T., Coucelas, L., & Timsit, K. (n.d.). *Thematic Report: Blockchain and Digital Identity*. The European Union Blockchain Observatory and Forum. Retrieved From https://www.eublockchainforum.eu/sites/default/files/report_identity_v0.9.4.pdf (P. 8)

257. Shrier, D., Wu, W., & Pentland, A. (2016). Blockchain & Infrastructure (Identity, Data Security). *Massachusetts Institute of Technology Connection Science & Engineering*, *Part 3 Section II*. Retrieved from connection.mit.edu

258. Gruner, A., Muhle, A., & Meinel, C. (July, 2018). On the Relevance of Blockchain in Identity Management. Retrieved from https://arxiv.org/pdf/1807.08136.pdf

259. Gruner, A., Muhle, A., & Meinel, C. (July, 2018). On the Relevance of Blockchain in Identity Management. Retrieved from https://arxiv.org/pdf/1807.08136.pdf

260. https://mspoweruser.com/microsoft-passport-will-be-retired-as-a-brand-once-again/

261. Kassem, J. A., Sayeed, S., Marco-Gisbert, H., Pervez, Z., & Dahal, K. (2019). DNS-IdM: A Blockchain Identity Management System to Secure Personal Data Sharing in a Network. *Applied Sciences*, *9*(15), 2953. doi: 10.3390/app9152953

[262]. Surur, Rahul, & Anmol. (2016, June 29). Microsoft Passport Will Be Retired as a Brand Once Again. Retrieved from https://mspoweruser.com/microsoft-passport-will-be-retired-as-a-brand-once-again/.

[263]. Jones, M. B. (2007). A One-Page Introduction to Windows CardSpace. *Microsoft Corporation*. Retrieved from https://www.microsoft.com/en-us/research/wp-content/uploads/2017/05/CardSpace_One-Pager.pdf

[264]. Hanrahan, T., *Analysis of Windows Cardspace Identity Management System* (2011). Regis University Thesis. 469. Retrieved From https://epublications.regis.edu/theses/469

[265]. Hanrahan, T., *Analysis of Windows Cardspace Identity Management System* (2011). Regis University Thesis. 469. Retrieved From https://epublications.regis.edu/theses/469

[266]. U-Prove Overview. (2012, February 25). Retrieved from https://www.microsoft.com/en-us/research/project/u-prove/.

[267]. U-Prove Overview. (2012, February 25). Retrieved from https://www.microsoft.com/en-us/research/project/u-prove/.

[268]. Alpar, G. (2010). U-Prove Cryptography. Retrieved from http://www.cs.ru.nl/~gergely/objects/u-prove.pdf

[269]. OpenID Connect FAQ and Q&As. (2015, April). Retrieved from https://openid.net/connect/faq/.

[270]. OpenID Connect FAQ and Q&As. (2015, April). Retrieved from https://openid.net/connect/faq/.

[271]. OpenID Connect FAQ and Q&As. (2015, April). Retrieved from https://openid.net/connect/faq/.

[272]. Mainka, C., Mladenov, V., Schwenk, J., & Wich, T. (2017). SoK: Single Sign-On Security: An Evaluation of OpenID Connect. *2017 IEEE European Symposium on Security and Privacy (EuroS&P)*. doi: 10.1109/eurosp.2017.32 (P. 1)

[273]. What is OpenID? (2009, December). Retrieved from https://openid.net/what-is-openid/.

274. Mainka, C., Mladenov, V., Schwenk, J., & Wich, T. (2017). SoK: Single Sign-On Security: An Evaluation of OpenID Connect. *2017 IEEE European Symposium on Security and Privacy (EuroS&P)*. doi: 10.1109/eurosp.2017.32 (P. 15)

275. Li, W., Mitchell, C. J., & Chen, T. (2019). OAuthGuard: Protecting User Security and Privacy with OAuth 2.0 and OpenID Connect. *Proceedings of the 5th ACM Workshop on Security Standardisation Research Workshop, SSR19*. doi: 10.1145/3338500.3360331 (P. 1-2)

276. Mainka, C., Mladenov, V., Schwenk, J., & Wich, T. (2017). SoK: Single Sign-On Security: An Evaluation of OpenID Connect. *2017 IEEE European Symposium on Security and Privacy (EuroS&P)*. doi: 10.1109/eurosp.2017.32 (P. 15)

277. Li, W., Mitchell, C. J., & Chen, T. (2019). OAuthGuard: Protecting User Security and Privacy with OAuth 2.0 and OpenID Connect. *Proceedings of the 5th ACM Workshop on Security Standardisation Research Workshop, SSR19*. doi: 10.1145/3338500.3360331 (P. 1-2)

278. Mainka, C., Mladenov, V., Schwenk, J., & Wich, T. (2017). SoK: Single Sign-On Security: An Evaluation of OpenID Connect. *2017 IEEE European Symposium on Security and Privacy*. doi: 10.1109/eurosp.2017.32 (P. 15)

279. Li, W., Mitchell, C. J., & Chen, T. (2019). OAuthGuard: Protecting User Security and Privacy with OAuth 2.0 and OpenID Connect. *Proceedings of the 5th ACM Workshop on Security Standardisation Research Workshop, SSR19*. doi: 10.1145/3338500.3360331 (P. 1-2)

280. Lyons, T., Coucelas, L., & Timsit, K. (n.d.). *Thematic Report: Blockchain and Digital Identity* (p. 14). The European Union Blockchain Observatory and Forum. Retrieved From https://www.eublockchainforum.eu/sites/default/files/report_identity_v0.9.4.pdf

281. Montes, M. (2018). Resolving Refugee Crisis Through Blockchain Technology. *Far Eastern University Law Review*. Retrieved from https://www.academia.edu/35361457/Blockchain_Resolving_Refugee_Crisis

282. Montes, M. (2018). Resolving Refugee Crisis Through Blockchain Technology. *Far Eastern University Law Review*. Retrieved from https://www.academia.edu/35361457/Blockchain_Resolving_Refugee_Crisis

283. Lesavre, L., Varin, P., Mell, P., Davidson, M., & Shook, J. (2019). A Taxonomic Approach to Understanding Emerging Blockchain Identity Management Systems. *National Institute of*

Standards and Technology: U.S. Department of Commerce. doi: 10.6028/nist.cswp.01142020 (P. 1)

284. Dunphy, P., & Petitcolas, F. A. (2018). A First Look at Identity Management Schemes on the Blockchain. *IEEE Security & Privacy*, *16*(4), 20–29. doi: 10.1109/msp.2018.3111247 (P.12)

285. Lesavre, L., Varin, P., Mell, P., Davidson, M., & Shook, J. (2019). A Taxonomic Approach to Understanding Emerging Blockchain Identity Management Systems. *National Institute of Standards and Technology: U.S. Department of Commerce*. doi: 10.6028/nist.cswp.01142020 (P. 2)

286. Dunphy, P., & Petitcolas, F. A. (2018). A First Look at Identity Management Schemes on the Blockchain. *IEEE Security & Privacy*, *16*(4), 20–29. doi: 10.1109/msp.2018.3111247 (P. 3)

287. Haddouti, S. E., & Kettani, M. D. E.-C. E. (2019). Analysis of Identity Management Systems Using Blockchain Technology. *2019 International Conference on Advanced Communication Technologies and Networking (CommNet)* (p. 4). doi: 10.1109/commnet.2019.8742375

288. Lesavre, L., Varin, P., Mell, P., Davidson, M., & Shook, J. (2019). A Taxonomic Approach to Understanding Emerging Blockchain Identity Management Systems. *National Institute of Standards and Technology: U.S. Department of Commerce*. doi: 10.6028/nist.cswp.01142020

289. Lesavre, L., Varin, P., Mell, P., Davidson, M., & Shook, J. (2019). A Taxonomic Approach to Understanding Emerging Blockchain Identity Management Systems. *National Institute of Standards and Technology: U.S. Department of Commerce*. doi: 10.6028/nist.cswp.01142020

290. Rana, R., Zaeem, R. N., & Barber, K. S. (2019). An Assessment of Blockchain Identity Solutions: Minimizing Risk and Liability of Authentication. *IEEE/WIC/ACM International Conference on Web Intelligence*. doi: 10.1145/3350546.3352497

291. Sovrin™: A Protocol and Token for SelfSovereign Identity and Decentralized Trust. (2018). *A White Paper from the Sovrin Foundation*, *Version 1.0*. Retrieved from https://sovrin.org/wp-content/uploads/Sovrin-Protocol-and-Token-White-Paper.pdf (P. 7)

292. Sovrin™: A Protocol and Token for SelfSovereign Identity and Decentralized Trust. (2018). *A White Paper from the Sovrin Foundation, Version 1.0* (p. 7). Retrieved from https://sovrin.org/wp-content/uploads/Sovrin-Protocol-and-Token-White-Paper.pdf

293. Sovrin™: A Protocol and Token for SelfSovereign Identity and Decentralized Trust. (2018). *A White Paper from the Sovrin Foundation, Version 1.0* (p. 7). Retrieved from https://sovrin.org/wp-content/uploads/Sovrin-Protocol-and-Token-White-Paper.pdf

294. Lesavre, L., Varin, P., Mell, P., Davidson, M., & Shook, J. (2019). A Taxonomic Approach to Understanding Emerging Blockchain Identity Management Systems. *National Institute of Standards and Technology: U.S. Department of Commerce*. doi: 10.6028/nist.cswp.01142020

295. Lesavre, L., Varin, P., Mell, P., Davidson, M., & Shook, J. (2019). A Taxonomic Approach to Understanding Emerging Blockchain Identity Management Systems. *National Institute of Standards and Technology: U.S. Department of Commerce*. doi: 10.6028/nist.cswp.01142020

296. Lesavre, L., Varin, P., Mell, P., Davidson, M., & Shook, J. (2019). A Taxonomic Approach to Understanding Emerging Blockchain Identity Management Systems. *National Institute of Standards and Technology: U.S. Department of Commerce*. doi: 10.6028/nist.cswp.01142020

297. Lesavre, L., Varin, P., Mell, P., Davidson, M., & Shook, J. (2019). A Taxonomic Approach to Understanding Emerging Blockchain Identity Management Systems. *National Institute of Standards and Technology: U.S. Department of Commerce*. doi: 10.6028/nist.cswp.01142020

298. Lesavre, L., Varin, P., Mell, P., Davidson, M., & Shook, J. (2019). A Taxonomic Approach to Understanding Emerging Blockchain Identity Management Systems. *National Institute of Standards and Technology: U.S. Department of Commerce*. doi: 10.6028/nist.cswp.01142020

299. Sporny, M., Longley, D., & Chadwick, D. (2019, November 19). W3C Developer Portal: Verifiable Credentials Data Model 1.0. Retrieved from https://www.w3.org/TR/vc-data-model/#dfn-credential.

300. W3C Developer Portal: Decentralized Identifiers (DIDs) v1.0. (2019, December 9). Retrieved from https://www.w3.org/TR/2019/WD-did-core-20191209/.

301. W3C Developer Portal: Decentralized Identifiers (DIDs) v1.0. (2019, December 9). Retrieved from https://www.w3.org/TR/2019/WD-did-core-20191209/.

302. W3C Developer Portal: Decentralized Identifiers (DIDs) v1.0. (2019, December 9). Retrieved from https://www.w3.org/TR/2019/WD-did-core-20191209/.

303. Lesavre, L., Varin, P., Mell, P., Davidson, M., & Shook, J. (2019). A Taxonomic Approach to Understanding Emerging Blockchain Identity Management Systems. *National Institute of Standards and Technology: U.S. Department of Commerce.* doi: 10.6028/nist.cswp.01142020 (P. 40)

304. Lyons, T., Coucelas, L., & Timsit, K. (n.d.). *Thematic Report: Blockchain and Digital Identity* (pp. 15-16*).* The European Union Blockchain Observatory and Forum. Retrieved From https://www.eublockchainforum.eu/sites/default/files/report_identity_v0.9.4.pdf

305. Dunphy, P., & Petitcolas, F. A. (2018). A First Look at Identity Management Schemes on the Blockchain. *IEEE Security & Privacy, 16*(4), 20–29. doi: 10.1109/msp.2018.3111247

306. Kassem, J. A., Sayeed, S., Marco-Gisbert, H., Pervez, Z., & Dahal, K. (2019). DNS-IdM: A Blockchain Identity Management System to Secure Personal Data Sharing in a Network. *Applied Sciences, 9*(15), 2953. doi: 10.3390/app9152953

307. Dunphy, P., & Petitcolas, F. A. (2018). A First Look at Identity Management Schemes on the Blockchain. *IEEE Security & Privacy, 16*(4), 20–29. doi: 10.1109/msp.2018.3111247

308. Kassem, J. A., Sayeed, S., Marco-Gisbert, H., Pervez, Z., & Dahal, K. (2019). DNS-IdM: A Blockchain Identity Management System to Secure Personal Data Sharing in a Network. *Applied Sciences, 9*(15), 2953. doi: 10.3390/app9152953

309. Kassem, J. A., Sayeed, S., Marco-Gisbert, H., Pervez, Z., & Dahal, K. (2019). DNS-IdM: A Blockchain Identity Management System to Secure Personal Data Sharing in a Network. *Applied Sciences, 9*(15), 2953. doi: 10.3390/app9152953

310. Dunphy, P., & Petitcolas, F. A. (2018). A First Look at Identity Management Schemes on the Blockchain. *IEEE Security & Privacy, 16*(4), 20–29. doi: 10.1109/msp.2018.3111247 (

311. Dunphy, P., & Petitcolas, F. A. (2018). A First Look at Identity Management Schemes on the Blockchain. *IEEE Security & Privacy, 16*(4), 20–29. doi: 10.1109/msp.2018.3111247

312. Haddouti, S. E., & Kettani, M. D. E.-C. E. (2019). Analysis of Identity Management Systems Using Blockchain Technology. *2019 International Conference on Advanced*

Communication Technologies and Networking (CommNet). doi: 10.1109/commnet.2019.8742375

[313]. Offerman, A. (2018, February 16). Swiss City of Zug issues Ethereum blockchain-based eIDs . Retrieved from https://joinup.ec.europa.eu/collection/egovernment/document/swiss-city-zug-issues-ethereum-blockchain-based-eids.

[314]. Offerman, A. (2018, February 16). Swiss City of Zug issues Ethereum blockchain-based eIDs . Retrieved from https://joinup.ec.europa.eu/collection/egovernment/document/swiss-city-zug-issues-ethereum-blockchain-based-eids.

[315]. Sovrin™: A Protocol and Token for SelfSovereign Identity and Decentralized Trust. (2018). *A White Paper from the Sovrin Foundation, Version 1.0*. Retrieved from https://sovrin.org/wp-content/uploads/Sovrin-Protocol-and-Token-White-Paper.pdf

[316]. Haddouti, S. E., & Kettani, M. D. E.-C. E. (2019). Analysis of Identity Management Systems Using Blockchain Technology. 2019 International Conference on Advanced Communication Technologies and Networking (CommNet). doi: 10.1109/commnet.2019.8742375

[317]. Haddouti, S. E., & Kettani, M. D. E.-C. E. (2019). Analysis of Identity Management Systems Using Blockchain Technology. *2019 International Conference on Advanced Communication Technologies and Networking (CommNet)*. doi: 10.1109/commnet.2019.8742375

[318]. Kassem, J. A., Sayeed, S., Marco-Gisbert, H., Pervez, Z., & Dahal, K. (2019). DNS-IdM: A Blockchain Identity Management System to Secure Personal Data Sharing in a Network. *Applied Sciences, 9*(15), 2953. doi: 10.3390/app9152953

[319]. Dunphy, P., & Petitcolas, F. A. (2018). A First Look at Identity Management Schemes on the Blockchain. *IEEE Security & Privacy, 16*(4), 20–29. doi: 10.1109/msp.2018.3111247

[320]. Dunphy, P., & Petitcolas, F. A. (2018). A First Look at Identity Management Schemes on the Blockchain. *IEEE Security & Privacy, 16*(4), 20–29. doi: 10.1109/msp.2018.3111247

[321]. Haddouti, S. E., & Kettani, M. D. E.-C. E. (2019). Analysis of Identity Management Systems Using Blockchain Technology. *2019 International Conference on Advanced*

Communication Technologies and Networking (CommNet). doi: 10.1109/commnet.2019.8742375

322. https://sovrin.org/wp-content/uploads/Sovrin-Governance-Framework-V2-Master-Document-V2.pdf

323. Sovrin Governance Framework V2 Master Document V2. (April, 2019). *Sovrin Foundation: Governance Framework Working Group*. Retrieved from https://sovrin.org/library/sovrin-governance-framework/

324. Dunphy, P., & Petitcolas, F. A. (2018). A First Look at Identity Management Schemes on the Blockchain. *IEEE Security & Privacy*, *16*(4), 20–29. doi: 10.1109/msp.2018.3111247

325. Gruner, A., Muhle, A., & Meinel , C. (July, 2018). On the Relevance of Blockchain in Identity Management. Retrieved from https://arxiv.org/pdf/1807.08136.pdf

326. Sovrin™: A Protocol and Token for SelfSovereign Identity and Decentralized Trust. (2018). *A White Paper from the Sovrin Foundation, Version 1.0*. Retrieved from https://sovrin.org/wp-content/uploads/Sovrin-Protocol-and-Token-White-Paper.pdf

327. Community, V. O. N. (2019, January 21). About Verifiable Organizations Network (VON). Retrieved from https://vonx.io/about/.

328. Dunphy, P., & Petitcolas, F. A. (2018). A First Look at Identity Management Schemes on the Blockchain. *IEEE Security & Privacy*, *16*(4), 20–29. doi: 10.1109/msp.2018.311124

329. Kassem, J. A., Sayeed, S., Marco-Gisbert, H., Pervez, Z., & Dahal, K. (2019). DNS-IdM: A Blockchain Identity Management System to Secure Personal Data Sharing in a Network. *Applied Sciences*, *9*(15), 2953. doi: 10.3390/app9152953

330. Dunphy, P., & Petitcolas, F. A. (2018). A First Look at Identity Management Schemes on the Blockchain. *IEEE Security & Privacy*, *16*(4), 20–29. doi: 10.1109/msp.2018.3111247

331. Dunphy, P., & Petitcolas, F. A. (2018). A First Look at Identity Management Schemes on the Blockchain. *IEEE Security & Privacy*, *16*(4), 20–29. doi: 10.1109/msp.2018.3111247

[332]. Dunphy, P., & Petitcolas, F. A. (2018). A First Look at Identity Management Schemes on the Blockchain. *IEEE Security & Privacy*, *16*(4), 20–29. doi: 10.1109/msp.2018.3111247

[333]. The Future of Bank Identity & Authorization. (n.d.). *ShoCard Case Study with Bank Aljazira*. Retrieved from https://shocard.com/case-studies/

[334]. The Future of Bank Identity & Authorization. (n.d.). *ShoCard Case Study with Bank Aljazira*. Retrieved from https://shocard.com/case-studies/

[335]. The Future of Credit Reporting. (n.d.). *ShoCard Case Study with Creditinfo*. Retrieved from https://shocard.com/case-studies/

[336]. Digital ID & Authentication Council of Canada. (n.d.). DIACC Website About Page. Retrieved from https://diacc.ca/about-us/.

[337]. The Economic Impact of Digital Identity in Canada Understanding the Potential for Considerable Economic Benefits and the Cost of Inaction. (2018). *DIACC Member Consult Hyperion*. Retrieved from https://diacc.ca/wp-content/uploads/2018/05/Economic-Impact-of-Digital-Identity-DIACC-v2.pdf

[338]. The Economic Impact of Digital Identity in Canada Understanding the Potential for Considerable Economic Benefits and the Cost of Inaction. (2018). *DIACC Member Consult Hyperion*. Retrieved from https://diacc.ca/wp-content/uploads/2018/05/Economic-Impact-of-Digital-Identity-DIACC-v2.pdf

[339]. Andre Boysen Video.

[340]. The Economic Impact of Digital Identity in Canada Understanding the Potential for Considerable Economic Benefits and the Cost of Inaction. (2018). *DIACC Member Consult Hyperion*. Retrieved from https://diacc.ca/wp-content/uploads/2018/05/Economic-Impact-of-Digital-Identity-DIACC-v2.pdf

[341]. Boysen, A. (2017). How Blockchain Is Changing Digital Identity [video]. IBMBlockchain YouTube Channel. Retrieved from https://youtu.be/EQ5PGPIjrtI

[342]. Boysen, A. (2017). How Blockchain Is Changing Digital Identity [video]. IBMBlockchain YouTube Channel. Retrieved from https://youtu.be/EQ5PGPIjrtI

[343]. Boysen, A. (2017). How Blockchain Is Changing Digital Identity [video]. IBMBlockchain YouTube Channel. Retrieved from https://youtu.be/EQ5PGPIjrtI

[344]. Boysen, A. (2017). How Blockchain Is Changing Digital Identity [video]. IBMBlockchain YouTube Channel. Retrieved from https://youtu.be/EQ5PGPIjrtI

[345]. Boysen, A. (2017). How Blockchain Is Changing Digital Identity [video]. IBMBlockchain YouTube Channel. Retrieved from https://youtu.be/EQ5PGPIjrtI

[346]. Boysen, A. (2017). How Blockchain Is Changing Digital Identity [video]. IBMBlockchain YouTube Channel. Retrieved from https://youtu.be/EQ5PGPIjrtI

[347]. Boysen, A. (2017). How Blockchain Is Changing Digital Identity [video]. IBMBlockchain YouTube Channel. Retrieved from https://youtu.be/EQ5PGPIjrtI

[348]. Boysen, A. (2017). How Blockchain Is Changing Digital Identity [video]. IBMBlockchain YouTube Channel. Retrieved from https://youtu.be/EQ5PGPIjrtI

[349]. Boysen, A. (2017). How Blockchain Is Changing Digital Identity [video]. IBMBlockchain YouTube Channel. Retrieved from https://youtu.be/EQ5PGPIjrtI

[350]. Boysen, A. (2017). How Blockchain Is Changing Digital Identity [video]. IBMBlockchain YouTube Channel. Retrieved from https://youtu.be/EQ5PGPIjrtI

[351]. Boysen, A. (2017). How Blockchain Is Changing Digital Identity [video]. IBMBlockchain YouTube Channel. Retrieved from https://youtu.be/EQ5PGPIjrtI

[352]. Boysen, A. (2017). How Blockchain Is Changing Digital Identity [video]. IBMBlockchain YouTube Channel. Retrieved from https://youtu.be/EQ5PGPIjrtI

[353]. Boysen, A. (2017). How Blockchain Is Changing Digital Identity [video]. IBMBlockchain YouTube Channel. Retrieved from https://youtu.be/EQ5PGPIjrtI

[354]. Boysen, A. (2017). How Blockchain Is Changing Digital Identity [video]. IBMBlockchain YouTube Channel. Retrieved from https://youtu.be/EQ5PGPIjrtI

355. Boysen, A. (2017). How Blockchain Is Changing Digital Identity [video]. IBMBlockchain YouTube Channel. Retrieved from https://youtu.be/EQ5PGPIjrtI

356. SecureKey. (n.d.). Partner Directory Page. Retrieved from https://SecureKey.com/partner-directory/.

357. Lundkuist, C., Heck, R., Torstesson, J., Mitton, Z., & Sena, M. (2016). Uport: A Platform for Self-Sovereign Identity (Draft Version) (p. 8). Retrieved from http://blockchainlab.com/pdf/uPort_whitepaper_DRAFT20161020.pdf

358. Sovrin™: A Protocol and Token for SelfSovereign Identity and Decentralized Trust. (2018). A White Paper from the Sovrin Foundation, Version 1.0. Retrieved from https://sovrin.org/wp-content/uploads/Sovrin-Protocol-and-Token-White-Paper.pdf

359. Wong, K. L. X., & Dobson, A. S. (2019). We're Just Data: Exploring China's Social Credit System in Relation to Digital Platform Ratings Cultures in Westernised Democracies. Global Media and China, 4(2), 220–232. doi: 10.1177/2059436419856090

360. Wong, K. L. X., & Dobson, A. S. (2019). We're Just Data: Exploring China's Social Credit System in Relation to Digital Platform Ratings Cultures in Westernised Democracies. Global Media and China, 4(2), 220–232. doi: 10.1177/2059436419856090

361. Redefining the Story of Privacy. (n.d.). Retrieved from https://hu-manity.co/ and https://hu-manity.science/

362. Smith, C. H. (2014, May 21). Tax, Debt, Wage and Fiat Slavery: How the Elites Extract Wealth from the People. Retrieved from https://www.globalresearch.ca/tax-debt-wage-and-fiat-slavery-how-the-elites-extract-wealth-from-the-people/5383129

363. Smith, C. H. (2014, May 21). Tax, Debt, Wage and Fiat Slavery: How the Elites Extract Wealth from the People. Retrieved from https://www.globalresearch.ca/tax-debt-wage-and-fiat-slavery-how-the-elites-extract-wealth-from-the-people/5383129

364. Kurt, D. (2020, January 29). How Currency Works. Retrieved from https://www.investopedia.com/articles/investing/092413/how-currency-works.asp

[365]. U.S. Government Accountability Office, (2019, April 10). The Nation's Fiscal Health: Action Is Needed to Address the Federal Government's Fiscal Future. Retrieved from https://www.gao.gov/americas-fiscal-future?t=federal_debt

[366]. Bureau of Economic Analysis. (2019, February 28). Gross Domestic Product, Fourth Quarter and Annual 2018 (Initial Estimate): U.S. Bureau of Economic Analysis (BEA). Retrieved from https://www.bea.gov/news/2019/initial-gross-domestic-product-4th-quarter-and-annual-2018

[367]. Plecher, H. (2019, December 9). Global GDP 2014-2024. Retrieved from https://www.statista.com/statistics/268750/global-gross-domestic-product-gdp/

[368]. The Federal Reserve. (2020, February 12). FAQs: How much U.S. currency is in circulation? Retrieved from https://www.federalreserve.gov/faqs/currency_12773.htm

[369]. Ravn, I. (2015). Explaining Money Creation by Commercial Banks: Five Analogies for Public Education. *Real-World Economics Review*, *71*, 98. ISSN: 1755-9472

[370]. Klein, M., & Shambaugh, J. C. (2019, March 6). How Fast Did the Economy Grow Last Year? Retrieved from https://econofact.org/how-fast-did-the-economy-grow-last-year

[371]. Johnston, M. (2020, October 15). Why Banks Don't Need Your Money to Make Loans. Retrieved from https://www.investopedia.com/articles/investing/022416/why-banks-dont-need-your-money-make-loans.asp

[372]. Ravn, I. (2015). Explaining Money Creation by Commercial Banks: Five Analogies for Public Education. *Real-World Economics Review*, *71*, 98. ISSN: 1755-9472

[373]. Reserve Bank of Australia. (2018, October 9). Inflation and Its Measurement: Education. Retrieved from https://www.rba.gov.au/education/resources/explainers/inflation-and-its-measurement.html

[374]. Kurt, D. (2020, January 29). How Currency Works. Retrieved from https://www.investopedia.com/articles/investing/092413/how-currency-works.asp

[375]. Pejic, I. (2019). *Blockchain Babel: The Crypto Craze and the Challenge to Business* (p. 145). London: Kogan Page Limited.

[376]. Shrier, D., Wu, W., & Pentland, A. (2016). Blockchain & Infrastructure (Identity, Data Security): Part 3. *Massachusetts Institute of Technology: MIT Connection Science*. Retrieved from https://www.getsmarter.com/blog/wp-content/uploads/2017/07/mit_blockchain_and_infrastructure_report.pdf

[377]. Beck, R., & Müller-Bloch, C. (2017). Blockchain as Radical Innovation: A Framework for Engaging with Distributed Ledgers as Incumbent Organization. *Proceedings of the 50th Hawaii International Conference on System Sciences (2017)*. doi: 10.24251/hicss.2017.653

[378]. Ali, R., Barrdear, J., Clews, R., & Southgate, J. (2014). Innovations in Payment Technologies and the Emergence of Digital Currencies. *Bank of England Quarterly Bulletin*, *54*(3). Retrieved from https://econpapers.repec.org/article/boeqbullt/0147.htm

[379]. Ali, R., Barrdear, J., Clews, R., & Southgate, J. (2014). Innovations in Payment Technologies and the Emergence of Digital Currencies. *Bank of England Quarterly Bulletin*, *54*(3). Retrieved from https://econpapers.repec.org/article/boeqbullt/0147.htm

[380]. Dannen, C. (2017). *Introducing Ethereum and Solidity: Foundations of Cryptocurrency and Blockchain Programming for Beginners* (pp. 47-48). New York: Apress.

[381]. Dannen, C. (2017). *Introducing Ethereum and Solidity: Foundations of Cryptocurrency and Blockchain Programming for Beginners* (pp. 47-48). New York: Apress.

[382]. Kagan, J. (2020, January 29). Credit Card Posting. Retrieved from https://www.investopedia.com/terms/c/credit-card-posting.asp

[383]. Grüschow, R. M., Kemper, J., & Brettel, M. (2016). How Do Different Payment Methods Deliver Cost and Credit Efficiency in Electronic Commerce? *Electronic Commerce Research and Applications*, *18*, 27–36. doi: 10.1016/j.elerap.2016.06.001

[384]. Grüschow, R. M., Kemper, J., & Brettel, M. (2016). How Do Different Payment Methods Deliver Cost and Credit Efficiency in Electronic Commerce? *Electronic Commerce Research and Applications*, *18*, 27–36. doi: 10.1016/j.elerap.2016.06.001

[385]. G. Engelmann, G. Smith and J. Goulding. (2018). The Unbanked and Poverty: Predicting Area-Level Socio-Economic Vulnerability from M-Money Transactions. IEEE International Conference on Big Data, Seattle, WA, USA, 2018, pp. 1357-1366.

[386]. G. Engelmann, G. Smith and J. Goulding. (2018). The Unbanked and Poverty: Predicting Area-Level Socio-Economic Vulnerability from M-Money Transactions. IEEE International Conference on Big Data, Seattle, WA, USA, 2018, pp. 1357-1366.

[387]. Lenzer, R. (2012). The 2008 Meltdown and Where the Blame Falls. Retrieved from https://www.forbes.com/sites/robertlenzner/2012/06/02/the-2008-meltdown-and-where-the-blame-falls/#140b87c2a72a

[388]. Hall, M. (2020, January 29). Who Was to Blame for the Subprime Crisis? Retrieved from https://www.investopedia.com/articles/07/subprime-blame.asp

[389]. Kalotay, K. (2013). The 2013 Cyprus Bailout and the Russian Foreign Direct Investment Platform. *Baltic Rim Economies Quarterly Review, 3*. Retrieved from https://www.researchgate.net/publication/236981651_The_2013_Cyprus_bailout_and_the_Russian_foreign_direct_investment_platform/stats

[390]. Kalotay, K. (2013). The 2013 Cyprus Bailout and the Russian Foreign Direct Investment Platform. *Baltic Rim Economies Quarterly Review, 3*. Retrieved from https://www.researchgate.net/publication/236981651_The_2013_Cyprus_bailout_and_the_Russian_foreign_direct_investment_platform/stats

[391]. Kalotay, K. (2013). The 2013 Cyprus Bailout and the Russian Foreign Direct Investment Platform. *Baltic Rim Economies Quarterly Review, 3*. Retrieved from https://www.researchgate.net/publication/236981651_The_2013_Cyprus_bailout_and_the_Russian_foreign_direct_investment_platform/stats

[392]. Brown, B., Rhodes, D., Davis, A., Campbell, R., & Balashova, A. (2019, January 3). Genesis Block: The First Bitcoin Block Was Mined Ten Years Ago Today. Retrieved from https://blockexplorer.com/news/genesis-block-first-bitcoin-block-mined-ten-years-ago-today/

[393]. Payments U.K. *The Second Payment Services Directive, a Briefing from Payments UK*. Medici Insights, 15 June 2015, paymentsystemsconsultancy.com/download/payments-uk-the-second-paymentservices-directive-psd2-briefing-july-2016/.

[394]. Pejic, I. (2019). *Blockchain Babel: The Crypto Craze and the Challenge to Business*. London: Kogan Page Limited. (P. 143-148)

395. Hassani, H., Huang, X., & Silva, E. (2018). Digitalisation and Big Data Mining in Banking. *Big Data and Cognitive Computing*, *2*(3), 18. doi: 10.3390/bdcc2030018

396. Hassani, H., Huang, X., & Silva, E. (2018). Digitalisation and Big Data Mining in Banking. *Big Data and Cognitive Computing*, *2*(3), 18. doi: 10.3390/bdcc2030018

397. Raskin, M., & Yermack, D. (2016). Digital Currencies, Decentralized Ledgers, and the Future of Central Banking. *NBER Monetary Economics Program* (p. 14). doi: 10.3386/w22238

398. Ibrahim, A. (2018). Does Blockchain Mean Higher Transparency in the Financial Sector? *Revista De Contabilidad y Dirección*, *27*, 81. Retrieved from https://accid.org/wp-content/uploads/2019/04/Does_Blockchain_mean_higher_transparency_in_the_financial_sect orlogo.pdf

399. Dubey, V. (2019). FinTech Innovations in Digital Banking. *International Journal of Engineering Research & Technology (IJERT)*, *8*(10), 600. Retrieved from https://www.researchgate.net/publication/337137167_FinTech_Innovations_in_Digital_Banki ng/stats

400. Ibrahim, A. (2018). Does Blockchain Mean Higher Transparency in the Financial Sector? *Revista De Contabilidad y Dirección*, *27*, 80. Retrieved from https://accid.org/wp-content/uploads/2019/04/Does_Blockchain_mean_higher_transparency_in_the_financial_sect orlogo.pdf

401. Rolph, D. (2018, July 15). Here's Where We Are 10 Years After Busts, Bailouts and Broken Dreams. Retrieved from https://www.forbes.com/sites/duncanrolph/2018/07/15/heres-where-we-are-10-years-after-busts-bailouts-and-broken-dreams/#25576a967124

402. PricewaterhouseCoopers (PwC). (2017). Global Fintech Report 2017, Redrawing the Lines: FinTech's Growing Influence on Financial Services. Retrieved from https://www.pwc.com/jg/en/publications/pwc-global-fintech-report-17.3.17-final.pdf

403. Bordo, M. D. (2007). A Brief History of Central Banks. *Federal Reserve Bank of Cleveland*. Retrieved from https://www.clevelandfed.org/en/newsroom-and-events/publications/economic-commentary/economic-commentary-archives/2007-economic-commentaries/ec-20071201-a-brief-history-of-central-banks.aspx

[404]. Schindler, J. (2017). FinTech and Financial Innovation: Drivers and Depth. *Finance and Economics Discussion Series*, *2017*(081). doi: 10.17016/feds.2017.081

[405]. Schindler, J. (2017). FinTech and Financial Innovation: Drivers and Depth. *Finance and Economics Discussion Series*, *2017*(081). doi: 10.17016/feds.2017.081

[406]. Al-Essa, M. (2019). Thesis: The Impact of Blockchain Technology on Financial Technology (FinTech). *MSc in Business Innovation and Informatics*. doi: 10.13140/RG.2.2.27279.12961

[407]. Shaulova, E., & Biagi, L. (2019, May). FinTech Report 2019 (p. 6). Retrieved from https://www.statista.com/study/44525/fintech-report/

[408]. Shaulova, E., & Biagi, L. (2019, May). FinTech Report 2019 (p. 6). Retrieved from https://www.statista.com/study/44525/fintech-report/

[409]. Shaulova, E., & Biagi, L. (2019, May). FinTech Report 2019 (p. 5). Retrieved from https://www.statista.com/study/44525/fintech-report/

[410]. Plasma R&D Team. (2018, September). PlasmaDLT & PlasmaPay. White Paper. Retrieved from https://plasmapay.docsend.com/view/pcbc7a4

[411]. Legal documents of PlasmaPay. (2018, September 5). Retrieved from https://plasmapay.com/legal-documents

[412]. Moon, C. (2019, September 17). Average Cost of Online Trading. Retrieved from https://www.valuepenguin.com/average-cost-online-brokerage-trading#trading-fees

[413]. Robinhood Team. (n.d.). Trading Fees on Robinhood. Retrieved February 20, 2020, from https://robinhood.com/support/articles/360001226846/trading-fees-on-robinhood/

[414]. Dubey, V. (2019). FinTech Innovations in Digital Banking. *International Journal of Engineering Research & Technology (IJERT)*, *8*(10). Retrieved from https://www.researchgate.net/publication/337137167_FinTech_Innovations_in_Digital_Banking/stats (P. 599)

[415]. Lendoit Team. (n.d.). Frequently Asked Questions. Retrieved February 20, 2020, from https://lendoit.com/faq/

[416]. Narayanan, A., Bonneau, J., Felten, E., Miller, A., & Goldfeder, S. (2016). Forward. Bitcoin and Cryptocurrency Technologies: A Comprehensive Introduction. Princeton: Princeton University Press.

[417]. Al-Essa, M. (2019). (Thesis.) *The Impact of Blockchain Technology on Financial Technology (FinTech)* (pp. 67-68). doi: 10.13140/RG.2.2.27279.12961

[418]. Pejic, I. (2019). *Blockchain Babel: The Crypto Craze and the Challenge to Business* (p. 33). London: Kogan Page Limited.

[419]. Al-Essa, M. (2019). (Thesis). *The Impact of Blockchain Technology on Financial Technology (FinTech) (p. 86)*. doi: 10.13140/RG.2.2.27279.12961

[420]. Al-Essa, M. (2019). (Thesis). *The Impact of Blockchain Technology on Financial Technology (FinTech) (p. 86)*. doi: 10.13140/RG.2.2.27279.12961

[421]. Chen, Y., & Bellavitis, C. (2020). Blockchain Disruption and Decentralized Finance: The Rise of Decentralized Business Models. *Journal of Business Venturing Insights, 13*. doi: 10.1016/j.jbvi.2019.e00151

[422]. Whitepaper: Key Highlights and Observations. (2017). *CGI Global Payments Research*. Retrieved from https://www.cgi.com/en/media/white-paper/banking-capital-markets/global-payments-research

[423]. Shaulova, E., & Biagi, L. (2019, May). FinTech Report 2019 (p. 24). Retrieved from https://www.statista.com/study/44525/fintech-report/

[424]. Pejic, I. (2019). *Blockchain Babel: The Crypto Craze and the Challenge to Business* (p. 151). London: Kogan Page Limited.

[425]. Pejic, I. (2019). *Blockchain Babel: The Crypto Craze and the Challenge to Business* (pp. 151-152). London: Kogan Page Limited.

[426]. Shaulova, E., & Biagi, L. (2019, May). FinTech Report 2019 (p. 24). Retrieved from https://www.statista.com/study/44525/fintech-report/

[427]. Pejic, I. (2019). *Blockchain Babel: The Crypto Craze and the Challenge to Business* (p. 115-116). London: Kogan Page Limited.

[428]. Pejic, I. (2019). *Blockchain Babel: The Crypto Craze and the Challenge to Business* (p. 115-116). London: Kogan Page Limited.

[429]. Pejic, I. (2019). *Blockchain Babel: The Crypto Craze and the Challenge to Business* (p. 115). London: Kogan Page Limited.

[430]. Pejic, I. (2019). *Blockchain Babel: The Crypto Craze and the Challenge to Business* (p. 111). London: Kogan Page Limited.

[431]. Webster, K. (2017, April 10). Mobile Pay Hype: Apple Pay Adoption Down. Retrieved from https://www.pymnts.com/news/payment-methods/2017/apple-pay-adoption-down-and-so-is-the-hype-mobile-pay-usage/

[432]. Pejic, I. (2019). *Blockchain Babel: The Crypto Craze and the Challenge to Business* (p. 108-115). London: Kogan Page Limited.

[433]. Payment Methods Report 2019: Innovations in the Way We Pay. (2019, June 28). *The Paypers*. Retrieved from https://thepaypers.com/reports/payment-methods-report-2019-innovations-in-the-way-we-pay-2/r779461

[434]. Clement, J. (2019, December 16). Number of Apple Pay Users Worldwide 2019. *Statista*. Retrieved from https://www.statista.com/statistics/911914/number-apple-pay-users/

[435]. Al-Essa, M. (2019). Thesis: The Impact of Blockchain Technology on Financial Technology (FinTech). *MSc in Business Innovation and Informatics*. doi: 10.13140/RG.2.2.27279.12961

[436]. Pejic, I. (2019). *Blockchain Babel: The Crypto Craze and the Challenge to Business* (p. 107-108). London: Kogan Page Limited.

437. Clement, J. (2019, December 16). Number of Apple Pay Users Worldwide 2019. *Statista*, 24. Retrieved from https://www.statista.com/statistics/911914/number-apple-pay-users/

438. French, S. (2018, May 31). China Has 9 of the World's 20 Biggest Tech Companies. Retrieved from https://www.marketwatch.com/story/china-has-9-of-the-worlds-20-biggest-tech-companies-2018-05-31

439. Girasa, R. (2019). *Regulation of Cryptocurrencies and Blockchain Technologies: National and International Perspectives* (p. 248). Palgrave Macmillan.

440. Girasa, R. (2019). *Regulation of Cryptocurrencies and Blockchain Technologies: National and International Perspectives* (p. 248). Palgrave Macmillan.

441. RippleNet: Ripple's Global Payments Network. (2020). Retrieved from https://ripple.com/ripplenet

442. RippleNet: Ripple's Global Payments Network. (2020). Retrieved from https://ripple.com/ripplenet

443. RippleNet: Ripple's Global Payments Network. (2020). Retrieved from https://ripple.com/ripplenet

444. Al-Essa, M. (2019). Thesis: The Impact of Blockchain Technology on Financial Technology (FinTech). *MSc in Business Innovation and Informatics*. doi: 10.13140/RG.2.2.27279.12961 (P. 44)

445. Santander Bank. (2019). What is One Pay FX? Retrieved from https://www.santander.com/en/stories/one-pay-fx-blockchain-for-streamlining-international-transfers

446. Rega, F. G., Riccardi, N., Li, J., & Carlo, F. D. (2018). Blockchain in the Banking Industry: An Overview. doi: 10.13140/RG.2.2.25542.32328

447. Santander Bank. (2018). Santander Launches the First Blockchain-Based International Money Transfer Service Across Four Countries. *Madrid, 12 April 2018, Press Release.* s

448. Bashir, I. (2018). *Mastering Blockchain: Distributed Ledger Technology, Decentralization, and Smart Contracts Explained* (p. 245). 2nd edition. Birmingham: Packt.

449 R3 Team. (2018). What Is a CorDapp? Retrieved from https://docs.corda.net/cordapp-overview.html

450 Bashir, I. (2018). *Mastering Blockchain: Distributed Ledger Technology, Decentralization, and Smart Contracts Explained* (pp. 495-503). 2nd edition. Birmingham: Packt.

451. We.Trade. (2018). Banking Partners. Retrieved from https://we-trade.com/banking-partners

452. We.Trade. (2018). Frequently Asked Questions: Business. Retrieved from https://we-trade.com/faq

453. Keller, F. (2018, April 19). Blockchain-Based Batavia Platform Set to Rewire Global Trade Finance. Retrieved from https://www.ibm.com/blogs/blockchain/2018/04/blockchain-based-batavia-platform-set-to-rewire-global-trade-finance/

454. Rega, F. G., Riccardi, N., Li, J., & Carlo, F. D. (2018). Blockchain in the Banking Industry: An Overview. doi: 10.13140/RG.2.2.25542.32328

455. Grealish, A. (2019). The Flywheel Set in Motion . *Ripple's Blockchain in Payments Report 2019* . Retrieved from https://ripple.com/insights/blockchain-in-payments-report-2019-flywheel-set-in-motion/

456. Perez, Y. B. (2015, July 5). Santander: Blockchain Tech Can Save Banks $20 Billion a Year. Retrieved from https://www.coindesk.com/santander-blockchain-tech-can-save-banks-20-billion-a-year

457. Society for Worldwide Interbank Financial Telecommunication & Accenture. (2016). Position Paper: SWIFT on Distributed Ledger Technologies Delivering an Industry Standard Platform Through Community Collaboration. Retrieved from https://www.swift.com/insights/press-releases/swift-and-accenture-outline-path-to-distributed-ledger-technology-adoption-within-financial-services

[458]. Pejic, I. (2019). *Blockchain Babel: The Crypto Craze and the Challenge to Business* (p. 70). London: Kogan Page Limited. (P. 70)

[459]. Allison, I. (2015, September 11). Nick Szabo: If Banks Want Benefits of Blockchains They Must Go Permissionless. Retrieved from https://www.ibtimes.co.uk/nick-szabo-if-banks-want-benefits-blockchains-they-must-go-permissionless-1518874

[460]. Du, W. (D., Pan, S. L., Leidner, D. E., & Ying, W. (2019). Affordances, Experimentation and Actualization of FinTech: A Blockchain Implementation Study. *The Journal of Strategic Information Systems*, *28*(1), 50–65. doi: 10.1016/j.jsis.2018.10.002

[461]. Du, W. (D., Pan, S. L., Leidner, D. E., & Ying, W. (2019). Affordances, Experimentation and Actualization of FinTech: A Blockchain Implementation Study. *The Journal of Strategic Information Systems*, *28*(1), 50–65. doi: 10.1016/j.jsis.2018.10.002

[462]. Beck, R., & Müller-Bloch, C. (2017). Blockchain as Radical Innovation: A Framework for Engaging with Distributed Ledgers as Incumbent Organization. *Proceedings of the 50th Hawaii International Conference on System Sciences (2017)*. doi: 10.24251/hicss.2017.653

[463]. Beck, R., & Müller-Bloch, C. (2017). Blockchain as Radical Innovation: A Framework for Engaging with Distributed Ledgers as Incumbent Organization. *Proceedings of the 50th Hawaii International Conference on System Sciences (2017)*. doi: 10.24251/hicss.2017.653

[464]. Society for Worldwide Interbank Financial Telecommunication & Accenture. (2016). Position Paper: SWIFT on Distributed Ledger Technologies Delivering an Industry Standard Platform Through Community Collaboration. Retrieved from https://www.swift.com/insights/press-releases/swift-and-accenture-outline-path-to-distributed-ledger-technology-adoption-within-financial-services

[465]. Ibrahim, A. (2018). Does Blockchain Mean Higher Transparency in the Financial Sector? *Revista De Contabilidad y Dirección*, *27* (p. 82). Retrieved from https://accid.org/wp-content/uploads/2019/04/Does_Blockchain_mean_higher_transparency_in_the_financial_sect orlogo.pdf

[466]. Ibrahim, A. (2018). Does Blockchain Mean Higher Transparency in the Financial Sector? *Revista De Contabilidad y Dirección*, *27* (p. 82). Retrieved from https://accid.org/wp-

content/uploads/2019/04/Does_Blockchain_mean_higher_transparency_in_the_financial_sect
orlogo.pdf

467. Rouhani, S., & Deters, R. (2019). Blockchain Based Access Control Systems: State of the Art and Challenges. *IEEE/WIC/ACM International Conference on Web Intelligence.* doi: 10.1145/3350546.3352561 (P. 1-2)

468. US Legal, Inc. (n.d.). Access Control Mechanism [National Security] Law and Legal Definition. Retrieved from https://definitions.uslegal.com/a/access-control-mechanism-national-security/

469. Rouhani, S., & Deters, R. (2019). Blockchain Based Access Control Systems: State of the Art And Challenges. *IEEE/WIC/ACM International Conference on Web Intelligence* (p. 1). doi: 10.1145/3350546.3352561

470. Rouhani, S., & Deters, R. (2019). Blockchain Based Access Control Systems: State of the Art And Challenges. *IEEE/WIC/ACM International Conference on Web Intelligence* (pp. 1-2). doi: 10.1145/3350546.3352561

471. Maesa, D. D. F., Mori, P., & Ricci, L. (2019). A Blockchain Based Approach for the Definition Of Auditable Access Control systems. *Computers & Security, 84,* 93–119. doi: 10.1016/j.cose.2019.03.016

472. Maesa, D. D. F., Mori, P., & Ricci, L. (2019). A Blockchain Based Approach for the Definition Of Auditable Access Control systems. *Computers & Security, 84,* 93–119. doi: 10.1016/j.cose.2019.03.016

473. Rouhani, S., & Deters, R. (2019). Blockchain Based Access Control Systems: State of the Art And Challenges. *IEEE/WIC/ACM International Conference on Web Intelligence* (p. 1). doi: 10.1145/3350546.3352561

474. Rouhani, S., & Deters, R. (2019). Blockchain Based Access Control Systems: State of the Art And Challenges. *IEEE/WIC/ACM International Conference on Web Intelligence* (pp. 1-2). doi: 10.1145/3350546.3352561

[475]. Xu, R., Chen, Y., Blasch, E., & Chen, G. (2019). Exploration of Blockchain-Enabled Decentralized Capability-Based Access Control Strategy for Space Situation awareness. *Optical Engineering*, *58*(4), p. 6-9. 1. doi: 10.1117/1.oe.58.4.041609

[476]. Xu, R., Chen, Y., Blasch, E., & Chen, G. (2019). Exploration of Blockchain-Enabled Decentralized Capability-Based Access Control Strategy for Space Situation awareness. *Optical Engineering*, *58*(4), p. 22. 1. doi: 10.1117/1.oe.58.4.041609

[477]. Xu, R., Chen, Y., Blasch, E., & Chen, G. (2019). Exploration of Blockchain-Enabled Decentralized Capability-Based Access Control Strategy for Space Situation awareness. *Optical Engineering*, *58*(4), pp. 16, 21-23. 1. doi: 10.1117/1.oe.58.4.041609

[478]. Xu, R., Chen, Y., Blasch, E., & Chen, G. (2019). Exploration of Blockchain-Enabled Decentralized Capability-Based Access Control Strategy for Space Situation awareness. *Optical Engineering*, *58*(4), pp. 16, 21-23. 1. doi: 10.1117/1.oe.58.4.041609

[479]. Xu, R., Chen, Y., Blasch, E., & Chen, G. (2019). Exploration of Blockchain-Enabled Decentralized Capability-Based Access Control Strategy for Space Situation awareness. *Optical Engineering*, *58*(4). doi: 10.1117/1.oe.58.4.041609

[480]. Chai, H., Leng, S., Zhang, K., & Mao, S. (2019). Proof-of-Reputation Based-Consortium Blockchain for Trust Resource Sharing in Internet of Vehicles. *IEEE Access*, *7*, 175744–175757. doi: 10.1109/access.2019.2956955

[481]. Chai, H., Leng, S., Zhang, K., & Mao, S. (2019). Proof-of-Reputation Based-Consortium Blockchain for Trust Resource Sharing in Internet of Vehicles. *IEEE Access*, *7*, 175744–175757. doi: 10.1109/access.2019.2956955

[482]. Kursh, S. R., & Gold, N. A. (2018). Adding FinTech and Blockchain to Your Curriculum. *Business Education Innovation Journal*, *8*(2). Retrieved from http://eds.b.ebscohost.com/eds/detail/detail?vid=0&sid=6e892f21-344d-4685-a5dc-05b1907c96c8@pdc-v-sessmgr05&bdata=JnNpdGU9ZWRzLWxpdmUmc2NvcGU9c2l0ZQ==#AN=120450011&db=bsx

[483]. Es-Samaali, H., Outchakoucht, A., & Leroy, J. (2017). A Blockchain-Based Access Control for Big Data. *Computer Science*. Retrieved from

https://www.semanticscholar.org/paper/A-Blockchain-based-Access-Control-for-Big-Data-Es-Samaali-Van/d855e20457cf20a2d8e6b7b0f7e18905529cf6ae

484. Es-Samaali, H., Outchakoucht, A., & Leroy, J. (2017). A Blockchain-Based Access Control for Big Data. *Computer Science*. Retrieved from https://www.semanticscholar.org/paper/A-Blockchain-based-Access-Control-for-Big-Data-Es-Samaali-Van/d855e20457cf20a2d8e6b7b0f7e18905529cf6ae (P. 143)

485. Es-Samaali, H., Outchakoucht, A., & Leroy, J. (2017). A Blockchain-Based Access Control for Big Data. *Computer Science*. Retrieved from https://www.semanticscholar.org/paper/A-Blockchain-based-Access-Control-for-Big-Data-Es-Samaali-Van/d855e20457cf20a2d8e6b7b0f7e18905529cf6ae (P. 143)

486. Es-Samaali, H., Outchakoucht, A., & Leroy, J. (2017). A Blockchain-Based Access Control for Big Data. *Computer Science*. Retrieved from https://www.semanticscholar.org/paper/A-Blockchain-based-Access-Control-for-Big-Data-Es-Samaali-Van/d855e20457cf20a2d8e6b7b0f7e18905529cf6ae (P. 143)

487. Es-Samaali, H., Outchakoucht, A., & Leroy, J. (2017). A Blockchain-Based Access Control for Big Data. *Computer Science*. Retrieved from https://www.semanticscholar.org/paper/A-Blockchain-based-Access-Control-for-Big-Data-Es-Samaali-Van/d855e20457cf20a2d8e6b7b0f7e18905529cf6ae (P. 143)

488. Es-Samaali, H., Outchakoucht, A., & Leroy, J. (2017). A Blockchain-Based Access Control for Big Data. *Computer Science*. Retrieved from https://www.semanticscholar.org/paper/A-Blockchain-based-Access-Control-for-Big-Data-Es-Samaali-Van/d855e20457cf20a2d8e6b7b0f7e18905529cf6ae (P. 144)

489. Brafman, O., & Beckstrom, R. A. (2006). *The Starfish and the Spider: The Unstoppable Power of Leaderless Organizaitons* (pp. 185-189). London: Portfolio.

490. Brafman, O., & Beckstrom, R. A. (2006). *The Starfish and the Spider: The Unstoppable Power of Leaderless Organizaitons* (pp. 185-189). London: Portfolio.

491. Brafman, O., & Beckstrom, R. A. (2006). *The Starfish and the Spider: The Unstoppable Power of Leaderless Organizaitons* (pp. 185-189). London: Portfolio.

[492]. I-SCOOP. (2020, February 17). IIoT: The Industrial Internet of Things (IIoT) Explained. Retrieved from https://www.i-scoop.eu/Internet-of-things-guide/industrial-Internet-things-iiot-saving-costs-innovation/industrial-Internet-things-iiot/

[493]. Maroun, E. A., & Daniel, J. (2019). Opportunities for Use of Blockchain Technology in Supply Chains: Australian Manufacturer Case Study. *Proceedings of the International Conference on Industrial Engineering and Operations Management* (p. 1606).

[494]. Hellwig, D. P. (2019). The Feasibility of Blockchain for Supply Chain Operations and Trade Finance: An Industry Study. *American Council on Germany* (p. 18).

[495]. Hellwig, D. P. (2019). The Feasibility of Blockchain for Supply Chain Operations and Trade Finance: An Industry Study. *American Council on Germany*.

[496]. Kaynak, B., Kaynak, S., & Uygun, O. (2020). Cloud Manufacturing Architecture Based on Public Blockchain Technology. *IEEE Access, 8*, 2163-2177. doi:10.1109/access.2019.2962232

[497]. Zhang, Y., Zhang, P., Tao, F., Liu, Y., & Zuo, Y. (2019). Consensus Aware Manufacturing Service Collaboration Optimization Under Blockchain Based Industrial Internet Platform. *Computers & Industrial Engineering, 135*, 1025-1035. doi:10.1016/j.cie.2019.05.039 (P. 2)

[498]. Kaynak, B., Kaynak, S., & Uygun, O. (2020). Cloud Manufacturing Architecture Based on Public Blockchain Technology. *IEEE Access, 8*, 2163-2177. doi:10.1109/access.2019.2962232

[499]. Provenance Team. (2020, February 04). Traceability versus Transparency: What's the Difference and Which One Should My Brand Be Focused on? Retrieved from https://www.provenance.org/news/movement/traceability-versus-transparency-whats-the-difference-and-which-one-should-my-brand-be-focused-on

[500]. Provenance Team. (2020, February 04). Traceability versus Transparency: What's the Difference and Which One Should My Brand Be Focused on? Retrieved from https://www.provenance.org/news/movement/traceability-versus-transparency-whats-the-difference-and-which-one-should-my-brand-be-focused-on

[501]. O'Connell, L. (2020, February 03). Value of the Global Luxury Goods Market 2019. Retrieved from https://www.statista.com/statistics/266503/value-of-the-personal-luxury-goods-market-worldwide/

[502]. Dujak, D., & Sajter, D. (2018). Blockchain Applications in Supply Chain. *SMART Supply Network EcoProduction,* 21-46. doi:10.1007/978-3-319-91668-2_2

[503]. Dujak, D., & Sajter, D. (2018). Blockchain Applications in Supply Chain. *SMART Supply Network EcoProduction,* 21-46. doi:10.1007/978-3-319-91668-2_2

[504]. Maroun, E. A., & Daniel, J. (2019). Opportunities for Use of Blockchain Technology in Supply Chains: Australian Manufacturer Case Study. *Proceedings of the International Conference on Industrial Engineering and Operations Management* (p. 1609).

[505]. Maroun, E. A., & Daniel, J. (2019). Opportunities for Use of Blockchain Technology in Supply Chains: Australian Manufacturer Case Study. *Proceedings of the International Conference on Industrial Engineering and Operations Management* (p. 1606).

[506]. Maroun, E. A., & Daniel, J. (2019). Opportunities for Use of Blockchain Technology in Supply Chains: Australian Manufacturer Case Study. *Proceedings of the International Conference on Industrial Engineering and Operations Management* (p. 1609-1610).

[507]. Zhang, J. (2019). Deploying Blockchain Technology in the Supply Chain. *Blockchain and Distributed Ledger Technology (DLT)* (p. 3). doi:10.5772/intechopen.86530

[508]. Zhang, J. (2019). Deploying Blockchain Technology in the Supply Chain. *Blockchain and Distributed Ledger Technology (DLT)* (p. 1). doi:10.5772/intechopen.86530

[509]. Secretary-General of the OECD. (2007). The Economic Impact of Counterfeiting and Piracy (p. 5). *OECD 2007.* doi:10.1787/9789264037274-en

[510]. Kralingen, B. (2018, January 23). IBM, Maersk Joint Blockchain Venture to Enhance Global Trade. Retrieved from https://www.ibm.com/blogs/think/2018/01/maersk-blockchain/

511. Pandey, R. (2019). A Tryst of ERP with Blockchain (pp. 5-6). (Self Published). doi:10.13140/RG.2.2.19466.31682

[512]. Pandey, R. (2019). A Tryst of ERP with Blockchain (pp. 6-7). *(Self Published)*. doi:10.13140/RG.2.2.19466.31682

[513]. Barcnji, A. V., Barenji, R. V., & Sefidgari, B. L. (2013). An RFID-Enabled Distributed Control and Monitoring System for a Manufacturing System. *Third International Conference on Innovative Computing Technology* (pp. 498-503). doi:10.1109/intech.2013.6653649

[514]. Radmand, P., Talevski, A., Petersen, S., & Carlsen, S. (2010). Taxonomy of Wireless Sensor Network Cyber Security Attacks in the Oil and Gas Industries. *24th IEEE International Conference on Advanced Information Networking and Applications* (pp. 949-957). doi:10.1109/aina.2010.175

[515]. Abeyratne, S. A., & Monfared, R. (2016). Blockchain Ready Manufacturing Supply Chain Using Distributed Ledger. *International Journal of Research in Engineering and Technology, 5*(9). doi:10.15623/ijret.2016.0509001

[516]. Pandey, R. (2019). A Tryst of ERP with Blockchain (pp. 6-7). (Self Published). doi:10.13140/RG.2.2.19466.31682

[517]. Pandey, R. (2019). A Tryst of ERP with Blockchain (p. 15-16). (Self Published). doi:10.13140/RG.2.2.19466.31682 (P. 15-16)

[518]. Kuvvarapu, R. (2018). Research on Application of Blockchain in Cloud ERP Systems. (Masters Thesis). doi:10.13140/RG.2.2.27098.80327

[519]. Barenji, A. V., Guo, H., Tian, Z., Li, Z., Wang, W. M., & Huang, G. Q. (2018). Blockchain-Based Cloud Manufacturing: Decentralization. *IOS Press*. doi:10.3233/978-1-61499-898-3-1003

[520]. Wu, D., Rosen, D. W., Wang, L., & Schaefer, D. (2015). Cloud-Based Design and Manufacturing: A New Paradigm in Digital Manufacturing and Design Innovation. *Computer-Aided Design, 59*, 31-33. doi:10.1016/j.cad.2014.07.006

[521]. Wu, D., Rosen, D. W., Wang, L., & Schaefer, D. (2015). Cloud-Based Design and Manufacturing: A New Paradigm in Digital Manufacturing and Design Innovation. *Computer-Aided Design, 59*, 31-33. doi:10.1016/j.cad.2014.07.006

[522]. Barenji, A. V., Guo, H., Tian, Z., Li, Z., Wang, W. M., & Huang, G. Q. (2018). *Blockchain-Based Cloud Manufacturing: Decentralization*. IOS Press. doi:10.3233/978-1-61499-898-3-1003

[523]. OPC Foundation. (2019, January 31). Industrial Data Space (IDS). Retrieved May 24, 2020, from https://opcfoundation.org/markets-collaboration/ids/

[524]. I-SCOOP. (2020, May 19). Industrial Data Space: The Secure Data Exchange Model for Industrial IoT. Retrieved May 24, 2020, from https://www.i-scoop.eu/industry-4-0/industrial-data-space/

[525]. Fraunhofer Company. (2018). IDS Reference Architecture Model: Industrial Data Space, Version 2. *International Data Spaces Association*. Retrieved from https://www.fraunhofer.de/content/dam/zv/de/Forschungsfelder/industrial-data-space/IDS_Referenz_Architecture.pdf

[526]. Fraunhofer Company. (2018). IDS Reference Architecture Model: Industrial Data Space, Version 2. *International Data Spaces Association*. Retrieved from https://www.fraunhofer.de/content/dam/zv/de/Forschungsfelder/industrial-data-space/IDS_Referenz_Architecture.pdf

[527]. Gallay, O., Korpela, K., Tapio, N., & Nurminen, J. K. (2017). A Peer-to-Peer Platform for Decentralized Logistics. *Proceedings of the Hamburg International Conference of Logistics* (p. 24). ISBN:9783745043280

[528]. Li, Z., Barenji, A. V., & Huang, G. Q. (2018). Toward a Blockchain Cloud Manufacturing System as a Peer to Peer Distributed Network Platform. *Robotics and Computer-Integrated Manufacturing, 54*, 133-144. doi:10.1016/j.rcim.2018.05.011

[529]. Li, Z., Barenji, A. V., & Huang, G. Q. (2018). Toward a Blockchain Cloud Manufacturing System as a Peer to Peer Distributed Network Platform. *Robotics and Computer-Integrated Manufacturing, 54*, 133-144. doi:10.1016/j.rcim.2018.05.011

[530]. Li, Z., Barenji, A. V., & Huang, G. Q. (2018). Toward a Blockchain Cloud Manufacturing System as a Peer to Peer Distributed Network Platform. *Robotics and Computer-Integrated Manufacturing, 54*, 133-144. doi:10.1016/j.rcim.2018.05.011

[531]. Li, Z., Barenji, A. V., & Huang, G. Q. (2018). Toward a Blockchain Cloud Manufacturing System as a Peer to Peer Distributed Network Platform. *Robotics and Computer-Integrated Manufacturing, 54*, 133-144. doi:10.1016/j.rcim.2018.05.011

[532]. Li, Z., Barenji, A. V., & Huang, G. Q. (2018). Toward a Blockchain Cloud Manufacturing System as a Peer to Peer Distributed Network Platform. *Robotics and Computer-Integrated Manufacturing, 54*, 133-144. doi:10.1016/j.rcim.2018.05.011

[533]. Reed Albergotti, F. (2020, April 04). Ford and GM Are Undertaking a Warlike Effort to Produce Ventilators. It May Fall Short and Come Too Late. Retrieved from https://www.washingtonpost.com/business/2020/04/04/ventilators-coronavirus-ford-gm/

[534]. Baumung, W., & Fomin, V. (2019). Framework for Enabling Order Management Process in a Decentralized Production Network Based on the Blockchain-Technology. *Procedia CIRP, 79*, 456-460. doi:10.1016/j.procir.2019.02.121

[535]. Baumung, W., & Fomin, V. (2019). Framework for Enabling Order Management Process in a Decentralized Production Network Based on the Blockchain-Technology. *Procedia CIRP, 79*, 456-460. doi:10.1016/j.procir.2019.02.121

[536]. Baumung, W., & Fomin, V. (2019). Framework for Enabling Order Management Process in a Decentralized Production Network Based on the Blockchain-Technology. *Procedia CIRP, 79*, 456-460. doi:10.1016/j.procir.2019.02.121

[537]. Baumung, W., & Fomin, V. (2019). Framework for Enabling Order Management Process in a Decentralized Production Network Based on the Blockchain-Technology. *Procedia CIRP, 79*, 456-460. doi:10.1016/j.procir.2019.02.121

[538]. Bahga, A., & Madisetti, V. K. (2016). Blockchain Platform for Industrial Internet of Things. *Journal of Software Engineering and Applications, 09*(10), 533-546. doi:10.4236/jsea.2016.910036

[539]. Zhang, Y., Zhang, P., Tao, F., Liu, Y., & Zuo, Y. (2019). Consensus Aware Manufacturing Service Collaboration Optimization under Blockchain Based Industrial Internet Platform. *Computers & Industrial Engineering, 135*, 1025-1035. doi:10.1016/j.cie.2019.05.039

[540]. Zhang, Y., Zhang, P., Tao, F., Liu, Y., & Zuo, Y. (2019). Consensus Aware Manufacturing Service Collaboration Optimization under Blockchain Based Industrial Internet Platform. *Computers & Industrial Engineering, 135*, 1025-1035. doi:10.1016/j.cie.2019.05.039

[541]. Bahga, A., & Madisetti, V. K. (2016). Blockchain Platform for Industrial Internet of Things. *Journal of Software Engineering and Applications, 09*(10), 533-546. doi:10.4236/jsea.2016.910036

[542]. Marr, B. (2018). The Amazing Ways Tesla Is Using Artificial Intelligence and Big Data. Retrieved from https://bernardmarr.com/default.asp?contentID=1251

[543]. Tesla Car Software Updates. (2020, March 26). Retrieved from https://www.tesla.com/support/software-updates

[544]. IBM. (2018, January). Maersk, IBM to Form Joint Venture to Digitize Supply Chains. Retrieved from https://www-03.ibm.com/press/us/en/pressrelease/53602.wss

[545]. Maersk Digital Solutions. (2019, July). Tradelens Blockchain-Enabled Digital Shipping Platform Continues Expansion with Addition of Major Ocean Carriers Hapag-Lloyd and Ocean Network Express. Retrieved from https://www.maersk.com/news/articles/2019/07/02/hapag-lloyd-and-ocean-network-express-join-tradelens

[546]. Zhang, J. (2019). Deploying Blockchain Technology in the Supply Chain. *Blockchain and Distributed Ledger Technology (DLT)* (pp.11-12). doi:10.5772/intechopen.86530

[547]. Provenance Team. (n.d.). Empowering Small Food Producers with Digital Transparency Tools. Retrieved from https://www.provenance.org/case-studies/grass-roots

[548]. Maroun, E. A., & Daniel, J. (2019). Opportunities for Use of Blockchain Technology in Supply Chains: Australian Manufacturer Case Study. IEOM Society International - *Proceedings of the International Conference on Industrial Engineering and Operations Management* (pp. 1603-1604). IEOM Society International.

[549]. Provenance Team. (n.d.). Case Studies. Retrieved May 26, 2020, from https://www.provenance.org/case-studies

[550]. Deshmukh, A. (2019). The Last-Mile of Trust: Unconventional Methods to Secure Blockchain Supply Chains. *Preprint Version*. doi:10.13140/RG.2.2.33051.31523

[551]. A Novel Blockchain-Based Product Ownership Management System (POMS) for Anti-Counterfeits in the Post Supply Chain, 17465-17467.

[552]. A Novel Blockchain-Based Product Ownership Management System (POMS) for Anti-Counterfeits in the Post Supply Chain, 17465-17467.

[553]. Westerkamp, M., Victor, F., & Küpper, A. (2019). Tracing Manufacturing Processes Using Blockchain-Based Token Compositions. *Digital Communications and Networks*. doi:10.1016/j.dcan.2019.01.007 (P. 1)

[554]. George, C. (2020, May 15). Diamond Provenance at Every Link of the Value Chain. Retrieved from https://www.everledger.io/diamond-provenance-at-every-link-of-the-value-chain/

[555]. Dujak, D., & Sajter, D. (2018). Blockchain Applications in Supply Chain. *SMART Supply Network EcoProduction,* 21-46. doi:10.1007/978-3-319-91668-2_2

[556]. Westerkamp, M., Victor, F., & Küpper, A. (2019). Tracing Manufacturing Processes Using Blockchain-Based Token Compositions. *Digital Communications and Networks*. doi:10.1016/j.dcan.2019.01.007

[557]. Drastic Falls in Cost Are Powering Another Computer Revolution. (2019, September). Retrieved from https://www.economist.com/technology-quarterly/2019/09/12/drastic-falls-in-cost-are-powering-another-computer-revolution

[558]. Juels, Ari & Pappu, Ravikanth & Parno, Bryan. (2008). Unidirectional Key Distribution Across Time and Space with Applications to RFID Security. *IACR Cryptology ePrint Archive*. 2008. 44.

[559]. A Novel Blockchain-Based Product Ownership Management System (POMS) for Anti-Counterfeits in the Post Supply Chain, 17465-66.

[560]. A Novel Blockchain-Based Product Ownership Management System (POMS) for Anti-Counterfeits in the Post Supply Chain, 17468-17471.

[561]. A Novel Blockchain-Based Product Ownership Management System (POMS) for Anti-Counterfeits in the Post Supply Chain, 17469.

[562]. A Novel Blockchain-Based Product Ownership Management System (POMS) for Anti-Counterfeits in the Post Supply Chain, 17473.

[563]. A Novel Blockchain-Based Product Ownership Management System (POMS) for Anti-Counterfeits in the Post Supply Chain, 17473.

[564]. A Novel Blockchain-Based Product Ownership Management System (POMS) for Anti-Counterfeits in the Post Supply Chain, 17474.

[565]. Westerkamp, M., Victor, F., & Küpper, A. (2019). Tracing Manufacturing Processes Using Blockchain-Based Token Compositions. *Digital Communications and Networks* (pp. 3-4) doi:10.1016/j.dcan.2019.01.007

[566]. Westerkamp, M., Victor, F., & Küpper, A. (2019). Tracing Manufacturing Processes Using Blockchain-Based Token Compositions. *Digital Communications and Networks* (p. 3) doi:10.1016/j.dcan.2019.01.007

[567]. Westerkamp, M., Victor, F., & Küpper, A. (2019). Tracing Manufacturing Processes Using Blockchain-Based Token Compositions. *Digital Communications and Networks* (pp. 3-7) doi:10.1016/j.dcan.2019.01.007

[568]. Westerkamp, M., Victor, F., & Küpper, A. (2019). Tracing Manufacturing Processes Using Blockchain-Based Token Compositions. *Digital Communications and Networks* (p. 6) doi:10.1016/j.dcan.2019.01.007

[569]. Westerkamp, M., Victor, F., & Küpper, A. (2019). Tracing Manufacturing Processes Using Blockchain-Based Token Compositions. *Digital Communications and Networks* (pp. 2, 5-8) doi:10.1016/j.dcan.2019.01.007

[570]. Westerkamp, M., Victor, F., & Küpper, A. (2019). Tracing Manufacturing Processes Using Blockchain-Based Token Compositions. *Digital Communications and Networks* (p. 9) doi:10.1016/j.dcan.2019.01.007(P. 9)

[571]. Westerkamp, M., Victor, F., & Küpper, A. (2019). Tracing Manufacturing Processes Using Blockchain-Based Token Compositions. *Digital Communications and Networks* (p. 3) doi:10.1016/j.dcan.2019.01.007

[572]. FOAM Website. (n.d.). Retrieved from https://foam.space/

[573]. Narayanan, A., Bonneau, J., Felten, E., Miller, A., & Goldfeder, S. (2016). *Bitcoin and Cryptocurrency Technologies: A Comprehensive Introduction* (pp. 221-225). Princeton: Princeton University Press.

[574]. Narayanan, A., Bonneau, J., Felten, E., Miller, A., & Goldfeder, S. (2016). *Bitcoin and Cryptocurrency Technologies: A Comprehensive Introduction* (pp. 242-272). Princeton: Princeton University Press.

[575]. Narayanan, A., Bonneau, J., Felten, E., Miller, A., & Goldfeder, S. (2016). *Bitcoin and Cryptocurrency Technologies: A Comprehensive Introduction* (pp. 272-274). Princeton: Princeton University Press.

[576.] Narayanan, A., Bonneau, J., Felten, E., Miller, A., & Goldfeder, S. (2016). *Bitcoin and Cryptocurrency Technologies: A Comprehensive Introduction* (pp. 272-274). Princeton: Princeton University Press.

[577]. Narayanan, A., Bonneau, J., Felten, E., Miller, A., & Goldfeder, S. (2016). *Bitcoin and Cryptocurrency Technologies: A Comprehensive Introduction* (pp. 272-274). Princeton: Princeton University Press.

[578]. Slockit Website. (n.d.). Retrieved from https://slock.it/

[579].Chronicled Website Homepage. (n.d.). Retrieved from https://www.chronicled.com/

[580]. Dujak, D., & Sajter, D. (2018). Blockchain Applications in Supply Chain. *SMART Supply Network EcoProduction,* 21-46. doi:10.1007/978-3-319-91668-2_2

[581]. Li, Z., Barenji, A. V., & Huang, G. Q. (2018). Toward a Blockchain Cloud Manufacturing System as a Peer to Peer Distributed Network Platform. *Robotics and Computer-Integrated Manufacturing, 54*, 133-144. doi:10.1016/j.rcim.2018.05.011

582. Yeoman, A., Ryburn, A., Wood, P., Steel-Baker, D., Johansson, K., & Stiles, R. (2018, May 15). CLOUD Act: Law enforcement access to cloud data. Retrieved from https://www.lexology.com/library/detail.aspx?g=bf886d54-10fb-4b94-ada4-5fcd2936e811

583. Dujak, D., & Sajter, D. (2018). Blockchain Applications in Supply Chain. SMART Supply Network EcoProduction, 21-46. doi:10.1007/978-3-319-91668-2_2

584. Gallay, O., Korpela, K., Tapio, N., & Nurminen, J. K. (2017). A Peer-To-Peer Platform for Decentralized Logistics. *Proceedings of the Hamburg International Conference of Logistics* (p. 21). ISBN:9783745043280 (P. 21)

585. Zyskind, Guy & Nathan, Oz & Pentland, Alex. (2015). Enigma: Decentralized Computation Platform with Guaranteed Privacy.

586. ProPublica. (2017, December 07). Red Cross Built Exactly 6 Homes For Haiti with Nearly Half a Billion Dollars in Donations. Retrieved from https://www.huffpost.com/entry/red-cross-haiti-report_n_7511080

587. Seth, S. (2020, November 13). Central Bank Digital Currency (CBDC) Definition. Retrieved from https://www.investopedia.com/terms/c/central-bank-digital-currency-cbdc.asp

588. Flipside Crypto. (2019, October 15). The 0.1%-0.9%-99% Rule of Blockchains. Retrieved from https://medium.com/flipsidecrypto/the-0-1-0-9-99-rule-of-blockchains-dad628634fee

589. Cosmos Team. (n.d.). Internet of Blockchains. Retrieved from https://cosmos.network/intro#what-is-tendermint-core-and-the-abci

590. Cosmos Team. (n.d.). Internet of Blockchains. Retrieved from https://cosmos.network/intro#what-is-tendermint-core-and-the-abci

591. Habermeier, R. (2018, June 12). Polkadot: The Parachain. Retrieved from https://medium.com/polkadot-network/polkadot-the-parachain-3808040a769a

592. Wood, G. (2019, October 30). Polkadot, Substrate and Ethereum. Retrieved from https://medium.com/polkadot-network/polkadot-substrate-and-ethereum-f0bf1ccbfd13

593. Polkadot Team. (n.d.). Run a Validator (Polkadot). Polkadot Wiki. Retrieved from https://wiki.polkadot.network/docs/en/maintain-guides-how-to-validate-polkadot#vps-list

594. Plasm Network. (2020). *Validator Guide*. Retrieved from https://docs.plasmnet.io/workshop-and-tutorial/validator-guide

595. R. Billy (Cosmos) (personal communication, October, 10, 2020).

596. Boneh, D. (2020, May 13). Dan Boneh: Blockchain Primitives: Cryptography and Consensus. Retrieved from https://youtu.be/V0JdeRzVndI

597. Bashir, I. (2018). *Mastering Blockchain Distributed Ledger Technology, Decentralization, nd Smart Contracts Explained* (p. 511). 2nd edition. Birmingham: Packt.

598. The Ethereum Foundation. (2020). The Eth2 Upgrades. Retrieved from https://ethereum.org/en/eth2/

599. The Ethereum Foundation. (2020). Shard Chains. Retrieved from https://ethereum.org/en/eth2/shard-chains/

600. The Ethereum Foundation. (2020). Proof-of-Stake (PoS). Retrieved from https://ethereum.org/en/developers/docs/consensus-mechanisms/pos/

601. The DFINITY Foundation. (2018). DFINITY Foundation: Internet Computer. Retrieved from https://DFINITY.org/

602. DFINITY. (2020, December 10). Dominic Williams on the Internet Computer, DFINITY's Plan to Redesign the Internet. Retrieved from https://medium.com/DFINITY/dominic-williams-Internet-computer-DFINITY-plan-to-redesign-the-Internet-5604b3861dbe

603. Jones, S. (2020, July 08). CanCan Demo: Motoko on the Internet Computer. Retrieved from https://www.youtube.com/watch?v=_MkRszZw7hU&t=12s

604. Garg, I. (2020, July 01). DFINITY Showcases a Decentralized TikTok Made in Under 1000 Lines of Code. Retrieved from https://cryptobriefing.com/DFINITY-showcases-decentralized-tiktok-1000-lines-code/

605. DFINITY-Education. (n.d.). DFINITY-Education/data-structures. Retrieved from https://github.com/DFINITY-Education/data-structures

606. Dixon, C. (2021, January 15). Who Will Control the Software That Powers the Internet? Retrieved from https://a16z.com/2021/01/14/Internet-control-crypto-decentralization-community-owned-operated-networks/

607. Jones, S., & Williams, D. (2020, April 03). DFINITY | Vision for a Simplified IT Stack. Retrieved from https://www.youtube.com/watch?v=hiZ-EPwG9uQ&t=126s

608. Chopra, R. (July 24, 2019). *In re Facebook, Inc*. Commission File No. 1823109 (p. 8). Washington D.C.: Federal Trade Commission.